GCSE
Business Studies A
for AQA

CW00954172

Arthur Jenkins & David Hamman

With Contributions by
Barry Heywood & Martin Forster

Hodder & Stoughton

A MEMBER OF THE HODDER HEADLINE GROUP

British Library Cataloguing in Publication Data

A catalogue record for this title is available from the British Library

ISBN 0 340 77268 9

First published 2001

Impression number 10 9 8 7 6 5 4 3 2
Year   2005   2004   2003   2002

Typeset by GreenGate Publishing Services, Tonbridge, Kent.

Printed and bound in Italy for Hodder and Stoughton Educational, a
division of Hodder Headline plc, 338 Euston Road, London NW1 3BH

Contents

Contents

This book has been written specifically for the AQA GCSE in Business Studies, Specification A. However, it is a general textbook and the content covers all GCSE specifications and much of GNVQ. It is also of value to AS students, or others, who have not previously studied business studies, but want a good grounding in the subject.

The book is divided into units. Each unit covers a topic area. Units are not intended to be individual lessons. The amount of time devoted to a particular unit is a matter for the individual teacher. Indeed, some units contain more work than others and have been sub-divided. Each unit or sub-division is accompanied by exercises, many of which are based on short case studies, with questions of a similar style to those used in the AQA (A) examination. Outline responses to the questions are detailed in the accompanying teachers' book.

The order of the units more or less follows that in which topics are set out in the AQA (A) specification. We recognise that the majority of teachers have their own approach to teaching business studies, so by following the specification's order of topics, teachers are free to cover the subject in the way that best suits their particular teaching style.

We see this book as providing a 'one-stop' resource for the AQA (A) specification. The text has been written and the exercises devised to provide material across the ability range, enabling teachers to use the book at a number of different levels. The text is accessible to students of more limited ability while providing sufficient material for the more able to extend their knowledge and understanding.

The AQA (A) specification is unique in that it adopts a 'core plus options' approach, similar to that of the former SEG syllabus. A section is included that outlines the kind of subject matter that might be covered in the option part of the specification. In the new specification there are more options, specified in much less detail than in its predecessor, thus giving teachers and students much greater flexibility.

Throughout the book there are useful tips containing hints on examination technique. There are also sections devoted to coursework and to making use of the case studies. These sections are addressed to students. Further advice to teachers is contained in the teachers' book.

We wish to record our thanks to Bev Sylvester Evans and Clare Wilson at the AQA's Guildford offices for their encouragement and very considerable support in planning this book. We are also grateful to Llinos Edwards, Diana Bateman and the team at Hodder and Stoughton for their support, encouragement and technical expertise.

Arthur Jenkins
David Hamman
Barry Heywood
Martin Forster

The authors and publisher are grateful to the following for permission to reproduce illustrative material:

A1 REPORTS Cover of 1990 Myanmar Briefing. Used in November 1990 newsletter, page 250; Bank of England, page 79; Bank of England Museum, page 20; The Body Shop, page 83; E Botham & Sons Whitby, Yorkshire, page 101; © BP plc, page 86; BP Annual Report and Accounts 2000, page 79; Adrian Brooks, for The Body Shop, page 70; British Telecom, page 83; Centrica, page 79; CIS, pages 67 and 68; Citroën UK, pages 106, 186, 205 and 260; The Co-operative College, page 67; *Daily Express* (12/12/00), page 90; David Moody Haulage Ltd, page 66; Eriksson, page 261; © European Communities, 1997, page 27; European Parliament, page 24; European Parliament – Photo Roose Aviation, page 26; Eurostar Group Limited, page 6; Farmer's Union of Wales, pages 246 and 250; the *Financial Times* (8/3/01), pages 30 and 90; Photographic Dept, Ford Motor Company Limited, pages 101 and 102; Freight Transport Association, page 6; Gardiner/Greenpeace, page 14; Gazidis/Greenpeace, page 15; Gnash Communications, page 161; Health & Safety Executive, page 242; Ikea, page 170; John Lewis Partnership, page 60; Jonny Thompson, page 152; LA Fitness, page 146; the London Stock Exchange plc, page 156; Crown copyright reproduced with permission from HMSO, page 144; Magnet Kitchens, page 33; Matoff/Greenpeace, page 6; McDonald's, page 228; MRP Photography and Design, page 5; New Look, page 146; Nimtsch/Greenpeace, page 40; P & O Stena Line Ltd, page 6; PA Photos, pages 244 and 245; Parcel Force, page 75; Parliamentary Education Unit, page 19; Peter/Agripicture.com, page 113; Reuters New York, page 90; J Sainsbury plc, pages 83 and 118; Secretary of State, Department of Trade and Industry, page 22; René Solari, page 106; Tesco Photographic Unit, pages 50, 51, 94, 146, 261; Tesco Stores Ltd, page 83; *The Guardian*, pages 90 (12/5/01) and 144 (27/1/01); © Times Newspaper Limited (3/12/00), page 90; Tonbridge & Malling Borough Council, pages 46, 56, 74 and 95; Tunbridge Wells Borough Council, page 144; West Kent College, pages 232 and 233.

Pages 40, 43, 50, 54, 55, 59, 71, 74, 119, 127, 128, 152, 177, 185, 186, 205, 206, 237, 243, 249, 260, 275 © Greengate Publishing Services

Game voucher kindly provided by EB Stores Group Ltd, page 146.

Every effort has been made to trace copyright holders but this has not been possible in all cases; any omissions brought to our attention will be corrected in future printings.

The Business Environment | 1

Unit 1.1   Why business is needed

Barter →	exchanging goods for other goods without the use of money.
Business →	an organisation formed to supply goods or services, at the right time and in the right quantities to satisfy its customers' needs.
Choice →	when resources can be allocated in various ways.
Consumer →	the final buyer or user of a product or service.
Customer →	a person who buys goods and services from a supplier.
Demand →	the amount of a product that will be bought at a specified price at a given time.
Exchange →	the buying and selling of goods and services.
Needs →	those human wants that are essential to human survival. The main needs are food, clothing and shelter.
Opportunity cost →	a want which is not satisfied when limited resources force a choice to be made.
Profit →	the difference between the price a trader pays for goods and the price at which they are sold.
Resources →	everything that is needed to produce goods and services.
Scarcity →	exists when the resources available are not sufficient to satisfy human wants.
Trade →	the exchange of goods and services for money.

Why business is formed

People use hundreds of different things every day. As individuals, we cannot possibly provide all the things that we want and use. We have to buy most of them. It is the job of business to get the goods and services we want to us, the **consumers**, at the right time, in the right place and in the right amounts. Some businesses sell directly to the consumer. Others sell to other firms, or provide services such as transport, finance or storage. Other businesses build things like factories, bridges or houses. They all have the same purpose, to provide their **customers** with what they want.

Activities

1 Draw up a list of the goods and services you and your family use on most days.

2 How many of the things on your list are made, grown or carried out by either you or a member of your family?

3 How many things on your list are made or grown in:
   a this country;
   b overseas?

4 How many of the things on your first list must you have, because you cannot do without them?

Wants and needs

At any one time, people usually want more things than they can have. Once we have satisfied one set of **wants**, we think of other wants. Our wants are unlimited. (See Figure 1.1.)

Some wants are so important that we cannot do without them. We need them to survive. These needs are for:

- food;
- shelter;
- clothing.

These needs include things like warmth and clean water.

Needs — Water, Food, Clothing, Shelter, Warmth

Wants — Jewellery, Holidays, Television/Video, Sports Car, Kitchen Appliances

Figure 1.1 Needs and wants

The number of wants that we can satisfy depends on the **resources** we have. Most people think of their resources in terms of money. But resources are not just money. Resources include other things, such as land, equipment, time, or a person's skills and talents. Whether wants can be satisfied or not also depends on how easy it is to get the things we want. Even the richest people cannot always have everything they want at exactly the moment they want them.

Scarcity

At any one time, there are only a limited number of resources available. There is, for example, only so much wheat being grown in the world. There are a limited number of mills that can turn the wheat into flour. A person, government or business only has so much money. It will take time to grow more wheat, build more mills or to earn more money. This means that at any one time, resources are **scarce**.

Making choices

Wants are unlimited. Resources are scarce. So, all our wants cannot be satisfied at once. We have to decide which wants are most important. We have to make a **choice**.

The amount of choice we have varies. Those with fewest resources have to spend a greater part of them on food, clothing and shelter. Poor people may spend all their resources on these necessities. They have very little choice. Rich people spend a very small part of their resources on necessities. They have more choice.

The more resources we have, the more choices we enjoy and the easier it is to make those choices.

Opportunity cost

A choice is made when limited resources are used for one thing instead of another. When we make a choice there is something that we do without. The wants that are not satisfied are sacrificed. It can be said that part of the cost of the item we choose is the item we did without. This is known as **opportunity cost**.

Suppose someone has £15 and a number of wants, including buying a CD or saving the money towards a holiday. That person cannot satisfy both wants and must make a choice. If they choose the CD, the true cost is the lost opportunity of saving the money towards a holiday. The opportunity cost of saving the money is the CD that was not bought.

Figure 1.2 Opportunity cost

This is an important idea in business. At any one time a business only has limited resources. They can be used in many ways, so a choice has to be made. A piece of land, for example, could be sold for housing, or used to build an office block or a factory. If it is used for a factory, the opportunity cost will be the housing and office block that are not built. A business will choose how to use its resources on the basis of where the highest profit can be made. Governments also make choices about how they spend taxpayers' money. For every decision to use resources there is an opportunity cost.

Exchange, trade and business

Very few people can provide all the things they want for themselves. We satisfy as many wants as we can from our own resources. Any resources left over are used to satisfy as many of our other wants as possible from elsewhere. This gives rise to **exchange**.

In simple societies the surplus resources are in the form of goods or work. Surplus goods are exchanged for other goods or work. The exchange of goods for other goods is called **barter**. No money is needed. It is hard to make such systems work well, especially when a large number of goods and services are involved.

- You have to find someone who wants the surplus goods you have. At the same time that person has to have a surplus of goods that you want. There has to be a 'double co-incidence' of wants.

- It is hard to work out a basis on which to agree an exchange. For example, suppose a farmer has a surplus of wheat and wants fish, while a fisherman has a surplus of fish and wants wheat. They meet and agree to exchange. They also have to agree how many fish a quantity of wheat is worth.

In modern societies people sell their work in exchange for money. They use the money to buy goods and services that are the result of other people's work. This exchange of goods and services in return for money is **trade**.

Business has developed to make the systems of exchange and trade work effectively. A business is an organisation formed to supply goods or services. To satisfy customers' wants, it must supply them at the right time and in the quantities needed. In return for satisfying its customers, a business earns a profit.

Demand

People's wants are many and varied. Some wants are very important and essential to survival. Others are little more than dreams and may never be satisfied. Business is only interested in those wants that people are willing to spend money on. When people are willing to buy goods and services, and have the resources to do so, there is a **demand** for those goods. Demand is always at a price. If the price is too high people will choose not to buy a product. Usually, the lower the price the greater will be the demand.

Activities

1
  - Sarah has five surplus chickens. She wants to exchange them for an axe to cut firewood. She has no spare time as she runs a busy farm.
  - Danny has an axe he no longer uses. His roof leaks and he is prepared to give the axe away to someone who can mend the roof.
  - John is an unemployed builder and is hungry!

  a Explain how all three people would be better off if they were to trade their surplus goods or skills.
  b What is meant by the 'double co-incidence' of wants? Use the story in this question to explain what the term means.
  c How would a system of money have made the transactions in the story easier to sort out?

2 Ramesh is given £50 for his birthday. There are three things he would like to do with this money:
  - buy a £50 computer game;
  - buy a month's pass for a local theme park, which costs £50;
  - save the money and put it towards buying a snooker table.

  Explain Ramesh's situation by using these terms:

  scarcity   choice   resources   opportunity costs

  ### ICT Activity
  Wordprocess your answer to question 2. Illustrate your answer using clipart images.

3 A market trader starts the day with 100 melons for sale. The fruit will be rotten by the next day, so it will need to be thrown away if it is not sold. The trader is not sure how much he should charge for the melons. He does not have the information in the table, but decides to sell the melons for £1.50 each.

Price melons offered for sale	Number of people prepared to buy a melon at this price
50p	200
75p	150
£1.00	100
£1.25	70
£1.50	40

a How many melons will be wasted if he sells them for £1.50 each?

b Why would you not advise the trader to sell the melons for 50p?

c What is the highest price he should charge to sell all of his melons?

d If he wanted to get as much money as he could from selling the melons, what price should he charge?

ICT Activity

Place the data in the table onto a spreadsheet and produce a suitable graph. The price of the melons should be on the vertical (side) axis.

Unit 1.2 Classification of business

1.2a Production

Assets →	all the things owned by a business or by an individual.
Capital →	the funds invested in a business that enable it to buy the physical assets it needs.
Capital intensive →	where production depends heavily on capital equipment and much less on other factors of production.
Chain of production →	the stages through which a product passes during production, before it reaches the consumer.
Enterprise →	the ability to identify business opportunities and to take risks in business.
Factors of production →	the resources used in production. They fall into four groups: land, labour, capital and enterprise.
Labour →	the human resources used in economic activity.
Labour intensive →	where the cost of labour is a high proportion of the total costs of production.
Land →	the factor of production that includes natural resources (e.g. soil, minerals, fish) as well as the land surface.
Primary production →	the first stages of production, in which natural resources are extracted from the earth. It includes agriculture, fishing, forestry, mining and oil extraction.
Production →	the creation of goods and services to satisfy human wants. It includes all the stages involved in getting those goods and services to the consumer.
Secondary production →	the second stage of production, in which raw materials and other primary goods are processed through manufacturing.
Tertiary production →	the third stage of production, involving the provision of services to other industries and to the public.

→ Key terms

Production

Most business activity is concerned with **production**. Production is more than just making things. It also involves organising resources to create goods and services to satisfy human wants. Production includes all the stages involved in getting goods and services to the consumer. It includes any activity that helps to meet wants for which there is a demand.

Production can be divided into three stages, often called:
- primary production;
- secondary production;
- tertiary production.

Industries whose main activity falls into one of these types are called primary, secondary or tertiary industries.

Primary production

Trawler fishing is an example of a primary industry

Primary production or industry

Primary production makes use of natural resources. Examples are fishing, mining, forestry and farming. These involve taking something from the land. They are therefore often called extractive industries. Once the natural resources have been used they cannot be replaced. **Primary production** was the earliest form of industry.

Secondary production or industry

The second stage in production. In this type of production goods are manufactured or processed. This stage includes construction and public utilities such as gas, electricity and water. **Secondary industry** involves changing raw materials into goods and services.

- It may obtain raw materials from primary industry and process them (make them into something different). For example, the dairy industry receives milk from farmers and processes it to produce cheese or butter.
- It may combine the products of several manufacturers to create a new and different product. For example, computer manufacturers buy components from several other manufacturers and combine them to make computers.

Tertiary production or industry

This is the third stage in production. **Tertiary industry** supplies services to other industries or to the public. This 'business sector' helps the primary and secondary industries to run smoothly by providing:

- distribution services through wholesaling and retailing. It also provides marketing services through, for example, advertising and promotion;
- support services such as banking, insurance, transport and communication.

The chain of production

The stages through which a product passes on its way to the consumer is often called the **chain of production**. Goods may:

- contain raw materials provided by primary industry;
- be manufactured by secondary industry;
- be distributed and sold to the consumer by tertiary industry.

Transport is a tertiary industry

The Business Environment

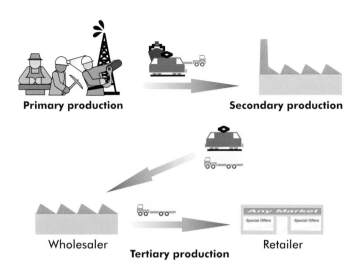

Primary production   **Secondary production**

Wholesaler   **Tertiary production**   Retailer

Figure 1.3 Chain of production

The chain of production differs from product to product. The stages are not always distinct. For example, transport and insurance are usually needed at each of the three stages. The chain of production also shows that firms and industries depend on one another. A hold-up anywhere along the chain will affect other firms along it.

Factors of production

All production contains elements called the **factors of production**. These factors are as follows.

- **Land** consists of everything that stands or grows on the earth's surface and anything that is of use and value below and above the earth. It therefore includes the land surface, buildings and natural resources such as the soil, oil, coal and fish. Land is in fixed supply, and cannot be moved.
- **Labour** is the human resources used in production. Labour provides mental as well as physical skills. It includes those willing and able to work but who are currently not employed as well as those actually working.
- **Capital** is the resources used by the owners to run a business. Capital is more than just money. When owners start a business they use money to buy things to use in the business. For example premises, equipment, stocks of raw materials and goods for sale. These are the **assets** of the business and are equal to

the capital. When a business closes down the assets are sold. Any money left over, after debts have been paid off, is the capital. It belongs to the owners.
- **Enterprise** is the initiative needed to start a business. It also means taking the risks involved in running a business. The reward is profit.

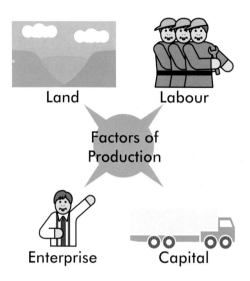

Land   Labour

Factors of Production

Enterprise   Capital

Figure 1.4 Factors of production

Production is a mix of these factors. The amount of each factor in the mix will vary, depending on the type of product. Some industries, such as oil refineries and chemical producers, use a great deal of machinery and equipment and very little labour. They are called capital-intensive industries. The hotel and catering industries employ a lot of labour and relatively little capital and are called labour intensive.

> ### BUSINESS ASPECTS
>
> The proportion of the working population engaged in each of the sectors of production has changed in the UK during the twentieth century. It is said that this indicates the economic maturity of a country. In highly developed countries the bulk of the working population works in the tertiary sector. In less developed economies most people are working in the primary sector.

1 Draw a table with these headings and place each industry into the correct column.

Primary production	Secondary production	Tertiary production

Carpet making   Quarrying   Retailing
Farming   Insurance   Computer manufacture
House building   Forestry   Transport

Case Study

2 Henry's Fish Farm

Henry McDonald decides to start a salmon farm on Loch Hope in a remote part of Scotland. He spends £150,000 on fish pens, fish eggs, a workshop, fish food and equipment, such as pumps and nets. Henry realises once the pens and equipment have been bought that his largest expense is employing five workers to look after and feed the growing fish. After the fish have been reared, Henry intends to sell them to restaurants and shops in the London area.

Explain the meaning of the terms below. Use the Henry's Fish Farm case study to help you.

a assets   *b* capital *c* enterprise
d tertiary industry   *e* labour *f* land
g primary production *h* labour intensive

3 List all the different industries involved in allowing you to be able to buy a burger and fries at a fast-food restaurant. Show clearly which of these industries are primary, which secondary and which are tertiary sector businesses.

ICT Activity

Using Paint or a DTP (desktop publishing) packages convert the list you produced for question 3 into a flow chart. Your flow chart should show how each industry produces something that another industry needs.

Use a colour code to indicate whether each industry/product is in the primary, secondary or tertiary sector.

Part of a possible chart is shown below.

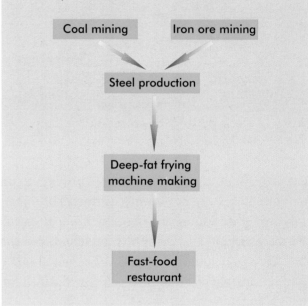

Case Study

4 Rosie's Flowers

Rosie Brown started her florist shop 'Rosie's Flowers' after being made redundant. She used the money she received to buy a shop just outside the town centre. Rosie buys her flowers from a specialist flower warehouse twice a week and sells them as bunches or wreaths to her customers. Container lorries bring the flowers from large-scale Dutch growers to the warehouse.

Rosie is not very happy about the location of her shop. It is on a quiet road about a 10-minute walk from the centre of town. She gets far fewer customers than she expected. She would like to trade in the town centre, but shops there are very expensive to buy or rent.

Rosie is considering two ways to improve her sales:

- opening a stall at a lay-by on a busy road going out of town; or
- starting to sell flowers by post. Customers would order by telephone and the flowers would be sent in special boxes to keep the flowers fresh and delivered the next day.

a Explain why Rosie's Flowers can be seen as both a secondary and a tertiary business.

b Describe the different factors of production that Rosie is likely to need to run her business.

c Rosie depends on other firms for the success of her own. Explain the term 'interdependence' by referring to Rosie's business.

d Draw the different chains of distribution that the flowers go through from the Dutch growers to Rosie's customers. You should include the shop, mail order and roadside customers.

e Consider both of Rosie's ideas for increasing the number of flowers that she sells. Discuss both the advantages and disadvantages of each of her two suggestions, and recommend which one Rosie should choose.

Unit 1.2 Classification of business

1.2b Economic systems

Capitalism →	an economic system where resources are owned and controlled by private persons and organisations and allocated by market forces. The government interferes as little as possible.
Command economy →	another name for a planned economy.
Market economy →	an economy in which the allocation of resources is decided by market forces. The government intervenes as little as possible.
Mixed economy →	one that is made up of both private sector and public sector enterprises.
Planned economy →	an economy in which the government decides on how resources are allocated, what will be produced, where, and in what quantities.
Private sector →	all businesses and organisations that are not owned or run by the state.
Private enterprise →	trading bodies that are privately owned either by individuals or by companies.
Public enterprise →	trading organisations owned and controlled by central or local government.
Public sector →	economic activity that is carried out by either national or local government.

Public sector

Some goods and services are best controlled by either national or local government. They are said to be supplied by the **public sector**. The public sector consists of organisations owned and controlled by local councils and central government. The public sector is made up of two parts.

1 The part that provides services to the public:
   - services provided by central government, for example defence and education;
   - services provided by local councils, for example refuse collection and street lighting.

2 Trading organisations that sell a product or a service to the public. They are often called **public enterprise** companies, and include:
   - trading bodies that are owned and controlled by the state, for example Parcel Force;
   - departments of local authorities that charge people who use a service, for example local council swimming baths and leisure centres.

Since privatisation in the 1980s and early 1990s, there are relatively few of these public enterprise companies left.

Public sector	Private sector
Central government departments	Sole traders
Local government departments	Partnerships
BBC	Private limited companies
Post Office	Public limited companies
Parcel Force	Co-operatives
Government agencies, e.g.	Franchises
Employment Agency	Voluntary organisations
Benefits Agency	
Learning and Skills Councils	
Office of Fair Trading	

Private sector

Any business that is not owned by the state is in the **private sector**. Most businesses that are in the private sector are owned by individuals or by companies.

Economic systems

Businesses operate within an economic system. The economic system of a country sets the rules by which that country's businesses are run. It decides what goods and services are produced. In other words, the system decides how scarce resources are used. There are three main types of economic system.

Market economy

In this type of economy goods and services are produced and sold at a certain price. If enough people want the goods or services, and are prepared to pay that price for them, they will all be sold. The producer will make a profit. If not enough people are willing to buy at that price, the goods will not be sold. The producer will make a loss and may go out of business. The resources they used will go instead to make other things that are wanted. In a market economy, supply and demand decide what goods are made and how resources are used.

In a market economy the government interferes as little as possible. This does not mean that businesses can do what they like. They have to work within the law. But the government makes rules to ensure firms act fairly and to prevent consumers from being exploited.

Planned economy

In this type of economy most things are decided by the state. The government makes all the decisions about what goods will be produced, in what quantities and where. It decide how resources will be allocated. The wages of workers and the prices of goods are decided by the government. Cuba and North Korea are two of the few remaining examples of a planned economy. Planned economies are also called **command economies**.

Mixed economy

Under this system part of the economy is run by private business and the rest is controlled by the state. Most countries have a mixed economy. The amount of private business varies from country to country. In all countries the government provides at least some services, such as education, defence, roads and street lighting. The UK is an example of a mixed economy. So too are the USA and members of the European Union.

Activities

1 Think about your journey into school or college today. Give examples of services and goods you saw or used that are provided by the state, rather than by private companies.

2 Services will usually only be provided by the private sector if they will earn a profit for the owners of the businesses. For instance, it would be very hard to make a profit out of running a private fire service. By the time a householder had negotiated a price for putting a fire out, the house would have burned down.

Some people believe that private companies could undertake some of the services provided by the police. Working in groups, discuss the jobs done by the police that could be performed by a business. Explain how it would be possible to earn a profit from these services.

3 In Britain, some services are provided both by the state and by the private sector. Schools are an example of this dual system. The government provides state schools, and private organisations also run fee-paying independent schools. Copy out and complete the empty spaces in the table below to show the main differences between these two types of schools.

	State schools	Independent schools
How are these schools financed?		
Who decides what is taught in these schools?		
What factors determine who attends these schools?		

ICT Activity

Instead of drawing the table, produce it on a computer using either a spreadsheet or tables in a wordprocessing package.

4 Cuba!

Since the early 1990s, most former communist countries have become market economies. There are just a handful of countries left that have refused to become capitalist. Cuba is an example.

Cuban industry is still run by the state, which decides what goods are needed and how they will be produced. Critics say that the Cuban people have no incentive to be enterprising or to work hard because they do not benefit from their efforts. As a result of this, and the US embargo (ban) on trade with Cuba, the economy is weak with many people living at poverty levels.

Supporters of communism argue that, for a poor country, Cuba has an excellent education system. Illiteracy has virtually disappeared and Cubans are well protected by a state welfare system that provides pensions and health care.

a What type of economic system operates in Cuba?

b Cuba's industries are not meant to be profit making. Explain how the industries might become more efficient if they were run by private firms aiming to make a profit.

c Why do you think the Cuban government has used many of the country's scarce resources to provide a good standard of education?

d The USA refuses to trade with Cuba because it disagrees with communism. Explain how this embargo might affect Cuba's industries.

ICT Activity

Write a short report on how Cuba is slowly allowing more foreign firms to trade there. Use the Internet to research your response. A website that you might find helpful is www.cubafirst.com.

Unit 1.3 The environment in which business operates

1.3a The local environment

Brownfield site →	a site available for building which has been cleared of previous buildings.
Census →	a survey of the population carried out by the government every ten years.
Demography →	the study of the structure and make up of a population.
Environment →	the natural setting or conditions in which human activity takes place.
Greenbelt →	area of open countryside around towns in which new building is not generally allowed.
Greenfield site →	a building site that has not previously been built upon and is probably in the countryside.
Infrastructure →	the network of essential services that support a community and business.
Planning permission →	the approval given by a local council to allow a building to be built or changed.
Pollution →	damage caused to the environment by contaminating the air, water or earth with chemicals, fumes or noise.
Utilities →	the industries that provide gas, electricity and water services.

Demographics

Firms only produce goods if they expect to sell them. They have to take a number of factors into account before starting production. Among the things they need to know is the make up of the population:

- the age distribution of the population – the number of people in each age group;
- how many people are of working age, retired or unemployed;
- how many people between 18 and 25 are still in education or working;
- the numbers of males and females there are in each age group;
- the kinds of households that people live in, for example the number of people who live alone, or in families of various sizes;
- the trends in these figures – whether certain groups in the population are increasing or getting smaller in size.

This kind of information is called **demography**. The information is collected and published in the UK by the National Office of Statistics. It collects the information every ten years in a national **census**.

Demographic information is used by businesses to help them decide what market to aim at. Changes in the age distribution of the population may make them decide to change their target market. Many clothes retailers, for example, have changed their target market from the under-25s to the 30–35-year-old age group. They have done this because there are more 30–35-year-old than 25-year-old people.

Changes in the local population affect businesses in an area. For example, the closing of coal mines in the early 1990s had a big effect in mining areas. Often the local pit was the main employer. Its closure led to local unemployment. This meant that local people had less money to spend in shops and other businesses. Some of those businesses therefore also closed. Because of a shortage of work some people of working age moved away from the area to find work. These were usually the fitter and younger people. The population that remained was older and unable or unwilling to find work. The kinds of businesses and services needed by an older population are different from those needed where there are many young people.

Population figures can also be used to help firms decide where to locate a business. Firms need to know whether the kind of labour they need is available in a particular place now and in the future.

Infrastructure

The **infrastructure** is the network of essential services that support a community. It includes:

- basic services such as electricity, water and gas;
- communication services such as roads, railways, air links, telephone networks and postal services.

The quality of these services in an area is very important to businesses. The infrastructure affects firms in a number of ways. Good road and communication systems mean that firms can:

- deliver goods to their customers quickly;
- respond to and communicate quickly with customers and suppliers;
- receive deliveries of raw materials and components more easily.

These factors help firms to keep a good relationship with their customers and suppliers. They also help to keep a firm's costs down. Firms that use air transport and railways benefit from being close to an airport or rail links.

Firms in town centres need to have good roads leading into and out of the town. They also want plenty of car parking spaces for their customers and for their workers. However, roads are busy in towns and car parking is expensive. Many firms have moved to out-of-town sites and shopping centres.

Reliable services are vital to all businesses. A breakdown in a service can cost firms many thousands of pounds a day. Not all firms use all the utilities, but a breakdown in a service causes problems for everyone, including consumers. For example factories may lose production and cause orders to be delivered late. An electricity power cut may force shops to close. Restaurants cannot prepare and cook food if they lose water, gas or electricity.

Environment

Among the things that affect the environment are:

- the quality of the air, especially in towns;
- the quality of water in rivers and the seas around the coast;
- what we see around us;
- the numbers of wild animals, birds and plants.

Activities such as the national grid building new pylons, or a water company flooding an area to build

Road transport is not always reliable! Traffic hold-ups can cause delays

The Business Environment

Electricity pylons can have a dramatic impact on the environment

a new reservoir, have a big effect on the environment. Billboards and posters at the side of the road can ruin a landscape.

In recent years worries about the environment have increased. People are concerned about the long-term effects of **pollution** of all kinds:

- holes in the ozone layer;
- global warming;
- modern farming methods;
- depletion of finite resources.

Many of these things are affected by business activity. Some of the problems are a result of mistakes made in the past, before the effects were known. For example, the use of coal in power stations led to a build up of sulphur dioxide in the atmosphere and caused acid rain. The use of CFCs in fridges, plastic foam and in aerosol cans led to holes in the ozone layer.

The breaks in the ozone layer and the build up of carbon dioxide from factories, power stations and vehicles have resulted in global warming. Clearing large areas of tropical rainforest to provide more land for farming and timber have also helped to cause global warming.

Modern farming methods have resulted in hedgerows being dug up to make room for large agricultural machinery. The greater use of weedkillers and pesticides has badly damaged the habitats of many species of wild plants, birds and animals. The balance of nature has been upset.

Smoke, fumes, smells and noise produced by factories are not the only causes of **pollution**. It is also caused by dumping waste of various kinds in the sea, in rivers and in holes in the ground. Keeping pollution under control is expensive and raises costs. Higher costs reduce a firm's ability to compete.

Modern packaging methods can cause pollution through litter and lead to waste disposal problems. Firms are encouraged to use materials that can be recycled, since it reduces waste and the amount of energy used. It also helps to conserve finite resources. These are resources that, once they have been used, cannot be replaced. Once a particular tree is cut down, or a quantity of oil, coal, metal ore or gas has been taken out of the ground, they have gone for ever. However, new trees can be grown.

Planning

Buildings have a very big impact on the environment. They can be ugly and not fit in with the other buildings around them. One of the biggest worries is the way housing and industrial building has spread out of towns into the countryside. More and more houses are needed, and firms prefer to build new factories and offices on **greenfield** sites rather than on old, **brownfield** sites. As a result, building has spread into the **greenbelt**, resulting in 'urban sprawl'.

To control all types of building, **planning permission** must be obtained from the local council. It is needed before any new building starts, and for a change in the use of an existing building. This is intended to prevent ugly, unsuitable buildings from being built, and to make sure that new buildings are fit for their purpose.

Planning permission has to be applied for long before building work starts. Big projects may take several months of talking to the local council officials before the application is made. Decisions are made by a planning committee of councillors. They may amend a scheme, or put conditions on their approval.

Environmental policies

Many firms try to control the effect of their activities on the environment. They may have an environmental policy that sets targets for:

- the way they handle and dispose of waste, for example by recycling waste paper or by fitting smoke-control equipment to factory chimneys, or not letting waste get into rivers;
- the way energy is used by setting up a programme for energy saving;
- the use of 'environmentally friendly' materials, for example by using only packaging materials that can be recycled, or raw materials that come from sustainable and renewable sources.

Such policies may be the result of government or European regulations. There are also international treaties that set targets. These initiatives are meant to make sure business accepts its responsibilities for the environment.

Activities

1 Explain why businesses often prefer to build on greenfield sites.

2 A local authority has decided to contract out its refuse collection service to a private company using competitive tendering.
   a Explain how competitive tendering works.
   b How could the local authority ensure that the firm that wins the contract performs the job to the correct standard?

3 Burgerland is a fast-food restaurant chain. The company has applied for planning permission to build one of its restaurants in the suburbs of a city. The city council rejects the application. List as many reasons as you can why planning permission may have been refused.

ICT Activity
Find out how your local authority helps businesses in the area where you live. Most local authorities have websites where you can read about the support that they offer local firms. An example is www.lincolnshire.net/business/busstartup. You may want to look at what your own local council offers.

4 Some areas have more unemployed people than others. Explain how high levels of unemployment in an area can affect the local government.

5 In order to raise the money it needs, a local authority is considering two options:
   - sell some schools' playing fields to a housing development company;
   - raise admission charges at the council-run sports centre.

   a Discuss why these options might not be popular with local people.
   b What else could a local council do to raise money?

6 Explain the ways in which these industries can have an effect on the local environment:

a farming;

b electricity.

□ Case Study

7 Hydro-Spa

Hydro-Spa is a private company that runs several fitness and leisure clubs. Members of these clubs pay an annual fee of about £500 and they are also charged a small amount for using the facilities. In addition to the usual pool and leisure facilities, many of Hydro-Spa's clubs have beauty salons and hairdressers.

Hydro-Spa is considering opening a new centre, and two possible locations are being considered: Alderston and Counby. The business asks a researcher to provide demographic information about these two towns. Their results can be found in Tables 1 and 2. It then asks for advice on which of the two towns is the more suitable for locating one of its clubs.

Table 1: Number of residents in each age group (and % of total)

Age of population	0–16	17–30	31–45	46–60	60+
Alderston	3,520 (18%)	4,250 (22%)	5,530 (28%)	3,740 (19%)	2,570 (13%)
Counby	4,810 (25%)	2,890 (15%)	2,150 (11%)	4,730 (25%)	4,440 (23%)

Table 2: Number of households in each socio-economic group (and % of total)

Socio-economic groups	A Higher management and professional	B Intermediate management and professional	C1 Junior management	C2 Skilled manual workers	D Semi-skilled and unskilled workers	E State pensioners, casual workers, unemployed
Alderston	910 (13%)	1,270 (17%)	2,570 (35%)	1,260 (17%)	790 (11%)	480 (7%)
Counby	680 (7%)	800 (8%)	2,370 (23%)	2,180 (21%)	2,670 (26%)	1,540 (15%)

Use this demographic information to decide which location is the more suitable. Write a report to Hydro-Spa to explain your choice.

Your report should contain these things:

● comments on the demographic breakdown of the two towns – graphs of the data would be helpful to explain your points;

● a discussion of what other information would help you form an opinion on which location is better;

● a clear recommendation on which of the two towns you think would make the better location for Hydro-Spa.

Unit 1.3 The environment in which business operates

1.3b External factors: government

Bank of England →	the central bank for the UK. It is publicly owned but is technically independent of the government.
Economic growth →	the increase in a country's wealth over a period of time.
Fiscal policy →	the government's policy for raising money through taxes and for spending money on services.
Inflation →	a general increase in the level of prices, and a related decrease in the value of money.
Interest →	the cost of borrowing money. It is usually stated as a percentage of the amount borrowed.
Interest rate →	the rate charged for borrowing money over a period of time.
Legislation →	law that is made by parliament. It is contained in Acts of Parliament and includes regulations made under an Act.
Monetary policy →	the government's policy on the control of inflation and economic growth through control of a country's money supply.
Money supply →	the total amount of cash, bank deposits and credit in the economy.
The budget →	the annual forecast of what the government expects to collect in taxes and to spend on services during the next financial year.

Business does not work in isolation. A business has to take into account many things that affect it, but over which it has no control. These include:

- laws and regulations;
- government policy;
- what its competitors are doing;
- what is happening in the rest of the world.

In this unit we will look at the first two of these influences.

Laws and regulations

Business has to work within the law. There are some laws that apply mainly to business. They fall into four main types:

- laws that provide rules for the way businesses work, for example the Companies Acts;
- laws that control the way businesses deal with other businesses, for example the law of contract;
- laws that control the way businesses deal with their workers, or potential workers, for example the Health and Safety at Work Act, Equal Pay Act, Sex Discrimination Act;
- laws that protect consumers, for example the Sale of Goods Acts, Food and Drug Acts.

An increasing number of laws and regulations are based on European Union regulations. Once the UK adopts an EU law, that law becomes part of UK law and has to be enforced. For example, the Working Time Regulations limits the working week to 48 hours. People can volunteer to work longer but very strict records have to be kept. European laws overrule UK law where there is a difference between them.

Where it is necessary to learn something about these laws, they will be dealt with later in the book.

Government policy

The economic policy of a government has a big effect on business. There are four main areas of government economic policy:

The Business Environment

- employment policy;
- fiscal policy;
- monetary policy;
- competition policy.

The Houses of Parliament

Employment policy

All governments want to keep unemployment as low as possible. By providing grants and other incentives they encourage companies to create jobs. They do this by:

- working to get overseas companies to set up bases in this country;
- encouraging firms to set up new branches or to move to areas of high unemployment;
- setting up development agencies. These work with local councils and the government to bring new investment into an area.

Employment policy can also change the relationship between workers and their employers.

UK governments have tried to encourage more flexible working practices. Between 1979 and 1997, laws were brought in to reduce the influence of trade unions. More recently, some of these laws have been modified and the European Union's Social Chapter has been adopted. The minimum wage and the Working Time Directive have improved the rights of workers. On the other hand, firms' costs have increased.

Fiscal policy

This is the name given to the government's spending, taxation and borrowing plans. These plans are set out each year in **the budget**, which is usually held at the beginning of March.

Government spending is of three main kinds:

- spending on goods and services, for example the government buys stationery, computers and medicines for the health service and rents buildings. It also employs civil servants, judges, police officers, members of the armed forces and many others;
- capital spending, for example building new roads, schools, hospitals or ships for the Navy;
- transfer payments, including spending on benefits such as family benefit, disability and unemployment benefits, and state pensions.

These services are paid for through taxes. There are three main kinds of taxes:

- taxes on the income of individuals and companies collected by the Inland Revenue – income tax for individuals and corporation tax for companies;
- National Insurance contributions – these are not strictly a tax but work in a similar way. Contributions are paid by both employers and employees;
- taxes on expenditure collected by Customs and Excise, for example Value Added Tax (VAT).

The government also borrows money. Money from taxes does not come in regularly throughout the year. Government services may cost more than is collected in taxes. The government borrows when it runs short of money. This government borrowing is called the Public Sector Borrowing Requirement (PSBR). There is only so much money available to lend. If the government borrows money there is less available for firms to borrow. This causes **interest rates** to rise. Firms may then be less willing to borrow money.

Monetary policy

This is government policy on the control of the total supply of money in the economy. Money supply has three main parts:

- all the notes and coins circulating in the country;
- deposits in banks and building societies;
- the total amount owing through credit and borrowing.

The main method of controlling the money supply is through interest rates. In 1997 the government passed

The Bank of England

control over interest rates to the **Bank of England**. The Bank is advised by the Monetary Policy Committee (MPC), which is an independent group of experts. They meet every month to fix a central rate, called the Bank of England base rate. The banks and building societies change their interest rates in line with the Bank of England's.

There are two reasons why the government wants to control the supply of money:

- to manage the speed at which the economy grows;
- to control inflation.

Interest rates are the main tool for doing both of these.

When there is growth in an economy, firms expand and invest in new plant and equipment. Employment increases and labour becomes scarce. Firms raise wages and salaries to attract the labour they need. This makes people better off. However, it may result in a general rise in prices. This means there is inflation.

Inflation is not a good thing because the value of money falls. A given sum of money will buy fewer goods. When inflation is high, prices rise quickly and money falls in value faster. Inflation is caused in two ways:

- **Cost-push inflation** happens when prices are pushed upwards by increases in costs. An increase in the price of raw materials or wages increases a firm's costs. To keep their profits at the same level, firms raise prices.

- **Demand-pull inflation** happens when there is an increase in the demand for goods. If people decide they want more goods, sellers may not be able to increase the supply of those goods quickly. More goods are being demanded than sellers can supply. Sellers may put up their prices in an attempt to make the demand equal to their ability to supply the goods.

One way of controlling inflation is to put up interest rates. When interest rates rise:

- the cost of borrowing money rises;
- firms cut their borrowing as quickly as possible and stop investing in new plant and equipment;
- consumers are less willing to borrow money to buy goods on credit, and mortgages cost more;
- consumers have less money to spend so the demand for goods falls. Firms need less labour, and unemployment begins to rise.

Interest rates also affect people's willingness to save. When interest rates are high people may choose to spend less and save more. Some people, for example pensioners, depend on interest on their savings as part of their income. When interest rates are low they have less money to spend.

The ideal result of monetary policy is steady economic growth with little or no inflation.

Competition policy

Competition policy has two main purposes:

- to prevent unfair business practices that limit competition;

to encourage businesses to grow, especially small and medium-sized firms (SMEs).

Examples of unfair business practices that the government tries to stop include:
- firms in the same industry getting together to fix prices – cartels;
- manufacturers forcing retailers to sell goods at prices they fix;
- overcharging;
- incorrect and inaccurate labelling.

Such actions reduce consumers' choice. This limits competition. If the public has any reason to complain about a firm's business methods they can contact the Office of Fair Trading. The Office of Fair Trading may investigate the complaint and make a firm stop the unfair practice.

Competition is reduced if one firm, or a small group of firms, becomes very powerful in a market. If a firm has more than a 25% share of a market, it has a monopoly. A monopoly may be in a position to fix a high price for its goods. It may keep the price high by limiting the supply of its products. Firms that use their power against the interests of consumers may be referred to the Competition Commission.

Many new jobs are provided by expanding small and medium-sized firms. The government supports growth through a number of schemes. These usually aim to help with training, developing new products, and by supporting firms that have a good idea for getting their product on the market.

BUSINESS ASPECTS

Fiscal policy
When the government increases or reduces spending there is a 'knock-on' effect. When it buys more goods and services or increases capital expenditure, there is:
- a business opportunity for suppliers;
- a possible reduction in unemployment;
- an increase in the amount of money that is put into the economy, meaning that people have more money to spend.

Capital projects take a long time to plan. There is a long delay before capital spending has any effect on business.

Increases in benefits and pensions mean that those who receive them have more money to spend in shops and elsewhere.

When the government takes on more staff it reduces unemployment. It may, however, compete with business for the labour.
The government may also reduce spending. For instance, in recent years the government has reduced defence spending. This has had a big effect on makers of defence equipment and suppliers of other goods and services to the armed forces. Unemployment increased as suppliers reduced their workforces and members of the armed forces were made redundant.

Changes in taxation affect businesses. For example, a change in the rate of VAT affects prices and therefore sales. Firms have to change payroll details if income tax or National Insurance rates change. This affects their costs.

A fall in income tax means that people have more money to spend. They may spend it in the shops, on having a holiday, or possibly buying a new house.

Monetary policy
Inflation makes a country's products uncompetitive. When prices rise above a certain point consumers stop buying home-produced goods, preferring to buy cheaper imported goods. This affects the exchange rate and the balance of payments.

Interest rates are important to businesses and affect them in a number of ways:
- All businesses have to borrow money. Interest rates are the price firms have to pay for loans. Interest is part of a firm's costs. An increase in interest rates raises total costs. A firm has to decide whether to reduce its profits or pass on the higher costs by putting up prices.

- When interest rates are high companies are unwilling to invest in new buildings and equipment.
- The total cost of buying goods on credit rises when interest rates increase. Sales of goods bought on credit fall. For example, sales of televisions, washing machines and other expensive household goods are affected. Sales of houses tend to fall when interest rates are high, and rise when interest rates are low.
- Higher interest rates also have an indirect effect on firms. When interest rates are high consumers' mortgage payments rise. They therefore have less money to spend and stop buying certain goods and services. This will affect the producers of those goods.

High interest rates make a country's currency attractive to investors. This pushes up the exchange rate. If the exchange rate for the pound is high, it makes the price of British goods abroad expensive. Firms that export overseas find it harder to sell their product. At the same time imported goods become cheaper.

Competition policy

The government's policy on business development is set out in its Competitiveness White Paper.

Department of Trade and Industry

Governments want to encourage businesses to develop and grow. British business has to work in an environment where:
- goods have to be of high quality;
- there is competition from low-cost countries;
- changes in technology are happening very quickly;
- the growth of e-commerce is changing the way business is done;
- firms have to compete on a global scale.

Only business can create jobs. All the government can do is provide policies that support business. Through its competition policy the government:
- invests in science and engineering research and development;
- encourages innovation;
- encourages companies to cooperate, especially companies working in new technology;
- helps small businesses to grow by setting up an Enterprise Fund, and to understand and adopt new technology;
- supports and encourages training, especially in technology and information and communications technology;
- encourages greater flexibility and openness in business by trying to reduce unfair and anti-competitive behaviour, and working to remove trade barriers internationally.

Activities

1 a Explain why you think there is a need for a national minimum wage law.
  b Some people do not want Britain to have a minimum wage. Give reasons why they may hold this view.

2 The government is sometimes criticised for making it difficult for businesses to operate. If you ran a small business explain why you would not be pleased if new health and safety laws were passed.

The Business Environment

3 The government is trying to reduce the number of unemployed workers. It is considering three ways of achieving this:

- giving businesses money (grants) to take on more employees;
- reducing the amount of tax people have to pay on their wages;
- lowering the rate of interest.

Explain how each of these suggestions could help to reduce the level of unemployment. Then comment on why each of the ideas may not actually help create jobs.

4 What is meant by a Public Sector Borrowing Requirement (PSBR)? What can the government do to reduce the amount that it needs to borrow in future years?

5

Daily News   *Business Page*

The government recognises that the economy is expanding too rapidly and there is a chance of high inflation. At its recent monthly meeting, the Bank of England has decided against increasing interest rates. The Bank of England felt that it was not the right time to increase interest rates, as not all businesses were doing well.

Business writers believe that the Chancellor of the Exchequer will be forced to use fiscal policies in the next budget to reduce the level of demand in the economy.

a What is the government budget?
b Which of these pieces of evidence would suggest that the economy is expanding:
- house prices rising;
- more businesses starting up;
- an increase in the level of unemployment;
- an increase in the inflation rate;

- banks being unwilling to lend money;
- a decrease in the output of goods and services?

c Why do governments not like high inflation?
d Explain why items such as tobacco and petrol have more tax on them than other things.

ICT Activity

Research how the percentage rate of inflation has changed over the last 30 years. You can find this information at www.statistics.gov.uk. With this information, produce a graph to show the changes in the rate of inflation. Then create a poster containing the graph. The poster should be suitable for teenagers who have never studied business studies.

❑ Case Study

6 Japanese firm asks for money from UK government

In 1999 the Japanese car manufacturer Nissan asked the UK government for £100m in aid. Nissan's Sunderland plant is one of the company's most efficient and profitable. But Nissan said it wanted the money to help its less profitable plants in Japan and Europe. The request for the money caused uproar, not just because the Sunderland plant made a profit of £23m in 1998, but also because Renault, Nissan's main shareholder, is partly owned by the French government.

a Give reasons why Nissan might have decided to produce cars in Britain rather than export vehicles from Japan to the UK.
b Why does the UK government encourage foreign firms to move to Britain?
c Discuss whether the government should give Nissan the money it wants.

Unit 1.3 The environment in which business operates

1.3c External factors: the European Union

→ Key terms

CAP →	the Common Agricultural Policy.
Currency →	the unit of money used within a country. In the UK the currency is the pound sterling.
EC →	the European Community. It is the trading and economic part of the European Union.
ECB →	the European Central Bank. It controls interest rates and monetary policy for countries using the Euro as their currency.
EU →	the European Union.
Euro →	the unit of currency that will replace the national currencies of the 11 countries that have joined the single European currency. It will come into full effect in 2002.
Euroland →	the 11 countries that will use the Euro as their unit of currency – Austria, Belgium, Finland, France, Germany, Ireland, Italy, Luxembourg, Netherlands, Portugal and Spain.
European Commission →	the civil service of the European Union. It manages the day-to-day running of the EU and recommends European laws.
European Council of Ministers →	the main law-making body of the EU. It consists of the heads of government of member countries, and meets every six months. Sometimes other ministers meet, depending on what is being discussed.
European Parliament →	an elected body that reviews and comments on proposals made by the European Commission, and approves the EU budget.
Exchange rate →	the price at which one currency can be bought and sold in exchange for another currency.
Quota →	a limit on the quantity of a product that can be produced or traded in.

Businesses in the UK have to take into account what is happening in the rest of the world. Many British firms buy and sell goods and services all over the world. They are therefore affected by what happens to the economies of other countries. They also have to follow rules laid down through international agreements. The European Union is the main international body that affects business in the UK.

What is the European Union?

The European Union is like a club. It currently has 15 member countries. When it was formed in 1957, it was known as the European Economic Community (EEC). This name was later shortened to the **European Community (EC)**. The UK joined in 1973. In 1993 the members of the EC formed the Single Market. This meant that people, goods, services and capital could move freely between the member countries. The Community still exists for trading matters.

The European Union was set up under the Maastricht Treaty when the members agreed to set up a single European currency. The UK decided to wait before joining the single currency, which is known as the Euro.

Figure 1.5 Map of Europe showing the members of the European Union

How is the EU organised?

There is no European government. All the main decisions are made by the **European Council of Ministers**. Government ministers from each of the member countries meet in the Council.

The Council discusses policies that have been put forward by the **European Commission**. This is the civil service of the EU. There are 20 Commissioners, who each head a department, based in Brussels. Each of the member countries has at least one Commissioner.

Proposals for new laws are considered by the **European Parliament**. The members are called MEPs and are elected every five years. The number of MEPs that a country has is based upon its size. The UK has 87 members.

How does the EU affect us?

Here are a few of the ways that membership of the EU affects the UK.

Trading

- Firms have a home market of over 370 million people.
- EU-based firms can buy and sell goods and services in any of the other countries, as if they were trading in their own country.
- Goods can move freely within the EU so that there is a greater choice of goods for consumers.

The European Commission

The EU's Civil Service.
20 Commissioners, at least one from each member state.
Each heads up a department.
Functions

- Manages day-to-day running of the EU
- Makes sure Community rules and decisions are carried out properly
- Carries out decisions made by the Council of Ministers
- Proposes new policies   *Harry Potter*
- Only Commission can propose new European laws
- Can make some policy decisions e.g. competition policy

Council of Ministers

Consists of Ministers from each member country. Ministers attending vary, depending on what is being discussed, e.g. if trade the Trade Ministers attend, if finance the Finance Ministers.
Functions

- Discuss policy put forward by the Commission
- Only body that agrees policy for EU
- Approves and passes European laws, but only after European Parliament

European Parliament

Members called MEPs, elected every 5 years.
Most of its work done through specialist committees.
Powers are limited:

- is consulted on new laws, can suggest changes, but cannot stop them going through
- has a say in the appointment of the Commission
- has the right to dismiss the Commission
- must approve the Community budget

Figure 1.6 The three main European institutions

EU headquarters in Brussels

- Capital can move freely between EU countries. This makes it easier for firms to invest in or take over firms in the rest of the EU.
- Competition policy sets out rules about how firms compete with one another. The EU regulates takeovers and mergers. For example, when BMW took over Rover the deal had to be approved by the Commission.
- The EU is a major provider of funds for research and development.

Consumer protection

- There are common standards for the quality and safety of goods. For example, there are strict rules about the safety of the materials used in toys.
- Minimum standards of hygiene in the preparation, display and handling of food are laid down.
- Goods must be clearly labelled. For example, all food products must have a 'best before' label, and there are rules about displaying prices and showing the ingredients, colouring and additives used.

Travelling and working

- EU citizens can travel freely from one member country to another. All they need is a passport or identity card.
- Visitors from one EU country to another can buy goods as if they were residents. The goods must be for their own use and not for re-sale.
- Citizens can work, study or live in any of the member countries. EU citizens can apply for jobs in any

EU country and must be treated the same as residents. They can also set up businesses anywhere within the EU.
- Qualifications gained in one member country are recognised by the others.
- The UK has now signed the Social Chapter. This sets out rules concerning, for example, working hours, working conditions and health and safety.
- The Social Fund provides money for training for the unemployed, young people, women and the disabled, to help them to get jobs.

The environment

The EU policies on the environment lay down minimum standards and rules, for example:

- standards for emissions from cars and factories, in order to lower pollution;
- standards for water quality and the cleanliness of beaches.

Farming

The Common Agricultural Policy (CAP):

- decides the price farmers are paid for their products;
- tries to stop over-production by fixing quotas for certain products;
- aims to make sure people buy farm goods produced in the EU rather than those imported from the rest of the world.

Regional help

Poorer regions get help through the Regional Development Fund to improve the infrastructure and to help create jobs.

The European Parliament, Strasbourg

The Business Environment

Fishing

The Common Fisheries Policy aims to conserve and manage fish stocks. It also protects fishermen's jobs.

- To stop overfishing, the Common Fisheries Policy sets quotas for how many fish of a certain type can be caught.
- There are rules about where fish may be caught and what type of net must be used.
- There is a common pricing system, intended to guarantee regular supplies of fish at reasonable prices.

European Monetary Union

When people travel from one country to another they have to change their money into the local **currency**. Banks charge a commission for exchanging money. The rate of exchange varies each day. You never know for certain how much your money is worth in another currency. This can be a big problem for business since the price of goods varies according to the **exchange rate**. Businesses never know for certain how much they will have to pay for the goods they buy, or receive for the goods they sell.

The Euro

To try to get over these problems, most member states aim for monetary union. This means replacing national currencies with a single currency. The final stages in the introduction of the single currency began with:

- the naming of the new single currency as the **Euro**;
- deciding which countries met the criteria to join the Euro, and
- setting up of the **European Central Bank (ECB)**.

So far, 12 countries have joined the Euro. They are often referred to as **Euroland**. The ECB is run by a governing council made up of representatives of the 12 Euroland countries. Since January 1999:

- the ECB has been responsible for a single monetary policy and for fixing a single interest rate for all the Euroland countries;
- the rates at which the currencies of the participating countries are converted between each other and into Euros have been fixed for all time;
- exchange rates are quoted in terms of the Euro, not in national currencies;
- trade that does not involve cash can take place either in Euros or in the national currencies;
- prices in shops are shown in Euros and in the national currency.

The last stage in the introduction of the single currency will begin in January 2002 at the latest.

- Euro bank notes and coins will come into circulation and replace those of national currencies.
- Within six months national currency notes and coins will be replaced.

Advantages of a single currency

- Travellers do not have to change money when they move from one country to another.
- Money is saved. People do not have to pay commission each time currency is exchanged.
- Goods are priced in one currency only, making it cheaper for firms to produce catalogues and price lists.
- Businesses know exactly how much they have to pay for the goods and services they buy, and receive for those they sell.
- As a result there is less risk in trading with countries within the Euro zone.

1 Ikea more expensive in Britain

Ikea, the Swedish designer-furniture chain, is charging British customers up to 75% more for some of its beds, wardrobes and sofas than French consumers. It was discovered that customers wishing to buy several household items might find it cheaper to travel to France to buy them.

Item	British price	French price	Difference
Hagali bed frame	£109.00	£61.65	£47.35
Kubist book case	£604.00	£454.92	£149.08
Roberto chair	£22.00	£12.33	£9.67

This discovery has upset consumer groups. Some have asked the Department of Trade and Industry (DTI) to do something about it. They want companies that trade in several countries to have to publish international price lists. This way consumers can compare prices in different countries. Shoppers in France receive the same Ikea catalogue as British shoppers (except for the language difference), only the prices are cheaper.

a Give possible reasons why Ikea decided to charge more for its furniture in Britain than in France.

b Britain's membership of the EU allows consumers to buy anywhere in Europe. Why might UK consumers still not buy in the cheapest country?

c Explain the reasons why some countries are able to produce goods, such as furniture, cheaper than others.

2 Fish Fryers Association

An organisation that represents Britain's fish and chip shops, the Fish Fryers Association, announced in December 1999 that the price of the traditional meal of fish and chips was likely to go up. The association blamed the European Union (EU) for this increase.

EU fisheries ministers had met that month and agreed to reduce the amount of fish each country could catch – called its quota. The ministers felt that stocks of fish in the sea were falling too quickly. They said that unless something was done about it there would soon be no fish left to catch.

The fall in quotas meant that fishermen had to reduce the amount of fish caught. Some had to cut back by as much as 60%. Particularly hard hit was cod, which is mainly caught in the Irish and North Seas. Cod is the most popular fish sold in chip shops.

Elliott Morley, the British fisheries minister, said that the EU was prepared to offer £30 million to compensate fishing fleets for loss of their income. But, he added, something had to be done to keep stocks of fish for the longer-term future of the fishing industry.

Environmental groups, such as Greenpeace, welcomed the cuts. They felt that overfishing was the result of modern fishing techniques. Less pleased were the fishermen, who stood to lose their jobs, and the trawler owners who would have to watch their expensive boats tied up for long periods.

a How can the Fish Fryers Association help fish and chip shops?

b Why were fish stocks falling so rapidly?

c List the arguments for and against the EU introducing fish quotas.

d Explain why a reduction in fish quotas can result in increases in the price of fish.

e Discuss whether the problem of overfishing could be solved without the involvement of the EU.

Unit 1.3 The environment in which business operates

1.3d External factors: international

Agent →	a firm or person who has been given the power to act on behalf of another person or company, often in an overseas country.
Balance of payments →	the difference between the total amount earned from buying and selling goods and services overseas.
Balance of trade →	the difference between the total value of **goods** imported and the total value of **goods** exported by a country.
Exports →	goods and services sold to overseas buyers.
Exchange rate →	the rate at which one currency is exchanged for another.
Globalisation →	the tendency for companies to see their business as being conducted on a worldwide scale. It also recognises that decisions made in one country can have an effect on the rest of the world.
Imports →	goods and services bought from another country.
Invisibles →	services such as banking and insurance bought and sold overseas.
Multinational →	a company that has its head office in one country but has branches or factories in a number of other countries.
Parent company →	a company that owns and controls one or more subsidiary companies.
Trade gap →	the difference between the total value of goods exported and the total value of goods imported.
Subsidiary →	a business that is owned and controlled by another company (a parent company).
Unit cost →	the average cost of producing one unit of output.
Visibles →	physical goods that are bought (imports) and sold (exports).

The European Union affects firms and people in many ways. But the UK also buys and sells goods and services in countries outside Europe. Because trade with other countries is important to the UK, it is affected by events in the rest of the world. For example, the economies of Thailand, South Korea and Malaysia ran into trouble in 1997. The Russian economy more or less collapsed in 1998. Many British firms, including banks, had huge losses. It also caused large falls in share prices around the world.

Events in the rest of the world affect all countries. Decisions made by governments and firms in one country affect governments and firms in other countries. For example, when the USA changes its interest rates, it can cause changes in the rest of the world.

Exports

Exports are goods and services sold to other countries. Exports mean that money comes into a country from overseas firms or people. When tourists from overseas visit the UK, or foreign firms borrow money from a UK bank, or people fly on British Airways, the money they spend is part of UK exports.

Imports

Imports are goods and services bought from other countries. Imports mean that money goes out from one country to another.

Why firms trade overseas

The reasons why firms export goods:

- Firms may want to grow. By exporting they can increase the number of customers, sales and profits.

- A firm may not be using its machinery and its workers to the full. When this happens it has spare capacity. By exporting it may get enough extra sales to use up this spare capacity.
- An increase in sales may mean that unit costs fall. If so, profits increase.

The reasons why UK firms may import goods or services:

- The UK does not produce all the raw materials and food it needs and uses.
- Raw materials or components may not be produced in a country, for example the UK does not have any bauxite, needed to make aluminium.
- Raw materials of the right quality may not be available. For example, the UK has coal deposits but they may not be suitable for some uses because they contain too much sulphur.
- It may be cheaper to buy supplies from abroad. Wages are lower in less developed countries, so the goods produced are cheaper.
- The choice of goods available to consumers is increased. For example, fruit and vegetables from many parts of the world can be bought in supermarkets.

The benefits of trading with other countries:

- Very few countries can supply everything they need for themselves. Foreign trade fills the gaps.
- It allows a country to specialise in those things that it does best. For example, the UK is a major provider of banking and insurance services in the world.
- A country can earn foreign currency from exports to pay for the goods it imports.
- Foreign trade helps to develop good relations with other countries.

Balance of payments

Imports result in money leaving a country. Exports earn money for a country. This flow of money into and out of a country is measured through the **balance of payments**. It is published every month.

The balance of payments is the difference between the total amount earned from buying and selling goods and services. It measures the differences in two things:

1 The total value of **goods** exported and imported. The difference between the two figures is called the **balance of trade**. This is known as the balance in visibles, because goods are things that can be seen. Usually the UK imports more goods than it exports. The difference between imports and exports is called the **trade gap**.

2 The total value of exports and imports of **services**. Examples of such services include banking, insurance and tourism. Because these things cannot be seen, they are called **invisibles**.

Exchange rates

Like any other commodity, money can be bought and sold. The price of changing one currency for another is called the exchange rate. In the UK we state the price in terms of the pound sterling. When British people travel or do business abroad they want to know how many dollars, French francs or other currency they will get for £1. If £100 buys 160 dollars or 1,000 French francs the exchange rate will be $1.6 to the pound or FF10 to the pound.

The exchange rate is important. It sets the price UK firms have to pay for foreign goods and the price overseas buyers have to pay for UK goods and services. Foreign sellers of goods expect to be paid in their own currency.

Example

A British firm buys and sells goods in Germany. The German supplier will expect to be paid in marks.

Suppose the exchange rate is £1 = 2.1 marks.

German goods priced at 2,100 marks will cost the British buyer £1,000. £1,000 of British goods will sell in Germany for 2,100 marks.

If the exchange rate falls to £1 = 2 marks, the German goods cost the British importer £1,050. £1,000 of British goods will sell in Germany for 2,000 marks.

If the exchange rate rises to £1 = 2.2 marks, the German goods cost the British importer £954.50. £1,000 of British goods will sell in Germany for 2,200 marks.

Exchange rates vary from day to day. As shown in the example above, changes in the exchange rate can make a big difference in what importers have to pay for goods and services. In the same way, it has an effect on how much exporters receive for the goods they sell abroad.

If the value of the pound is high against other currencies, exports from the UK are expensive and imports are cheap. When the value of the pound is low, exports are cheap and imports are expensive. The value of the pound therefore affects the balance of payments.

Globalisation

In recent years there has been a growth in the number of firms that operate all over the world. They see the world as one, very big, market. Coca-Cola can be found almost anywhere in the world. Ford cars and lorries, Microsoft, Shell petrol and Kentucky Fried Chicken are other examples. These are very large firms with branches all over the world. This trend for very big firms to operate on a global scale is known as **globalisation**.

Globalisation has come about mainly because of better worldwide communications. The growth of the Internet and satellite telephone systems have made it easier and cheaper for people and firms to keep in contact worldwide.

- Firms can keep in touch at any time with branches anywhere in the world, through computer networks that are easy to set up.
- Firms can advertise and sell their goods anywhere in the world on the Internet.
- They know instantly about any change that is likely to affect them, wherever it happens.

Multinationals

Very large companies such as BP, Glaxo Wellcome, Unilever and Sony are based in one country. But they own factories and branches, or **subsidiaries**, all over the world. They are known as **multinational** companies. Some of them are huge. Very often their turnover (sales) is bigger than the national income of some of the countries in which they operate.

Multinationals are usually too big to be run just as one company. They have a parent company which controls the business as a whole. This is the company's headquarters.

The day-to-day running of the business is carried out through the subsidiaries. The parent company owns at least 51% of the shares. They may be companies taken over by the parent company, or they may be companies the parent company has set up to run part of the business. Very often the subsidiary trades under its own name. Most of the profits from the subsidiaries are paid to the parent company.

Advantages of multinationals

- They bring investment into a country, that poorer countries cannot afford for themselves. This may include roads and other infrastructure.
- They help countries to exploit their natural resources.
- They may train local people and improve and increase a country's skills. They may introduce new methods and new technology. Japanese car makers, for example, brought new technology and management methods to the British car industry.
- They employ local people and pay taxes. This improves a country's wealth and standard of living.
- If the goods they produce are exported they help a country's balance of payments.

Disadvantages of multinationals

- They can decide to move production from one place or country to another. They make decisions based on their own interests. They do not take into account the effects on a country's economy, such as the loss of taxes and jobs.
- Because of their importance to the economy, some people think they have too much power and political influence.
- Host countries have no control over the investment decisions of multinationals. A decision to invest in another country can have a huge impact on a country.
- Most of their profits are returned to the country where they are based, therefore a host country may not benefit very much from them.
- The jobs they create are often low-level jobs. They tend to exploit the low labour costs in less developed countries. They often bring in people from their own country to do the skilled and management jobs.

BUSINESS ASPECTS

Overseas sourcing

Firms make their profits by buying goods as cheaply as they can and selling them at a higher price. Business is very competitive. There is very little scope for varying the price of a product of a certain type and quality. So a firm's profits largely depend on its ability to buy or manufacture the goods it sells as cheaply as possible.

Most of the UK's large clothing retailers, such as Next, Principles, Laura Ashley and Marks & Spencer, buy their supplies from abroad. They often buy from the Far East and from eastern and central European countries, where labour costs are much lower than in the UK. They are able to buy good quality goods cheaper than they can in the UK.

Many manufacturers have moved their factories to countries where labour costs are low, often closing factories in high-cost countries. Other manufacturers do not make anything themselves. They rely entirely on foreign-owned manufacturers to whom they subcontract their production.

Difficulties in trading overseas

Buying and selling overseas is always more difficult than trading in the home market. Large firms deal with these problems by having offices in the countries they trade with. These are the kinds of difficulties a firm might face when trading overseas.

- **Distance** – when a firm first buys and sells abroad it is hard to get accurate information about the overseas firms that it hopes to deal with. Will the goods being imported arrive on time? Will they be of the right quality? Will the exported goods be paid for? If there are problems, it can be hard to sort them out over a long distance. To overcome these and other problems, firms may have an agent to represent them abroad. The agent is local and knows which firms are good and reputable.
- **Language** – in most cases overseas firms do not have English as their first language. Letters and other communications, exporters' price lists and sales literature have to be translated, adding to costs.
- **Transport risks** – the further goods have to travel the greater the risk of damage or loss. The cost of transport has to be paid, and adds to the cost of the goods. Included in the transport costs are the costs of insurance.

- **Different regulations** – goods must meet different regulations and standards in each country. For example, left- and right-hand drive cars; the different rules about voltages and the type of plug that must be supplied with electrical goods. Exporters have to make sure their goods meet these different standards and regulations. Firms selling in a number of different countries may have to have several different versions of the same product. This again adds to costs.
- **Cultural sensitivities** – firms have to take into account the different cultures and religions of the countries they are selling to. They have to be careful that the goods they sell do not contain anything that offends the local culture.
- **Packaging** – this may have to be printed in a number of different languages. Care has to be taken that there is nothing on or in the packaging that might cause offence.
- **Exchange costs** – every time a firm makes a transaction in a foreign currency it involves a cost. The banks charge a commission each time money has to be exchanged.

Balance of payments

The balance of payments figures published every month are in two parts. In this unit, only one part has been described. This is known as the current account. It shows the difference between the total value of exports and imports of goods and services.

But this is only part of the picture. There are other large sums of money that come in to and go out of a country. These are movements of capital. Very large sums are invested overseas by banks, companies and individuals. In the same way large sums of money are invested in the UK from overseas. These movements of funds are shown in the capital account of the balance of payments.

1 Look at the picture. How many of the items in it might have been imported from abroad?

2 Say whether these represent imports or exports for Britain:
- *a* selling a Jaguar car to an American;
- *b* buying a bottle of Australian wine;
- *c* buying a car made in Germany;
- *d* a UK insurance company selling insurance to a Canadian firm;
- *e* profits earned by a UK chemical factory operating in Belgium;
- *f* a Japanese holidaymaker paying her London hotel bill;
- *g* British Airways selling a ticket to an Indonesian man for a flight from Jakarta to Sydney.

3 What is meant by:
- *a* a visible export;
- *b* a trade gap?

4 Powerwash

Washing machine manufacturer Powerwash buys-in German electric motors and uses Swedish steel when producing its appliances. The cost of these components for each machine it makes is shown below.

Electric motor	80DM
Steel	120SKr

DM = German marks

SKr = Swedish kroner

Powerwash charges an average price of £300 for its machines. Many of the appliances are sold abroad.

At the moment the exchange rate is:

£1 buys 2.5DM or 10SKr

a Calculate how much Powerwash has to pay (in pounds) for each motor, and for the steel needed to make a washing machine.

b After one year, the exchange rates change to £1 = 2.00DM = 12SKr. Calculate what happens to the price that Powerwash has to pay now for a motor, and for the steel needed to make a washing machine.

c Changes in the exchange rate affect Powerwash. Write a report to the board of directors of Powerwash outlining the problems caused by exchange rate changes.

5 Many European countries have tried to make trading between each other easier by using the same unit of currency, the Euro. Explain how a single European currency can help countries trade.

ICT Activity

Use information from the website www.euro.gov.uk and http://europa.eu.int/euro to write a short account of the Euro. Use pictures of the notes and coins to illustrate your writing.

Unit 1.3 The environment in which business operates

1.3e External factors: other firms

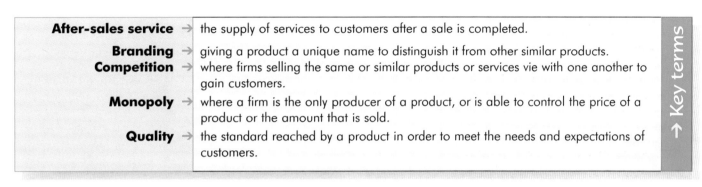

After-sales service →	the supply of services to customers after a sale is completed.
Branding →	giving a product a unique name to distinguish it from other similar products.
Competition →	where firms selling the same or similar products or services vie with one another to gain customers.
Monopoly →	where a firm is the only producer of a product, or is able to control the price of a product or the amount that is sold.
Quality →	the standard reached by a product in order to meet the needs and expectations of customers.

→ Key terms

Competition

Most of the goods and services people buy are sold by a number of firms with similar products. Firms contest with one another to get people to buy their products. This is known as **competition**. Each firm tries to gain an advantage over its competitors.

The sort of competition a firm faces depends on the nature of the business. There are three levels of competition:

Local

This is where firms compete within a locality. Most of the businesses are small, and locally owned and run. They compete with other locally owned businesses. However, many small towns have branches of nationally owned companies which also compete with the local firms. Local competition may be increased by people travelling outside their locality to branches of large, national firms, such as supermarkets.

National

This is where firms sell their goods or services nationally.
- Firms based in one location might compete with other firms by selling nationally. Most manufacturing and insurance firms fall into this category.
- Banks and large retail chains compete nationally through having branches in most parts the country.

For example, Dixons, Next, Halfords, HSBC Bank and Safeway.

International

This is where firms also sell their goods or services overseas. They compete with home-based firms and other foreign firms. Firms facing international competition can be divided into three types:
- Firms based in the UK that export goods made in the UK. For example, Rolls Royce sells its aero engines to airlines all over the world. Firms that export usually have a sales office in the main countries they sell to. Smaller firms use agents based in the overseas countries.
- Firms that compete by taking over firms based in other countries. They can then operate in those countries as a home-based company. They pay local taxes but their profit is returned to the country where the parent company is based. For example, the American supermarket chain Wal-Mart has taken over Asda in the UK.
- Firms that set up branches or subsidiaries in other countries. They too operate as if they were a home-based company. For example, Nissan and Toyota have set up manufacturing plants in the UK. When they export cars, the value of the exports count towards the UK balance of payment.

Firms compete with one another in a number of ways:

Price

Firms try to keep their prices equal to, or slightly below, those of their competitors. If one firm cuts its prices its competitors try to match the price cut so that they do not lose customers. On the other hand, when a competitor raises prices, other firms may keep their prices the same to try to win some customers.

Quality

When people buy a product they expect it to be of a certain quality so that it:

- is suitable for the purpose for which it was bought;
- lasts for a reasonable length of time.

The quality of goods and services is usually measured at a price. The more consumers are prepared to pay the better the quality they expect to receive. People expect better quality components and a more luxurious finish when they buy a VW Golf GTi car than they do from the basic model. Quality is measured against similar products of a similar price. Firms therefore compete on the basis of quality within a range of prices.

After-sales service

Sellers of goods want to keep in touch with their customers after a sale has been completed. They offer a range of services that include:

- guarantees;
- a repair and maintenance service, as in the case of cars, televisions and other durable goods;
- an updating service, for example for trade directories or the latest version of computer software;
- help lines, as offered by software providers, Internet Service Providers and computer sellers.

Customer loyalty

Firms want consumers to be loyal to their product by repeat buying of their goods. They can achieve this by offering good quality, reliable goods that are good value for money. They can also make their product unique by giving it an identity of its own. This is done by **branding**, which means giving a product a special name. The name is registered so that no one else can use it. For example, Marks & Spencer uses the St Michael brand name.

Product

Competition is a result of a number of similar products being available that can perform the same functions. The goods and services of each producer are substitutes for those of other producers in the same market. Producers try to keep their products up to date. This is why car makers make small changes to their models every year. Producers try to get ahead of their competitors by:

- introducing new models;
- gaining a technical advantage;
- changing the packaging of a product or the way a service is presented.

Each time a competitor gains an advantage through a change in its products, its rivals respond as quickly as they can.

To stay competitive, firms have to be innovative and bring out new products. To stay ahead of their competitors firms must plan ahead so that they always have new products in the pipeline. This means spending money on research and development and keeping up to date with technology.

Monopoly

Competition depends on there being a number of firms selling the same or similar products. Sometimes a firm, or small group of firms, can become so powerful in a market that they can:

- fix prices, which will be higher than if there were competition;
- limit the amount of the goods on the market so as to keep prices high.

When this happens, it is called a monopoly. In the UK, the law defines a monopoly as existing when a firm controls more than 25% of the market for a product. In general, monopolies are considered to be against the interests of consumers.

BUSINESS ASPECTS

Buying

The prices at which goods and services are bought are a major part of a firm's costs. They affect a firm's ability to compete. If it can buy more cheaply than its rivals, a firm may make a larger profit. It also has more scope for cutting its prices to gain an advantage. Firms are often criticised for their buying policies:

- Large firms are accused of exploiting smaller suppliers by naming the price at which they will buy goods or services. The big firm's order may form a large proportion of the small company's total output. The small firm may become dependent on its large customer for its work and profits. The large firm may use this position and expect even lower prices when the order is next renewed. The small firm may have little choice but to either accept the lower prices or go out of business.
- Companies often 'export jobs' to countries where poor, uneducated people are paid very low wages for working long hours. These are mainly Asian, central and eastern European countries. Goods are cheaper in these countries since their labour costs are lower. The goods are often of a very high quality made in modern factories that are technically advanced.

Price cutting

Firms sometimes cut prices to gain a temporary advantage over their competitors. There is, however, a limit to the amount by which firms can cut their prices. If they cut their prices to below the cost of making them, they make a loss. Even the richest firms can only afford to make a loss for a short time.

Price cutting can lead to a 'price war' where firms have several rounds of price cuts to try to win an advantage.

Branding

Very often there is little or no difference between one firm's product and that of another firm. Sometimes a firm may make two similar products that compete with one another. In both cases the firms try to make the products different in the minds of buyers by branding them. Branding means giving the goods or services a name that makes them appear unique. For example, Proctor & Gamble produces the washing powder Ariel; Unilever produces Persil. There is very little difference between the two products. They both do the same job and have similar ingredients. But, in the minds of the public, they are different in every way.

A firm may have a number of different brand names. Cadburys, for example, produces a number of different products made from chocolate – Roses, Whispa and many more. Through branding, a product becomes totally different from that of its competitors, however similar they may be in other ways. Branding a product gives the owners of the brand a monopoly for that product. However, there are usually substitutes with other brand names that stop the producer exploiting the market.

Activities

1 What is meant by 'price competition'?

2 How else can firms compete with each other besides lowering their prices?

3 Give five reasons why a motorist may not always buy the cheapest car that is available.

4 A chocolate manufacturer decided to bring out a new type of chocolate bar. Describe the ways in which the bar could be made to appear different from other bars already on the market.

ICT Activity

Use a DTP software package to illustrate the chocolate bars you have described in question 4. Invent some suitable advertising slogans to go next to each picture.

5 Computer manufacturer PC Bytes finds that its sales have been falling recently. The company pays a researcher to look into the problem. The researcher's findings show that the prices of Bytes' computers are higher than most of its rivals. The researcher suggests that rather than trying to compete by lowering its prices, Bytes should try other ways of getting back its market share. Explain the strategies Bytes might use.

6 a Explain how the Internet has increased the amount of competition that bookshops face.

b Describe why Internet booksellers can charge lower prices than bookshops.

7 Mobile phones have been around for a relatively short time, but in that time there have been many improvements made to them.

    a Describe some of the changes in mobile phones that have taken place over the last few years.

    b Why would these changes have been less likely to happen if there were only one mobile phone company?

8 Sarah Jones needs to travel from Newcastle-upon-Tyne to London for a business meeting. The meeting will last between 12.30 pm and 3.30 pm. She researches the different ways of travelling. Her findings are shown in the table.

Travelling between Newcastle and London

	Coach	Plane[1]	Train[2]	Car[3]
Cost	£30	£125	£75	£55
Time taken each way	5 hrs	2 hrs	3½ hrs	4½ hrs
Frequency of service	Every hour	Every two hours	Every 45 minutes	n/a

Notes
1 Includes time & cost of getting to and from the airports
2 1st class £120
3 Includes carpark fee in London

    a Explain the advantages to Sarah of each method of travelling to London.

    b The coach company that does the Newcastle to London run wants to make itself more attractive to business passengers. Describe what it could do to get more business people to travel by coach.

c Discuss how your answer to b might affect the coach company's profits.

Case Study

9 Microsoft found not to be operating in the public interest

In 2000 the computer software giant, Microsoft, had to appear in the American courts. It was accused of being unfair to its competitors. Anyone who bought Microsoft Windows also received its Internet Explorer. This meant that customers no longer needed to buy an Internet browser from another company. It was said that Microsoft was becoming too powerful and too much of a monopoly. It was accused of stopping fair competition. When this occurs it is the customer that suffers.

It was suggested that the lack of competition meant that Microsoft had no real incentive to improve its products. Microsoft denied these charges. It replied that it had done a lot of work to develop its software products and the fact that consumers bought the products showed that they wanted them. The courts decided that Microsoft was not operating 'in the public interest' and fined the company.

    a Make a list of the things that a business could do which might not be 'in the public interest'.

    b Explain whether you think Microsoft behaved badly in the way it sold its Internet Explorer.

    c In what ways do consumers benefit from industries having competition?

Unit 1.3 The environment in which business operates

1.3f Impact of business decisions

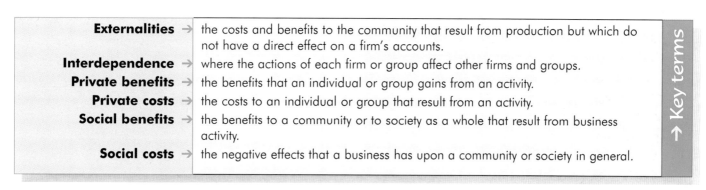

Externalities →	the costs and benefits to the community that result from production but which do not have a direct effect on a firm's accounts.
Interdependence →	where the actions of each firm or group affect other firms and groups.
Private benefits →	the benefits that an individual or group gains from an activity.
Private costs →	the costs to an individual or group that result from an activity.
Social benefits →	the benefits to a community or to society as a whole that result from business activity.
Social costs →	the negative effects that a business has upon a community or society in general.

Business is part of the society in which it operates. The decisions firms make affect the communities of which they are a part. They may have an effect on society as a whole. Business is said to have social responsibilities. It is expected to take them into account when making decisions.

Interdependence

Every business depends on its customers. Customers depend on businesses to provide them with the goods and services they need. All companies depend on their workers and the workers depend on their employers. Companies depend on other companies, for example for their supplies or for transport and insurance. Countries are unable to provide for themselves all the raw materials, goods and services they use. The UK depends on other countries to buy its exports. It also depends on other countries for supplies of raw materials and many of the goods and services it uses.

People, firms and countries have become specialised. One result of specialisation is that few people, organisations or countries can provide for all their own needs themselves. They are therefore more dependent on others to meet their needs. Specialisation has made people, communities, companies and countries more **interdependent**.

A decision by one firm affects other firms. For example, if a firm changes a supplier it may mean job losses

Figure 1.7 Interdependence

at the old supplier and new jobs at the new one. A firm that closes a factory affects employment in an area. This in turn affects shops and other local businesses. Decisions made by consumers can affect whether a business is successful or not. Actions by workers in one part of a firm affect those in other departments. Government decisions affect all business. For example, changes in taxes mean extra administrative work for firms, thus increasing their costs.

Private costs and benefits

In any business decision there will be costs and benefits that have to be weighed up. The costs of making a new

Two of the environmental costs of business – traffic congestion, and river pollution caused by industrial waste

product include the extra raw materials and workers needed. The benefits include a higher share of the market and extra profits. Firms have to decide whether the benefits are greater than the costs. If they are, they will go ahead and make a profit. Most of those costs and benefits affect only the company. They are therefore known as **private costs** and **private benefits**.

Social benefits

Many decisions made by firms affect the community around them. These days we expect firms to take account of their responsibility to the community. Some decisions have a positive effect on the community and are known as **social benefits**.

- Firms create employment. This is important when a new firm moves into an area, particularly if it is an area where there is high unemployment.
- Employees use their wages and salaries to buy goods and services from other local businesses. Those local businesses will be busier and may make more profit. They too may employ more people as a result.
- The standard of living of the area will be improved because more people have more money.
- Sometimes firms improve road access or provide new amenities.
- Firms may have policies that result in improvements to the environment. This might be landscaping a site, or purifying waste water before it enters a river.

These social benefits do not benefit the firm directly. They do not add to the firm's profits. Some, for example the environmental benefits, may add to a firm's costs. The benefits go to those *outside* the firm.

Social costs

Other decisions made by firms have a negative effect on the community. These effects are called **social costs**.

- Pollution, through smoke or discharging waste into rivers. Some industrial work is noisy.
- Disposal of toxic waste.
- Impact on the local landscape – large buildings or electricity pylons in areas of rural beauty can spoil the views.
- Traffic problems, for example heavy lorries moving in and out of a site day and night.
- There may be traffic noise and congestion, especially at the beginning and end of the working day.
- When a firm closes down there can be a big effect on the local community, particularly in places where it is the only major employer. Unemployment increases, which in turn affects other businesses.

These costs are external to the firm. That is, they do not involve the firm in any direct expenditure. They have no effect on a firm's profit and loss account.

Social costs are hard to measure and to put a money value on. They often result in money costs to other people, or to local or central government. For example, traffic congestion caused by a business may necessitate changes in road layout, paid for by the local council; people living near a noisy factory may have to pay for double glazing.

Externalities

The costs and benefits to the community discussed above, which may have little direct effect on the business concerned, are often grouped together and called **externalities**.

Activities

1 What is a cost–benefit analysis?

2 Outline what the externalities (social costs and benefits) are in each of these cases:

The Business Environment

a An insurance company builds an impressive award-winning building for its London head office.

b British Nuclear Fuels opens a new power station to produce cheap electricity.

c A pharmaceutical company conducts extensive research to try to find a cure for cancer.

d Oxfam opens a new store selling art and craft items produced in less developed countries.

3 Describe the different types of pollution that can be caused by industry.

4 Using the concepts of private and social costs and benefits, explain why some firms feel that it is worthwhile to pollute the environment.

5 What action might the government take to stop firms causing pollution?

6 The example below shows the interdependence between manufacturers and suppliers. Complete the missing links for the two other relationships.

Depends on suppliers for materials, so it can produce goods and make a profit

Rely on firms to pay for their supplies promptly so they can continue in business

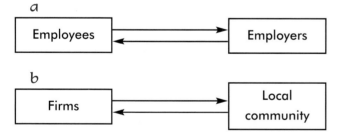

7 Garden World
Garden World is a manufacturer of expensive wooden garden furniture. It has been based in a small town near the Scottish Borders for about 30 years. Over the last few years business has been thriving and the firm is finding it increasingly difficult to get skilled workers. The premises are becoming too small and many

Case Study

local residents are complaining about the noise from the factory and its lorries.

Most of Garden World's customers live in the south of England. As its products are bulky and heavy, transport is becoming an increasing cost to the firm. Garden World's accountant has suggested that the business closes down and moves to a greenfield site 300 km to the south.

This way the business will be closer to its market. Another option is to move to a brownfield location. There is a site available that once contained a chemical factory. The land here is badly polluted.

a Explain the difference between a greenfield and a brownfield site.

b Garden World decides to produce a cost–benefit analysis. Copy out the CBA table below and add other points you feel should be included.

	Costs	Benefits
Private	• The cost of building the new factory	• Savings made on transport costs
Social	• The loss of jobs would affect the local community	• The firm would improve the brownfield site

ICT Activity

Produce the cost–benefit analysis using tables in Word or on a spreadsheet.

c It is easy to calculate the value of some of the costs and benefits involved. Others are more difficult to measure. Explain why some costs and benefits are difficult to put values on.

d Discuss whether Garden World should be concerned about the social costs created by the move to the south of England.

Unit 1.4 Agencies that support business

Most firms need help and support from time to time. Much of this support and advice comes from government departments and agencies. It also comes from other firms in the same business, trade associations, and bodies like the CBI that cover all industries.

Department of Trade and Industry (DTI)

Department of Trade and Industry

Most of the government's advice and support for business is given by the DTI. It aims to help companies of all sizes to be more productive and to take up new ideas and methods. It tries to do this by encouraging new businesses to start up, and companies to grow by:

- investment;
- developing new skills and using new technology;
- research and development;
- adopting best practice;
- taking up business opportunities abroad.

Small companies

The DTI tries to help small businesses through, for example, the Small Business Service and the Small Firms Loan Guarantee Scheme. This guarantees loans from banks to firms that are unable to provide the banks with the security they want.

Exporting

The DTI helps exporters:

- by working closely with the Foreign Office, which has a Commercial Officer in most British embassies and a Consul in most main towns throughout the world. Through this network, firms can get detailed information about overseas markets and export opportunities;
- by providing tailor-made market research and sales leads;
- by helping to identify reliable agents overseas;
- by setting up trade missions to overseas countries.

Regulation

The DTI supports industry by helping to make sure that the public has confidence in firms and in the way they are run. The DTI regulates the way companies are run.

- It can investigate and prosecute firms or their directors if they break company law.
- The DTI can ask the Office of Fair Trading (OFT) to examine firms that act unfairly.
- Mergers and takeovers can be examined by the OFT. On its advice, the DTI may refer them to the Competition Commission.

Export Credit Guarantees Department (ECGD)

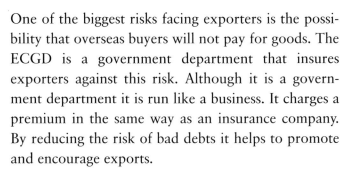

One of the biggest risks facing exporters is the possibility that overseas buyers will not pay for goods. The ECGD is a government department that insures exporters against this risk. Although it is a government department it is run like a business. It charges a premium in the same way as an insurance company. By reducing the risk of bad debts it helps to promote and encourage exports.

Department for Education and Employment (DfEE)

Department for Education and Employment

This large government department provides a wide range of services that are available to businesses.

- Control of all full-time education and qualifications. It also funds vocational education through further education colleges, and higher education (which offers more advanced training and qualifications).
- Overall supervision of the Learning and Skills Councils. These offer training and enterprise services through a variety of local providers, at all levels.
- The New Deal, that encourages unemployed people back to work. Grants are provided to help employers meet the wage and training costs of employing young and long-term unemployed people.

- Running Job Centres through which employers can advertise job vacancies.

Business Link

This national network offers a 'one-stop' business advice and support service. It specialises in offering professional advice to small and medium-sized companies. It gives them access to appropriate expertise on everything a person might need to run their own business.

Regional Development Agencies (RDAs)

The nine agencies covering England came into being in April 1999. Agencies for Scotland and Wales had already existed since the mid-1970s. They work closely with the local councils in their region. They are funded by central government, European grants and other sources. They offer grants and other incentives to firms. Their objectives are:

- the economic development and physical/social regeneration of their region – they aim to bring in new industries, to improve social conditions and to bring derelict land into use;
- to provide support for business, and increasing investment and competitiveness in their region;
- to improve skills by encouraging firms to train people, especially in new skills and in skills where there are shortages;
- to promote employment;
- to promote sustainable development.

The Confederation of British Industry (CBI)

The CBI is the main business organisation in the UK. It is independent, non-political and non-profit making. It gets most of its funds through the subscriptions its members pay. Its objective is to create and sustain the conditions that allow UK businesses to compete and succeed both in the UK and abroad.

The CBI draws its members from all sectors of industry and commerce and all parts of the UK. Member

A derelict brownfield site in an industrial area

companies are of all sizes, from very large multinational companies through to very small firms. Between them, its member organisations employ 6 million people. It is therefore able to speak for UK business and be its main voice. It can put forward the needs of business and commerce to the government, parliament, Europe and also to local councils through its regional offices.

By acting as a pressure group, the CBI enables its members to:

- influence and help to shape government policy;
- have a voice in Europe and internationally;
- influence public opinion about the importance of industry to the country's wealth;
- get up-to-date information on policies that affect business people;
- attend conferences on matters that concern business.

The CBI also carries out regular surveys of its members. They show trends in business confidence and performance. These are widely used by the government and economists.

Chambers of Commerce

The British Chambers of Commerce (BCC) is a network of local chambers of commerce. It provides a voice for local businesses. Each chamber is an association of business people that represents and promotes business interests in its area. Chambers of commerce provide their members with a wide range of services:

- providing information about European grants and how to apply for them, also other sources of funding and grants;
- providing information about overseas law, regulations, documentation and details of business opportunities and contracts. Also, general help on overseas trading;
- helping to find agents and suppliers at home and abroad;
- organising trade missions overseas to open up new business opportunities;
- offering training services across a wide range of activities, including exporting and health and safety;
- selling services relatively cheap, such as translation services, energy, telephone, fleet and fleet breakdown services. Some services are provided through specialist companies owned by BCC that sell to members at below commercial rates.

Trade associations

These are associations whose members are drawn from a particular trade or industry. Examples include the National Farmers Union and the Road Hauliers Association. The Association of British Travel Agents is a trade association that also acts as a regulator for the travel industry.

Trade associations give members of an industry:

- a means of sharing information that is of common interest;
- a way of promoting the industry;
- a means of putting the industry's point of view to the government and other legislative bodies, for example the European Union, on matters such as new regulations, laws and taxes. They act as pressure groups.

Voluntary organisations

There are a number of charities that support new businesses, especially those being set up by young people. Two of the best known are:

- **Princes Trust** – offers help to the unemployed and temporary or part-time workers between the ages

of 18 and 30. Young people with a business idea, who cannot get finance to start up, may be offered a low-interest loan of up to £3,000 and test marketing grants of up to £250, and advice from a volunteer local business person during the first three years of trading. Specialist advice is also available.

- **Livewire** – a charity sponsored by Shell which helps 16 to 30-year-olds to start and develop their own businesses.

Activities

1 Describe the type of help and advice a person might need when setting up a business.

2 What problems might a firm have when selling its goods abroad that it would not necessarily have if it were selling in the UK?

3 Explain two ways in which the DTI helps small businesses.

Case Study

4 **Confederation of British Industry (CBI)**

The CBI, the organisation that represents UK businesses, asked the Chancellor of the Exchequer to look at ways of making it easier for manufacturing companies to survive.

The leader of the CBI, pointed out that the gap between manufacturing and service industries was becoming very wide. He was worried that Britain was heading towards a two-speed economy. He said that the service sector was growing rapidly but manufacturing was becoming less important.

The CBI suggested that the Chancellor could help manufacturers by spending money on improving the rail and road systems. This would make it cheaper for manufacturers to transport their goods around the country.

The CBI said it would also like to see people saving less, and using the money to buy manufactured goods. Lowering the amount of interest people get on their savings could encourage them to spend more.

a Give some examples of manufacturing and service industries.
b How exactly would a better system of roads and railways help manufacturers?
c What problems could arise if there was a decline in manufacturing in Britain?
d Explain how a decrease in the rate of interest would affect consumers and savers.
e Suggest reasons why service industries are becoming so important in Britain.

ICT Activity

Use the Internet to find out how the CBI is able to help businesses. Write an account of your findings. The website is www.cbi.org.uk.

5 IKKI Designs

Talented young fashion designer Beverley Sloly launched her business, IKKI Designs, in March 1997. Based in Birmingham, IKKI Designs specialises in everyday clothes for women, as well as tailored suits for special occasions. Beverley was unemployed for two years prior to starting her venture, and was only able to obtain part-time cleaning work.

In order to help her start her business the Prince's Trust agreed to give Beverley a £1,500 grant and a loan for £1,000.

IKKI Designs is a successful, expanding business. Beverley made wedding outfits for guests attending Victoria Adams and David Beckham's wedding in 1999, and her long-term plan is to open her own retail premises.

"Running your own business enables you to take control of your life. I look back to my period of unemployment, and realise just how much I have achieved. Without the Prince's Trust I wouldn't be where I am today," says Beverley.

a Why do young people find it particularly difficult to start a business?
b Beverley received both a grant and a loan from the Prince's Trust. Explain why it was important that she was expected to pay some of the money back.
c Besides providing funds, what other support could the Prince's Trust have offered to Beverley?

Unit 1.5 Markets, demand, supply and prices

→ Key terms

Demand →	the amount of a good or service that will be bought at a stated price over a certain period of time.
Equilibrium →	the point at which the supply and demand for a product in a market are equal.
Market →	the place where those wishing to buy goods make contact with those who have those goods to sell.
Market forces →	the operation of supply and demand in deciding what goods and services are produced and the price at which they are sold.
Price →	the amount of money for which goods are bought and sold.
Supply →	the volume of goods and services producers are willing to supply at a given price.

Markets

The word 'market' usually brings to mind crowded stalls selling many different kinds of goods. Sellers will be shouting to attract customers and offer bargains.

A local open-air market

This sums up pretty well what is meant by a **market**. In business terms, a market is a place where:
- buyers and sellers meet;
- there are a large number of buyers and sellers;
- there is a choice of goods of a particular kind – several stalls sell apples or jeans;
- a change in prices in one part of the market is quickly followed by a similar change in the other parts of the market. If one stall-holder drops the price of apples, the other stall-holders do the same to retain their share of the customers.

A market can be:
- a physical place, for example a town's fish market; Lloyds of London is a market for insurance;
- a group of people who want, or are willing to buy, a product of a certain type within a price range. Thus there is a small market for Gucci shoes, which is quite different from the market for Hush Puppies.

Markets can be broken down into several different groups or sectors. For example, the market for cars can be broken down into private buyers and company-car buyers.

Goods and services are always bought and sold at a price. The prices of goods and services in the market are decided by the supply and the demand for them. This is what people mean when they say that **market forces** fix prices.

Demand

When buyers in the market are ready to actually buy goods, there is a demand for those goods. Demand is always at a price. People decide to buy (demand) goods only when they think those goods are 'worth it'. Some people are willing to pay a high price for a product. Others are only prepared to pay quite a low price. Usually, as the price of a product falls, so more people are willing to buy it.

This can be shown on a graph, called a demand curve. Below is a demand curve for shoes.

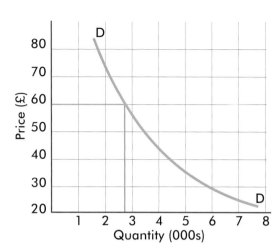

Figure 1.8 Demand curve for shoes

The demand curve usually slopes down from left to right because the demand rises as the price falls.

Demand is always given in terms of a period of time. A business needs to know how *often* the goods are demanded. If a family's demand for baked beans is six cans, what does it mean? Is it every day, every month or every year?

Supply

In a market there has to be someone willing to sell goods and services to meet demand. The price at which they can sell their product determines whether a firm is willing to supply the market. When a firm supplies goods or services it expects to sell them at a price that covers its costs, and provides a reasonable profit.

The price at which a product can be sold also determines the quantity of a product that is available in a market. When the price is high, producers are more willing to supply in large quantities. The efficient firms will then make a large profit. Even the inefficient ones make some profit.

In the same way, when prices are low producers are less willing to supply the market, and do so in smaller quantities. Only the most efficient firms can make a profit. The less efficient firms leave the market.

This link between price and the quantity supplied can be shown on a supply curve. The curve slopes upwards from left to right because producers are willing to supply more goods as the price rises.

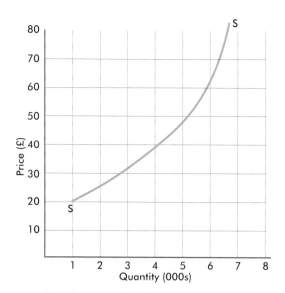

Figure 1.9 Supply curve for shoes

Prices

Supply and demand react to price in opposite ways, as shown by Figure 1.10.

Figure 1.10 How supply and demand react to price

How, then, are the prices paid by consumers arrived at? In theory the price of a product settles at a point where supply and demand are equal. This point is called the **equilibrium** point.

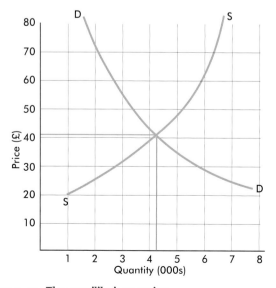

Figure 1.11 The equilibrium point

At this point there are just enough goods or services supplied to meet the demand. All the suppliers make a reasonable profit. Everyone who wants to buy the goods is able to do so, at a price which they consider to be good value for money.

We shall see later that, in practice, firms base their prices on a number of other factors as well.

Activities

1 Explain what is meant by the 'demand' for a product.

2 Dreamtime USA is an independent UK travel agent that specialises in arranging holidays for British people in Florida. Describe the four things that determine how many people want to go on Dreamtime's holidays.

3 Bettina works part-time at her local fruit and vegetable market. She quickly discovers that as soon as one stall reduces its prices towards the end of the day, the others quickly follow and lower their prices too. Bettina had a bright idea and explained it to the boss.

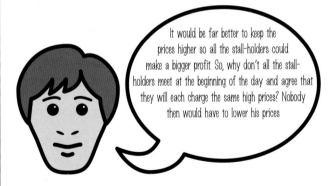

It would be far better to keep the prices higher so all the stall-holders could make a bigger profit. So, why don't all the stall-holders meet at the beginning of the day and agree that they will each charge the same high prices? Nobody then would have to lower his prices

a Why is it that after one stall-holder lowers his or her prices, the others lower theirs as well?

b Why are the prices of vegetables at the market more likely to fall later in the day than at the beginning?

c Explain why Bettina's idea may not be as good as she thinks it is.

4 What is meant by the 'equilibrium' price?

5 Price changes
In autumn, a farmer decides what crops to grow in his fields the following year. To help him decide he looks at how much each crop is being sold for at the moment.

First year

Vegetable	Price per tonne
Carrots	£150
Cabbage	£180
Broccoli	£220

He realises that he will get roughly the same number of tonnes per hectare of land for each vegetable, so he decides to grow broccoli. Many other farmers also decide to grow broccoli, so next year there is a surplus of broccoli and its price falls.

Second year

Vegetable	Price per tonne
Carrots	£190
Cabbage	£220
Broccoli	£120

a Why does the farmer decide to grow broccoli in the first year?

b Draw the supply and demand curve for broccoli for both years.

c Explain why you think the price of both cabbage and carrots has gone up.

ICT Activity
Draw a bar chart to compare the changes in prices of the vegetables for the two years.

The Business Environment

Unit 1.6 Location

→ Key terms

Brownfield site	→	a site that has been previously built upon and cleared for development. Such sites are usually found in urban areas.
Economies of scale	→	the effects on the costs of a business that result from an increase in its size.
External economies of scale	→	the benefits that a firm gains from being located in the same area as other, similar industries.
Greenbelt	→	an area of land surrounding towns, on which new building is restricted by law. It is usually agricultural land.
Greenfield site	→	a site that has not previously been used for building.
Planning permission	→	the approval of plans for new buildings or extensions to existing buildings that must be obtained from a local authority before building can begin.
Rent	→	the payment made for hiring the use of land or property for an agreed, fixed period of time.
Subsidies	→	payments made by the government to firms to encourage them to take certain actions. For example, to choose a particular location for a factory or warehouse.
Trade association	→	an organisation whose members are drawn from a particular industry or trade.

Choosing where to site a business is one of the most important decisions a firm has to make. Some businesses, such as computer services, can be set up almost anywhere. Others have to choose their sites carefully. This unit looks at some of the main reasons why firms are based where they are.

Cost of sites

The price a business has to pay for a site varies, depending on:

- how close it is to a town centre;
- for how long the site is needed;
- which part of the country it is in.

Firms have to decide whether to buy or rent a site. Sites are expensive to buy; renting one is cheaper. There are fewer sites available to buy than to rent. This limits the choice of sites to buy. Firms may not want to lock up capital in land and buildings. Owning a site makes it harder to move in the future. Many sites are owned by specialist property companies who may have also built the premises.

Firms that intend to stay in one place for a long time might think it worth buying a site. But a business that is expanding rapidly may expect to move in, say, five years' time. It would not be worthwhile for this kind of firm to buy a site.

Sites in town centres are more expensive than those on the edge of town, whether to rent or to buy. This is why many business parks and retail shopping centres have been set up on the outskirts of towns. The cost of a site is usually higher near large towns and cities than close to small towns.

The cost of buying or renting sites is lower in some parts of the country than in others. Land for industrial or commercial development is more expensive in relatively prosperous areas. In general, similar sites are more expensive in the south and south-east of England than in other parts of the UK. Other factors, such as grants, also affect the costs of locating in a particular place.

Availability of sites

Land is scarce, and there are restrictions on building in the **greenbelt** on the outskirts of towns. Firms that need a **greenfield site** have a limited choice. How easy it is to obtain planning permission is also a big factor.

New offices to rent at a site in Kent

Firms may have special requirements such as a large, flat site, near to the coast, close to water and fuel supplies and with access to motorways. This restricts even further the choice of possible sites.

The cost of land and property is important. As we have seen, land is expensive in town centres and in prosperous areas. Firms are therefore often attracted to areas of high unemployment, where there are usually more sites available and they are relatively cheap. The land available is often reclaimed. It may have

A greenfield site ready for development, with the infrastructure in place

been occupied by older industries that have now closed. Such cleared land is called a **brownfield site**.

Transport costs

The cost of transport is important in deciding where to locate a business. Transport costs depend on:

- the kinds of raw materials a firm uses;
- the nature of the goods produced;
- the nearness to motorways, railways and ports.

In some industries raw materials are bulky and heavy and need a lot of space. Such goods have a low value for their weight, and are expensive to transport. For example, iron ore is a bulky raw material that has so much waste that it is reduced in quantity by four-fifths during processing. To keep transport costs low, the iron and steelworks at Port Talbot and Llanwern in South Wales are located on the coast, as near as possible to the source of iron ore. They have their own jetties where imported iron ore is unloaded directly into the plant. Oil refineries are located near the coast for the same reason. Sawmills are usually close to forests, and brickworks are near their clay supplies.

Other firms produce goods that are more bulky than the raw materials that go into making them, for example furniture. To save on transport costs such goods are usually produced near to the market.

Firms need to get goods to their customers as quickly as possible. They also need to get their supplies delivered without delay. Traffic in towns causes costly delays. Firms therefore prefer to locate on the outskirts of towns, near good transport links. This is why many distribution centres are located close to motorway junctions. Other firms are located close to ports or railway terminals.

Transport costs in some industries are not important in deciding where to locate. For instance in the electronics industry, components and products are transported easily and cheaply. The value of the final product is high compared with the transport costs, so such industries can be located anywhere.

Markets

- Industries that serve the public directly must be located close to their market. Examples include service industries such as retail banks and shops, hairdressers and solicitors.

- Some products, like bread, have to be produced on the day they are sold, and are therefore made close to their market.
- In the past, perishable goods such as vegetables and milk had to be produced close to their market. Better transport, refrigeration and processing have made this less important.
- Component suppliers sell to producers of other products. Thus many producers of car components are based near the major car-producing plants, since these are their customers.

Government influence

The government and local councils try to attract new industries to certain areas. Among the incentives they offer are:

- grants to encourage new industries under the government's regional policies. These grants are often targeted at areas of high unemployment. They may be paid for partly out of European Union regional development funds;
- subsidies, such as rent-free property for the first two years, or low-rent properties;
- new factory or office units for rent or sale that are already built, thus saving on building costs;
- making sites available that may already be cleared, with roadways and main services installed, and already with planning permission;
- making planning permission for new sites easier to obtain.

Most local councils have departments set up to attract businesses to their area. In some areas Regional Development Agencies have been set up. They use government money to attract new industries to their areas. For example, the Welsh Development Corporation attracted the LG Electronics plant to South Wales.

Geography and natural resources

Climate and soil conditions are important in deciding where certain crops are grown. Flowers are grown in the Scilly Isles because of the mild climate. The growing conditions for fruit and vegetables are good in Kent and the Vale of Evesham. Hydroelectric power stations need a good supply of water and a steep gradient.

A brownfield site ready for clearance

Tradition

Some older industries are concentrated in certain areas of the country. The reasons why they were first set up in those areas may have disappeared, but they were probably based near their raw materials' supply, or the fuel to power their machinery. For this reason:

- the engineering industry grew in the West Midlands close to the raw materials and coal needed for its steam-driven machinery;
- brewing was based in Burton-on-Trent because of the quality of the water there;
- the Lancashire cotton industry grew close to the ports of Liverpool and Manchester, where the raw cotton arrived from America.

Once an industry is established in an area it tends to stay there. Other companies grow up around the established industries to supply machines, components and other services they need. New firms entering the industries may still be drawn to the traditional areas.

Supply of labour

Labour costs are probably the biggest single cost item for most firms. A good supply of cheap labour draws new firms to an area. Firms are attracted to areas of high unemployment where wages are likely to be lower than in, for example, south-east England.

Once an industry is well established in an area, new firms may want to set up in that area. They are attracted by the pool of trained and skilled workers. This may save training costs. For example, a firm manufacturing heavy clothing may be attracted to the Leeds area because there is already a supply of trained pattern cutters and sewing machinists.

Nearness to other firms

Firms in some industries need to be in close touch with other members of their industry. The financial services industry is based mainly in the City of London. There they are close to the Bank of England and the Stock Exchange. Although these firms are in competition, they work closely together. They have, for example, developed and use common computer systems.

There are benefits for firms if an industry is based in one area:

- specialist suppliers and services develop to meet the needs of the industry;
- there is a supply of specialised and skilled labour;
- the local college may develop specialist courses for the industry;
- the industry may sponsor the local university to carry out research on its behalf;
- a trade association may develop to represent the industry.

These are all examples of external **economies of scale**.

Owner's choice

Most businesses in the UK are small, and run by their owners. The owners may be unwilling to move their business away from their local area. Once a business is established, even if it grows, there is little reason to move to another area.

Activities

1 Give three things that a furniture maker might take into account when deciding where to locate her business.

2 Explain two reasons why it costs more to buy land in Greater London than in other parts of the country.

3 A carpet manufacturer is considering where to build its factory. There are two choices: a place where there are other carpet makers and another location where there is no competition nearby. Explain an argument in favour of moving to each of these two places.

4 The government sometimes encourages firms to move to areas where there are high levels of unemployed workers. Say how each of these things will help get firms to move to these areas:
   a building a new motorway into the area;
   b offering the firm a £50 a week subsidy for each worker it employs;
   c making planning permission easier to obtain in the area.

5 **Watson Stationery**

Watson Stationery produces high quality writing and printer paper that the company mainly sells abroad. The lease on its factory building is about to expire and the business needs to move to another location very shortly. Christine, the company owner, has discovered two possible sites for the company: Arrington which is only 4 km from the firm's original factory, and Bobleigh which is 400 km away in an area of natural beauty, but has high levels of unemployment. Christine researches the costs of the two places. The main points of Christine's reports are given below.

Arrington: The main advantage is that there will be no need to recruit and re-train workers, as existing workers will be able to continue to work for the company. The land prices are high though (£180,000) and it would cost £200,000 to build a suitable factory. It would also cost £20,000 to be able to present a strong case to the local council to get planning permission. The running costs will be quite high; labour will cost £120,000 a year, but transport will be quite low at £60,000 each year as Arrington is close to the ferry ports. Raw materials will cost the firm £100,000 each year. The yearly cost for electricity will be £20,000.

Bobleigh: If the business moved here, it would have to pay to recruit and train new staff, which would cost £40,000. Land, though, is far cheaper and would only cost £100,000, and there would be no cost at all of getting planning permission; the local council is keen to get new business into the area. It would cost about £10,000 less than at Arrington to build a similar factory as builders are cheaper to employ, and annual labour to run the factory would cost £90,000. Transport, however, would be more expensive at £100,000 each year because vans would have further to travel. Electricity costs would be the same in both places and raw materials a little cheaper at £90,000 as the firm would be closer to the supplier.

Copy out these tables then, using the information given above, complete the costing tables.

Setting-up costs	Arrington	Bobleigh
Planning permission costs		
Cost of buying land		
Factory building		
Recruiting and training staff		
Total cost of setting up		

Annual running costs	Arrington	Bobleigh
Electricity charges		
Labour		
Raw materials		
Transport to market		
Total annual running costs		

a Why might the workers find it difficult to move if the company transferred to Bobleigh?

b What other costs, not mentioned in the report, should be taken into account by Watson's?

c What external economies of scale might the Bobleigh site have?

d Which option would you recommend Watson's to take? Explain your answer by referring to the completed tables.

e If the government offered to give Watson's a subsidy of £40,000 each year for 10 years if it moved to Bobleigh, how would this affect your answer to d?

6 Cost of a coke controlled by the climate

Everyone knows that the price of ice-cream tends to be higher on warm days. But this practice is not restricted to ice-cream sellers. Coca-Cola is experimenting with a new type of vending machine that increases the price it charges for chilled cans of coke as the weather gets warmer. The reason for this is not to exploit consumers, Coca-Cola says, but to avoid vending machines emptying too quickly on hot days. Coca-Cola insists that it could equally be interpreted as a way of lowering prices on cold days.

a Besides ice-cream and soft drinks, give two other products and two services where demand depends on the weather.

b Explain, using the concepts of supply and demand, how the price of a can of Coca-Cola would change as the weather gets warmer.

c Besides lowering the price of its drinks at different times of the year, how might Coca-Cola smooth out the demand for its drinks?

Unit 2.1 Business ownership and funding

Unit 2.1a Sole trader

		→ Key terms
Capital →	the funds invested in a business that enable it to buy the physical assets it needs.	
Discount →	an amount of money deducted from the selling price of a product.	
Division of labour →	the splitting of a job or process into a number of smaller parts.	
Finance →	the money needed to run a business or project.	
Operating capital →	the capital needed to meet the day-to-day running costs of a business.	
Private sector →	businesses that are not owned or run by the state.	
Public sector →	economic activity that is carried out by either national or local government.	
Sole proprietor →	a person who owns and controls their own business.	
Sole trader →	someone who operates in business as an individual.	
Specialisation →	where a job, or part of a job, needs to be done by someone with special skills or tools.	
Start-up capital →	the finance needed to get a business started.	
Unlimited liability →	where the owner is personally responsible for all the debts of the business.	

Public and private sector

Businesses are either in the private sector or the public sector.

- Public sector businesses are owned by public bodies such as central and local government.
- Private sector businesses are owned by individuals or groups of private people. Most businesses are in the private sector.

This flower seller's business is in the private sector

What is a sole trader?

The largest and most common kind of business in the UK is the **sole trader** or **sole proprietor**. Anyone who is in business on their own account is a sole trader. All sole traders have certain things in common:

- one person – the sole proprietor – provides the **capital** and owns the business;
- that person controls the business and makes all the decisions;
- the owner takes all the risks related to the business and takes all the profit.

Sole traders are to be found in all kinds of businesses:

- They may run shops, offer bed and breakfast accommodation or offer specialist services such as hairdressers, plumbers or electricians.
- They are often in highly specialised trades which do not attract enough business to interest larger firms.
- They often do work that needs highly specialised skills or tools. It may not be worthwhile for large firms to employ people with such skills, or to buy specialist tools, since they would only use them

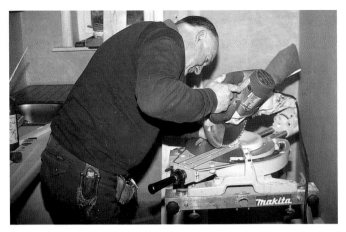
A carpenter is a sole trader

occasionally. Instead certain jobs are put out to small specialist firms, for example in the engineering industry.

Not all sole traders are very small businesses. Some may employ quite a large number of people.

Starting a business

Many businesses start as sole traders. People often set up their own business because they want to be their own boss. Others see a business opportunity and start in a small way. Some grow to be quite big companies. Most stay as sole traders, often because the owner does not want the business to grow too big.

People who start their own business must be hard working, willing to work long hours and to take risks, and enjoy responsibility. They also need to have a business idea. Ideas for a business come in many ways:

- spotting a gap in the market, for example a need for a mobile hairdresser in a rural area or where there are a number of elderly people who cannot travel;
- being often asked by people for a service, for example a carpenter who is asked to make wooden toys for friends' children at Christmas;
- turning a hobby into a business, for example a violinist who repairs violins;
- having a skill and deciding to set up in business as, for example, a plumber or plasterer.

The business idea and the size of the market should be researched before starting the business.

You need finance to start a business. This is the business **start-up capital**. It is used to pay for premises, buy stock or materials, buy a van if necessary, and any-thing else needed to get the business started. Initially you may need very little money; the family car can be used for transport, tools may have been bought already and the kitchen table can be the office. The owner may provide most of the capital from savings, preferring to borrow any extra money from friends or family rather than from a bank. An overdraft might be arranged with a bank to cover emergencies.

Running the business

When a new business starts up it is unlikely to earn enough money to cover all its day-to-day running costs straight away. These include:

- the cost of replacing stock once the starting stock is sold;
- the owner's weekly wage that he or she needs to live on;
- the cost of heating, lighting, advertising, telephones, rent, rates and staff wages.

To meet these everyday costs the owner needs to have **operating capital**. This is in addition to the start-up capital needed. Once the business is established, it should earn enough money to pay its running costs.

Benefits of being a sole trader

1 It is very easy to set up in business as a sole trader. There are only a few requirements, for instance:
   - a business name that should be different from that of any other business;
   - any licences that may be necessary, for example to sell alcohol or tobacco or to run a disco;
   - planning permission from the local council if there is a change in the use of premises;
   - the Inland Revenue has to be told because the new owner will be taxed differently as a self-employed person;
   - registration with Customs and Excise for VAT.
2 The sole trader has total control over the business and makes all the decisions. The owner decides what goods or materials to use or buy, when to open and close and whether to employ staff.
3 Decisions can be made quickly without having to ask anyone else, although advice may need to be taken on some things. Customers and staff like to deal with the boss because they can get answers to questions quickly and easily.

4 The owner does not have to share the profits with a partner or shareholders. This may encourage the owner to work harder. There is a direct link between the amount of work put into a business, its success and the money earned by the owner.

5 Very little **capital** may be needed to start up the business. The amount needed varies according to the type of business. It is much more expensive to set up a restaurant than to start a plumbing business, where little more than tools is needed.

It is a very flexible form of business. If it does not work out, it is relatively easy to switch to something else.

Drawbacks of being a sole trader

1 The main disadvantage is **unlimited liability**. This means that the sole proprietor has to pay for all the debts incurred by the business. There is no real difference between the owner's personal money and the money tied up in the business. If the business makes a loss the owner is personally liable to pay the debts. In an extreme case the owner might have to sell personal or family property to pay off business debts. There is no limit to the owner's personal liability for the debts of the business.

2 Because their businesses are usually small, sole traders find it hard to compete with larger firms.

- Small firms cannot buy their supplies on such good terms as larger firms. The big firms buy in large quantities and are given a bigger discount by suppliers for bulk buying.

A local shopping centre

- Small firms do not gain the benefits of specialisation and the economies of scale. Every employee has to do a range of jobs, so they are unable to break up operations through the **division of labour**.

3 Sole traders that want to expand their business often find it hard to get the finance to do so. There is a limit to the amount friends and family can lend. The banks tend to charge sole traders a higher rate of interest because they cannot offer enough security for loans.

4 The sole proprietor is tied to the business. If the owner is ill there may be no one to take over responsibility. Taking a holiday may mean closing the business while the owner is away.

Benefits

- I'm my own boss
- I didn't need much capital to get started
- I make all the decisions
- I get all the profits, and I don't have to share them with anybody
- I can open and close and come and go as I please

Drawbacks

- Unlimited liability – I could lose my house, the lot
- Its hard competing with the big boys, no one will give me their discounts
- We have to do everything ourselves
- The bank charges me more interest than the big firm down the road
- I can never get away, every night and weekend I have to do my books
- I'd love a holiday, but we can never get away

Figure 2.1 Benefits and drawbacks of being a sole trader

Business Structure, Control and Organisation

Profit-taker	Risk-taker
Sole owner	Long hours
Decision maker	Unlimited liability
Own boss	Finance raising
Flexibility	No holidays

Figure 2.2 The two sides of being a sole trader

Activities

1 Write out this passage, filling in the missing words from the list in the box.

Sole traders

Sole traders are examples of _____ sector businesses. They are also known as sole _____ . The main feature of a sole trader is that one person both owns and _____ the business. The owner takes all of the _____ in running the business but receives all the _____ . The sole trader has unlimited _____ , which means he or she is responsible for all the business's _____ .

> risks   manages   debts   proprietors
> private   liability   profits

2 List the reasons why sole traders might find it difficult to raise finance.

3 Many sole traders fail before the business is five years old. Describe reasons why sole traders are more likely to fail than larger businesses.

4 Explain why the following businesses might be better run as a small firm than a large organisation:
  a stained-glass designer;
  b childminder;
  c village shop.

Case Study

5 Lampshades

Joanne has a part-time business selling lampshades on a market stall. She has a stall each Saturday, for which she pays £40 daily rent. The trading day lasts from 8.30 am to 4.30 pm. Joanne also gives £15 to her daughter to help her set up and close down the stall, and to allow Joanne a short break for lunch.

The lampshades are bought from a wholesaler for £9 each, though the company will give a 10% discount if more than 40 shades are bought at one time. Joanne tries to keep her stock level at an absolute minimum, so she only buys what she thinks she will sell on any one day. She has no other costs to her business.

Experience has taught Joanne that the number of shades she sells each Saturday depends solely on the price she asks for the shades. She has created this demand schedule to help her planning.

Price of lampshades	Number bought each Saturday
£10	42
£12	35
£14	30
£16	23
£18	15
£20	12

At the moment Joanne runs the only lampshade stall in the market. There are rumours, however, that another stall-holder is intending to diversify into lampshades in the near future.

While Joanne enjoys her business, she does not expect to make a fortune out of it. She believes that as long as she is making at least £8 an hour profit, then it is worth her time.

Imagine you are a small business advisor and Joanne has come to you for help. She has asked you to comment on her business. She is particularly concerned about the threat of competition and is wondering if it is worthwhile keeping the stall.

Your job is to give the business a 'health check' and produce a report on what you think. You should look at these points:

- the price Joanne should charge to get the maximum profit from selling the lampshades;
- Joanne's attitude towards stock control;
- what could be done if another stall starts selling lampshades;
- whether she should give up the business.

ICT Activity

Produce your report for Joanne using a computer.

6 Snow Bound

Snow Bound is a ski-equipment hire business owned by former geography teacher, Pete Knight. Pete used to organise his school's annual skiing holiday. Appalled at the prices the students had to pay to hire skiing clothes, Pete persuaded the headteacher to use school funds to buy a stock of clothing. It could then be hired out at more reasonable rates. Other schools soon heard about Pete's enterprise and asked if they could hire the clothing for their ski trips.

After a few years, Pete realised that there was an opportunity to run his own business hiring out skiwear. Keeping his 'day job' as a teacher, he arranged a bank loan for £20,000. He used this money to buy stocks of ski clothes. He then advertised his service by sending a mailshot to schools in the area.

He was able to keep his costs down by storing his stock in a spare room in his house and

using his bedroom as an office. After four successful years he took the important decision to give up his teaching job and run the business full time. He was able to rent a small warehouse to store his stock and to get back the use of his house. He started to advertise his service in national educational newspapers to gain a larger market.

He is also considering arranging school skiing trips in the future.

a What did Pete do to make sure that the risks he took in starting Snow Bound were as low as possible?

b Why was Pete able to undercut other skiwear hire businesses when he started Snow Bound?

c As a sole trader, Pete has 'unlimited liability'. Explain what this term means.

d What advantages would the larger ski hire companies have over Snow Bound?

e Despite being a successful business, there is no reason why it will continue to do as well in years to come. Describe three things beyond Pete's control that could cause problems for Snow Bound in the future.

f Pete informed his local council that he was running a business from home. Fortunately they granted him planning permission. Describe the circumstances under which a new business might not be given planning permission.

g Not everyone could be as successful as Pete. What personal qualities do you feel Pete has that allow him to do well as a sole trader?

ICT Activity

Produce a letter that Pete might use to advertise his business. Find the names and addresses of a number of local schools then mailmerge them to create personalised letters.

Unit 2.1 Business ownership and funding

Unit 2.1b Partnerships

		→ **Key terms**
Deed of Partnership →	a written document that sets out the business relationship between members of a partnership.	
Limited partner →	a member of a partnership who has unlimited liability. Such partners invest money and have a share of the profits, but play no part in running the firm.	
Partnership →	where two or more people own a business together with a view to making a profit.	
Sleeping partner →	a member of a partnership who invests money in the firm but plays no part in its running.	

One of the options open to sole traders who want to expand their business is to take on one or more partners. The business then becomes a **partnership**. This is quite a big step because it changes the ownership and the way a business is run.

What is a partnership?

A partnership exists when two or more people own a business together with a view to making a profit.

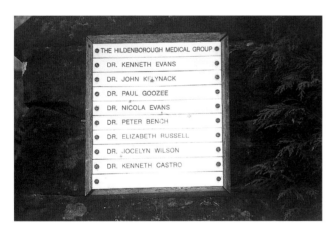

A medical practice is an example of a partnership

- Each partner is a part owner of the business and has a right to take part in its running.
- Ordinary partners have unlimited liability. If the business fails they can each lose all their personal wealth, not just the money they invested in the business.
- A maximum of 20 partners is allowed in a general partnership. Solicitors, accountants and estate agents can have more than 20 partners.

- In law it is assumed that capital, profit and responsibility are all shared equally by the partners. If the partners want to do something different from this they must draw up a legal document which sets out the terms of the partnership. This is called a deed of partnership.

Sleeping partners or **limited partners** may invest money in a business but take no part in its running. They do not have unlimited liability. However, they lose this protection once they play any part in running the business. Sleeping partners and limited partners are both quite rare.

Why form a partnership?

- To finance expansion of a sole trader's business. A sole trader's own resources will be limited. So too will the money that friends and family are willing to lend. Borrowing money from the bank is expensive.
- To obtain capital for a business. Many businesses start out as partnerships. It may take more capital to set up a business than one person can raise.
- To get someone to share the work and the responsibility of running the business.
- To add new skills to the business. Partners can specialise in certain aspects of the business.

Deed of partnership

This is a very important document and is the contract that sets out the terms of the relationship between the partners. It includes:
- the rights and duties of each of the partners;

- the names of the partners and the purpose of the partnership;
- how much money (capital) each partner has put into the business;
- how profits and losses are to be divided – usually in the same proportion as the share of capital. A partner that has put in 20% of the capital will usually get 20% of the profits;
- how disputes between partners are to be settled and the number of votes each partner has at partnership meetings;
- how the partnership would be wound up, and what happens if one of the partners dies or wants to leave, or a new partner comes into the firm;
- other matters, such as how often partners can withdraw their share of the profits (drawings). It also states if interest is to be paid on capital, and whether partners are to be paid a salary in addition to their share of the profits.

If there is no deed of partnership the law assumes that each partner is equal. Profits are therefore shared equally however much money each of the partners has put into the business.

Benefits of partnerships

1 It is an easy way to bring in extra capital if a sole trader wants to expand a business. Two or three people can usually raise more money than one person to start a new business. There can be up to 20 partners, so quite large amounts of capital can be brought into the business.

John Lewis is a well-known example of a partnership

2 Costs are shared. For this reason it is cheaper for five doctors to share premises than for each of them to have their own practice. Problems, management and responsibility are all shared. This reduces strain on the partners and may allow them more time for leisure.
3 It may be easier to make decisions because 'two heads (or more) are better than one'.
4 The business details of the partnership can be kept private. Accounts are not published so no one, except the tax authorities, can find out how much profit the business is making or how much each partner earns.
5 Partners can specialise in particular aspects of the business. A firm of accountants might have a partner that specialises in tax matters while another deals with small businesses.
6 New blood, new ideas and new skills can be attracted by offering a partnership. It is also used by some firms to reward hard work and loyalty and as a method of 'bringing on' future senior managers.

Drawbacks of partnerships

1 The main disadvantage is that each partner has unlimited liability. Each is personally liable for the debts of the business as a whole. Thus a partner could lose all their private wealth, even if the problem was nothing to do with them. Someone owed money by the firm can sue the partnership or choose to sue just one partner. If that partner had to pay the debt, he or she would have to get the other partners to pay up their share of the money owed.
2 Partnerships can still run short of capital, especially if they want to expand the business. Partners may have invested all they can afford when they joined the partnership. They may not want to add more partners because more people will share the profits.
3 Differences of opinion can lead to the break up of the partnership. There can be difficulties if one partner is seen not to be pulling his or her weight.
4 A partner can bind the business and the other partners to doing something the other partners do not agree with. A careless or 'rogue' partner can cause financial problems for the business and the other partners.

Business Structure, Control and Organisation

5 There is no continuity. If one partner leaves the partnership or dies, the partnership comes to an end. If the partners that are left want to carry on in business they must form a new partnership. A partnership cannot be passed on to someone else or sold. This is because it is a personal contract or agreement between the partners.

6 It is hard for partners who want to withdraw from a firm to get their money back.

Benefits of working as partners:
- more start-up capital
- shared costs
- shared decision-making
- wider range of skills
- more ideas.

Drawbacks of working as partners:
- unlimited liability
- have to share profits
- limited capital
- one partner's actions can ruin the business
- no continuity
- hard to get money back.

Figure 2.3 Partners

Activities

1 Both partners and sole traders have unlimited liability. Explain why unlimited liability is probably more of a risk to partners than it would be to a sole trader.

2 Suggest a reason why there is a legal limit on the number of partners in a partnership.

3 Imagine that you and a friend decide to form a partnership and go into business together. Between you, discuss any concerns you may have in running the business. Write a deed of partnership that would overcome any worries each of you may have about working together.

4 'A deed of partnership is not needed when the partners have a good working relationship.' Comment on how true you believe this statement to be.

Case Study

5 Needlecraft

Mary and Tracey met at art college when they were both students and have remained firm friends ever since. While at college Tracey developed a flair for making stylish, inexpensive jewellery. She found she had no trouble selling her jewellery to other students. Mary had studied textile design and had used her time at college to develop her embroidery skills using sewing machines.

When they left college Mary started her own sole-trader business that she called Needlecraft. She was able to put into practice the skills she had learned at college to produce attractive wall hangings and quilted pictures. These were then sold through specialist art shops and at craft fairs. While not making a fortune, Mary was just about able to make a living from the business. Tracey, on the other hand, had started working as a trainee manager at a supermarket, a job she did not particularly like.

At one of their nights out, Mary suggested that Tracey should give up her job and join her in the art business. Mary suggested that Tracey had learned valuable management skills as a trainee manager and could contribute a lot to the business in addition to her skills of jewellery making. Mary also hinted she would like to have the support of another person in the business.

a Why was it important that Mary and Tracey knew each other well when they formed their partnership?

b Mary seemed to want the support of somebody else in the business. Give examples of how partners can offer each other support.

c Mary and Tracey were able to bring different strengths to the partnership.
  i State what these strengths might be.
  ii Explain why it is important that partners have different skills.

d Discuss reasons why Tracey may have concerns about going into partnership with Mary.

6 John Lewis Partnership

Not all partnerships are small businesses; there are some that are extremely large. The retailer John Lewis is an example of a large partnership. The company owns a chain of department stores throughout Britain, and the Waitrose supermarket chain. More than 50,000 of the people who work at John Lewis and Waitrose are partners in the business. As a result the company is managed in a quite different way from other large businesses.

John Spedan Lewis, the founder of the company, believed that you get the best from people when they feel happy and secure. He saw a partnership as being a much fairer way of running a business than having the traditional boss/employee relationship. People who worked at John Lewis would also be more likely to be loyal if they were partners in the business.

Part of the company's annual profits are put back into the business so it is able to expand. The rest of the profits are shared between the

partners as their annual bonus. Partners, no matter how junior, are entitled to have their questions answered about how the company is being run. Each John Lewis partner is said to have profit, knowledge and power.

John Lewis has a carefully arranged system so that every partner can have some say in the running of the business. Each partner has the opportunity to discuss any concerns he or she may have with a manager. Partners can express their views through an elaborate democratic structure, including a Central Council, which elects three members of the Trust and five members of the Central Board. The company produces a regular journal, *The Gazette*, which gives partners details of how well the shops are doing each week. Partners can write letters to *The Gazette* that will be answered by one of the directors.

a Explain how John Lewis is different from other companies.

b How does John Lewis allow the partners to know what is happening in the business?

c Describe the benefits to John Lewis of having a loyal workforce.

d Not everyone who works at John Lewis likes the idea of being a partner in the business. Discuss the possible reasons for this.

e Very few businesses are organised along the lines of John Lewis. Suggest reasons why the traditional manager/employee relationship is more popular elsewhere.

ICT Activity

Write a short article for John Lewis's *Gazette* explaining the benefits that the company offers its partners. Information can be found on the company's website: www.john-lewis-partnership.co.uk

Unit 2.1 Business ownership and funding

Unit 2.1c Limited companies

	Key terms
Annual General Meeting (AGM) →	a meeting of ordinary shareholders that must be held by a public limited company at the end of every financial year.
Annual Report and Accounts →	a report that limited companies must produce at the end of every financial year. It must be approved by the AGM and a copy sent to the Registrar of Companies.
Articles of Association →	the internal rules that govern the running of a limited company.
Directors →	people elected by the shareholders to the board of directors of a company, to run the firm on their behalf.
Dividends →	the share of a company's profits that is paid to shareholders.
Economies of scale →	the reduction in the costs of a business that are a result of an increase in a firm's output or size.
Incorporation →	the process that gives an organisation a separate legal existence of its own.
Joint stock company →	a company that is jointly owned by its shareholders.
Limited liability →	when the liability of the shareholders in a company is limited to their original investment if the company should fail.
Memorandum of Association →	a document that must be drawn up when forming a limited company. It states briefly the main details of the company that may be needed by external bodies.
Shareholders →	holders of shares in a limited company, in which each is a part owner of the company.
Shares →	the units into which the capital of a limited company is divided.

Due to the high risk of investing in them, sole traders and partnerships find it hard to raise capital to expand their businesses. People are afraid they might lose everything they own if the business fails. **Limited liability** overcomes this fear and encourages people to invest in industry and commerce. It enables limited companies to be formed. All the members of a limited company have limited liability.

Limited liability

Limited liability lets people invest money in businesses without risking their personal wealth. If a business fails, the liability of investors is limited to the amount they put into the business. For example, if someone invests £500 in a limited company that fails, then the most that person can lose is that £500. No more money can be claimed by those that are owed money by the firm.

Shareholders

There are people who want to put money into a business but do not want to take part in running it. They hope their money will earn more than they would get by leaving it in a bank. They invest money by buying **shares** in a company. They become **shareholders**. They partly own the business but play no part in the day-to-day running of it.

When a company sells shares it is dividing its capital into equal parts. Every share gives the holder an equal share in the ownership and profits of the company. This is why shareholders have one vote per share at company meetings. **Dividends** (the shareholders' share of the profits) are also paid at so much per share. Companies are owned jointly by the shareholders, which is why they are called **joint stock companies**.

Types of limited company

There are two types of limited company:
- the private limited company, which has the letters Ltd at the end of its name;
- the public limited company, which has the initials PLC at the end of its name.

Both types of firm must include either 'Ltd' or 'PLC', as the case may be, after their company names. This tells those that do business with them that they have limited liability. There may be some risk in dealing with them, as the owners are not liable to pay off the firm's debts.

How public and private limited companies differ

Private company
- There must be at least two shareholders.
- There must be at least one **director**.
- Shares are issued but may not be sold to the public.
- Shares cannot be transferred freely. Shares can only be transferred with the agreement of the other shareholders.
- It must hold an **Annual General Meeting (AGM)** and send a copy of the accounts to shareholders and to the Registrar of Companies every year.

Public company
- It must have a minimum capital of £50,000.
- The company must have at least seven shareholders, although only two people are needed to sign the **Memorandum of Association.**
- Shares are sold to the public.
- The company must hold an Annual General Meeting where the directors present the **Annual Report and Accounts**. The meeting approves the accounts and appoints directors. A copy of the Annual Report and Accounts must be sent to the Registrar of Companies at Companies House in Cardiff. The accounts can be inspected there by anyone with an interest in them.

Incorporation

All limited companies are incorporated. This means that they have a separate legal existence of their own. In law, the company becomes separate from the people that own it. The company can be sued and it can sue others in its own name. It can commit crimes, such as fraud, and it can be fined, but not sent to prison.

Setting up a limited company

Every limited company must be registered with the Registrar of Companies. Before a limited company can start to trade it must send certain documents to the Registrar.

Memorandum of Association
This must include:
- the company name, including either Ltd or PLC;
- the address of the company's registered office;
- a statement that the shareholders have limited liability;
- the amount of each type of share it can issue (its authorised capital);
- the objects of the company – what its activities are intended to be.

The company will probably say its authorised capital is greater than it really needs. This allows it to raise more capital in the future without the cost of changing its Memorandum.

The objects clause is very important. A company cannot legally do things that are not covered by its objects clause. It is therefore in a company's interest to keep it as general as possible.

Articles of Association
This sets out the rules for running the company. For example, the voting rights of shareholders; when the Annual General Meeting will be held; how profits will be distributed; the number, rights and duties of directors.

Certificate of Incorporation
Once the Registrar is satisfied that all the formalities have been properly completed, the Certificate of Incorporation is issued. This makes the company a separate entity in law. At this point a private company can begin to trade.

Prospectus
Before a public company can sell its shares to the public it has to issue a prospectus. This gives details of the history of the company, its future plans and estimates of future profits. It must be truthful and give the public an honest basis on which to decide to invest. The law and the Stock Exchange lay down what the prospectus must contain.

Trading Certificate
A public company may not start trading until it has sold shares. A company must have enough capital to

pay its debts and to trade effectively. When the Registrar of Companies is happy that the company has raised the capital it needs, a Trading Certificate is issued. Only then can it begin to trade.

Advantages of private companies

1 They can be set up quite cheaply. Setting up a private company is the ideal way to run a small business. Many private companies are family owned and run. They have most of the freedom and flexibility of the sole trader and partnership, but without the risks of unlimited liability.
2 Small private companies can raise capital more easily. Limited liability makes people more willing to invest in them and they can also borrow money more easily. It also provides a basis for later growth into public companies.
3 There is continuity because the company has a separate legal identity. The business does not come to an end when one of the owners dies or pulls out of the business.
4 The owners are able to keep control of the business because they can choose the shareholders.

Drawbacks of private companies

Because shares are not sold on the open market:
- it can be hard for investors to get their money back when they want to;
- people may be unwilling to buy shares in a private company.

Compared with a sole trader or partnership:
- there are more controls over the way the business is run;
- there is less privacy because accounts have to be sent to the Registrar of Companies.

Advantages of public companies

1 The market for shares is highly organised through the Stock Exchange. Shareholders who want their money back can sell their shares easily. This makes people more willing to invest in PLCs. It is easy to check how much shares in a company are worth. The price at which shares are sold is shown in newspapers every day.
2 Large amounts of capital can be gathered in one organisation. Very large companies can be formed that are able to compete on a global basis. Some industries need very large amounts of capital, so only very large companies can run them. For example, the petrol and chemicals company BP has capital of nearly £30 billion.
3 Because they can be very large, public companies are able to benefit from **economies of scale**. They can afford to pay high salaries to attract top quality staff. They can also employ specialist staff.
4 Banks are more willing to lend to companies that have large share capital.
5 Anyone wishing to do business with a public company can check its Annual Report and Accounts. They can find out about the company and see if it is financially sound.

Drawbacks of public companies

1 In practice, the ordinary small shareholder has very little influence on the way a company is run. In many companies most of the shares are owned by insurance companies and pension funds. These financial institutions have huge voting power, leaving the small shareholder with very little say.
2 Ownership, management and control become separated. The owners take no part in the day-to-day management of the company; this is done by paid employees. The managers may have different goals from the owners. The management structure needed to run a large firm may be very complex.
3 Public companies are very strictly controlled by law, and regulated by the Department for Trade and Industry.

There are fewer limited companies than any other kind of business organisation. However, their total value is far greater than that of any other form of business. Although there are some very big partnerships with branches all over the world, they are an exception, for example the accountants Price Waterhouse Coopers. All the major businesses are limited companies.

Activities

1 Produce a list of five companies you know which have limited liability. They will have either PLC or Ltd after their names.

2 Copy out the passage below, inserting the correct words from those in the box.

Owning businesses

People who invest money in a business are called _____ . This means that they part of the company, even though they may not want to have any day-to-day _____ of the business. Instead they elect _____ to look after their interests. The part of the company's profits they receive is called their _____ . To be able to sell shares a company must be _____ . This means it has _____ liability.

> directors   control   shareholders   own
> dividend   limited   incorporated

3 Explain why people would be worried about putting money into a business that did not have limited liability.

4 List three questions which shareholders might ask at their company's Annual General Meeting (AGM).

ICT Activity

Monitor the share prices over a five-week period of three well-known companies quoted on the Stock Exchange. Place the results on a spreadsheet and draw a graph to show how the prices have changed. Add comments to the graph to try to account for any changes that have occurred.

---

5 D Moody Ltd

D Moody Ltd is a family business started by David Moody in the early 1950s. The business began with one lorry bought with the money Mr Moody received when he left the RAF. Mr Moody used the lorry to make deliveries of coal to local houses. He later bought a tipper, so bulk deliveries could be made to larger coal users, such as power stations and factories.

In the late 1960s Moody's noticed a decline in the demand for coal. To help, the business started to transport agricultural grain around the country and began selling building materials from their yards. The miners' strike in the 1980s virtually ended coal deliveries for the business and it looked elsewhere for income. Moody's decided to expand the building material part of the business. The company also joined with other similar firms to form a next-day delivery parcel courier network, called Focus.

The company gained limited liability status in the mid-1960s and family members own all the shares. Since David's retirement, his son, Alan, heads the company. The business provides work for many members of the Moody family, including Alan's own daughter and son. Some people in the business can see advantages to D Moody merging with some of the other parcel carriers in the network and forming a public limited company. However, not everybody at Moody's is keen on this move.

a Suggest reasons why there has been a decline in the demand for coal since the 1960s.

b Use the information in the case study to show how Moody's has adapted to a changing market.

c Describe the documents D Moody Ltd would need to allow it to become a public limited company.

d Why might some of Moody's shareholders be concerned about the suggestion to go public?

Business Structure, Control and Organisation

Unit 2.1 Business ownership and funding

Unit 2.1d Co-operatives

→ Key terms

Consumer	→	the final buyer or user of a good or service.
Consumer co-operative	→	an organisation, owned by its members, set up to provide members with good, honest products at a fair price. Members share its profits and have a say in the way it is run.
Customer	→	a buyer of goods and services from a supplier.
Dividend	→	the share of a co-operative's profits that is paid to its members.
Mutual societies	→	businesses, usually insurance companies or building societies, that exist to provide services to members and whose profits are used for the benefit of members.
Producer co-operative	→	a group of producers who join together to market, promote and distribute their products for their mutual benefit.
Worker co-operative	→	a group of workers who set up or buy into a business and share in its ownership, management and control.

A co-operative is a form of business that is owned by its members. The members may be its customers, its workers or a group of producers who cooperate to sell their produce.

Features of co-operatives

Co-operatives share many aspects of a limited company.

- They have limited liability and a separate legal existence from their members, that is, they are incorporated.
- The members provide the capital by buying shares. The shares are not sold on the Stock Exchange. They have to be sold back to the co-operative.
- They share profits in the form of dividends.
- Members have a say in running the business by voting at the Annual General Meeting (AGM). The AGM covers the same kind of business as that of a limited company. Voting is different from that of a limited company in that members have one vote each, no matter how many shares they have.

The co-operative movement

At one time the co-operative movement was strong in the UK, across a wide range of different goods and services. Almost every region and large town had its own retail co-operative society. The retail societies owned the Co-operative Wholesale Society that supplied them with most of the goods they sold. There is also a Co-operative Bank and the Co-operative Insurance Society (CIS).

The Co-op has changed dramatically since it began as a small grocers shop over 150 years ago

CIS building in Manchester

Over the last 30 years the retail societies have found it hard to raise capital to build large out-of-town stores and to compete with supermarkets and specialist shops. However, the Co-operative Bank and the CIS have continued to do well.

Co-operatives are still an important form of business in the UK, though they are more common in other countries, especially less-developed countries.

Types of co-operative

Consumer co-operatives

These are the local Co-op shops. They are owned by their customers, the consumers. The first shop started at Toad Lane in Rochdale in 1844 with 28 members. Sixty years later there were 1.7 million members in nearly 1,500 different societies all over the UK. Today, societies have merged into about 50 large, mainly regional societies. They still keep their original aim, to

sell 'pure food at fair prices and with honest weights and measures, rather than simply for profit'. In the past, profits were divided according to the amount spent; this was the dividend, or the 'divi' as it was known. These days, the dividend may be paid out or, more usually, used to keep prices down. The Co-operative Insurance Society and the Co-operative Bank are also consumer societies.

Worker co-operatives

These are formed by the people that work in a business. A group of workers may buy out their firm because it is about to close down. As in other co-operatives, decisions, profits and risks are all shared equally. Capital is provided by the members who buy shares, with the rest coming from borrowing. Decisions are taken at meetings of all the members, who usually have one vote each. Worker co-operatives do not often have industrial relations problems and members work hard for their firm. The main drawbacks are:

- it can be difficult to raise capital;
- how to deal with new workers joining the firm – should they put capital into the business, and for how long should they work in the firm before getting a share of the profits?
- if the firm gets bigger, more people take part in making decisions and it becomes harder to get agreement.

Producer co-operatives

These are groups of producers that get together to sell and distribute their products. They are often found in agriculture. By working together and pooling their resources members are more effective than when they are each acting on their own. The advantages are:

- products can be jointly marketed and packaged;
- the producers may set up their own transport company to distribute the produce;
- they can get together to buy supplies such as seed and fertiliser;
- they can buy equipment jointly and share its use.

Another example of a producer co-operative is a group of craftsmen getting together to buy a building and dividing it into workshops, with perhaps a shop to sell their products.

Other co-operatives

Any group set up for the benefit of its members and controlled by its members, and who share the profits and make decisions democratically, is a co-operative.

Other than the CIS, many insurance companies in the UK were set up in this way. **Mutual** building societies are another example, the biggest of which is the Nationwide. Many of these insurance companies and building societies have been de-mutualised. This means that instead of sharing profits for the benefit of members, profits are paid to shareholders. They have become ordinary limited-liability companies with many of the building societies becoming banks.

Credit unions are another type of co-operative. In this case a group of people pay savings into a fund, probably every week. The money earns interest but can be taken out when needed. The money is used to make loans to members at a low rate of interest. Credit unions are often set up by people who do not like banks or who may find it hard to borrow money from banks.

Activities

1 What does it mean if an organisation is described as being 'mutual'?

2 Co-operatives and public limited companies have some things in common and some things that are different.
   a Give two similarities between the two types of organisation.
   b Give two differences between them.

3 Workers co-operatives are often formed when a business is about to close down. Suggest reasons why the workers may feel they could make a success of the business when the previous managers were unable to do so.

4 The Co-operative Bank has a reputation for not dealing with companies that have the ability to harm people. For example, it will not lend money to tobacco companies and firms that trade with countries that have poor human rights records. Explain how taking this position might affect the Co-operative Bank's profits.

Case Study

5 CWS and CRS

The co-operative movement started in 1844 when 28 poor Rochdale mill workers formed a grocery club so they could buy food and household goods at cheaper prices than elsewhere. The idea was that any profits made would be given back to those who shopped there. From these humble beginnings the co-operative movement was formed.

At their peak, Co-op stores between them controlled about 25% of the retail market. Since the growth of the big supermarkets such as Asda and Tesco, this share has rapidly declined. There followed a period when Co-ops merged in order to survive the competition from the giant supermarkets.

The two biggest co-operative organisations, the CWS and the CRS (the Co-operative Wholesale Society and the Co-operative Retail Services) have recently had talks about a possible merger. Both organisations have a long history, but have watched their market share being taken away by the supermarkets.

Finding it difficult to compete with the cut-price supermarkets, many Co-ops have tried to find a new market as convenience stores. Customers of these stores are often prepared to pay slightly higher prices. Co-ops are also looking at developing other non-food areas such as their travel agencies.

a What were the two factors that encouraged the CWS and CRS to consider joining together?
b Explain how merging can allow smaller Co-ops to be in a stronger position to compete with the supermarkets.
c Why might people be prepared to pay more for goods at a convenience store?
d Why do you think supermarkets such as Tesco and Asda have been able to take so much of the Co-op's market share?

Unit 2.1 Business ownership and funding

Unit 2.1e Franchises

For someone thinking of starting a business, one of the options open to them is to buy a **franchise**. Franchises are advertised regularly in the business sections of newspapers. There are also exhibitions where people interested in starting a franchise can get more information and talk to firms selling franchises. Firms that offer franchises (**franchisors**) are careful to ensure that the people who buy a franchise (**franchisees**) are able to run the business well. The name and reputation of the franchisor is at stake. Franchises are most common in the service sector.

What is a franchise?

A franchise is where an exiting company (the franchisor) lets someone else (the **franchisee**) use its business idea and name. The franchisor charges a fee that is usually in two parts:

- a basic fee to buy the franchise;
- a percentage of the franchisee's profits from the business.

In return for the fee, the franchisee buys a **licence** to carry out the business of the franchisor. Every franchise should look like and work in exactly the same way as the franchisor.

Features of franchises

- The franchisee buys the right to use a known and successful name, logo and brand within a certain geographical area.

- The way premises are designed and how the name and logo are used are strictly laid down. Fixtures and fittings are standard so that premises are easily identified by the public. The Body Shop, McDonald's and Kentucky Fried Chicken shops look exactly the same all over the world.
- Staff uniforms are also standard. So too is the training that staff get.
- There is also training for the franchisee in the business systems and methods used by the franchisor.
- All supplies used in the franchise have to be bought from the franchisor.

Benefits of a franchise

To the franchisee

- It is easier to set up a business using a well-established and known name than it is to start from nothing.

The Make Your Mark Human Rights campaign in the window of The Body Shop, Brighton (© Adrian Brooks)

Burger King is a familiar example of a franchise

- Franchisees can start up and run their own business with a lower risk than normal. The failure rate for new franchises is much lower than for other new businesses.
- Franchisors provide support and help, particularly when the business first starts.
  - They lay down a minimum level of capital that the franchisee must have. This avoids having too little capital, one of the main causes of business failure.
  - Franchisees are given training before the business starts. They also get further training from time to time.
  - Franchisors are big enough to have their own specialist departments, for example marketing, accounting and research. These resources can be used by the franchisees.
- New franchisees get help, advice and support on how to run and develop the business.
- They benefit from national advertising and promotion.
- Each franchisee is given a geographical area and knows that there will not be another franchise by the same firm within that area.

To the franchisor
- The business can be expanded very cheaply. The costs of new premises, more staff and buying extra stock are met by the franchisee.

- The franchisee also pays towards the general costs of the business, such as advertising.
- The franchisor gains the economies of scale that come from buying in bulk from suppliers.
- Franchisees usually have to buy their supplies from the franchisor. This benefits the franchisor in two ways: it can buy goods in bulk, and therefore more cheaply, and it also makes a profit on the goods it sells to the franchisees.
- The business is probably more successful than if it opened more branches and took on more staff. The franchisees have a financial stake in the business and are working for themselves. They will therefore work hard to make it a success.

Drawbacks of a franchise
To the franchisee
- Franchises are not very flexible. The franchisor keeps tight control over the business so that the franchisees are not able to develop their businesses as they want.
- Franchisees are not able to sell their businesses without the agreement of the franchisor.
- A fixed share of the turnover has to be paid to the franchisor.

To the franchisor
- A franchisee may not provide a good service, which might damage the name of the franchisor.

Activities

1 Suggest reasons why companies might franchise their business ideas rather than produce the goods or provide the service themselves.

2 Explain two reasons why a fast-food restaurant might have a better chance of success as a McDonald's franchise than it would using the owner's name.

3 Why is staff training important for a franchise business?

4 Gastro-Dome

Sandra and her husband Ian started their first specialist vegetarian restaurant called Gastro-Dome in 1977 in Manchester. The restaurant opened at a time when people were becoming more health conscious and wealthier, and so could afford to eat out more often. The restaurant was an immediate success appealing to meat eaters as well as strict vegetarians.

More restaurants were opened and by the mid-1990s Sandra and Ian had a flourishing business of 16 restaurants located in major cities. Gastro-Domes became well-known nationally for their exciting cooking and relaxed, upmarket atmosphere. It was at this time that Sandra suggested, rather than opening up more restaurants, they should sell franchises to other businesses that wanted to trade under the Gastro-Dome brand.

Sandra and Ian knew that if franchising were to work, they would need to ensure that franchisees were able to maintain the high standards that had been set at Gastro-Domes. The couple recognised that they would need a clear set of rules. There would also need to be a system for checking that franchisees were keeping standards high.

a What made Gastro-Dome suitable for franchising?

b Explain how one careless franchisee could ruin Gastro-Dome's reputation.

c Produce a list of the rules you would expect Gastro-Dome franchisees to follow.

d Describe how you would ensure that each franchisee restaurant was checked to maintain standards.

e What type of training would new Gastro-Dome franchisees need?

5 Thrifty Car Rental

In 1997 two brothers, Andrew and Robert Burton, bought the UK part of the Thrifty car hire business. This gave the Burtons the right to sell Thrifty franchises in Britain. At first there were just 47 Thrifty franchises operating, which the Burtons hoped to increase to 100. As its name suggests, Thrifty operates at the economy end of the car hire business.

A car hire company that wants to trade under the Thrifty name must pay the Burton brothers £17,000 plus 3.5% royalty on its turnover. In return it gets a site from which to operate, the Thrifty brand image, training, money for a public relations launch and the ability to tap into the Thrifty network. Thrifty will also guarantee a certain geographical area in which to operate with no other franchises allowed within it.

According to the British Franchise Association (BFA) there are many advantages to being a franchisee. The franchising business has a well-established reputation, so less promotion is needed. The BFA also says that franchisees need less capital to get started and have the backing of a wide network of other franchisees. The chances of succeeding in business are much higher, with 94% of franchises reporting that they make a profit.

a List the advantages mentioned above of having a Thrifty franchise.

b Why is it important that Thrifty franchisees are guaranteed their own geographical area?

c If a franchisee had an annual turnover of £200,000, how much would the Burton brothers receive as royalties?

d Explain why a franchised Thrifty car hire business is more likely to be successful than one without the backing of the franchise.

ICT Activity

Many franchisers advertise on the Internet. Find an example of a franchise advertisement. List the advantages that the franchiser offers to franchisees. Examples of sites are: www.lds.co.uk and www.franchise-group.com.

Unit 2.1 Business ownership and funding

Unit 2.1f Public sector organisations

Central government →	the national government responsible for running a country.
Contracting out →	getting some of the work of an organisation done on its behalf by another company.
Compulsory competitive tendering →	a form of contracting out, where local authorities are required by law to invite private sector firms to supply services previously provided by themselves.
Financial institutions →	the name given to banks, insurance companies, pension providers and others who sell their financial services to business and the public. In the UK they are based mainly in the City of London.
Local government →	locally elected councils that provide a range of services within their locality.
Mixed economy →	an economy that is made up of both public sector and private sector enterprises.
Monopoly →	where a firm is the only producer of a product or is able to control the price of a product or the amount that is sold.
Planning permission →	the approval given by a local council to allow a new building to be constructed, or an existing one changed.
Private sector →	businesses that are not owned or run by the state.
Privatisation →	the sale or transfer of enterprises and services from the public to the private sector.
Public corporation →	a type of independent trading body for the control of state-owned enterprises, but which is not a government department.
Public sector →	economic activity carried out by either national or local government.
Regulator →	a person appointed by the government to supervise and control the activities of an industry.

The UK is a **mixed economy**. This means that it is made up of **public sector** and **private sector** enterprises. The public sector is made up of organisations that are owned and controlled by either **local** or **central government**. These organisations are of two main kinds:

- those that provide services;
- those that carry out some form of trading.

Within each of these groups, some things are provided by local councils and others by central government.

Services provided by local councils

The country is divided into local council areas. England and Wales are divided into county councils (e.g. Surrey and Essex) and metropolitan councils (e.g. Manchester and Birmingham). The county councils are further broken down into borough or district councils. Each council is elected by the people living within its area.

By law, councils have to provide services such as refuse collection, education, the fire service and the police, social services and local roads. They may also provide other services such as libraries and parks.

Not all councils provide all the services in their area. County councils provide some services, for example education, libraries, social services, the fire service and the police. Borough or district councils provide other services, such as refuse collection and environmental health services.

Metropolitan councils and the councils in some large towns provide all the services in their area. Where a council offers all services it is known as a unitary authority.

To pay for the services they provide, councils get their income from five main sources:

- grants from central government (revenue support grants);
- council tax, which is fixed by the local council and based on the value of property within its area;

Borough council offices

- unified business rate, which is based on the rateable value of property occupied by a business. The government fixes the actual rate on a national scale;
- fees and rents from things like cemeteries and leisure facilities;
- borrowed money – the amount councils can borrow is controlled by the government.

Every few years councils must invite private firms to put in bids for providing some council services. This system is known as **compulsory competitive tendering**. Council departments effectively have to bid against private firms to do their own jobs. Where jobs that used to be done by a council department are now provided by private companies it is known as **contracting out**. Examples of services that have been contracted out include refuse collection, gardening

Councils provide local leisure facilities, like this swimming pool

(for example in parks and on traffic islands) and school cleaning.

Trading activities of local councils

Local councils do not trade in the usual business sense. However, they do charge for some of their services. For example, they get fees for planning applications, and rent from properties and markets. They also charge admission fees to users of leisure centres and for events at the Civic Hall.

Planning permission

Every business is based within a local council's area. Before any new building can be constructed, or the use of an existing building changed, planning permission has to be given by the local council. The planning system is one of the main ways in which local councils affect business.

Services provided by central government

The government makes the policies that govern all public services. Some services are provided by the state direct to the public. Others are supplied by agencies on its behalf, including local councils.

Some services are best controlled by the state:
- those that should be provided on a national scale with everyone in the country being treated the same, for example the National Health Service, social services and the Inland Revenue;
- services that cannot be entrusted to anyone else, for example defence and national security.

There are also services that support the state. These are services that help the government to work effectively, for example the Office for National Statistics and the Central Office of Information.

Finally there are services that are offered by other organisations, but paid for out of taxes. These are bodies that need to be more flexible than government departments. Examples include English Heritage, Learning and Skills Councils, Small Business Service and the Arts Council. These are often called Quasi Autonomous Non-Governmental Organisations (QUANGOs). Each one is run by a board appointed by the government.

Public corporations

The government does very little direct trading itself. Where it trades commercially it does so through **public corporations.**

Public corporations are very like public limited companies. They have limited liability and only have one shareholder, the government. They are not government departments. They are financially independent of the state and are run by a board. Profits are 'ploughed back' into the business or used to reduce prices.

After the Second World War, a number of large and important industries were taken over and run by the state. Among them were the coal, iron and steel and railway industries, and the electricity, gas, telephone and water utilities.

In addition, there were a number of other state-owned firms including British Petroleum, Jaguar, Rolls Royce, British Aerospace and what is now Rover. These were all businesses that traded like any other company, except that they were owned by the state.

During the 1980s and early 1990s most public corporations were returned to the private sector through **privatisation.**

These days there are very few trading enterprises that are owned by the state. The main ones are the Post Office, Parcel Force and the BBC.

Privatisation

Privatisation is the sale or transfer to the private sector of activities that are part of the public sector. The term is used mainly in two ways:
- The sale of state-owned companies to private shareholders. Some of these have involved the high-profile sale of shares to the public, for example companies such as British Telecom, British Gas and the electricity and water companies. In other cases, private companies were asked to bid for state-owned companies. Jaguar was sold to Ford and Rover was sold to British Aerospace in this way.
- The contracting out of services, such as school cleaning and refuse collection, to private companies.

Many of the public corporations were the only suppliers of their product or service. They had a **monopoly.** This was true of the gas, telephone, water

Parcel Force – a public enterprise

and electricity utilities, and of British Rail, British Steel and British Coal. Many people were opposed to their sale, as they thought they were too important to the country to be put in the hands of private companies. Other publicly owned companies, such as Rover, Jaguar and Ferranti, had originally come into public ownership to save them being wound up.

Arguments for privatisation
- Civil servants do not have the right kind of experience to run businesses. They tend to be bureaucratic, and companies are run more efficiently by people who know about business.
- Private companies are able to raise capital more easily. They can attract investment from the **financial institutions.** The government cannot afford to invest the money that is needed into the businesses it owns.
- Competition is greater, and the public benefits by having cheaper and more efficient services.
- It results in wider share ownership. Many people who had never owned shares before bought shares in British Telecom, British Gas and the electricity and water companies.

Arguments against privatisation
- Some people view it as selling off the nation's assets.
- It is thought by some to be wrong to make profits out of basic services such as water, heat and light.
- It is substituting a private monopoly for a state monopoly. The state ran the companies for the benefit of the consumer. Private monopolies have to make a profit. They are therefore more likely to exploit consumers. This is why there are regulators to control the privatised utilities.

Regulators

Gas, water, electricity, telecommunications and the railways were privatised

under Acts of Parliament. Under the Acts the government has to appoint a **regulator** for each industry. The regulator's job is to protect the interests of consumers. The privatised companies' profits must be large enough to provide reinvestment, but without exploiting the public. It is also the job of regulators to bring competition into the industries. New companies also come under their control. Examples of regulators include OFWAT, OFGEM and OFTEL.

Activities

1 Explain the difference between the public and private sectors.

2 State whether these industries belong to the public or private sector, or can be found in both.
   a roads   b estate agents
   c healthcare   d policing
   e housing   f commercial radio

3 What is a unitary authority?

4 Explain how the objectives of a public corporation might change if it were to be privatised.

5 Write out the following passage, putting the words listed below in their correct places.

   At one time, local authorities provided all services themselves using _____ labour. Now authorities need to _____ out services to private firms using competitive _____ . In the 1980s many of the public corporations were _____ . This meant that people could buy _____ in these organisations. A public corporation would often have a _____ , which meant it had no real competitors.

   | shares   direct   monopoly   privatised
     tendering   contract |

Case Study

6 Electricity

The electricity industry has three separate functions:

Generation: producing electricity at a power station;

Transmission: sending the electricity at very high voltages along the national grid;

Distribution: taking the electricity from the national grid to individual houses, factories, etc.

The UK electricity industry was privatised mainly during 1990 and 1991. Before privatisation, the supply of electricity was the responsibility of public sector organisations. In England and Wales the job of generating electricity was governed by a single organisation, with each regional board distributing the electricity and selling it to the people in its area.

In Scotland there are just two electricity companies: ScottishPower and Scottish Hydro-Electric. Both of these companies carry out each of the three functions described above. They even produce enough electricity to export some of it to England.

A new law was passed in 1998 that allowed all users to buy their energy needs from any supplier. Consumers no longer had to buy from their local supplier. This allowed ScottishPower to look beyond Scotland for its customers.

a Explain how the ownership of the electricity companies changed in the early 1990s.

b Draw a diagram to show the types of organisations needed to produce electricity and get it to customers in England and Wales.

c Describe the ways in which ScottishPower benefited from privatisation.

d Some people believe that privatisation of the electricity industry is wrong. Write an account giving the arguments against privatisation.

Unit 2.2 Ownership, management and control

Key terms	
Annual General Meeting (AGM) →	a meeting of ordinary shareholders that must be held by a public limited company at the end of every financial year.
Board of directors →	a committee elected by the shareholders of a limited company to run the business on their behalf. It decides company policy and makes all important decisions.
Director →	a person elected by the shareholders to the board of directors of a limited company.
Executive director →	a director of a limited company who is also a senior manager responsible for one of the firm's main functions (departments).
Financial institutions →	the name given to banks, insurance companies, pension providers and others which sell their financial services to business and the public. In the UK they are based mainly in the City of London.
Fund managers →	firms that specialise in managing the investments of private individuals, usually in stocks and shares.
Manager →	a person responsible for the organisation and control of an activity, or group of activities, in a firm.
Non-executive directors →	part-time directors who play no part in the day-to-day management of the business. They give neutral advice and are paid a fee for their time.
Ordinary shares →	the main type of share issued by a limited company. Each share represents a part ownership of the company and gives the holder a right to vote at the Annual General Meeting.
Preference shares →	a type of share issued by a limited company. The holders are part owners of the company, and are entitled to a fixed rate of dividend. They have no say, however, in company business.
Shareholders →	holders of shares in a limited company. Each shareholder is a part owner of the company.

This unit looks at three important aspects of business:
- **ownership** – the people or organisations to whom the business actually belongs, usually those that provide the capital;
- **management** – those who run the business day to day;
- **control** – in the hands of those who decide policy and who make the final decisions.

Sole traders and partnerships

In the case of sole traders, the ownership, management and control of the business are all in the hands of one person, the owner or sole proprietor.

In a partnership, the ownership, management and control of the business are shared between the partners.

Limited companies

In larger private companies and all public limited companies, ownership, management and control are usually separated.

- **Shareholders** own the company. Public limited companies are owned by thousands of shareholders. They cannot all have a say in the way the business is run.
- **Directors** direct or control the business. They are elected by the shareholders to run the company on their behalf.
- The directors then appoint **managers** to do the day-to-day running of the business.

In a small private limited company, one person, family or small group of people own all or most of the shares.

Figure 2.4 Ownership, control and management

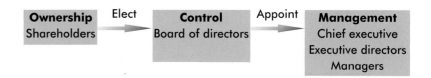

The owners, directors and managers of the company are probably the same people.

Shareholders

There are two main types of share that a company can issue:

Preference shares

- They earn a fixed rate of dividend.
- Owners of these shares are the first shareholders to have their money paid back if the company is wound up.
- They are not as risky as ordinary shares, so holders do not have a vote at the Annual General Meeting.

Ordinary shares

- The dividend they earn varies according to the company's profits.
- If the company is wound up, the owners of these shares get their money back only after everyone else that is owed money has been paid.
- Holders of ordinary shares carry a higher risk. They can, therefore, vote at the Annual General Meeting.

The number of each type of share that a company is allowed to issue is set out in the Memorandum of Association. Not all companies issue preference shares. Where they do, there will usually be more ordinary than preference shares.

All ordinary shares are equal. Each share gives its owner an equal share in the ownership and control of the company. Shareholders have one vote at general company meetings for every share they hold.

Every share may be equal, but not every shareholder is equal. A holder of 1,000 shares owns 10 times more of the company than the holder of 100 shares. That person also has 10 times more votes and 10 times more control.

In most firms only a small proportion of the shares are held by private individuals. The biggest holders of shares are **financial institutions** and **fund managers**. They hold thousands of shares in large companies. They gather fairly small amounts of money from individuals and invest it on their behalf. Recent governments have tried to widen share ownership through privatisation and schemes like Personal Equity Plans (PEPs) and Individual Savings Accounts (ISAs). PEPs and ISAs are run by fund managers.

One shareholder may hold more shares than any other shareholder. The majority shareholder has a large say in the way the company is run, but does not control it. If the other shareholders got together they would be able to out vote that one shareholder. Anyone holding 51% or more of the shares in a company has a controlling interest in the firm.

Annual General Meeting (AGM)

This must be held every year by law. It is held after the end of the financial year. At this meeting the shareholders must:

- approve the Annual Report and Accounts;
- appoint auditors for the accounts;
- approve the dividend to be paid to shareholders;
- appoint directors (they are usually appointed for three years at a time).

As the owners, the shareholders, in theory, have control over the business. In fact the AGM is the only real chance the shareholders have to question the directors on the way the company is being run.

Board of directors

It is not possible for all the owners of a limited company to take part in its running. Instead, the shareholders elect directors to run the business on their behalf. The directors are also shareholders, although they do not have to be big shareholders in the firm. The directors meet as a **board of directors**. The directors must, in law, act in the best interests of the company and the shareholders.

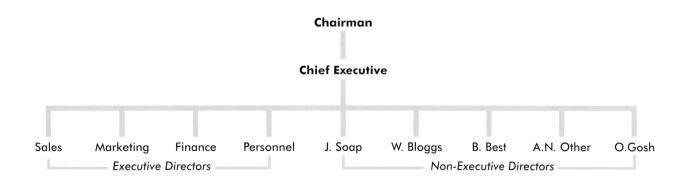

Chairman

Chief Executive

Sales	Marketing	Finance	Personnel	J. Soap	W. Bloggs	B. Best	A.N. Other	O.Gosh
Executive Directors					*Non-Executive Directors*			

Figure 2.5 The board of directors

Company reports

The number of directors varies with the size of the firm. A private limited company must have a minimum of one director. Public limited companies must have at least two directors.

The board of directors is usually made up of four people or groups of people:

- The chairperson, who runs meetings, leads the company and speaks on behalf of the board of directors to outside bodies.
- In large companies, the most senior manager in the firm is also a member of the board. He or she is known as the managing director or, more likely these days, the chief executive.
- Other senior managers may also be directors. They are the top managers of important departments such as finance, marketing, personnel or sales. These are **executive directors**.
- The other members of the board are **non-executive directors**. The company does not employ them. They are part-time and are usually paid a fee for their time. They play no part in the day-to-day running of the firm. They are often also directors of other companies. Their main task is to make sure the firm is being run in the best interests of the shareholders. They are usually very experienced managers and can give specialist and neutral advice. They may also act as a brake on the executive directors, for example preventing them from taking too many risks.

The board of directors makes all of the most important decisions affecting the company, for example:

- it decides on policy for the company;
- it also decides the long-term (three to five years) aims of the company – this is the company's strategic plan. Together with the objectives it provides a framework for managers to work within;
- it sets the company's objectives and targets;
- it keeps the performance of the company under constant review.

Activities

1 List the differences between ordinary and preference shares.

2 Explain why the owners of a large business are not the same people as those who control it.

3 Give as many reasons as you can why an individual might buy shares in companies.

4 Outline three questions that a shareholder might ask a board of directors at the Annual General Meeting.

5 Why is it unlikely that a shareholder is able to have any influence on how his or her company is run?

6 Copy and complete each of these sentences using a word from the box below.

a The people who own a limited company are its _____ .

b The day-to-day running of a business is the responsibility of the _____ .

c To look after their interests, shareholders appoint _____ .

d The money paid to a shareholder is called a _____ .

e Somebody on the board of directors not employed by the company is called a _____ .

f Owners who get a vote at the AGM are _____ .

g If an owner of a business is guaranteed a fixed return each year, he or she is a _____ .

h If a person or organisation has a controlling interest in a business it is called a _____ .

preference shareholder   majority shareholder
shareholders   ordinary shareholders   dividend
managers   directors   non-executive director

ICT Activity
Use the Internet to find some company reports. Use the information you find to produce a briefing sheet suitable for someone interested in buying shares.

Case Study

7 Fine Pine

Fine Pine is a private limited company. It manufactures pine furniture that is sold throughout the country. Karen Tay and her friend Julie Marshall started the business as a partnership. It became a private limited company about five years ago. There are 40,000 ordinary shares in the business, and they are owned by:

Case Study

Director's name	Position held	Status	No. of shares
Karen Tay	company founder	chief executive	12,000
Richard Tay	founder's husband	non-executive director/ financial advisor	2,000
Julie Marshall	co-founder	executive director	8,000
Sayeed Hussain	sales manager	executive director	5,000
Ian Chetwynd	production manager	executive director	5,000

In the past, Fine Pine has encouraged its workers to buy shares in the company. Employees and former employees, therefore, own the remaining 8,000 shares. The company has not issued any preference shares.

Last year the business distributed an £80,000 profit to shareholders.

a How much was paid as a dividend on each share?

b If Karen and Richard wanted to gain a controlling interest in the business, how many shares would they have to buy?

c Explain why it is unlikely that Karen and Richard would be able to gain a controlling interest.

d Give reasons why Fine Pine has Richard Tay as a non-executive director.

e Why might a company such as Fine Pine not want to issue preference shares?

f Discuss whether it is a good idea to allow employees to buy shares in the company for which they work.

ICT Activity
Produce a pie chart to show the distribution of shares at Fine Pine.

Unit 2.3 Business objectives

2.3a Objectives

Figure 2.6 Business objectives

Every company has to have some goals to aim for. These goals are the company's **objectives**. They state what the company hopes to achieve in the long run. Companies' objectives vary according to the nature of the business and the principles on which they are based.

General objectives

There are some objectives that are so basic that they form part of every company's objectives:

- survival;
- making a profit.

Every company wants to survive and stay in business. It is important to everyone connected with a business that it survives. If a firm fails, those that invested in it lose money and the people who work for it lose their jobs. Jobs may also be lost in other firms that dealt with the failed business.

No business can survive for long without covering all its costs. It must at least **break even**. A firm breaks even when the money it earns from sales just covers all its costs. Those costs include the price of raw materials, wages and salaries, and general costs such as rates, telephones and interest on loans. To be sure that they stay in business, companies must also make a **profit**.

A profit is made when goods and services are sold for more than the cost of buying or making them. The profit should be big enough to pay dividends to shareholders and to put some money into reserves for reinvestment.

The size of the profit varies from firm to firm. In practice, most firms' objective is to maximise profits. That is, to make as big a profit as possible.

Other objectives

Many objectives are worthwhile in themselves, but they also have the effect of helping to maximise profits. These include:

- To increase **turnover**, that is to increase the value of total sales. Higher sales usually mean higher profits.
- To use resources efficiently, meaning to keep waste to a minimum. For example, a clothing manufacturer lays its patterns in such a way that the amount of cloth wasted is kept to a minimum. It also means using labour efficiently, employing just enough people to do the job. Firms must also strive to get the most out of their equipment. They may operate shift working so as to make use of expensive machinery for 24 hours a day. Efficient use of resources cuts costs, and leads to higher profits.
- To increase market share, that is their share of the total sales of a product. This adds to the firm's prestige. It also gives it more control over prices in the marketplace.
- To be a global force. Many firms wish to sell their products all over the world. Selling globally increases turnover and may improve efficiency and market share, as well as profits. In industries that need a lot of capital this may be the only way to grow. Becoming a global force in the petroleum industry was one reason why BP and Amoco merged.

There are other objectives that do not have to be related to profit:

- To improve quality – customers buy goods on the basis of 'value for money'. This means that they expect goods of a certain price to be of a certain quality. Cars are often sold on their 'build quality'. Firms with a reputation for quality must maintain the standard that they have set themselves. Other firms may want to raise their position in the market by raising quality.

- To improve customer satisfaction – customers only repeat buy if they are satisfied with the goods and services they bought. This is especially true in the service industries. Customers are unhappy with the train operating companies because trains run late or are cancelled. Improving customer satisfaction is important in getting more people to use trains.
- To improve prestige or image – firms like Harrods and Rolls Royce are concerned with keeping up their reputation for high quality. Other firms try to improve their image by, for example, showing concern for the environment.
- Staff welfare – many firms regard their staff as their most important resource. They often spend large sums of money on staff welfare.

Nature of objectives

Objectives should not be empty statements. The objectives should be what drives a business. They are often translated into targets. For example, a company may set a target of a 5% growth in turnover. These targets can then be broken down into departmental targets. Objectives and targets should be:

- realistic and attainable – there is no point in having impossible objectives;
- measurable – if an objective cannot be measured, people will not know if they have reached it;
- reviewed regularly – firms are affected by a range of external factors over which they have no control. For example, a rise in interest rates may mean that sales on credit fall. This might make a target impossible to achieve. If there is a regular review, the target can be revised to make it more realistic and achievable;
- given a time limit – the objective has to be reached in a certain time;
- known to everyone – people must know what is expected of them.

Why set objectives?

- It helps decision making, ensuring decisions are well thought through and given proper consideration.
- It motivates employees by focusing on target setting.
- It allows a company to measure progress.
- It ensures that all parts of the firm are working towards the same goals and are coordinated.

Our core purpose is to create value for customers to earn their lifetime loyalty.

The Body Shop

'To meaningfully contribute to local, national and international communities in which we trade, by adopting a code of conduct which ensures care, honesty, fairness and respect.'

J Sainsbury plc

Our objectives:

- To provide shareholders with good financial returns by focusing on customers' needs, adding value through our expertise and innovation, and investing for future growth.

- To provide unrivalled value to our customers in the quality of the goods we sell, in the competitiveness of our prices and in the range of choice we offer. ...

BT's mission, our central purpose,

is to provide world-class telecommunications and information products and services, and to develop and exploit our networks, at home and overseas, so that we can:

- meet the requirements of our customers,
- sustain growth in the earnings of the group on behalf of our shareholders, and

make a fitting contribution to the community in which we conduct our business.

Some mission statements

Mission statements

A **mission statement** is a general statement that tries to summarise what an organisation stands for. It sets out the principles on which the company is based. It should state a point of view that can be shared by everyone in the organisation. It is often quite short, and may form the basis for the firm's more detailed objectives.

Business ethics

These are the general moral or ethical standards by which companies are run. Most firms want to run their business honestly. They also want to run it in a way that is fair to their workers, shareholders, customers and suppliers. Some industries and companies have detailed standards that they work to.

Many industries have a Code of Practice or a Code of Conduct that has been agreed by the industry as a whole. For example, the banking industry and most professional bodies such as doctors, accountants and solicitors.

Individual firms may have a set of principles that controls the way the firm does business, for example:

- The Body Shop does not sell cosmetics that have been tested on animals;
- some big supermarkets do not sell food that contains genetically modified (GM) ingredients;
- many furniture manufacturers only use sustainable and renewable resources, such as wood from managed forests.

Activities

1 Explain the difference between a business's mission statement and its objectives.

2 A Stoke-on-Trent taxi business decides to have the mission statement:

'to be the most customer-friendly taxi service in Staffordshire'.

a How might the firm make its employees and customers aware of the mission statement?

b Explain why it is important that the firm's workers and customers know the business has a mission statement.

c The taxi firm is taking a risk having this mission statement. Discuss the problems that could arise because of the mission statement.

3 A business sets itself two objectives:

- to increase the dividends paid to its shareholders;
- to increase the size of the company by taking over smaller companies.

Explain why trying to realise one of these objectives could cause the other to fail.

4 You are the chief executive of a large public limited company. You receive the following e-mail from one of the company shareholders. Compose a suitable reply to this shareholder. You will need to explain in your e-mail why Daffrey's donates money to charity.

From:	pwilson@urchin.net
Sent:	Monday, 15 January 2001
To:	chiefexec@daffreys.co.uk
Cc:	chairman@daffreys.co.uk
Subject:	Company donations to charity

Chief Executive

I was annoyed to read in the newspaper that Daffrey's is to donate £125,000 to the 'Computers for Schools' appeal. As a Daffrey's shareholder I cannot remember being consulted about this donation. I rely on my Daffrey's dividend to support myself in my retirement. I object strongly to my cash being given away in such a manner. If I want to give to charity, I will do so myself. I do not need someone to do it on my behalf.

Peter Wilson

Case Study

5 Cadbury-Schweppes

Like any limited company, the directors of Cadbury-Schweppes have to consider its shareholders when its business objectives are set. The shareholders have put their money into the business and expect to see a return on this investment. 85% of the company's two billion shares are owned by institutions, such as banks and pension funds. Individuals, who may have put their life savings into the business, hold the remainder of the shares.

Case Study

Shareholders can earn money in two ways: the value of their shares can rise, and they receive a dividend each year. If Cadbury-Schweppes is performing well, more people will want to buy its shares, which will make them more expensive. So if shareholders decide to sell their shares, they may receive more money than they paid for them. Similarly, the amount shareholders are paid as their dividend each year will depend upon how profitable the company is.

Cadbury-Schweppes tries to reward its shareholders, and has set itself these objectives:

- to increase the amount each share earns by 10% each year;
- to double the value of shares every four years.

Cadbury-Schweppes has also tried to get its employees to think more about the needs of shareholders. They are encouraged to become more concerned about finding ways of helping the company make higher profits. Workers' pay is also partly linked to the amount of profit the company makes, and all employees are encouraged to become shareholders in the company.

a Explain how shareholders can earn money from their shares.

b Calculate how many of Cadbury-Schweppes' shares are owned by individual shareholders.

c Explain how the interests of Cadbury-Schweppes' workers are different from those of its shareholders.

d Why do you think that most individual shareholders in large companies do not go to the shareholders' AGM?

e How is Cadbury-Schweppes more likely to achieve its objectives if it encourages its workers to own shares in the company?

f Why is it important to Cadbury-Schweppes that its shareholders are happy with the company's performance?

Business Structure, Control and Organisation

Unit 2.3 Business objectives

2.3b Measuring success

→ Key terms

Cost price	→	the price at which a trader buys the goods that it then sells at a higher price.
Economies of scale	→	the effects on the costs of a business that result from an increase in its size.
Market share	→	the proportion of the total sales of a product gained by a company or brand.
Overheads	→	the general costs of running a business.
Productivity	→	the quantity of goods produced by a worker in a given time.
Stakeholders	→	everyone within and outside an organisation who has an interest in the way that organisation operates.

Stakeholders

The success of a business is important to all of those with an interest in its activities, be they individuals or groups of people. They all have a stake in the success of the business. They benefit if the company does well and suffer if the business fails. Some will be people or groups of people within the company, others will be external to the company.

Each **stakeholder** has a slightly different point of view – each one measures success in a slightly different way.

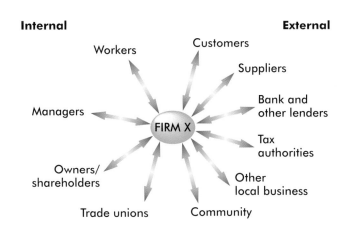

Figure 2.7 Stakeholders

The success of a business depends on the extent to which it has achieved its objectives in a particular year. It would be unusual for a firm to fully meet all of its targets. It should come close to meeting each target, otherwise they were probably not realistic or challenging enough.

Profitability

A firm's success is usually measured by the size of its profits. The higher a firm's profits the more successful it is seen to be. The term profit is used in two ways:

- the profit made on a single item when it is sold, that is, the profit per unit;
- the overall profit made by a firm on the total of its sales.

A firm is successful if its total profit is bigger than in the previous year. To make an overall profit a firm has to make a profit on most, if not all, the items it sells. It is from the profit on the separate items that it sells that it makes the money needed to cover the day-to-day costs of running the business. These costs include the wages, raw materials and general expenses such as heating and lighting, rent, interest on loans, telephones, computer systems, etc. It only makes a profit at the end of a year if it has made enough money to cover all these expenses. These general expenses of a business are often called the **overheads**.

The owners of a business are paid out of the profits. In a large business these will be shareholders who expect to get a dividend on their shares. The price of those shares will largely depend on how profitable the business has been. The ability of a business to borrow money from the banks also depends on its profitability. Being profitable is, therefore, more than just a measure of success.

Checking for explosive gases at a BP refinery in Texas

The opposite of profit is loss. Firms can stand making a loss in some years, but they cannot go on doing so year after year.

Other measures of success

There are many ways of deciding whether a business is a success or not. Profitability is only one of them. Each stakeholder has a different interest in a business, and therefore a different point of view on how to judge its success.

Growth

A business is thought to be successful if it becomes bigger. Larger firms sell more, they make bigger profits and have more resources. They benefit from **economies of scale**. It is easier for a big firm to survive when business is poor. Firms grow by either expanding on their own, or buying up other firms.

Market share

An increase in the share of the total market for a product shows that a firm is giving its customers what they want, and therefore is doing well.

Staying competitive

Firms have to be competitive or people do not buy their goods. They must make sure their prices and the quality of their products are at least as good as those of their competitors. Increasingly, even in home markets, firms also have to compete with overseas companies.

Improved efficiency

Firms improve efficiency by keeping their costs as low as possible. This in turn improves their profitability. Low costs make them more competitive.

Higher productivity

This means that a firm can produce more, with the same or fewer resources. Productivity is usually measured by how many units per worker are produced in an hour.

Return on capital

Shareholders and others who invest money in a business do so in order to earn an income from that money. They want as high a return on that money as possible. There is some risk in putting money into a business, and shareholders expect a reward for taking that risk. The income they earn has to be at least as high as they could earn by putting their money into a safe place such as a bank or building society.

Higher share prices

A company is successful if it is making a good profit and a good return on capital. If its future prospects are also thought to be good, the prices of its shares rise. A high share price shows that experts consider the firm to be successful.

Employment

A firm may increase the number of workers it employs to meet increased sales. This is a sign that it is doing well and is a benefit to the local community.

Environment

Many people judge a firm's success by the efforts it makes to reduce pollution. Firms are expected to lower their levels of smoke emission, toxic waste and noise. Neither their manufacturing processes nor their products should damage the environment. They should use materials from sustainable sources.

Community

Successful firms benefit the community of which they are a part by providing more and safer jobs. The people in those jobs will, in turn, spend more in local shops and on other services. This increases the prosperity of the whole community.

Non-profit making organisations

Some organisations, such as charities, do not aim to make a profit at all. Their success is measured by the extent to which they carry out their purpose, that is, to meet their objectives.

Activities

1 What is the difference between an internal and an external stakeholder?

2 Some people say that the only stakeholders who matter are the firm's shareholders and its customers.
   a Why are these two stakeholders seen as being so important?
   b What might a firm do to look after the interests of its:
      i employees:
      ii suppliers?

3 The directors of a firm set three targets for the organisation:

Profits: to improve upon last year's profit levels;

Environment: to reduce the level of pollution created by the organisation;

Efficiency: to reduce the overall wages bill by introducing more efficient ways of working.

Explain why it might be difficult to achieve all three objectives at the same time.

4 Occasionally, firms that have made very high profits are embarrassed and try to disguise just how much they have made. Explain possible reasons why they find high profits embarrassing.

❑ Case Study

5 Readycrete

Readycrete is a successful business that supplies ready-mixed concrete to building sites. The firm has recently received a request to provide sponsorship for the local football team. The team is having financial problems and is struggling at the bottom of its league table.

The team manager has asked Readycrete to sponsor the team with £20,000 per season, guaranteed for the next three years. In return Readycrete would be able to use the directors' box to watch matches and the firm would have its name printed on the players' shirts.

a Why do many sporting events seek sponsorship in this way?

b Explain two possible reasons why companies give money to sporting events or charities.

c You have been asked to produce a report on whether or not Readycrete should sponsor the football team. You should consider the deal from the viewpoint of each of the firm's stakeholders.

   i What are the benefits Readycrete might get?

   ii What are the problems associated with this deal?

Your report should end with a clear recommendation as to whether Readycrete should sponsor the football team or not.

❑ Case Study

6 Crusty's

Crusty's is a baker's shop owned and managed by Kerry Wilkinson. The shop is situated in a large shopping mall on the outskirts of a city, selling bread, sandwiches and cakes to shoppers. Kerry is keen to increase the turnover of the business, so a target is set at the beginning of each year. The manager realises that the target should be challenging to give the shop assistants something to aim for, but it should be achievable as well. Over the last few years Kerry has felt that the targets may have been set too high and this has led to her employees becoming demoralised.

Case Study

Turnover of Crusty's Bakery

Year	1997	1998	1999	2000	2001	2002	2003
Target for sales £000	250	290	320	360	400		
Actual sales £000	230	260	310	330	360		

a How can having an achievable target help businesses like Crusty's?

b Explain how having too high a target can cause problems for the business.

c Draw a suitable graph of this information. You may want to do this using a spreadsheet. Place a trend-line along the graph. (This is easily done using a spreadsheet.)

d The company is keen to set more realistic targets for 2002 and 2003. Use your graph to determine what these targets should be for these years. Explain your choice of targets carefully.

Case Study

7 BP

BP is one of the world's largest oil, gas and petrochemical producers. For many years the oil industry had a poor reputation for the damage it caused to the environment. Extracting crude oil from the ground, refining it and distributing the finished products such as petrol can cause environmental harm if not done with great care.

In the 1990s BP decided that it needed to be more aware of environmental issues. It began by setting itself targets for reducing the impact it had on the environment. BP looked at ways of reducing its levels of emissions of waste gases thought to contribute to global warming. The company set itself a target of a 10% reduction in the emissions of these gases – carbon dioxide and methane – by 2010. BP is also investing in solar power, an alternative form of energy production that may become significant in the future.

The company has also worked at becoming a better employer. Each employee receives an average of five days' training a year and strict health and safety rules have been introduced. Checks are made to see that the business has a balance of male and female workers and employees from different nationalities. In addition, BP makes funds available to support social projects. For example, BP's Grizzly Challenge provides money for 14–16-year-olds to improve their local environment in some of Scotland's most deprived areas.

BP has put considerable effort and expense into making and monitoring its improvements. It publishes the results of its findings widely. It also takes care to check how the public's image of BP compares with that of its competitors.

a Why is BP looking at alternative ways of providing energy?

b Describe how BP and other petrochemical companies can damage the environment.

c BP provides training for its employees. How does the company benefit from this training?

d Explain why it is important that BP does not upset its public image by damaging the environment or exploiting its workers.

ICT Activity

Look at BP's website at www.bp.com. List the ways mentioned by which BP is trying to improve its public image.

Unit 2.4 Business growth

2.4a Why and how firms grow

Agreed takeover →	where the directors of a company advise the shareholders to sell their shares to another company which then takes control of the business.
Assets →	everything that is owned by a business or a private individual.
Capital →	the funds invested in a business that enable it to buy the physical assets it needs.
Chain of production →	the stages through which a product passes during production, before it reaches the consumer.
Diversification →	when a business moves into new markets or new industries to reduce business risks. When one industry or market is weak others may prosper.
Economies of scale →	the effects on the costs of a business that result from an increase in its size.
Horizontal integration →	where a firm merges with or takes over another firm in the same line of business.
Hostile takeover →	where a company is taken over against the advice of its directors.
Joint venture →	where two or more companies join together to form a new company in order to carry out a business venture together.
Lateral integration →	where a firm moves into a different line of business that uses the same skills and methods. The products will be related but not the same.
Market leader →	the firm with the largest share of sales in a given market.
Market share →	the proportion of the total sales of a product gained by a company or brand.
Merger →	when two companies agree to join together to form a new company.
Sales turnover →	the total value of a firm's sales during a stated period of time.
Takeover →	when one firm gains control over another company by buying a majority of its shares.
Takeover bid →	an attempt by one company to gain a controlling interest in another company.
Vertical integration →	where a business joins with another that operates at a different stage in the chain of production.

Many large firms began as sole traders. The traditional way for the sole trader to expand has been to take on a partner, adding more partners as the firm grows. To raise still more **capital**, the firm then becomes a private limited company. Finally, to carry on growing and to raise more capital again, it sells shares to the public as a public limited company.

What is growth?

When firms grow they may do so in several ways:
- increased sales turnover;
- more people employed;
- higher profits;
- bigger market share;
- new markets opened at home and abroad;
- increased value of the assets, i.e. capital has increased.

Not all these things may happen when a firm grows. For example, sales may rise without more people being employed.

Why firms want to grow
- The directors are ambitious and want to have the biggest company in its line of business. They want the power and status that come from running a very large firm.
- To drive rival firms out of business. **Market share** increases and the firm becomes the **market leader** in its field. This increases its power in the market.
- To gain the benefits of **economies of scale**.
- Some industries need huge amounts of capital and need to be run by very large companies. For example, the pharmaceutical and petroleum industries.

Mergers and takeovers are often headline news

- Greater size may lead to larger profits and thus better returns for the owners. The price of shares in a public limited company may rise. This benefits the firm's shareholders.
- It is easier for large firms to protect themselves from a **takeover**. It is also easier for them to take over rival firms.
- Larger companies can survive more easily when business is poor. Large companies can borrow money more easily than smaller firms, and they probably also have greater reserves to call upon.

How firms grow

Firms grow in two main ways:

- through internal growth, using their own resources;
- through external growth by buying up or joining with other firms.

Internal growth

Most firms grow to some extent through internal growth. They increase their sales and production. In due course this may lead to them taking on more workers, buying more equipment and moving into bigger premises. Their profits also grow. They use at least some of these profits to pay for the expansion. This is often known as 'ploughing back the profits'.

External growth

A quick way for a firm to grow is to join with another firm to form a new, larger business. Firms can grow externally in four ways:

- mergers;
- takeovers;
- buying a business that is for sale;
- joint ventures.

Mergers

A **merger** is when two firms agree to join together to form a new company. Mergers are expected to mean higher sales, bigger market share and savings in costs. The savings in costs come from those parts of the two firms that overlap. For example, only one board of directors is needed. There is no need for two headquarters. Only one chief executive and central administration is needed. Savings in costs may lead to redundancies.

Takeovers

This is where a company buys control of another firm. The buyer gains control by buying more than 50% of the ordinary shares of the target company. Takeovers can be of two kinds:

- agreed takeover;
- hostile takeover.

The effects of a takeover are similar in many ways to those of a merger. The buyer increases sales turnover, market share and the value of its assets. Costs are cut by closing the parts of the business that overlap. Surplus premises are sold and jobs are lost.

In an **agreed takeover**, the directors of a company advise the shareholders to agree to sell their shares to a buyer. Usually the price offered by the buyer is higher than the market value of the shares at the time. There are a number of reasons why a firm might agree to be taken over:

- it may not have the resources to expand further on its own – it might not have the skills or the capital for the next stage in its growth;

a firm may have a better chance of surviving as part of another, larger business.

A **hostile takeover** happens when the directors turn down an offer to buy their firm. There is then a **takeover bid**. The bidder buys as many shares as it can on the open market. It goes against the advice of the target company's directors and makes an offer direct to the shareholders. Again, the price offered for the shares is higher than the market price before the bid was made.

Purchases

From time to time businesses are put up for sale by their owners. This is different from a merger or a takeover. In a merger two firms agree to form a new joint company. In a takeover one company buys another. In the case of a purchase a firm puts itself up for sale and waits to see who makes an offer to buy it. There are a number of reasons why a firm is put up for a 'trade sale' in this way:

- The owners of a private limited company may want to retire. They decide to sell the company so that they can get back their capital.
- A company bought in a takeover may own a number of other firms. The buyer may not want some of these other firms. They may not fit in with its plans, or with the rest of the business. So they are put up for sale.
- At one time it was thought that firms should have a spread of businesses in more than one industry. This was known as **diversification**. Nowadays, firms concentrate on their main or 'core' business. They sell off those parts of the business that are not part of their core activities.

Joint ventures

This is another way firms can grow and enter new markets. There are some business projects that are either too big, too expensive or too technically demanding for one company to carry out on its own. One way to get over these difficulties is through a **joint venture**. Two or more companies get together and set up a separate 'joint venture company' in which they own all the shares. Each company may have a different size of stake. The joint venture company is set up to carry out a specific task. Each company within the joint venture provides finance, staff and expertise.

The Channel Tunnel was built by a joint venture company. Airbus Industries is a joint venture of European aircraft manufacturers. Separately, they could not compete with Boeing and the other big American aircraft companies. As a joint venture, they have been able to outsell the American companies in some types of aircraft. Joint ventures are often set up with firms in less developed countries. This helps those countries to develop their industry and gives them skills they do not have. It is also an easy way for firms get a foothold in some new markets, for example China.

Integration

When firms expand through mergers or takeovers, they are said to integrate. There are three main types of integration:

- horizontal;
- vertical;
- lateral.

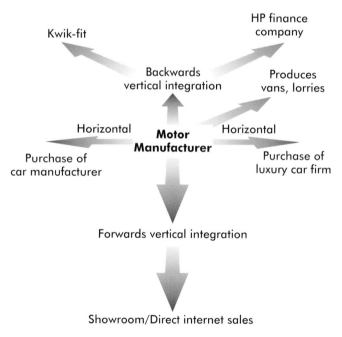

Figure 2.8 Integration

Horizontal integration

This is where a firm expands within the same kind of business. Ford buying Land Rover and Volvo are examples of **horizontal integration**.

Vertical integration

When a firm expands by buying another firm in the same industry, but which is at a different stage of the **chain of production**, it is called **vertical integration**. Firms can vertically integrate in two ways:

- Backward vertical integration: where a firm expands by buying a firm that is at an earlier stage in production. For example, a manufacturer might buy a firm that supplies it with raw materials or components.
- Forward vertical integration: where a firm expands by buying a firm that is at a later stage in the chain of production. For example, a firm manufacturing shoes might buy a chain of shoe shops through which to sell its shoes.

Lateral integration

This is when a firm expands by moving into a similar but different area of production. The product is different, but the skills and techniques needed are similar to those used in the existing business. For example, Ford makes cars and has integrated laterally to make lorries and vans.

Activities

1 One firm employs 100 people and another employs 40. Give reasons why we cannot say confidently that the company employing 100 workers is the larger one.

2 Some people assume that the bigger the firm, the greater the profits. Explain why this may not be true.

3 The board of directors of Richmond's, a traditional tea and coffee merchant, call an emergency meeting. It has become clear that their larger rival, Fast Brew, intends to take over the company. Several of the directors are hostile to the takeover bid. Others see that it might be a good thing for Richmond's.
   a Give two reasons why some of the directors may not want to be taken over by a larger company.
   b Explain why some of the directors favour being taken over by Fast Brew.
   c Why might Fast Brew want to take over a smaller competitor?

4 **Bass**
Bass plc is probably best known as a leading brewer, based in the Midlands town of Burton-on-Trent. William Bass started the business as a small brewery in 1777. Since then the company has expanded hugely. Some of the

expansion has been due to Bass building up its brewery so it can produce more beer. Much of Bass's expansion, however, is the result of the business taking over other companies. Bass has tried to take over companies with a strong brand image, including Tennent's, Carling, Caffrey's and Worthington.

The business has also moved out of its core business by going into other areas of drink manufacturing. Bass now owns the soft drinks manufacturer Britvic, which in turn is the owner of such names as Tango, Pepsi and Robinson's. In common with other breweries, Bass has also moved into the restaurant, hotel and bar industries. Its brands now include Harvester, Toby, All Bar One, O'Neills and Bar Coast. Bass either owns or franchises more than 2,500 hotels that trade under such names as Holiday Inn and Crowne Plaza.

a What is meant by a firm's 'core business'?
b What problems might Bass encounter when it moves into a new industry?
c Explain the advantages to Bass of keeping the taken-over company's name on the product rather than starting to use the Bass brand name.
d Copy the diagram below, inserting examples of each type of integration.
e Explain why breweries often take over hotels, restaurants and bars.
f Discuss whether a growing firm would be better advised to concentrate on expanding its core business, rather than diversifying into new industries.

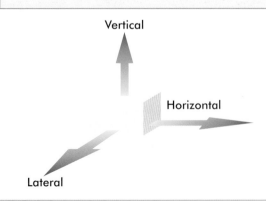

Business Structure, Control and Organisation

Unit 2.4 Business growth

2.4b The effects of growth

When a firm gets bigger, the costs of running it do not grow at the same rate. It may, for example, be able to double its production without having to have new premises. It is unlikely to need twice as much equipment, or offices that are twice as big. When firms grow they are able to use their resources more efficiently. This means they make some savings and gain some advantages simply by being bigger. These advantages are called the economies of scale. They form one of the main benefits of business growth. 'Scale' here means size. Economies of scale are of two kinds: internal and external.

Internal economies of scale

These are advantages that benefit a particular business.

- Large firms buy their supplies in larger quantities. They buy in bulk, often from a small number of suppliers. They can therefore buy their supplies more cheaply than smaller firms.

- They get the full benefit of **specialisation** and the **division of labour**. Larger firms are able to break down jobs so that workers do a narrower range of tasks. Workers become more specialised and more efficient in their job.

- Bigger and newer machines and equipment can be used. Bigger machines produce more, and larger firms can use these machines more effectively. Newer machines may be faster and more efficient. One worker may be able to look after several machines at the same time.

- Large firms find it easier to raise capital and to borrow money. They can offer more security. They can also borrow at lower rates of interest than smaller companies.

- Large firms can afford to spend more money on **marketing**, which may not be worthwhile for smaller firms. The costs are spread over higher sales. For example, a large firm may spend £50,000

Economies of scale from centralised distribution

on one national advertisement and get £500,000 worth of new business from it. The actual cost of each extra sale is very small.

- There are savings in management. A firm that doubles in size does not need twice as many managers. It can use the managers it has more effectively. It can also employ managers who are trained in specialised areas.
- Large firms can afford to carry out research and development. This means that they can spend large amounts of money to create new products. This helps them to keep their products up to date and to get ahead of their competitors.

External economies of scale

These are economies that benefit a number of firms in a particular industry. Some industries are concentrated in an area, for example carpet making around Kidderminster in the West Midlands. The production of china and earthenware goods is centred in the Potteries around Stoke-on-Trent. Suppliers are drawn to the same area. This concentration of similar firms in an area produces advantages to those firms. These are known as **external economies of scale**.

- Suppliers can specialise and gain some internal economies of scale. They benefit from the growth of the industry they supply.
- Having suppliers close by reduces delivery times and transport costs.
- When an industry is concentrated in an area, a pool of labour builds up with the specialist skills that the industry needs.

- Local colleges may develop specialist training courses to meet the needs of the industry.
- Other specialist services develop. For example, people who specialise in repairing the machines used in the industry, or specialist delivery firms. Local bank managers know the particular needs and difficulties of the industry.
- If an area has a good name for high quality goods, local firms benefit from that reputation. For example, Stourbridge in the West Midlands has a reputation for producing high quality cut-glass goods.
- Firms cooperate to promote their industry. They may set up a trade association or joint research and development from which they can all gain. For example, the motor industry has a research station near Nuneaton in Warwickshire.

Other benefits of growth

When a firm grows, its costs do not grow at the same rate. This is because some costs stay more or less the same over a wide range of production levels. For example, a firm can increase production a great deal without needing a new factory. Its rent and rates therefore stay the same. They are spread across a larger total production. As a result, the cost per unit produced falls, and therefore so does the average cost per item.

Example
Suppose a firm's rent and rates cost £5,000 a week. The firm increases production from 150,000 units to 250,000 units a week. The cost of the rent and rates are spread over an extra 100,000 units.

When production is 150,000 units a week, the cost per unit is £5,000 ÷ 150,000 = 3.3 pence per unit.

When production is 250,000 units a week, the cost per unit is £5,000 ÷ 250,000 = 2 pence per unit.

By growing through takeovers and mergers, firms avoid the risks of 'putting all their eggs in one basket'. If they wish, they can choose to move into new markets. They may sell new products that are different from those they deal in already, or they may decide to sell in new areas of the country, or in different countries altogether.

Trading in more than one industry is called **diversification**. By diversifying, firms hope to spread some of

Pubs are diversifying by moving into the restaurant and café business

the risks of business. The idea is that when one market is doing badly, others are doing well or less badly. Losses made in one industry or market can be offset by the gains made in other industries and markets that are doing well.

Companies that trade in a number of different industries that are not related are called **conglomerates**. A conglomerate is made up of:

- a parent company that owns and controls the conglomerate;
- subsidiaries that the parent company has bought or set up for a particular purpose.

Each subsidiary carries on trading as a separate company. Each has its own managers and accounts. The managers make all the day-to-day decisions, but within the overall policy set by the parent company.

Diseconomies of scale

Size does not always bring benefits. Size can also have disadvantages. Some costs can rise as an organisation increases in size. As an organisation gets bigger it becomes harder to manage. These difficulties are called the **diseconomies of scale.**

- To cope with extra size more layers of management may need to be added. Decisions are slowed down, since more people have to be consulted. As a result, making decisions becomes more expensive.

Business opportunities may be lost when it takes a long time to decide about something.

- Large firms are less flexible than smaller ones. They are not able to change their production quickly if there is a change in demand.
- Because the chain of command is longer in larger firms, communication is harder and slower. The amount of paperwork increases, adding to the cost of administration.
- Having more workers makes it harder to manage labour relations. There may be more disputes.
- Workers may feel remote and alienated from the firm, and not care so much about their work. Quality may then suffer.
- Large firms may have a number of branches in different parts of the country and the world. The head office is remote from most of these branches, and its relationship with them may suffer. As a firm becomes more spread out geographically, it becomes harder to control.

Downsizing and demergers

One way of getting over these disadvantages of size is to make a company smaller. The process of making it smaller is called **downsizing**. The company recognises it can be more efficient if it is smaller. This is often carried out by removing a layer of management (delayering). It may also mean reducing the number of sites, and concentrating on a smaller number of larger sites. It usually means that some workers are made redundant.

Large conglomerates may choose to make the business more viable by **demerging** some of their subsidiaries. This is the opposite of a merger. The parent company breaks up the group into separate parts. This can be done in three ways:

1 a trade sale, where the parent company lets it be known that one of its subsidiaries is for sale and invites other companies to buy it;

2 a management buyout, where the management of the subsidiary buys the firm from the parent company;

3 where a subsidiary is floated on the Stock Exchange. The subsidiary becomes a separate public limited company. Its shares are sold to the public and listed on the Stock Exchange.

1 Explain the difference between internal and external economies of scale.

2 Say whether these factors will result in internal or external economies of scale for a furniture maker:

 a the local further education college provides courses in upholstery;

 b a timber merchant offers a discount for large purchases of wood.

3 A firm operates from a small factory on which it pays £400 per week rent. If the business operates at its maximum capacity, 2,000 electric kettles can be made each week. At the moment it is working at 60% capacity.

 a Calculate how many kettles are being made each week at the moment.

 b Calculate the business's average cost (the cost per kettle) at its current output. Then show what will happen to average cost if the business was to operate at full capacity.

ICT Activity

Produce a poster of the brand names owned by the conglomerate Unilever. This information can be found on the company's website at www.unilever.com. Cut and paste images of the brand names on to your poster.

Case Study

4 Kingfisher

The retail group Kingfisher may not be a familiar name to many people, but they will have certainly heard of some of the well-known companies owned by this group. Kingfisher owns such famous names as Woolworths, B&Q, Superdrug, Comet, MVC and Big W.

Case Study

Some organisations choose to grow by diversifying into new, unrelated areas of business. These businesses become conglomerates and have the advantage of spreading their risk by operating in different markets. If there is a decline in one market, a conglomerate can be supported by its other areas of business. Kingfisher, however, prefers to concentrate on the retailing sector. This way it can obtain large economies of scale.

The different companies owned by Kingfisher are able to share the same distribution systems. This means fewer warehouses are needed. Kingfisher can also save money by sharing transport. Lorries can carry goods from all of Kingfisher's different businesses around the country.

In September 2000 Kingfisher made the surprise announcement that it planned to demerge the organisation into two parts: New Kingfisher and General Merchandise. While Kingfisher's DIY and electrical companies were doing well, Woolworths and some of its other companies were less successful. It was felt that by demerging the group into two parts, both sides of the business would be able to perform better.

 a Outline the meaning of these terms:
  i economies of scale;
  ii demerger.
 b Explain why brand names are important to Kingfisher.
 c Discuss possible reasons for the success of B&Q and the lack of success of Woolworths.
 d Describe the advantages that a conglomerate has over a business that expands within the same industry.
 e Discuss how Kingfisher might benefit from the proposed demerger.

Unit 3.1 Specialisation and the division of labour

De-skilling →	where a skill is no longer needed because a job is broken down into a number of smaller, separate parts. Advances in technology have had the same effect.
Division of labour →	the splitting up of a job into a number of smaller parts. Each part is then carried out by a different person.
Redundancy →	where workers are dismissed because their jobs are no longer needed.
Specialisation →	where people concentrate on a narrow range of activities. By doing so, they become expert in those tasks.

→ Key terms

In primitive societies, people do everything for themselves and try to provide for all their own needs. However, some are better than others at hunting, making clothes, building huts or growing crops. They are all better off if the good hunters hunt for everyone, the best farmers grow crops for the rest and the good hut builders build all the huts. This **specialisation** makes everyone better off. They all enjoy more food and better huts to live in. As societies develop the amount of specialisation carries on growing.

Specialisation is the breaking up of activities into separate parts or jobs. Each person carries out a specific job or task, and becomes a specialist in it. The people who do the jobs become expert in them. The range of skills and knowledge of each person gets narrower each time jobs are broken down.

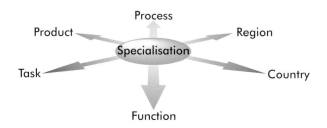

Figure 3.1 Specialisation

Forms of specialisation

Specialisation can be classified in a number of ways:

- **by product (or service)** where a firm produces a single product or service;
- **by process** where machines or equipment are used to carry out a particular process or job;

- **by task** where the job of making a product is broken down into a number of small parts. Each part of the process is carried out by different people. This gives rise to the **division of labour**;
- **by country or region** where a country or part of a country specialises in producing certain products. For example, Scotland produces Scotch whisky; South Korea produces engineering products;
- **by function** where a person specialises in a particular job or aspects of a job. For example, a plumber, or an accountant that specialises in tax matters.

Benefits of specialisation

- Through specialisation, enough work can be found for specialist machinery and equipment to be used. This means it is used more efficiently.
- Workers can concentrate on those things they do best, or enjoy doing the most.
- Expert knowledge and skills can be built up in a company, and can be developed through constant use.
- Resources can be concentrated where they are used best and most efficiently.

Drawbacks of specialisation

- It increases dependence. For example, firms become dependent on other specialist companies for their supplies and to transport, distribute and sell their products.
- Areas where there is one main industry become specialised. People become specialists in a narrow range of jobs. If that industry declines the whole area is

badly affected. Jobs are lost and other businesses are affected.

- People find it hard to move into other types of work that do not require their particular skills and knowledge.

Division of labour

The division of labour is just one aspect of specialisation. The division of labour is the breaking down of a production process into a number of separate, smaller tasks. Instead of a whole product being made by one person, it is made in a number of stages. Each stage is carried out by different people. They become specialists in a very narrow set of tasks. The number of stages varies. It depends on the size and complexity of the product.

Mass production methods in large factories are based on the division of labour. A job is broken down into a number of small operations. Each operation is carried out by a different person, usually on a production line. Because they only do that one operation every day, they become very fast and expert at that task.

Benefits of the division of labour

- Production is quicker and the total output is greater. It would probably take one person a day or two to build a washing machine. But the job can be broken down into perhaps 100 stages, with one person doing each stage. A washing machine can then be produced every minute or so. The total number of machines built is greater than if one person built each one.
- It is worthwhile for large firms to employ specialist workers, such as marketing executives or designers, since they are experts in their jobs.
- Workers become expert at their jobs. By repeating the same thing over and over again, their skills are increased. They can concentrate on the things they do best and become very efficient.
- Workers do not waste time moving from one job to another.
- The cost of training is less because a job can be learnt quickly. People are slower when they are learning to do a job. The cost of their wages may be greater than the value of the goods they produce. The shorter the learning time, the faster a worker will 'justify' his or her wages.

Drawbacks of the division of labour

- Jobs are so narrow that workers have no interest in what they are doing. They keep repeating the same thing over and over again and get bored.
- Workers may become careless because they are bored and not interested in their job. This can cause safety problems.
- Because each worker plays such a small part in making a product, they have no sense of responsibility for their work. The quality of their work may suffer as a result.
- The division of labour takes the skill out of jobs (**de-skilling**). As a result workers may not be able to do all aspects of a job. This can lead to a loss of craftsmanship. It also makes it easier to replace workers with machines. This is known as **automation**.
- Workers have very limited training and do jobs requiring a narrow range of skills. As a result, their skills cannot be used elsewhere. They would probably need to be re-trained if they lost their jobs.

Activities

1 Give examples of specialisation of labour that can be found in your school or college.

2 State the type of specialisation shown in these examples:
   a a dentist specialises in treating children;
   b a television manufacturer employs a worker to pack the televisions into boxes;
   c Bolivia in South America produces most of the world's tin;
   d a firm specialises in making the batteries used in mobile phones;
   e an agricultural company owns several combine harvesters to gather the crops for farmers.

3 In this unit, five different forms of specialisation are listed. Give examples of how each of the five forms of specialisation are used by a car-making company, such as Ford or Vauxhall.

4 Specialisation is often said to make work repetitive and boring.

  a Explain why many people believe that this is true.

  b Give examples of how specialisation could make work more interesting and rewarding.

Case Study

5 **Townsend Pottery**

Townsend Pottery decorates vases and bowls using traditional, hand-painted designs. The business used to manufacture its own vases and teapots, but now buys 'biscuit-fired' items from a supplier. Teams of six artists then carefully paint the vessels. Each artist concentrates on one aspect of the design. One person paints flowers, another borders, and so on. The vases are then coated with a glaze and given a second firing in a kiln. The company uses a courier service to take the finished products to shops selling upmarket ceramic artworks.

  a List all the examples of specialisation you can find in this case study. State what type of specialisation each one is.

  b Explain why Townsend Pottery might have decided not to produce its own clay vessels.

  c Why do you think Townsend Pottery does not mention to customers how it makes its pottery?

ICT Activity

Produce a flow chart on the computer to show the different stages of manufacture of a typical piece of Townsend's pottery.

Examination hints

- Always support your answers with examples. Examples help to show that you understand what you are writing about. They also provide evidence to support your point.

- Section A of the examination may ask questions about things that are not covered in the case study. This means that you have to revise all that you have learnt in your course not only those matters dealt with in the case study.

- Examples to support your answer to Section A questions can be drawn from any part of business studies. For example, there may be a definition in this section that is not covered by the case study. You are expected to find an example from what you see around you or from your reading.

Unit 3.2 Organisation of production

3.2a Methods of production

Production is the creation of goods and services to meet human wants. Every product, including services, passes along a **chain of production**. This unit looks in more detail at the part of the chain concerned with manufacturing, or secondary production.

Like all other aspects of production, manufacturing involves the use of the factors of production:
- land for premises;
- capital for the plant and equipment;
- labour;
- enterprise to organise all the other resources and take the risks.

The way these resources are organised depends on the kind of product that is being made. The way a product is made depends on the nature of the product and the demand for it. There are three main methods of production:
- job production;
- batch production;
- flow production.

Job production

This is the production of a 'one-off' product. The product is tailor-made to suit a particular person or purpose. The goods are only produced when there is an order for them. Products are not made in advance in the hope that someone will buy them. Craftsmen and people working on their own often use job production. For example, a tailor makes a suit to measure, or a cabinet maker makes a piece of furniture to a person's own design or to fit a particular space in a house. Services are often carried out on a job basis. For example, hairdressers, 'jobbing' gardeners and architects. Job production is often used for big projects such as building a bridge, a motorway or a multistorey office block.

A skilled tailor cutting out a suit. This is an example of job production

Benefits of job production
- Craft skills are retained and craftsmen have a chance to use their skills.
- Specialist knowledge and skills can be used.
- Every product can be different.

Drawbacks of job production
- Specialist labour is very expensive.
- Production is slow.
- The final product can be expensive.

Batch production

In **batch production** goods are produced in lots or batches. The goods produced are similar, or only differ in one respect such as colour. When one batch is finished, machines may have to be re-set before moving on to the next batch. Bread, cakes, jam and sweets are regularly produced in batches. There are other examples:
- goods made to order, where one order is completed before moving to the next one, for example printing a book;
- where the same machine is used to produce different things by changing the settings, for example a lathe that can produce several designs of chair leg;
- goods of the same design made in different sizes and colours, for example clothes.

Batch production

Benefits of batch production
- It can be used for both long and short 'runs'.
- Specialist machines and skills can be used.
- It is easy to produce a variety of sizes and colours of a product.

Drawbacks of batch production
- Production has to be stopped to re-set machines.
- Gaps in production lead to higher costs.

Flow production

Under this method, goods flow along a production or **assembly line**. They pass from one stage to the next, without a break, on a conveyor belt. The number of stages varies according to the product. In making a car there are hundreds of stages. There is a worker at each stage who does just one operation. They do the same thing all day, every day; perhaps adding or fixing one component. At each stage there is a constant stock of the components and tools needed. The assembly line keeps moving all the time, so workers have a limited time in which to do their part. Flow production is used in **mass production**.

Flow production is used for making large quantities of goods. It can only be used if it is possible to break production up into a number of different stages and operations. Flow production is used, for example, in making cars, washing machines and computers. It is also used in brewing, chemical manufacture and oil refining where it is often called continuous flow production. Very little human labour is used in these processes.

The Ford Model T – one of the first uses of flow production (see the case study on page 103)

Benefits of flow production

- Large quantities can be produced quickly and cheaply.
- Assembly lines can run for 24 hours a day and shift work introduced.
- Parts of the work can be automated, using robots.
- The goods produced should be of standard quality.

Drawbacks of flow production

- It needs very large factories and very costly machinery.
- Very large amounts of capital are required.
- Workers get bored doing the same thing all the time.
- Loss of concentration can lead to safety risks.
- Workers do not see the results of their work and may therefore take no pride in it.
- The production line sets the speed at which people work, causing stress.
- Workers are skilled in one, narrow job making it hard to transfer to other jobs.

Automation

This means replacing human labour with machines. The growth of computers and computer-controlled machines has speeded up the move to automation. Many aspects of mass production lend themselves to automation. Processes such as welding and paint spraying are better done by robots. They can do the job better and faster than humans. Automation is not used only in factories. It is widely used in offices and places like warehouses for stock control. It has resulted in the loss of many jobs. Some service industries, that rely on personal service, are not easy to automate, for example hairdressing and restaurants.

Benefits of automation

For employers:

- machines can be used 24 hours a day without a break. More can be produced because there is no break in production;
- computer-controlled machines can be easily reprogrammed to do other jobs;
- there are cost savings because less labour is needed.

For employees:

- working conditions are cleaner and less physical work is needed;
- those who program and maintain the machines are highly skilled. They need constant updating, and workers have greater training opportunities and job security;
- there may be fewer workers but those that remain may be better paid and have better job security.

Drawbacks of automation

For employers:

- not all companies have the capital to buy the very expensive equipment needed;
- there may be industrial relations problems when the equipment is introduced;
- introducing automation is costly because of the high costs of training people to use the equipment and redundancy payments to workers who may have to be laid off.

For employees:

- fewer people are needed so there is a high risk of redundancy;
- jobs may be de-skilled and skilled workers may become just 'machine minders';
- when a firm automates, fewer jobs are available.

Automation is used extensively in car making

1 Copy out and complete the table. Part has already been filled in for you.

Company	Examples of different factors of production needed		
	Land	Labour	Capital
Minicab firm	Place for office/ control centre	Drivers Radio operator Mechanics	Vehicles Radio system
Market gardener			
Firm of solicitors			
Leisure centre			

2 Decide which of the three production methods (job, batch or flow) would be the most suitable for the following companies. Explain your choices.

   a a building firm that has won a contract to build a new food technology block at a school;

   b a large manufacturer of breakfast cereals;

   c a maker of hi-fi and personal stereos.

3 Barcoding on supermarket products has not just allowed consumers to be given an itemised bill. The EPOS system has also improved supermarkets' stock control. Supermarkets find it convenient because they are able to reduce the amount of wastage caused by overstocking goods. Customers are pleased because they are less likely to find the products that they want out of stock.

   a Describe how barcodes have allowed supermarkets to become more efficient.

   b Explain why small shops are unlikely to have a barcoding system.

4 Ford Tin Lizzie

'You can have any colour you like,' Henry Ford is claimed to have said in 1908 about his new car, the Model T, 'so long as it's black.'

Case Study

The reason for the lack of choice was that Ford produced the Model T using flow production techniques. The idea of this type of production was not new, but Ford was the first to put the idea into practice. Before the Model T, cars had been made one at a time or in small batches.

Production of the Model T took place on an assembly line more than 300 metres long at Ford's Detroit factory. The cars moved around the plant at a slow speed. As the vehicles went from one worker to the next, the men would add another piece to the car. The work was repetitive and tended to be boring, but to compensate for this Ford paid the highest wages in the industry. Such was the demand for jobs at Ford's that the police had to be called to control the crowds when new jobs were advertised.

This method of production allowed the Model T to be sold for $825, which was far cheaper than other cars at the time. The car was within the reach of people who would otherwise not be able to afford to buy one.

These days most cars are made using the Ford technique. Some firms still keep to batch production methods, though their vehicles are a lot more expensive to buy.

   a Why was it necessary for Ford to sell just one colour of car?

   b What is meant by 'division of labour'?

   c Why did Ford have to pay high wages to his workers?

   d How was Ford able to charge a low price for the Model T, despite paying workers high wages?

   e Explain why a high level of supervision is needed when mass production methods are used.

   f Why do some car makers continue to make cars in small batches?

Unit 3.2 Organisation of production

3.2b Improving production

Mass production is a good way of producing large numbers of similar goods cheaply. However, there are disadvantages to mass production.

- Very long production lines take up a great deal of expensive land. In a car factory the assembly lines can be a km long.
- Production lines are very rigid. Making changes to them takes a long time and is very costly.
- To keep production lines flowing there have to be large stocks of parts. If stocks run out or there is a problem at one part of the line, production may have to stop. Those further down the line will then not be able work. This is very costly.
- Workers are isolated. They are strung out along an assembly line that they have to keep up with, doing one limited task. There is little chance to chat or talk about their work. They may feel they are being treated as little more than machines. This sense of isolation and of not being valued can lead to industrial relations problems.
- It is difficult to maintain standards of quality along the whole of the production line.

The Japanese have tried to find answers to these problems. Many of their systems began to be used in the UK when Japanese car makers started to manufacture here. They not only used the new systems in their own factories but insisted that their suppliers did too.

Cell production

In cell production the work is divided up into blocks or cells of work. Each cell is made up of a team of workers who work together to produce a complete part of the product or process. Each cell is given production and quality targets. The team members have to work together to improve their product and to solve any problems that arise in their part of the process. As a result they:

- have more control over the way they work;
- can see what they have produced and take pride in their work;
- are less bored and more interested in their work.

Examples of cell production can be found at Rover, Nissan and Honda, and at many of their suppliers.

Just-in-time (JIT)

The workers on a production line have to be kept well supplied with parts. Traditionally this meant holding large stocks of parts near to the production line. Holding large stocks is costly because they:

- tie up capital that could be used somewhere else;
- take up expensive floor space that earns nothing and could be better used in production.

These problems can be avoided using **just-in-time** (JIT). Under this system stocks of parts are delivered to the production line, at the point where they are going to be used, just before they are needed. JIT depends on having a highly organised system for ordering parts and materials. Users must work closely with their suppliers to get their supplies delivered at exactly the right time, that is, just in time. The growth in the use of computers and modern methods of communication has helped to make the system work. There are, however, risks with the system. If one supplier fails to get goods to the user on time there will be hardly any stock to fall back on. A delay in delivery due to traffic can bring production to a stop.

Lean production

This is a system that aims to keep all the resources used in production (inputs) to a minimum. Under the system, the size of the factory, and the number of workers, suppliers, stocks of parts and finished goods are all kept as small or as low as possible. Just-in-time is an example of **lean production**. The aim is to keep costs down and under strict control. It should mean better quality goods and higher productivity.

Kaizen

This is a system based on the Japanese word meaning 'continuous improvement'. However good a firm may be there is always room for improvement. Quality can be improved and costs brought down. Everyone has a part to play in improving the firm's products. All workers should be involved.

Under traditional methods the workers 'did what they were told'. But they may well know more than the managers about how things really work and how they could be improved. It makes sense to ask them for ideas on how production can be improved. Under kaizen, workers are asked for their views. Their ideas are taken seriously and are often acted upon.

Kaizen is often used in cell production. If there is a problem in a cell all the members of that cell share it. They work together to solve it. This means they all have to know about each other's jobs. They have to be flexible and **multi-skilled**, and be able to do whatever job needs doing. Old ideas of workers only being allowed to do a particular job do not apply.

Quality circles

Quality is important to all firms. The people who probably know best how to improve it are the workers making the goods. Many firms have set up quality circles to draw on this expertise. Groups of workers meet with supervisors and managers. They talk as equals, about ways of improving working practices and solving problems. Quality circles not only produce good ideas and improve efficiency. They also:

- give workers more interest in their work by becoming involved;
- allow workers to learn about other aspects of the business;
- improve communications;
- give workers the chance to understand their bosses' point of view better.

Benchmarking

Firms use **benchmarking** to measure their efficiency. They compare their performance with that of other firms in the same or similar industries. Among the things they may compare are:

- output per worker over a day, a week or a month;
- how long supplies of raw materials, components and finished goods are kept in stock;
- measurements of quality such as the number of rejects, or items that have to be corrected during production.

Firms can see quickly how far they are in front or behind their competitors. They can use the results to set future targets. Firms need to make these comparisons if they are going to compete effectively with firms in their own country and internationally.

Technology

Firms have to compete by producing goods and services as efficiently and as cheaply as they can. To do so they have to keep up to date. Technology changes very quickly. Firms nowadays have to change their equipment much more often than they used to. New machines are faster, more efficient, more reliable and cheaper to run. They help to produce more, better quality goods, more efficiently and at a lower cost. Most of the technology used in production and in the service industries is based on computers. Here are four example of how technology is used in production.

Robots

Robots are machines that can be programmed to do a task. They can also be reprogrammed quickly and easily to do other jobs. They are a form of automation and so usually replace people. They are widely used in mass production. For example, in the car industry they are used for jobs like spot welding and paint spraying. Three advantages of robots are that:

- they can work non-stop for 24 hours a day;
- they do not need to have tea breaks or holidays or even stop to change shifts;
- the quality of their output is always the same.

Computer-aided design (CAD)

This is where products are designed on computers. The product can be looked at from all angles in two and three dimensions. The design can be modified easily and cheaply. It is widely used in making complex products such as cars and aeroplanes.

- Designers no longer have to produce complicated drawings by hand, so design has been speeded up.
- CAD is also used to design each of the parts that make up the product.
- It is easy to check, using the computer, that the parts fit together properly in the final product.

Computer-aided manufacturing (CAM)

The data from CAD can be fed directly to certain machines. The data is used to program the machines to produce the parts concerned. The machines are called computer-numerically controlled (CNC) machines. They have a built-in computer that can be programmed to control the machine's operations. They can also be used separately from CAD.

Using a CAD program

Computer-integrated manufacturing (CIM)

This is where all, or large parts, of a manufacturing process is controlled by computers. In CIM a central computer can be used to control, for example, robots and the speed of a production line. It can also keep a record of parts as they are being used and the flow of new parts to the production line. It collects accurate data that can be used to make production more efficient.

Citroën C5x on the production line

Activities

1 Rearrange these terms so they are next to the definition that best fits.

Term	Explanation
Cell production	Arranging for supplies to arrive when they are needed and not holding large amounts of stock.
Kaizen	Using the best standards in the industry to see how well a firm is doing.
Lean production	A method of making goods using teams of workers working together.
Just-in-time	Always looking for ways of improving how the products are made.
Quality circles	A general term to describe ways of keeping costs of production as low as possible.
Benchmarking	Groups of workers and managers who meet to consider ways of improving the way products are made.

2 Draw the table below and complete the two empty columns.

Stock control

	How it works	Advantage
Traditional method	Firms buy large amounts of stock, which is stored at the factory until needed.	It is highly unlikely that supplies will run out and cause production problems.
Just-in-time		

---

3 Old Cobblers

Old Cobblers is a long-established family shoe-making business. Methods of production have changed little since it was founded 50 years ago.

The production method involved in making a new range of shoes can be represented by the stages shown in the diagram below.

Designer draws new shoe on drawing board

↓

Prototype is made by hand-cutting leather

↓

Prototype is tested by being worn by volunteer for 3 weeks

↓

If found to be suitable, sufficient leather is ordered to produce a run of 4,000 pairs

↓

Each employee works individually making one shoe size using batch production

↓

Quality controller inspects completed shoes

The directors of Old Cobblers have recently discovered that the quality controllers are rejecting a growing number of shoes for being below standard. The directors are also concerned that its competitors appear to be operating more efficiently than Old Cobblers.

a How could Old Cobblers measure the efficiency of the business?

b Suggest ways in which Old Cobblers might use more modern production methods to improve its efficiency.

c What problems might arise if the firm introduced new production methods into its factory?

4 Marconi

Marconi Electronic Systems (MES) produces target-tracking equipment for military aircraft and flight recorders (the 'black boxes') used in both commercial and military aeroplanes.

Government cutbacks in military spending in the 1990s meant that MES had to concentrate more on the private-sector side of its business. Unfortunately for MES, there was more competition in this area of business, so MES had to look at ways of producing goods more efficiently. In particular, MES tried to provide a high quality product at a competitive price, keeping the time between ordering and delivery (the lead time) as short as possible.

Manufacturing in MES was organised in a very traditional way. Specialist engineers worked individually on batches of items. They would take the items they needed to work on from the stores and return it when their particular tasks had been completed. When studies were undertaken it was discovered that this production method was very inefficient. It was also never clear who was responsible for checking that the final product was of a high standard.

The production manager decided to reorganise manufacturing into production cells. Here teams of workers were responsible for the production of a complete item. Instead of working

on their own, the engineers had to cooperate and rely on each other. A system of benchmarking was introduced. The engineers were encouraged to look at how they worked, so they could work as well as the best of their competitors.

At first, the workers were suspicious and reluctant to change the way that they worked. So MES had to convince its workers that it was in the best interest of everyone to change. A programme of re-training was started and workers were kept up to date on how well the company was doing. The new system proved to be very successful, allowing MES to be able to compete with other firms.

a What were the three things MES tried to improve?

b Explain what these terms mean:
- lead time;
- benchmarking;
- cell production.

c Explain why an engineer might have been reluctant to change the way he or she worked.

d Consider these three ways of communicating the importance of the changes to the engineers:
- a letter sent to each engineer explaining why the changes are being introduced;
- a large meeting where the engineers can pose questions to the production manager;
- a statement from the production manager pinned up on notice boards.

List the arguments for and against each of these methods as a way of persuading the workers to accept the changes.

e The company may have considered taking the new teams on a week-long outdoor pursuits course. Discuss whether you think this would be a good form of training for these workers.

Unit 3.3 Quality, production and marketing

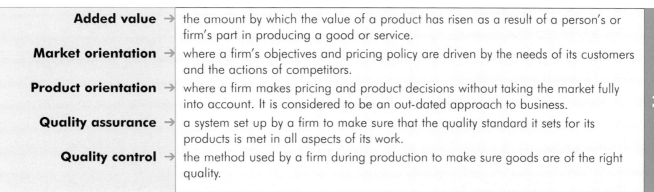

The only reason firms produce goods and services is to sell them either to the public or to other firms. Products have to be of the right **quality** and sold at a price that reflects that quality. If the product is of poor quality or too expensive it will not sell and the firm may fail.

Firms hope that consumers buy their products time and again. Consumers will only do so if the product is:

- reliable, that is it does what it is supposed to do;
- of the same quality whenever or wherever they buy it;
- reasonably long lasting;
- good value for money.

In other words, consumers expect the goods and services they buy to be of a certain quality. Quality is usually related to the price paid for the product. Higher priced goods and services are expected to be of better quality than cheaper goods. Goods and services must, by law, be fit for their purpose. This provides a minimum standard of quality that all goods and services must meet.

Apart from making sure their products comply with the law, firms have to decide for themselves what quality their goods or services are aiming for. All firms have ways of checking the quality of their product regularly.

Quality control

Traditionally, firms check the quality of goods during and at the end of manufacture using **quality control**

inspectors. They test samples of the product against certain measures. For a simple product, this is usually done only at the end. For more complex goods it is done at various stages during manufacture. Goods that have faults are either scrapped or put right before they move on to the next stage. A weakness of the method is that only a sample is taken, perhaps one in every 20 items. A lot of faulty goods can get through the system without being picked up. It can be a wasteful system if there are many faults and a lot of goods have to be scrapped.

Quality assurance

Firms set a standard of quality for all their products. Quality assurance is the system a firm sets up to make sure that this quality standard is met in all aspects of its work. Everyone working in the firm is expected to work to this standard. Quality assurance aims to ensure that faults do not happen. Quality then becomes the responsibility of all the workers, not just a few inspectors.

British Standards Institution (BSI)

The BSI draws up detailed specifications for a wide range of goods. These specifications are called 'standards'. The standards lay down details of the materials that have to be used and the way goods have to be made and tested. All goods made to a standard have the same basic specification. Firms producing goods

Quality control by inspection

to a BSI standard are allowed, after inspection by the BSI, to say so on their labels and advertisements. They are allowed to show the 'kitemark'. This helps to sell goods, since consumers know that they are made to a certain standard of quality.

Added value

Goods change as they pass through each stage of the production process. They are worth more at the end than they were at the beginning of each stage. This difference in value is called the **added value**. The added value includes the cost of materials, wages and expenses, plus an allowance for profit. Each stage in the chain of production adds value to a product.

Added value

Figure 3.2 Added value

Example

A computer manufacturer buys parts from a number of suppliers and combines them to make a computer. Each part on its own may be of very little use, but when put together with other parts, it makes a new, very useful, product. The computer manufacturer has added value. Each of the workers on the production line has also added value through their effort.

Added value is measured by the difference between the selling price, and the costs of the materials and labour that have gone into the product.

The idea of added value is important in business. In many ways the whole purpose of business is to add value. Adding value creates wealth, which benefits consumers and communities as well as firms. Consumers benefit in that they get a better choice of goods. Communities gain from the work provided and the incomes earned. The more value a business can add the more successful it is. Consumers gain because the price of the goods is kept down.

Production and marketing

Production is the process that adds value to goods. Raw materials and labour are brought together to create or assemble a product.

Goods and services are produced for a market. There is no point in producing products that people do not want to buy. Goods and services must meet a need that consumers will pay for. Products do not sell if they do not meet a need, or are too expensive or of poor quality. Producers must therefore find out what consumers want. Finding out people's needs and wants is an important part of marketing.

Product orientation

There are firms that have been producing the same product for years. They often take little notice of new trends or changes in taste. There are also firms that have a good idea and then go ahead and produce the product in the hope that it will sell. Such firms are said to be **product orientated** or product led. Product-led firms tell consumers what they can have, rather than consumers telling them what they want. This is rather risky and is now considered to be an old-fashioned approach.

Market orientation

Goods and services are sold in competitive markets. The size of the market for any one product is limited. Firms compete with one another for a share of that market. Firms in such markets have to be outward looking and try to give consumers what they want. Firms that respond to consumers' wants are **market orientated.**

Before they start to produce goods and services, market-orientated firms try to find out as much as they can about what consumers want, both now and in the future. They look for trends, study them and take them into account in their planning. They watch for changes in tastes and try to react quickly to them. This should mean that their products sell well. In practice this is not always the case. Finding out what people want is the job of market research.

Activities

1 Explain why it is in firms' own interests to sell good quality products.

2 Describe how the manufacturers of the following goods might check the products to ensure good quality:
   a a pair of jeans;
   b a CD game;
   c washing machines.

3 Outline two reasons why it might be better for workers to be responsible for the quality of the goods they produce, rather than inspectors.

4 The owner of a forest sells a blown-down oak tree to a sawmill for £100. The sawmill cuts the tree into planks, which are sold to a furniture maker for £250. The planks are made into four oak tables. These tables are then sold to a furniture retailer for £1,000. Members of the public then buy the tables for £400 each.

Use this example to explain the concept of 'value added'.

☐ Case Study

5 **Aston Martin**

The car maker Aston Martin takes a completely different approach to its product than most other car manufacturers. Companies like Vauxhall and Ford research the market very carefully, taking the consumers' needs into account when they design their cars. If, for instance, people are concerned about the high price of petrol, a company like Vauxhall might adapt its engines to make them more economical. Style and design are also considered from the customers' point of view. If it is fashionable to have a certain style of car, such as people carriers or four-wheel drive, the major car makers will always respond to what the market wants. Even the colours people want are taken very seriously.

Aston Martin is quite different. Its cars have changed very little over the years. More care is given to traditional designs and quality workmanship than to frequent changes in styling. The company goes to enormous lengths to ensure that their cars leave the factory in perfect condition. Quality checks are made at every stage of the production process. But quality does not come cheap. An Aston Martin car will probably cost more than ten times as much as a mass-produced car.

Aston Martin knows its cars are always in demand, so it sees no need to conduct market research. In fact, the demand for Aston Martin cars is so high, consumers may have to wait many months after ordering one before it is ready for collecting.

a Why is it important that major car makers, such as Ford and Vauxhall, spend money researching just what consumers are looking for in a car?

b Explain the concepts of product and market orientation using the case study.

c Why is Aston Martin able to have a different orientation from Vauxhall?

d Discuss whether it would be worthwhile for Aston Martin to move towards mass production to reduce the delivery time for its cars.

ICT Activity

Look at the website of BSI:

www.bsi.org.uk/bsi/products/kitemark.

Explain how the BSI kitemark can help consumers.

6 **Persil**

Read the article below and then answer the following questions.

a What error did Unilever make when it launched Persil Power?

b Why did Proctor & Gamble advertise its own product, Ariel, so heavily when the report on Persil Power became public?

c Comment on the view that manufacturers would be better off remaining with their old tried-and-tested products, and not taking risks by making changes to them.

Persil Washing Powder Said to Damage Clothes

The Consumers' Association (CA) is a group that checks on products and then advises the public on what is the best buy. In the mid-1990s CA claimed that Persil washing powder was responsible for damaging clothes. Persil is a major brand owned by the company Unilever. CA washed clothes many times with Persil and compared the results with garments washed in other powders. The Persil-washed clothes began to lose their colour and to show signs of wear much sooner than those washed with other leading brands of washing powder.

The damage had been caused because Unilever had included a new stain-removing chemical in Persil, which it called the 'accelerator'. The new stain-removing powder was launched as Persil Power. Unilever's US rival, Proctor & Gamble, immediately set about promoting its own leading soap powder, Ariel. The advertisements for Ariel showed clothes full of holes, which they claimed had been washed in Persil.

Unilever tried to limit the bad publicity by putting notices on packets of Persil, saying that care should be taken when using the powder. This did not work, though, and major supermarkets such as Tesco and Sainsbury stopped stocking Persil for a short time. Sales of Persil dropped by a half. Persil was once a market leader, but its reputation was lost because of the bad publicity.

Unit 3.4 Markets and marketing

3.4a The nature of markets

The word 'market' for most people means an exciting, noisy street market or market hall. But this is only one sort of market. Wherever buyers and sellers meet to buy and sell goods and services there is a market. It does not have to be a physical place such as a street market or a shop. It is still a market if goods and services are bought and sold by telephone or on the Internet. Some companies only sell in this way. For example, direct sales companies such as Direct Line insurance sell only by telephone; amazon.com sells books and egg.co sells financial services only on the Internet.

The term 'market' is also used for the group of people who buy, or might buy, a product. Products can have more than one market. For example, a certain model of car may be bought by a private individual or a com-

pany. These are two entirely separate markets even though the car is the same in every way. Each market has different needs and its own characteristics.

Types of market

The different kinds of markets can be classified in many ways, some of which are given here.

- **Local** – some goods and services are sold within an area. For example, services such as hairdressing and plumbing. The street market is a local market, drawing on people within, perhaps, a 30 km radius.
- **National** – goods and services are sold on a national basis. Marks & Spencer and Tesco, for example, have branches all over the country. Each branch sells mainly the same goods, many of which will be supplied from a central depot.
- **International** – goods and services are sold in other countries as well as at home. For example, BP sells petrol all over the world.
- **By sector** – for example:
  - trade sales (goods are only sold to other companies, not the public);
  - retail sales (goods are sold to the public through shops);
  - wholesale sales (goods are sold to retailers but not directly to the public).
- **By characteristics** – for example, according to age, product or geographical area.

All these different markets overlap. Companies sell their products in a number of different markets at the same time.

A cattle market

Market segmentation

Firms like to know as much as they can about the people who buy their goods or services. They spend a good deal of time and money analysing their markets. Within their overall market there are a number of different types or groups of customers. The breaking down of a market into different groups or types of customer is called **market segmentation**.

Firms have a number of different segments or markets for their product. Each segment is a group of buyers who share common features or characteristics. Firms may decide to aim their products at only one or two segments of the market. Each segment is a separate market that may need to be treated in a different way.

Markets can be segmented in many ways. Firms segment their market in the way that is most suitable for their products. The segments for leisure clothing are different from the segments for work wear. Here are some of the more usual ways to segment a market.

By population

In particular, according to:

- age – different age groups have different needs and spending habits;
- gender – some goods appeal to women only or men only, other goods appeal to both but may need to be sold in different ways;
- ethnic origin – firms need to be aware of the ethnic make up of the population and be careful not to offend people's customs and religious practices.

By income

Some products appeal to people on low incomes while luxury goods are bought by people with higher incomes.

Geographically

This means by area or region. Tastes often vary from one part of the country to another. Goods that sell well in Bournemouth may not sell as well in Newcastle or Carlisle.

By social factors

For example, there are an increasing number of single-person households and more single parents of both sexes. Firms often put people into social groups, often according to income. These groups are called socio-economic groups.

By buying habits

People may, for example:

- buy the same product each time and develop a brand loyalty;
- switch from one brand to another;
- always choose goods by their price;
- choose by the quality of goods;
- always want to have the latest fashion.

Changing market segments

Market segments are not fixed. They change in size and importance as the structure and distribution of the population changes. As the population changes the types of goods consumers want also change. Here are three examples of how changes in population may affect firms.

- The number of people in the 16 to 25 age group has fallen. At the same time, the number of people in the 25 to 35 age range has increased. Many of the firms that used to produce goods for the 16- to 25-year-old market have switched to the 25 to 35 age group. There are more of them, and they have more money to spend. This slightly older group want more fashionable, more expensive goods. They are setting up homes and are interested in furniture, gardening and DIY.
- There are more jobs for women, especially part-time jobs. There are also more women in professional and senior jobs. As a result shopping patterns have changed. For example, supermarkets are open until later. Sunday and late-night shopping are common.
- In the UK, the population is ageing. As a result more goods and services are being produced to meet the needs of older people. The proportion of people over 55 who are retired with good company pensions has risen. They often have time and money to spend on leisure. Other retired people are not so well off. They have less money to spend, and have to spend a bigger part of their money on necessities.

Niche markets

Market segments are usually quite large groups of consumers and form a broad market. There are some markets that are highly specialised with a small, narrow group of customers. Such markets are known as **niche markets**. They may be a specialised part of a larger market. They are often served by small, specialised firms since there are not enough customers to attract the interest of bigger firms. For example, the market for brass parts for models of steam engines built between 1875 and 1899 is a niche market. The model-making market, on the other hand, may be quite large.

Target markets

There are very few products that everyone has to have and therefore buys. Most firms choose certain segments of the market at which to aim their product. They decide which group of consumers they want as their **target market**.

Activities

1 Describe the types of people likely to form the market segment for these businesses:
   a Body Shop cosmetics;
   b computer games;
   c Jaguar cars;
   d extreme sport holidays.

2 An ice-cream manufacturer has relied upon a market segment of young children in the 3 to 13 age group. The company finds that this age group no longer is attracted to the ice-cream it produces. The firm feels that it needs to break into the young adult market (age 16 to 25). Describe how the firm could adapt its product and marketing approach to appeal to this group.

3 Economy Holidays

Economy Holidays is a business that arranges cheap holidays, mainly for lower income family groups, to resorts in Spain. It has found that although there has been an increase in the number of foreign holidays taken by British people, there has been a sharp decline in the number travelling with Economy Holidays.

The company undertakes some research on how its holiday market has changed over the last five years. The results are shown in the table below.

a Draw a series of graphs of the data. Use the graphs to forecast the figures for the next two years. (You will find this task easier if you are able to use a spreadsheet.)

b Use the graphs you have produced to help you write a report for Economy Holidays. The report should:
   i offer a possible explanation as to why the company's revenue has fallen over the last five years;
   ii provide Economy Holidays with suggestions on how it might change its market segment to avoid declining further.

Year	1997	1998	1999	2000	2001
Economy Holidays' annual revenue (£000)	£3,430	£3,150	£2,700	£2,470	£2,180
Average annual household income	£18,500	£19,300	£20,350	£22,180	£23,600
Average number of people per household	4.2	4.0	3.9	3.8	3.6
Average spending per household on foreign holidays	£650	£875	£960	£1,170	£1,340
Percentage of foreign holidays that are:					
short haul (Europe)	72%	65%	62%	59%	56%
medium haul (e.g. Florida, Israel)	18%	21%	23%	25%	26%
long haul (e.g. Australia, Indonesia)	10%	14%	15%	16%	18%

4 Gala Clubs

Gala Clubs is a private limited company. Originally owned by Bass Ltd, it was bought out by its managers in 1997. The core business of Gala Clubs is bingo. The company owns 150 bingo clubs throughout the country. When its owners decided to open a new large bingo club, Gala Clubs looked carefully at Ashton-under-Lyne, near Manchester as a possible site for this club.

Gala already had a bingo club at Ashton-under-Lyne, but its location was far from ideal. The club was based in an old cinema away from the town centre. There were four other bingo clubs locally and it had no convenient car parking facilities.

Gala Clubs believed that Ashton was a possible site for its new purpose-built bingo club, so it carried out extensive research into the demographic profile of the area. Ashton was found to have many advantages as a location:

- it had a large population (80,000 adults) which was growing at a rate of 1.7% each year;
- the town and surrounding area consisted mainly of people in socio-economic groups D and E;
- a higher than average percentage of the population said they played bingo (8.1% compared with the national figure of 6.3%);
- statistics from local breweries showed that the people in the area drank on average 225 pints of beer a year – higher than the national average.

There were some negative points, however:
- unemployment was higher than the national average;
- a large percentage of workers were employed in manufacturing;
- census figures showed that a higher than average percentage of the population came from ethnic groups. For cultural or religious reasons, these people are less likely to play bingo;
- car ownership was low, so many customers would have to rely on public transport.

Gala Clubs decided that the demographic profile of Ashton make it suitable for a large bingo hall.

a What is meant by:
- core business;
- management buyout (MBO)?

b How would you describe the market segment for bingo playing?

c Calculate the number of adults at Ashton who said they played bingo.

d Why were the following factors a concern for Gala Clubs:
- a high level of unemployment in Ashton;
- a large number of people employed in manufacturing?

e What type of demographic profile would be ideal for:
- an organic greengrocer;
- a new ten-pin bowling alley?

(Adapted from 'Case Studies with Business News', Fifth Edition, published by *The Times*.)

Unit 3.4 Markets and marketing

3.4b Market research

Desk research →	the collection of information from existing, published data.
Field research →	the collection of new and original information by going out into 'the field' and gathering it directly from the public.
Loyalty cards →	cards issued by supermarkets and other stores that give customers points when shopping at the store. The points can be used against future shopping bills. They give stores a great deal of information about regular customers' shopping habits.
Market research →	the collection of information about existing and potential markets for a product.
Market testing →	the selling of a new product in a limited area to see how well it sells and to highlight any possible problems.
Population →	in market research, it is used to mean a group of people who match certain criteria.
Primary research →	the first-hand collection of new and original information directly from the public.
Primary sources →	from where primary, or first-hand, information is collected.
Questionnaire →	a list of questions designed to produce answers about a defined set of issues.
Random sample →	a group of people selected by chance without taking the characteristics of the group, such as age or gender, into account.
Sample →	a small group of people taken as being representative of a much larger group.
Secondary research →	looking into and examining existing published information.
Secondary sources →	published material that is the subject of secondary research.
Survey →	a form of primary research where information is collected directly from a sample of the population either by questionnaire or by interview.
Test marketing →	where a product is first sold in a small, well-defined part of the market to test its popularity.

Firms need to know who buys their products, what the public thinks of them, and who is not buying their products and why. Finding out what consumers want and what they think about products is called **market research**.

Large firms have a marketing department to do at least part of their market research. Other firms hire agencies to do it for them. Even large firms use specialist firms for some parts of the work.

Reasons for market research

All firms, especially those that are market orientated, have to respond to the market. To do that they need information. The more information they have the more likely they are to judge correctly what the market wants. There are many things that firms need to know.

- Firms must study the trends in the population, incomes and the ways people spend their money. They consider what is happening now and estimate what may happen over the next three to five years. In this way they are able to look ahead. They can plan new products or the changes needed to keep their products up to date.
- They need to know who their customers are and what they and the rest of the public think about their products. If sales are falling they need to know why. Are customers satisfied with the product and the after-sales service? How can it be improved?
- Why do consumers buy one product rather than another? What kind of price are people willing to pay and what kind of quality do they expect for the price?
- It costs a great deal of money to bring out a new product, or to change an existing one. Firms

thinking of launching a new product need to check that people will buy it at the price they are hoping to sell it at. They should also find out how people react to the name and packaging of the product.

- After a product has been launched the producer needs to find out the public's reaction to it.
- Companies need to know as much as they can about their competitors, their goods and their plans for the future.

Sources of information

Firms collect the information they need from many different sources.

- Information already held within the firm. For example, monthly sales figures and the speed with which they sell stock.
- **Loyalty cards** give retailers huge amounts of information, for example data about what is being bought in their stores, the age and jobs of the customers, popular and unpopular goods, and regional differences.

Sainsbury's Reward Card gives the company valuable information about its customers. Customers can earn AIR MILES, save money on eating out and receive money off their grocery bills

- National information available from the government, trade associations and organisations such as Chambers of Commerce and the CBI.
- Information from market research surveys.

Desk research

This is where data is collected from existing published information. It involves sitting at a desk and going through reports and statistics that are widely available. Some of the information is held in libraries and some of it can be bought or is available by subscription.

Information obtained in this way is collected by **secondary research** from **secondary sources**. It is secondary because it is not collected first hand from the public.

Examples of secondary sources include:
- Official reports and statistics produced by the government, the European Union, local government and foreign governments. This includes census information and other statistics collected by the Office of National Statistics.
- Information from Chambers of Commerce, the CBI, the Institute of Directors, trade associations and trade magazines. This information is often available only to members, or it may be for sale to others.
- Company reports – limited companies have to send a copy of their Annual Report and Accounts to the Registrar of Companies. The reports can be read by anyone on payment of a small fee. It is a cheap way for firms to find out about their competitors.
- The Internet.
- Reports produced by specialist firms.
- Press reports.

Desk research has its limits. It is often hard to find the exact information needed. It is not unusual for the information to be fairly old and therefore out of date. This is often true of official statistics, where the latest figures available may be two or three years old. Some information can be expensive to buy, especially if it is produced by specialist firms.

Field research

This is where new and original information is collected in 'the field'. This means going out and collecting information directly from the public. Because the information is collected first hand, directly from members of the public, it is called **primary research** and is obtained from **primary sources**.

Examples of possible methods of primary research include:
- **Surveys** – where a sample of the public is questioned directly using **questionnaires** or interviews, by post or by telephone.
- **Observation** – where people's behaviour is watched and recorded. This method may be used to see how people move around a store or look at goods on a

Market research can be carried out by asking people questions in the street

shelf. The results may be used in designing store layouts and the way shelves are stacked.

- **Consumer panels** – where groups of people are brought together to sample and discuss a product. Their reactions are recorded and passed to the producer.
- **Testing** – where a new product is tried out in a small area to see how it sells. Any problems with the product or the way it is sold or presented can be solved before it is sold on a large scale. This is called **test marketing**.

Surveys

A survey is any direct attempt to find out people's opinion. Surveys are usually carried out through interviews or through a questionnaire.

The size of a survey depends on what is being investigated. They can be:

- national or local;
- general, where questions are asked about a number of things, for example a shopping survey;
- very specific, where questions are asked about one product or service.

Before carrying out a survey a firm must be clear about what it wants to know. It must not ask too many questions or people get bored or not give enough time

to answering the questions. Surveys can be carried out using two main methods:

- interviews (face to face or telephone);
- questionnaires (postal or door-to door).

There are four main types of questions used in surveys.

Open questions

These are questions that give people a chance to give their own views. For example, 'What do you think about holidays in England'.

Closed questions

In this type of question people are not given a chance to give their own opinion. Their answers are controlled by limiting the choice of answer they can give. People are asked to choose one answer from a list of possible responses. No other answers are allowed.

Example

Do you ever travel by train?	Yes	☐
	No	☐
How often do you travel by train?	Daily	☐
	More than once a week	☐
	Once a week	☐
	Once a month	☐
	Once a year	☐

Advantages of closed questions:

- people are willing to answer them because the tick boxes are easy to complete;
- they are easy to check and the data is easy to code for computer input;
- they are easy to summarise, analyse and turn into statistics.

Disadvantages of closed questions:

- it is not possible to write answers that cover all possible responses;
- there is no scope for people to express an opinion;
- people may not answer some questions because the answers offered do not fit with what they think.

Direct questions

These are questions that aim to gain an exact, specific answer. Most closed questions are direct.

Indirect questions

These are very open questions which allow for any answer. They are used only where attitudes are being looked at. They are very difficult to manage and are mainly used in personal interviews.

Interviews

Interviews are usually highly structured with the interviewer asking a prepared list of questions. There may be a limited choice of answers so that responses can be turned into statistics easily. For example, 'Do you think new Brand X washing powder makes your whites: whiter than before, the same as before, or less white than before?'.

Interviews by a person in a shopping centre are often of this kind. They are little more than questionnaires with a person asking the questions. Firms carrying out such surveys find they get a better response rate than when people have to fill in a questionnaire at home.

Questions can be less structured when people's attitudes, understanding and opinions are wanted. Here 'qualitative' rather than 'quantitative' responses are wanted. They are harder to sum up and to state as statistics.

The advantages of interviews are that:
- in-depth information can be obtained;
- people can be persuaded to agree to be questioned, so there is a good response rate.

The disadvantages are that:
- they are expensive;
- interviewers may interpret answers rather than record them accurately.

Questionnaires

For a questionnaire to be effective it has to be very carefully designed. It must not be too long or people will not answer it. The meaning of questions must be clear. Questions should not be biased or lead people towards a particular answer, for example 'Do you think it would be a good idea to…?'.

Questionnaires are not only used to ask the public about products. They are also used in business-to-business surveys. Questionnaires can take a lot of time to complete. For this reason, questionnaires are often used in postal surveys. People may be offered an incentive that has to be valuable enough to encourage them to fill them in.

Advantages of postal surveys:
- they are cheap;
- they can be targeted at certain groups;
- questions can be written in a way that is suitable for the target group;
- people who may not be willing to answer by telephone or face to face may be willing to complete a questionnaire, because they can remain anonymous.

Disadvantages of postal surveys:
- without incentives there is usually a very poor rate of response;
- questions can be misunderstood, unless they are very carefully constructed;
- the meaning of questions cannot be explained;
- the people who respond may not be typical.

Samples

It would cost far too much and take too long to survey the whole population. Instead, a survey is taken of a small group. This small group is called a **sample**. The results from the sample are taken to represent the views of all the people who share similar characteristics. For example, if 20% of the sample responds in a certain way, it is assumed that 20% of the whole population also has the same view. The way the sample is chosen partly depends on what the research is trying to find out. If the views of married 35-year-olds are wanted there is no point in asking single 18-year-olds or 70-year-old pensioners.

BUSINESS ASPECTS

Sampling

Market researchers would like to get a sample that exactly matches the target population for a product. There are various ways of choosing samples. Two methods are random sampling and structural sampling.

Random sample

This is a group of people chosen by chance. No account is taken of the age, gender, income or any other characteristic when choosing the sample. Everyone has an equal chance of being questioned. Selection is often quite crude, such as every tenth person who passes the researcher in the street. Random samples are not very accurate and not very useful for making comparisons. This is because the make up of the sample is different each time a new sample is selected. It varies according to where and when it is taken.

Structured sample

Here, some attempt is made to make sure that the sample reflects the population that the firm is trying to research. There are, for example, cluster areas that market research companies know, from experience, are typical of certain target markets.

Another form of structured sample is the quota. On the basis of secondary research, market research companies know the structure of the population. They can then give the researcher a quota of people to interview that exactly matches the composition of the market for a product. The researcher may thus be told to interview, for example:

10 males aged 16 to 20;
10 females aged 16 to 20;
20 couples aged 25 to 35;
15 couples over 40.

The researcher would then question the first people in each category they met, up to the number in the quota.

Population

This is a common word that is used in different ways in business studies. In market research it means a group of people who share certain characteristics or match certain criteria. For example, a firm manufacturing saws may wish to know how many left-handed carpenters there are. Once it knows the total of such people (the population) it can take a sample to test a new saw designed for left-handed carpenters.

Activities

1 Below are some questions taken from a market research survey into theatre visits. The questionnaire is very poor for many reasons. Examine each question and outline its weaknesses.

> **Market Research Questionnaire**
> a How old are you?
> b Do you go to the theatre often?
> c How much would you spend on a theatre ticket?
> - less than £6
> - £7–£9
> - £10–£13
> - more than £14
> d Why do you think people do not like going to the theatre? (tick one reason only)
> - it's too expensive
> - not heard of play
> - it's seen as snobbish
> - don't like going out

2 Keith is considering buying a newsagent's shop in a suburb of a large city. He decides to undertake some market research to attempt to discover if the business is likely to be profitable.

Explain what information he would find useful to have. Split this information into desk and field research.

ICT Activity

Use the Internet to find census information about the population of the area in which you live.

3 You work as a market researcher for a children's shoes manufacturer. The company is keen to determine what types of shoes will be most popular next year. The market segment for the shoes has already been identified as both boys and girls aged 3 to 12 from families in socio-economic groups ABC1.

As it is parents who buy the shoes, you decide to invite some parents to join a marketing consumer panel.

a Why does the shoe manufacturer want to know what will be fashionable next year?

b If you were in charge of running the consumer panel, explain how you would:

- select the parents to join this group;
- encourage them to participate in the research;
- arrange the panel so you get the information you need.

Case Study

4 Dyson

Dyson's vacuum cleaners caused quite a stir when the first model, the DC01, was launched in 1993. Unlike its competitors, the DC01 did not have a bag in which to collect household dust. The cleaner also looked very different with its bright plastic parts and the see-through dust-collecting compartment.

Market research had played an important part in developing the vacuum cleaner. James Dyson, the company founder, knew that normal cleaners lost efficiency when dust blocked their dust bags. So a machine that could work without bags was essential in creating a new style of vacuum cleaner.

Market research had shown that some people needed a machine that was light and easy to handle. They wanted a machine that could clean different surfaces and were concerned that all dust was captured, so allergy sufferers were not affected. Many said they liked the idea of the clear plastic dust compartment and the fact that the cleaner did not lose efficiency

Case Study

as it became full. Dyson also looked at what competitors were producing. Competitors' literature, Internet sites and trade journals were investigated carefully.

The market research also showed that many consumers misunderstood vacuum cleaner technology. It was thought that the bigger the motor in the vacuum cleaner, the better it would clean. Dyson knew that this was not the case. Rather than giving in to consumer pressure, James Dyson put a smaller, more economic motor into the DC03 model and changed the design to make it more efficient.

a Which of Dyson's research was field- and which desk-based?

b Explain how Dyson's used market research to produce a product that consumers wanted.

c What risk did Dyson's take in ignoring the consumer research on motor sizes?

d Dyson's vacuum cleaners were considerably more expensive than those of their competitors. How could market research have indicated to James Dyson whether consumers would be willing to pay extra for his vacuum cleaners?

ICT Activity

Go to the Dyson website (www.dyson.co.uk). Describe how the DC06 model has been developed to take into account the market research findings.

Examination hints

Use diagrams only when they help to make a point. Putting drawings into your answer will only earn marks if they add something to your answer. 'Pretty pictures' will not earn marks.

Organising to Achieve Objectives

Unit 3.4 Markets and marketing

3.4c Marketing and the marketing mix

Market leader →	the product or company that has the largest share of a market.
Market penetration →	the extent to which a firm has been able to gain market share. A high market penetration means a high market share.
Market share →	the proportion of the total sales of a product gained by a brand or a company.
Marketing →	a range of activities that ensure consumers get the products they want, in the right amounts, at the right price, in the right place and at the right time. Also, that they are fully informed of what is available.
Marketing mix →	the full range of activities a business may use to market its products. It consists of the 'four Ps' – product, price, place and promotion.
Place →	the part of the marketing mix that determines where goods are going to be sold and how they are going to get there.
Price →	the money paid when goods or services are bought and sold.
Product →	that which is made or supplied at the end of the production process. In marketing it is the goods or services available for sale.
Promotion →	the part of the marketing mix where it is decided how a product should be marketed or sold.

Marketing

We tend to think of **marketing** as selling goods and services. Marketing is more than this. It is a range of activities that makes sure consumers get what they want, in the right amounts, at the right time and at the right price. It also lets consumers know what goods and services are available so that they can make informed choices. The range of activities covered by marketing can be summed up as:

- identifying the size and type of consumers' needs and wants;
- deciding which markets to serve;
- deciding what goods and services to provide, and at what price;

} Based on market research

- informing consumers through promotion and advertising of products;
- getting goods and services to consumers through distribution systems.

Why firms market their products

Firms need to market their products because there are so many goods and services on the market. Firms spend money on marketing to let buyers know about their product and also to try to persuade them to buy it.

There are four main reasons why firms market their goods.

1 To increase sales. Generally, the more goods a firm sells the more profit it makes. This is because the more a firm sells the lower the cost per item becomes.

2 To increase **market share**. Market share is usually measured as a percentage of the total value of the sales of a product in a market. For some products, like cars, market share is better measured in terms of the volume of sales, that is, the number sold. The firm with the biggest market share is the **market leader**. Market share is a measure of a company's prestige and importance. It was a severe blow to Sainsburys' image when Tesco overtook it as the biggest supermarket group in 1996. When market share starts to fall a firm is losing customers to its competitors. It may mean it has to improve its product, change the price or improve its marketing.

3 Many firms run marketing campaigns to raise the image of the company and its products. Thus Rover has tried to change its image so that it is seen as producing high quality, prestige cars.
4 To keep the public informed of their products, especially new products.

The marketing mix

The **marketing mix** is the full range of activities that can be used by a business to market its products. This mix is usually referred to as the 'four Ps'.

1 **Product** – this is all aspects of the good or service itself. It is the name or branding, design, quality, appearance and any special features. Product also includes the number of sizes or models offered and the after-sales service.
2 **Place** – where the product can be bought and how it is distributed. The product must be at the right place at the right time.
3 **Price** – the price at which the product is sold. The price must let customers feel they are getting value for money while the sellers can make a reasonable profit. Among other things, the price of competing products is taken into account when deciding price.
4 **Promotion** – the methods used to sell a product, including advertising, other publicity, discounts, special offers, point-of-sale displays and direct marketing.

The marketing mix is different for every product. A new washing powder will be marketed in a different way from a motor insurance policy. The emphasis of the marketing mix depends on the target market for the product.

Marketing plan

Firms sell goods and services to make a profit. They want to make as big a profit as possible from each product they sell. To do this they have to blend each part of the marketing mix as effectively as possible. It is no use making a really good product without setting up a good system for getting it to consumers. Each part of the marketing mix is as important as the others.

Firms, therefore, draw up a detailed **marketing plan** that shows how each product is to be marketed. For example, it shows:

- the price of the product in each market;
- how it is going to be promoted, for example where it will be advertised, for how long and at what cost;
- how the product will be distributed.

The marketing plan must be updated from time to time all through the product's life.

Marketing department

Many firms have a **marketing department**. It looks after a firm's market research, the design of packaging, advertising, promotion and distribution. It is unlikely that the marketing department will do all these things itself. It may hire specialist agencies to do some of the detailed work. It works closely with them, and approves everything they do.

There is no point in offering goods and services that customers do not want to buy. The design, price and quality of products have to be what consumers want, or they do not sell. It is part of the marketing department's job to explain the needs and wants of customers to the design and production departments.

It is never certain that a product is going to sell. But by using market research, the firm can be as sure as possible that it will. The marketing department can save a firm money. Before a product is produced, the department tries to find out if it is what customers want and how much they are willing to pay for it.

In a way, the marketing department represents the customers' view within a firm. It acts as a kind of bridge between the customer and the production department.

Once it is decided to produce a product, the marketing department starts to plan how it is to be marketed.

1 Marvel Foods has developed a new range of ready-made traditional roast dinners. The firm is concerned that it sets the price for this new product at the right level. What could be the problems of selling the meals at:

a too high a price;

b too low a price?

2 Before Marvel Foods launches the ready-made roast meals on the market, it decides to test the popularity of the meals by selling them in one or two parts of the country first. Explain how this strategy could help Marvel Foods.

3 Market research conducted by Marvel Foods on its new ready-made meals has shown that they would appeal mostly to single people aged 20 to 35 in socio-economic groups B and C1. Discuss an appropriate way in which the meals could be promoted. Consider the media that might be used for advertisements, and a suitable image for portraying the product.

4 A business has put together an eight-stage marketing plan for its new range of low-fat chocolate biscuits.

These stages are listed below, but the order in which they should be carried out is mixed up. Rearrange the list into the most appropriate order.

1 Send out advertising literature to large wholesalers/ supermarket chains.

2 Investigate the competitors' products to see which low-fat biscuits are selling well.

3 Advertise the product on national television.

4 Arrange for a research agency to conduct a survey into the likely market segment.

5 Try out the product in two test areas.

6 Use market research results to decide what price to charge.

7 Agree the final price by looking at sales in the test areas.

8 Send out money-off vouchers in the test areas.

Case Study

5 Patak (Spices) Ltd

The Indian spice company Patak's was started in the late 1950s by LG Panthak. Mr Panthak had arrived in Britain from Kenya and raised money by selling Indian food from his house. When he had enough money he bought a small shop in North London. Besides prepared food, Patak's also sold ingredients needed for authentic Indian cooking such as chutneys, pickles and curry bases.

In the early days of the business, Patak's customers were limited to students and a few others who had a taste for Indian foods. However, there was a huge growth in interest in Indian food in Britain in the 1960s and 1970s with many new Indian restaurants opening. Patak's name was becoming better known, and the firm was able to exploit this in its advertising.

The market for Patak's products has now changed, and its customers are mainly those in the socio-economic groups ABC1 (professional people and those in the higher income groups), and those in the 25–44-year-old age bracket. It was found that older people were more cautious in their eating habits. In general, it has been found that people who buy these products have an adventurous side to their character.

Patak's is now the second largest company in the Indian food sector. Much of Patak's success can be explained because it is willing to spend time and money on market research. It knows the type of people who are its customers and ensures it makes the products they want to buy. By keeping in touch with the market, Patak's can also see if its customer structure is changing in any way. For instance, when it was discovered that an increasing number of customers were single or eating alone, the company started to produce smaller-sized packets. It was also found that the more convenient size encouraged other consumers to try out the product. Larger quantities were produced when it was discovered that many Indian restaurants were buying their cooking ingredients.

a What problems did Mr Pathak have when he introduced Patak's products in the early days of the business?

b Describe how the market for Patak's products has changed.

c Use the case study to explain the importance of market research to a business.

d Explain ways in which Patak's might have made its products appeal to a wider range of consumers.

ICT Activity

Using images found on the company's website (www.pataks.co.uk), design a poster to promote Patak's spices to the over-45 age group.

Examination hints

- Always write clearly. If the examiner cannot read what you write, you cannot be given credit for your work.
- Make your points as simply and as clearly as possible.
- Examiners cannot guess at what you mean. They can only mark what is in front of them. Do read what you have written to check if it is clear and makes sense.
- Get to the point of your answer as quickly as possible.
- Do not begin your answer by writing out the question. The examiner already knows the question, so do not waste time on doing something for which you will get no marks. Make any introductions as short as possible.
- AQA structure most questions. That means they break them down into parts to help you to plan your answer.
- Usually one part leads on to the next. Answer the parts in the right order, if you can.
- If you answer two parts of a question together in one answer do not worry.
- Do not do the work twice. Examiners are told to give you credit for your answer even if it is in the wrong part of the question.

Unit 3.4 Markets and marketing

3.4d Marketing mix: product and product life cycle

After-sales service →	the service supplied to customers after a sale is completed, for example a repair and maintenance service.
Branding →	giving a product a unique name to distinguish it from other products that may be similar in their use and purpose.
Guarantee →	a promise by a company to repair or replace a product, free of charge, if it should fail or go wrong within a stated period.
Logo →	a symbol or badge that enables the public to recognise a product or firm quickly and easily.
Own brand →	where a retailer sells its own brand of goods in its shops, or it has its own trademark, for example 'St Michael' in Marks & Spencer shops.
Market saturation →	when the market for a product is fully satisfied.
Packaging →	the materials used to protect and present a product.
Product differentiation →	where firms take steps to make their product appear different from similar products made by other firms.
Product life cycle →	a theory that states that all products go through a number of similar stages before sales drop to the point where they have to be withdrawn from the market.
Product mix →	all the range of goods produced by a firm.
Product range →	similar products produced by a single firm that compete with one another. They usually cater for different segments of the same market.
Test marketing →	selling a new product in a limited area to see how well it sells and whether there are any problems related to it.
Warranty →	another name for a guarantee.

Product

The **product** is the good or service that is being offered for sale. Thus the services sold by, for example, travel agents and banks are products. The product is the most important part of the marketing mix. Without the product there is no need for the other parts of the mix.

The term 'product' covers more than just the physical item or service offered. It also includes:

- the size, colour, style, design, quality and characteristics of the product;
- the name and packaging which are probably unique to that product;
- the guarantee on the product;
- the **after-sales service** that is available.

A selection from Cadbury's chocolate product range

Product mix

Large firms often produce several products that seem to be very alike and to compete with one another. Cadbury-Schweppes, for example, make a number of types of chocolate bar. This is Cadbury's chocolate bar **product range**. Each item in the range is targeted at a different segment of the market.

Cadbury-Schweppes also makes a number of other goods, including soft drinks, biscuits and chocolate drinks. The entire group of different goods that Cadbury-Schweppes produces is called its **product mix**.

Cadbury-Schweppes product mix

Product differentiation

When firms produce a range of goods that appear to be very similar, they have to try to make them seem different. Each of Cadbury's chocolate bars is different and is marketed in a different way. This emphasis on the differences between goods in the same product range is called **product differentiation**.

Firms want to show that their product is different from similar products made by other firms. They want to give each product an identity of its own. Providing this identity is a key part of the marketing mix. There are a number of ways that firms use to differentiate their product.

Name

Most products sold to the public are given a name. Giving a name to a product gives it an identity. To stop other firms from using it, a product's name is registered as a trademark.

Logo

Firms may have a symbol or badge they always use. For example, Lloyds TSB always has the black horse symbol at its branches and on its products. Firms always print the name of the firm and the name of a product in a certain way. The firm or the product can therefore be identified from the badge or symbol, or the way the name is printed. Thus Canon always prints the company name in exactly the same way on all its products. 'Coca-Cola' is always printed the same all over the world.

Design

Firms take a great deal of trouble to design their products so that they look different from similar products produced by other firms. Coca-Cola can be recognised from the shape of the bottle. Pepsi Cola can be recognised from the design on the can.

Content

What goes into making a product is an important part of a product's identity. Goods that are 'organic' are seen as different from similar non-organic products. Because people think they are purer and better for them, they are willing to pay a higher price for them.

Packaging

Packaging has two purposes. The first is to protect goods from damage. In marketing terms, it is also a way of presenting and selling goods. Packaging is one more way of giving goods an identity. Firms want people to recognise their product from its packaging, without having to read the label.

Products can be made to look attractive and eye-catching by their packaging. The same design and colour scheme are always used to identify the products. The packaging also gives consumers information about the product, for example the contents or cooking times. Things like perfume or aftershave are often given a very distinctive container.

Branding

Giving an identity to a product is called **branding**. Producers hope the public become loyal to their brand and always buy their product rather than any other. A brand can be the name of a product, such as 'Milk Tray'. It can also be the name of a company that markets a number of different products under its brand name. An example of such a brand is 'Virgin' that markets an airline, music shops and financial services under the 'Virgin' brand.

Some brand names are so well known that the product is known by that brand name, whoever makes it. Two well known examples are vacuum cleaners, that are sometimes known as 'Hoovers', while vacuum flasks are sometimes called 'Thermos' flasks.

Not all products are branded. General goods that do not have a brand name are called **generic goods**. Vegetables and fruit are generic goods. Paracetamol is a painkiller. It can be bought as a generic drug with no brand name, or as branded versions such as Anadin or Panadol.

Many retailers now sell goods under their own label or **own brand**. Supermarkets sell own-brand goods, usually more cheaply, alongside branded goods. Own-brand goods are often produced by the makers of branded goods. Some shops only sell their own-label goods, which often have the same name as the shop, for example Next or Principles.

The advantages of branding:
- it appears to widen consumer choice;
- shopping is simpler because products are easily identified and customers know what they are buying;
- consumers can be reasonably sure about the quality of the goods;
- goods can be advertised nationally.

Launching a product

This is when a new product is brought to the market. Firms need to have new products from time to time to keep their product mix up to date. Launching a new product needs a lot of careful planning and marketing.

As a new product approaches the production stage, the marketing department gets involved. It gives advice about consumer wants, and what kind of price buyers may be willing to pay. It also begins to market the product. Sales to the trade usually begin before the public is told about the product, and the trade press may test it.

The launch of a new product needs to be planned carefully to make sure there are enough supplies for people to buy. This means starting production some time before the launch. Stocks are built up and sent to sellers in advance.

A launch may be on a national basis, or sometimes companies test market the product in one region first. Any problems can then be ironed out before it is sold nationally. Products like cars may be launched over a 12-month period, in one or two countries at a time.

Product life cycle

No product goes on forever. All products have a limited life. The length of that life varies according to the nature of the product. The **product life cycle** is a theory that all products go through a number of similar stages before they come to the end of their life and have to be withdrawn from the market.

There are five stages in the product life cycle (see Figure 3.3).

Research and development stage

This is the stage when a new product is being designed and developed.
- Scientific and technical research may be needed, often with no guarantee of success. Design and development costs are high and may only be recovered if the product sells well. These costs include the 'tooling up' costs of buying or preparing the machinery and equipment needed to produce the product.
- The product is tested to make sure it works properly and is safe.
- There is also market research, and there may be **test marketing**.

This stage can last for several years and be very expensive. A new car model can take five years or more to develop. A new drug can take 10 or 15 years.

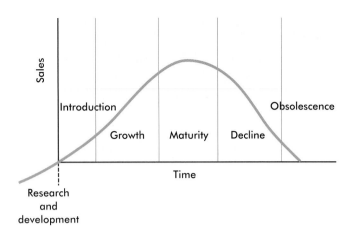

Figure 3.3 Product life cycle

Introduction

This is when the product is launched and placed on the market.

- There is heavy advertising and promotion of the product. Costs are high, probably higher than the sales revenue.
- How quickly it sells depends on the type of product. Sales may be slow because people are cautious about buying new goods. It may take time for people to get to know about the product.

Growth

This is the stage at which sales are growing quickly.

- Heavy advertising is probably still necessary.
- Sales revenue is building up. It is now probably greater than production and marketing costs. The product moves into profit.
- There may now be a growth in competition.

Maturity

This stage is probably longer than the introduction and growth stages.

- The product is well established in the market. It may have reached maximum market share. It may be at **market saturation** point.
- Sales are good, but growing only slowly, if at all.
- Advertising must continue to retain market share.
- The product is making a good profit.

Decline

This stage can be quite long. A firm may carry on producing because the product is still making a profit, even if this is falling. Ovaltine is in slow decline, but is still produced because there is a small market for it.

- Sales and market share are falling. The speed at which they fall depends on the type of product. Rival products are more up to date and attractive.
- Little or nothing is spent on advertising.
- Unit costs are low and the product still makes a profit.
- The product may become obsolete. The firm eventually decides to withdraw it from the market.

A number of factors affect the length of each stage and the total length of a product's life. They make it hard to predict the length of each stage.

- Technical changes affect some goods so that they become obsolete, for example vinyl records became obsolete when CD players were developed.
- External factors may affect the demand for a product and therefore the product life cycle. For example, health warnings and high taxation have affected tobacco products.
- Competitors bring out rival products that may be more advanced.
- The durability of the product affects the product life cycle.
- Fashion is one of the greatest factors in a product's life cycle. Clothing sales are obviously affected by fashion. Goods that are 'in fashion' grow and mature very quickly and then go into rapid decline to be replaced by the next fashion.

Goods that have a long life and only change slowly have a long time axis (see Figure 3.4). Fashion goods, such as clothing, have a short life. Clothes firms have at least two fashion changes a year. The product life cycle for clothing may, therefore, have quite a long sales axis but only a short time axis.

Extending the product life cycle

The length of a product's life cycle can be extended, especially at the growth and maturity stages:

- by making modifications to the product from time to time. Each year car manufacturers make small changes in design or specification;
- the product may be relaunched with a new promotion and advertising campaign;
- prices may be dropped to gain an advantage over competitors.

Organising to Achieve Objectives

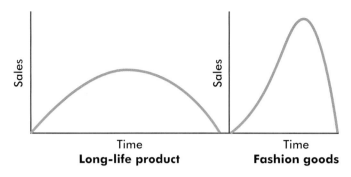

Figure 3.4 Two product life cycles

Activities

1 Using the Internet or a magazine, obtain a picture of a well-known product such as a type of shampoo or car. Mark on the picture how the manufacturer has differentiated the product so it is distinct from its competitors.

2 Cadbury-Schweppes produces several different types of chocolate products, some of which are listed in the table. From your knowledge of these products, complete the table below, showing the target market at which you think Cadbury-Schweppes is aiming the product.

Product	Likely target market
Buttons	
Miniature Heroes	
Dairy Milk	
Timeout	

3 Copy out the table below and give as many examples as you can of brand names for the types of products.

Product	Brand names
Sportswear	
Cars	
Bags, suitcases	
Musical instruments	
Cameras	
Washing machines	

4 Group activity

Fruit and vegetables do not tend to have a brand image. An importer of bananas decides to try to make his bananas distinct from those of his competitors.

a Explain why the fruit importer wishes to sell bananas that are distinguishable from those of his competitors.

b Brainstorm different ideas about how bananas can be made to appear distinctive.

c Comment on how realistic your ideas are. Select the best three ideas and produce an advertising poster to highlight these differences to the public.

Case Study

5 Italiano Coffee Machines

Italiano produces cappuccino coffee-making machines. Market research had informed the company that people would be more likely to buy a cappuccino maker if it were quicker and easier to use than the machines they make at the moment. Italiano spent two years developing a new type of easy-to-use coffee machine. The revenue the company expects to receive is shown in the following table.

Year	Revenue (£000)	Year	Revenue (£000)
1	−40	9	44
2	−25	10	45
3	8	11	42
4	28	12	34
5	43	13	18
6	46	14	12
7	48	15	
8	45		

a Place this data in a spreadsheet and use it to draw a suitable graph.

b Mark on the graph the different sections of the product life cycle.

6 Eidos

Lara Croft is the popular heroine in the Tomb Raider series of computer games. Most people would think that the software in which she appears would be the same all over the world. This is not the case. The manufacturer, Eidos, has had to adapt the game to suit the needs and preferences of different markets. In America, for instance, the games are made easier to play. Research showed that the average American youngster will play a computer game for perhaps just 10 minutes before getting bored and going to do something else. So the games have to be able to be conquered in a much shorter time than in Britain, otherwise players will lose interest.

Lara was found not to be an appealing character to the game-loving Japanese; she was thought to be too tall and too British. Japanese game players also did not like the way the flow of the game was stopped when the player loses all his lives. They prefer weapons to be taken off Lara or points deducted rather than have to restart the game. The last straw with Tomb Raider was the violence, which the Japanese saw as not being 'honourable' or 'justifiable'.

The high levels of violence in some computer games is a problem with many German players

and, if a game is to sell in America, there should be no hint of nudity: even zombies have to be fully clothed if the game is to be accepted by US parents.

(Adapted from: Mark Chadbourne, 'Why Lara Croft is too hot for the world to handle', *Independent*, 1 November 1999.)

a Devise a market research questionnaire that a games manufacturer could use to take account of cultural differences between countries.

b Besides cultural differences, what other problems might UK companies experience when selling their goods in markets abroad?

c Discuss the likely problems that a manufacturer of motorcycles could experience in trying to sell the same design of bike in several countries.

ICT Activity

Go to the website of a company that makes a wide range of products, such as www.unilever.com/br/bp or www.cadburyschweppes.com. List the products the company makes. Group the products which are of a similar type.

Examination hints

In Section B of the examination, make sure you use examples from the case study to support your answers. Examples taken from the case study provide evidence to support what you say in your answer.

Unit 3.4 Markets and marketing

3.4e Marketing mix: price

Competitive pricing	→	basing the price of a product on the prices charged by competitors.
Cost-plus pricing	→	basing the price of a product on the cost of producing it plus an allowance for profit.
Loss leader	→	a product that is deliberately sold for less than its cost price in order to attract customers.
Market-orientated pricing	→	pricing goods based on an analysis of a market through market research.
Mark-up pricing	→	pricing a product based on the cost of production plus a standard percentage (the mark-up) for profit.
Penetration pricing	→	setting a low price for a product in order to gain a good market share quickly. The price can be raised later, when a target market share has been won.
Predatory pricing	→	setting prices very low in order to gain a larger share of a market, or to drive competitors out of business. The price is raised later.
Price	→	the amount paid for goods and services.
Price discrimination	→	charging different customers different prices for the same product.
Skimming	→	setting the price of a new product very high while the goods are scarce. It is lowered later after 'skimming the cream'.

→ Key terms

Price is one of the main factors consumers take into account when they decide to buy a product. This means that price is a very important part of the marketing mix. Firms have to be very careful when deciding at what price to sell goods. If it is too high, consumers do not buy the product. If it is too low firms may not make a profit.

In theory, prices are fixed at the point where the supply and demand for a product are equal. In practice, there are many ways that firms can use to decide at what price to sell their products. Price largely depends on what targets a firm has set. These include:

- the level of sales or profit it is aiming at;
- the size of market share it wants;
- the cost of either making or buying the product. This cost must be covered if the firm is to stay in business. It also wants to make a profit, so it does not fix its prices so low that it makes a loss.

Firms must be consistent in their marketing mix. Once a target market has been chosen the whole marketing mix has to give consumers the same message. For the consumer, price is related to three factors:

- **Quality** – consumers match price to quality. They expect the price of good quality goods to be higher than that of lower quality goods. If a firm is marketing a product on its quality, the price should reflect that quality.
- **Image** – some goods have prestige value. People buy them because they reflect the image they project of themselves. Such goods include big or sporty cars and designer clothes. People are willing to pay more for goods that have 'pose value'.
- **Fair price** – consumers expect prices to be fair. People are not willing to pay high prices that they see as a 'rip off'. They are also suspicious of cheap goods, which may mean poor quality. People expect to get good value for money.

Cost-based pricing

Cost-plus pricing

Firms are in business to make a profit. They can base their prices on what competitors are asking and what the market wants, but this does not ensure a profit. Instead, price can be based on the cost of the product plus a percentage of the cost as profit. This is called cost-plus pricing.

Fixed costs £5.00

Variable costs
Fabric
Interlining
Buttons £15.00
Thread
Labour

Total cost price £20.00

Selling price £30.00

Figure 3.5 Costing a shirt

A shirt manufacturer knows the costs of making each shirt. There are costs that vary with the number of shirts produced, such as raw materials. There are other costs that are fixed, such as the cost of the premises. The cost of making a shirt can be worked out fairly accurately. The producer then adds a percentage for profit of, say, 50%.

Mark-up pricing

This is a common method of pricing in retailing. A retailer buys perhaps 100 different products from various manufacturers. The retailer has costs such as staff wages, heating and lighting plus rent and rates, and also needs to make a profit. With so many different lines it is impossible to split these costs between each product sold. The easiest thing is to add a fixed percentage to the cost of buying the goods. This fixed percentage is called a mark-up. The mark-up must be big enough to cover all the costs and leave enough for a profit.

Market-based pricing

Competitive pricing

Consumers are very aware of prices and are willing to 'shop around' for the best price. Therefore, firms have to be aware of the prices their competitors are charging. Firms that have higher prices than their competitors are likely to lose sales. This is why the supermarket chains send people around their competitors' shops to note the prices.

Firms look carefully at their competitors' prices, but that is only one factor in deciding their own prices.

- A firm may market its product as being of better quality or different, and therefore charge a different price.
- A new company may charge lower prices to get known in a market.
- No two firms are the same, and their costs are different. This may be reflected in the prices they charge.

Market pricing

This is also known as **market-orientated pricing**. In this case price is based on what market research shows people are willing to pay for a product. The price is therefore based on an analysis of the characteristics of each market in which the firm trades. To some extent the price is based on the prices of other goods in the same market.

There is a level of price that people are prepared to pay for a product. This is often called the price plateau. This level varies between different groups of buyers. A well-off middle class family will have a different idea about value for money from an unemployed family. Firms may try to meet the varying needs of different parts of the market by selling a range of goods in a number of price bands. For example, clothes with slight differences in quality may be sold at £10.99, £17.99 and £24.99.

Penetration pricing

A new manufacturer can find it hard to get its product accepted in an established market. The same is true for a new product. **Penetration pricing** may be used by new firms or for new products. It can be used by any business wanting to gain or improve its market share. Under this method of pricing, a firm fixes a low price in order to gain a foothold in the market. For a time, it accepts low profits. Once its target market share has been won it can raise its price and increase its profits. It is a risky strategy because those already in the market might also cut their prices and start a price war.

Predatory pricing

A company may set its prices very low to win a much larger market share. It may even try to drive its rivals out of business. Once it has captured the market it will probably raise prices. Supermarkets have been accused of **predatory pricing** when, as result of cutting their prices, small local shops have had to close. Fruit, vegetables and bread have been among the favourite targets.

Skimming

Many new products, especially those that are technology based, are sold at a very high price when they first come onto the market. Such goods have a high prestige value. Only the rich, and those willing to pay a high price to be among the first to own the latest model, will buy them. The price is reduced after a while so as to reach other parts of the market. That is, after 'skimming the cream' off the market.

Price discrimination

Firms may charge different customers different prices for the same goods or services. In other words, they discriminate between different groups of customers. By charging some customers more than others, firms can increase sales revenue and profits. They often make some, often small, difference between what the high-paying and the low-paying customers get. Firms can do this because some people can afford and are willing to pay more. In some cases there is an element of prestige to the higher paying group, for example in travelling First Class or Business Class on aeroplanes. Price discrimination is a form of market segmentation.

Example

Gas, electricity and telephone companies charge private customers different rates from those paid by business users. Mobile phone companies charge different rates according to the 'package' you buy.

The railways charge first class and standard class fares on the same train. The seats in first class compartments are bigger and more comfortable and they may serve free drinks. The running costs of the train would be almost the same if all the seats were standard class. The train operator makes a bigger profit on the first class seats.

Activities

1 Which pricing strategy is being described in situations a to d below?

  a The price is placed very low at first. As people get used to buying the product, the price is gradually increased.

  b The price is initially placed very high to take advantage of those consumers who want to be among the first to have the product. Later, the price falls to a level that will encourage more people to buy.

  c The price is kept artificially low, hoping to attract customers who will buy other goods as well as this one.

  d The purpose of this pricing strategy is to drive away competitors by undercutting their prices.

2 Examine these five situations. Decide which pricing strategies would be most appropriate in each case. Justify your choice.

  a A new series of weekly magazines based on the television series *The X Files* is to be launched. The series will consist of 52 issues and market research has shown that the magazine will appeal most to 14–23-year-olds. The publisher is planning to sell a hard-backed folder in which to store the magazines. How should she price the magazine and folder?

  b A pop promoter is to present the boy group Kool Soundz at Birmingham's NEC. The group is riding high at the moment with two records in the top ten. They have a large following of 12–16-year-old girls. As with most groups of this type, nobody expects them to last much longer than another year. What is the best pricing strategy for tickets for the concert?

  c A major supermarket chain has just brought out its own-label sparkling wine. It already knows that this type of wine is bought regularly by 25–40-year-olds and on special occasions by 41–60-year-olds. There are several other branded sparkling wines and champagnes on the market, some of which are stocked by the supermarket. How should the supermarket price the wine?

d A breakfast cereal manufacturer has put large amounts of money into developing a new type of muesli snack bar designed to be bought by people too busy or lazy to have breakfast at home. Its research has shown that many people who miss breakfast buy chocolate bars mid-morning to keep them going. What would be the best pricing strategy for the company?

e Curl Up and Dye is a ladies' hairdresser in a small town where until recently it enjoyed a monopoly position. The person who owns the business has built up a good reputation for good quality hairdressing. Another hairdresser has opened at the other end of the town, and is now offering a cheaper service. How should the owner of Curl Up and Dye respond?

□ Case Study

3 Price discrimination

Charging different prices for what is really the same product or service is more common than people may think. Virgin Trains and other railway operators were recently criticised for having too many different price systems. You paid more if you travelled before 9.30 am, there were standard and first class tickets, and reductions were available if you were young, old or travelling in a family. People said it was just too complicated a system to understand.

Retailers have also started to price discriminate. The DIY giant B&Q has for some time offered a 10% discount to over-60s who shop on Wednesdays. Other shops, cafés and garden centres offer older people a discount for mid-week shopping. Most theatres, cinemas and transport companies offer concessions to children, which is another example of price discrimination.

a Is the Royal Mail's first and second class postal service an example of price discrimination?

b Why do you think discounts for older shoppers tend to be offered during mid-week?

□ Case Study

c Why are business people asked to pay more than others when they travel on aeroplanes?

d Price discrimination would not work if the person getting the cheaper rate could then sell the product on to someone who was not entitled to the discount. How might companies avoid this situation?

□ Case Study

4 Flyaway Air

Flyaway Air is a small airline company that operates a fleet of 100-seat planes between London and New York. The company knows that the demand for seats depends on the price it charges. It has drawn up a table to show how many seats it would sell at different prices.

Price of seat	No. of customers willing to buy a ticket at this price	Revenue for selling tickets at each price
£400	20	£8,000
£300	30	£9,000
£250	50	£12,500
£200	80	£16,000
£150	100	£15,000
£100	130	£10,000

From this research the airline discovered that the most money it could get per flight was £16,000. That is, charging £200 to the 80 people prepared to pay that amount. Flyaway realised that there would be 20 unused seats on every flight.

Flyaway's marketing manager, Moira Ings, suggested that the company could sell the remaining seats at a cheaper price. If the 20 spare seats were sold at £150 each, it would fill the plane and bring in an extra £3,000 revenue. By selling at two prices the airline would make revenue of £19,000 – far more money than it could get with a single price.

Moira realised that the problem with this system would be having to persuade some people to pay more for their tickets than other passengers. She thought that this could be done by making the seats seem better (calling them business class, rather than economy) or by discriminating in some way. The airline could offer the cheaper seats to those prepared to book early (so discriminating against those who are unable to do so).

a What is meant by 'price discrimination'?

b Besides the ways mentioned in the case study, how else could Flyaway operate price discrimination?

c Why would it be difficult for Flyaway to discriminate on the grounds of its passengers' incomes? That is, the richer passengers are, the more they pay.

d If Flyaway charged two prices, £300 and £100, how much revenue would they make on each flight?

e If the airline decided to have three different prices for its flights, what prices should it charge to make the most revenue per flight?

Examination hints

- Look at the number of marks given to each part of a question.
- AQA shows the number of marks given to each part of every question. Questions that have low marks only need a short answer.
- The number of marks given to a question gives you an idea of how much time to spend on it. If it only carries 1 mark the examiner only wants a very short answer. One word may be enough. Higher mark questions want longer answers.
- Plan your time so that you spend most time on the questions that carry the most marks.
- There are 3 marks for definition questions in Section A of the exam. One mark is for the definition, 1 mark is for saying a little bit more about it, and 1 mark is for giving an example.
- Questions that have only 1 or 2 marks do not always have to be answered in a sentence.
- Questions that have more than 1 or 2 marks should always be answered in sentences.
- Remember that 5% of the marks are for good spelling punctuation and grammar. Writing good English affects your total marks. Good English may affect the grade you get.

Unit 3.4 Markets and marketing

3.4f Marketing mix: place

Place is where a product is finally sold to the consumer. Consumers expect to get the goods and services they want at the right place, when they want them and in the right amounts. Producers must choose where to sell a product and decide how it is to get to the point of sale. The goods must get to sellers in first-class condition and as quickly, cheaply and efficiently as possible. The route by which goods and services get to the consumer is known as the **chain of distribution**.

Transport

Transport is an essential part of the chain of distribution. It moves supplies of materials and parts between firms. It also gets goods to the point where consumers can buy them. The type of transport that is used depends on three main things:

- **Type of goods** – the form of transport depends on the size and weight of the goods; whether they are bulky, liquid, perishable, fragile or very expensive.
- **Cost** – varies with the type of load, size of load, (is it a train or lorry load?) and the distance. Firms use the cheapest form of transport that suits their needs. Road transport is cheap over short distances and for final delivery to the point of sale. Rail is cheaper over longer distances and for large, bulky loads.
- **Speed** at which goods are needed.
- **Security** if goods are valuable or expensive.

Retailers

A retailer is any point where goods are sold directly to consumers. Goods are sold in the small quantities that consumers want. Retailing is more than just shops and showrooms. It includes market stalls, vending machines and mail order. Services, such as hairdressing, printing, banking and insurance, are also sold retail. More recently, banks have used other ways to retail their services – through cashpoint machines, by telephone and on the Internet.

Wholesaler

The **wholesaler** provides a link between the retailer and the manufacturer, providing both of them with a service. These days, wholesalers are mainly used by small businesses.

Services to manufacturers

- Wholesalers buy in bulk from manufacturers who only have to deal with a few large orders from wholesalers and not with many small orders from retailers. This saves on clerical and distribution costs.
- They store goods until they are sold. Manufacturers need less storage space, cutting costs.
- They reduce manufacturers' risks. If the goods are not sold it is the wholesaler that suffers the loss, not the manufacturer.

Direct distribution: manufacturers to retailers

Manufacturers

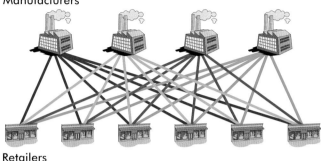

Retailers

Distribution using a wholesaler

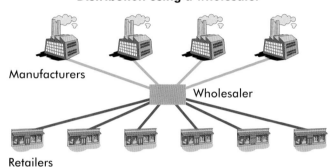

Manufacturers

Wholesaler

Retailers

Figure 3.6 Direct distribution and wholesalers

Services to retailers

- Wholesalers break bulk. This means they buy in large quantities from the manufacturer. They sell to retailers in the small quantities they want.
- They offer a choice of goods in one place. Goods from several manufacturers can be compared and bought at the same time. This saves having to write several orders and pay several firms.
- They can advise retailers on the latest products, special offers and lines that sell well.

The traditional role of the wholesaler is breaking down. Manufacturers often prefer to sell direct to retailers. In this way they keep control over the distribution of their products right up to the point of sale. However, the job of the wholesaler still has to be done. Manufacturers who sell direct to shops have to bear all the costs of storage and distribution. The large retail chains buy direct from manufacturers and have to have their own distribution warehouses.

Chain of distribution

There is no one chain of distribution that is used for all products. The way goods and services are distributed largely depends on the product. Goods that have a short life or are perishable are distributed differently

from durable goods like furniture, or services like insurance. The number of buyers and sellers involved is also a factor.

Examples of four chains of distribution

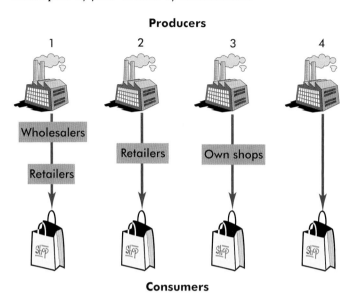

Figure 3.7 Chain of distribution

1 The traditional method. This is where the manufacturer sells goods to the wholesaler in very large quantities and cheaply. They add a mark-up to cover their costs and make a profit, and sell at a higher price to retailers. They in turn add their mark-up before they sell to consumers.

Wholesalers are mainly used by sole traders with small local shops or by shops selling specialist goods. There are also specialist wholesalers such as builders merchants, for example Jewson, who sell to small builders and tradesmen. Small manufacturers also use wholesalers.

2 Goods are sold by manufacturers directly to the retailer. Most of the large retail and supermarket chains buy goods in bulk directly from the manufacturer. They often buy in greater bulk than wholesalers. They may therefore get goods cheaper and pass on the savings in lower prices.

3 Goods are sold to the consumer through shops owned by the manufacturer. For example, Multiyork and Wesley Barrell both make furniture, which they sell through their own shops.

Firms like Next, Principles and Marks & Spencer do not make goods themselves, but they control the own-brand goods made for them and sold in their shops. They give the manufacturer an exact specification of what they want and the price they are willing to pay. Those goods are only available through their shops. They control every aspect of their manufacture and distribution.

4 Goods are sold directly to consumers by the producer. For example, farmers selling through farm shops, or nurseries selling through their own garden centres or by mail order. Racing Green and Lands End sell leisurewear direct by mail order.

Technology and the future

There are two main ways in which technology has affected the marketplace:

E-commerce

- This has made the marketplace much bigger. Access to the worldwide web means that goods can be bought easily from other countries. Consumers have more choice.

- Firms that sell on the net do not need expensive showrooms or shops in high-cost town centres. They only need a warehouse, which can be anywhere, usually where rents are low. They are able to under-cut prices in the traditional shops.

- In order to keep their market share, many shops also sell on the net. For example, Tesco has huge sales from their website. Many other big high street shops have also set up websites. It is a way of defending their market from new firms that only sell through websites. They also hope to gain market share from their rivals.

- New firms have entered well-established markets and increased competition. New methods of providing services have been developed. For example, there are banks like egg.com whose services can only be obtained on the net. Like the supermarkets, the traditional banks have also had to change their methods, or lose customers.

- The growth in mobile phones and digital television will all make shopping easier, reducing dependence on shops, changing shopping habits and increasing choice for consumers.

- The main method of payment for goods bought on the net is the credit card. Many people are worried about the security of their credit cards and are afraid to use the net for shopping.

- Business-to-business (B2B) Internet firms sell to other businesses and not to the public. This is attractive since the cost of goods is lower.

Distribution

The growth of computer systems has improved the way stocks are controlled and goods distributed. Almost all goods have barcodes which identify the country of origin, the maker and the product. Modern EPOS tills are linked to a barcode reader and to a computer. When goods are bought in a supermarket or large store a message is sent to a central computer. In this way firms know exactly how much of each product is sold in a given time. The computer will show what stock is left, and will order new supplies when stocks get low. This helps firms to keep stocks as low as possible and to ensure they do not run out of stock.

Activities

1 What are the functions of a wholesaler?

2 Why do many people prefer to use mail order rather than visit shops?

3 There has been a rapid growth in business-to-business trading on the Internet, known as B2B. However, Internet selling to consumers is progressing much slower. Give reasons why this might be the case.

4 Discuss how an increase in e-commerce would affect high streets in towns and business parks.

5 Copy and complete the table on the next page. The table looks at features affecting the transport needs of different goods. The example of smoked salmon has been done for you.

Value to bulk ratio: how valuable the product is in relation to the space it occupies. Jewellery would have a high ratio, but a shipment of coal a low ratio.

Need for security: how attractive the product is to thieves. A consignment of bottles of vodka would need high security, while a load of gravel would not present a big security problem. Some products need high security because they are dangerous (for example petrol).

Fragility: how fragile or easily damaged the product is.

Shelf life: how perishable the product is, or how important it is that the product is delivered quickly.

	Value to bulk ratio	Need for security	Fragility	Shelf life
Smoked salmon	High	Medium	Low	Low–Medium
Cigarettes				
Potatoes				
Cement				
Daily newspapers				
Cut-glass vases				
Music CDs				

Use your responses above to decide the best form of transport to use for carrying each product over a distance of 500 kilometres.

6 Eastern Shires Purchasing Organisation

Schools and colleges need to buy many different materials and equipment in order to function properly. Some of these items are obvious: textbooks are required, as are regular supplies of paper. Other items of equipment and consumables are also needed. Look around your own school or college. What do the managers of the school need to buy? Toilet paper, sports equipment, litter bins, computers, washing-up liquid, desks and benches: the list seems endless.

In some institutions it is left to budget holders (such as heads of department) to get the best deals when they need to buy their supplies. This puts a burden on members of staff, who probably have no special skills in negotiating prices with suppliers. Phoning around to check prices and ordering goods also takes a great deal of time.

To overcome these problems, in 1981 Leicestershire and Lincolnshire county councils set up the Eastern Shires Purchasing Organisation (ESPO). This organisation would buy materials for county council schools, social services and other departments. Since it started, many more authorities and charitable organisations have joined ESPO and it now has an annual turnover of £200m.

ESPO's specialist buyers are skilful in negotiating far better prices for materials than could an individual school. ESPO buyers visit suppliers and check the companies are suitable before agreeing to take their goods. Buying in bulk also means that economies of scale can be achieved. ESPO can also provide advice to its customers on which product is most suitable and which provides the best value for money.

a Draw a diagram to show how ESPO fits into the chain of distribution.
b Describe how ESPO can save money for schools and colleges.
c List the things an ESPO buyer might look for when visiting a supplier.
d Explain how an increased use of ICT could improve efficiency for a distribution organisation such as ESPO.

ICT Activity

Research the prices of a small group of items (for example sportswear or household goods) in a number of shops. Set up a database of these prices so comparisons can be made and the best value shown.

Unit 3.4 Markets and marketing

3.4g Marketing mix: promotion

Advertising →	an aspect of promotion in the marketing mix. Firms inform the public about their products and try to persuade them to purchase the products.
Advertising campaign →	a planned programme of advertising to promote an organisation, its products or services.
Discount →	an amount of money taken off the selling price of a product.
Loss leader →	a product that is deliberately sold for less than its cost price in order to attract customers.
Loyalty cards →	cards issued by supermarkets and other stores. They give customers points when they purchase goods at the store. The points can be used against future shopping bills. They give stores a great deal of information about regular customers' shopping habits.
Merchandising →	the methods used to display and promote goods at or near the point of sale. It is also used to describe the spin-off products and activities from, for example, films, football teams and pop stars.
Promotion →	a mix of methods designed to inform the public about a product and to persuade them to buy it.
Promotion pricing →	selling goods at special prices as part of a sales promotion campaign.
Public relations (PR) →	making sure that every part of a firm's relationships with outside bodies is good. These include customers, suppliers and the general public.
Sales promotion →	a special event or other short-term method used to persuade people to buy a product. Sales promotions, like special offers, all last for a limited time only.
Self-regulation →	where an industry sets up its own systems to try to control the activities of firms in the industry. Members are expected to follow a code of practice or a code of conduct. The schemes are voluntary.
Sponsorship →	the support given by firms to events, teams or individuals by providing finance, goods, publicity and other materials or services.

There is no point in making, pricing and distributing a product and then waiting for people to buy it. People only buy something if they know about it. It has to be promoted in order to:

- tell potential customers that the product exists, what it is like and what it can do;
- persuade people to buy the product.

Promotion is a mix of methods and activities designed to increase the sales of a product.

Advertising

Most people think that promotion means advertising, but advertising is only one aspect of promotion. Firms have four main reasons for advertising:

- to tell, or remind, consumers about their product. They also tell or show them how the product will meet their needs, and maybe where it can be bought;
- to persuade people to buy a particular article or service;
- to increase sales of a product and to improve its market share. This may mean targeting a new segment of the market;
- to launch a new product or create a new or improved image for an existing one.

By advertising, firms communicate with the public about their products. Advertisements are a kind of message that informs or persuades the people who receive it.

Organising to Achieve Objectives

Types of advertising

Informative

This kind of advertising is usually factual. Its main purpose is to inform the public. It does not set out to sell them something. For example:

- advertisements in trade papers giving technical information about a product;
- advertisements by a car maker telling owners about a fault on certain models and how to get it put right;
- job advertisements;
- public service advertisements, for example a government department telling the public about a new service or warning them of health risks (such as from smoking or drink driving); a local authority advertising road closures or planning applications.

Persuasive

This kind of advertising sets out to persuade the public to buy a particular product. It is closely linked to branding and aims to give the product an identity. It tries to convince people that:

- the product is special and better than other rival products;
- they need the product and that without it they are in some way worse off.

Defensive

This is where a company responds to a competitor's advertising claims. It fears that the rival may damage the company's reputation and win some of its customers.

Methods of advertising

Direct

This is where advertising is directed at chosen individuals. It often takes the form of mailshots or 'junk' mail, targeted at people of a certain age or income. The names have probably been taken from a database bought from a specialist agency. Other forms of direct advertising include catalogues, money-off vouchers and free samples.

Indirect

This is general advertising, aimed at the general public. It may also be targeted at a specific group, for example adverts in special-interest magazines aimed at people with a particular interest. Advertisements about computer-related products might be advertised in *PC World*, and advertisements for toys might be advertised during children's television programmes.

Most advertising is indirect and uses a wide range of media, as shown in Figure 3.8 below.

Advertising campaigns

When firms advertise it is usually part of an **advertising campaign**. This is a planned programme of advertising that promotes an organisation, its products or its services.

- There is a budget that sets out how much money can be spent on each type of advertising media.

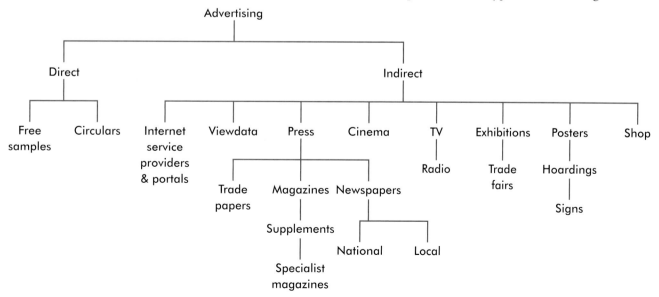

Figure 3.8 Advertising

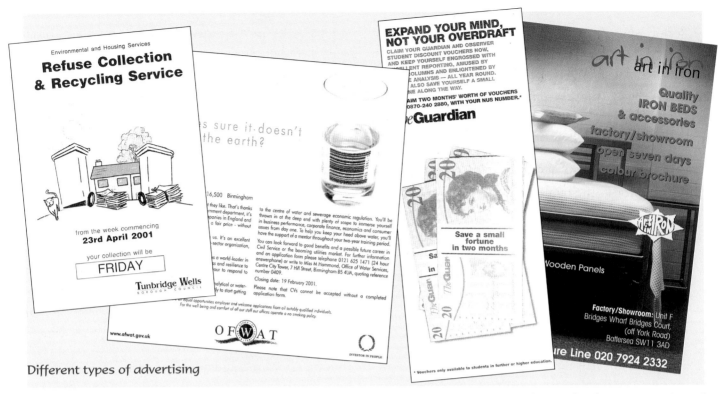

Different types of advertising

- It is aimed at a well-defined group.
- The media and methods used depend on the group targeted.
- The campaign lasts for a stated period of time.
- It should produce results that can be measured easily.

Advertising agencies

These specialise in giving advice on ways to promote a firm's products. They work with a firm to design advertisements and place them on television, on radio or in the press. They are paid for their work. They may also carry out market research, before and after an advertising campaign.

Benefits of advertising

- By choosing different places to advertise, it is possible to target different markets or customers. Day-to-day products are advertised in the popular press and on television. Local shops and services advertise local products. Goods aimed at people with a particular interest are advertised in magazines that specialise in that interest.
- Advertising may lead to increased sales and larger profits, and as a result to increased employment. An increase in sales means costs are spread over a larger output. Average costs will fall. This may be passed on to the customer as lower prices.

- An increase in demand may lead to economies of scale and a fall in costs.

Criticisms of advertising

- It may encourage habits and behaviour that are not good for people's health, for example smoking or drinking. It may encourage poor attitudes, like greed and envy.
- It may tempt people to buy things they cannot afford or do not need.
- Advertising increases firms' costs and may lead to higher prices.
- Firms may be tempted to make false claims for their products and to mislead the public.

Regulating advertising

To try to meet these criticisms, the Advertising Standards Authority (ASA) has been set up. It is formed and paid for by the advertising industry itself, for the voluntary **self-regulation** of the industry. It controls all advertising in the UK, except for that on radio and television.

- It tries to ensure that all advertisements are legal, honest and truthful.
- It lays down rules in the Codes of Advertising Practice and Sales Promotion. Anyone who publishes, orders or prepares advertisements is expected to follow the rules.

- It does spot checks to make sure the rules are being followed. Advertisers who are unsure about an advertisement can ask the ASA for advice before it is published.
- It investigates complaints from the public and can have advertisements withdrawn.
- The main criticisms are that it has no legal power to enforce its decisions. Because the advertising industry pays for it, the public may think it is biased.

Advertising on commercial television is controlled by the Independent Television Commission (ITC). Advertising on commercial radio is controlled by the Radio Authority. Unlike the ASA, both these bodies have been set up by Acts of Parliament. They both have codes of practice for advertising that cover the things that can and cannot be included in programmes.

Sales promotion

Any special event or other method used by a firm to boost its sales in the short term is a **sales promotion**. Not all sales promotions are aimed at the public; some are aimed at wholesalers or retailers. To get the best effect, a sales promotion only lasts for a limited time.

- **Special offers** – for example, 'two for the price of one'; 'buy a pack of three videos and get one free'; or '30% more' in the can of lemonade.
- **Free gifts** – for example, small toys are often included in cereal packets; or a free pen if you send for an insurance quotation.
- **Offers on packs** – for example, if you collect a number of tokens from a packet you can send away for a CD.
- **Free samples** – these are often used when a new product is being launched. A small, exact replica of the product is sent to households.
- **Money-off tokens** – these are used for new products as well as for well-known brands. People are given a voucher that gives them a certain amount, such as 10p, off their next purchase of the same product.
- **Competitions** – for example, 'Win a trip to Miami if you take out a subscription to XX magazine.' Or 'You will be entered for a £250,000 prize draw if you join our book club.'
- **Discounts** – This is where the price is reduced if a purchase is made before a certain date.
- **Sales** – at certain times of the year, all or most of the goods in a shop are sold at reduced prices. Traditionally, sales were always held in July and January, but nowadays they are held more often. They are a form of discounting. Sales are used to clear unsold stock and to make room for new stock. Selling out-of-date goods is bad for a firm's image, especially fashion goods. It is better to sell goods cheaply, and get something for them, rather than to keep them in the hope someone might buy them.
- **Loss leader** – a method usually used by retailers. To attract customers, they sell a product at less than cost price. It is heavily advertised at a very low price, selling it at a loss. They hope to attract people into their shops, and that once they are in the shops they will buy other goods at the normal price. Bread and sugar are often used as loss leaders.
- **Loyalty cards** – these are issued free by the large supermarkets and other store chains. Each time a customer buys goods at a branch of the store, points are earned. From time to time customers may be sent vouchers against the points. These vouchers have to be spent at the store's branches. Some stores do this every three months or when a certain number of points have been earned. Other firms allow customers to build up points to 'spend' when they like, such as at Christmas. The cards are issued to

Different types of promotion

give customers an incentive to keep going back to the same store. They also give the store a huge amount of data about their customers' shopping habits.

- **Point-of-sale displays** – these are displays in shops and shop windows. When there is a promotion, the goods might be stacked near the tills. Shops often have 'dump bins' where goods are piled into a container situated where customers are most likely to see them and buy the goods on impulse.

Merchandising

Merchandise is a general term used for the goods that are on sale. Merchandising is used to describe any kind of display or way of promoting goods, especially in shops. It includes window displays, display stands around the store, demonstrations and fashion parades. Recently, the term has also come to describe the spin-off sales from copyright materials. Examples include the sale of kit by football clubs, T-shirts and other goods by pop groups, and items, such as videos, related to films or television series.

Direct marketing

This is where goods and services are marketed directly to consumers. It includes personally addressed mail-shots, catalogues and other publicity like a free test drive of the latest new car. Door-to-door selling is also part of direct marketing, although fairly rare now. Firms usually target their direct marketing. If you take out household insurance with a company it will probably ask if you want a quotation for car insurance. Firms can also buy a database of a certain class or market segment from other firms.

Sponsorship

Firms are often keen to have their names linked to big events, to sports clubs and to individuals who are famous and successful. Thus we have the 'Lloyds TSB Six Nations Rugby Championship', the 'Nationwide League' and the 'Cornhill Test' series. Most football league clubs are sponsored by a firm. Plays at The Royal Shakespeare Theatre are sponsored by big firms. Leading athletes may be given kit by sports goods companies. Sponsors provide money and goods or services to those they support. Firms provide **sponsorship** because:

- they hope to get good publicity from being linked to big, popular events;
- their name becomes part of the title for the events they support, thus raising their public profile;
- they get good coverage from sponsored events on television and other media;
- the firm's name becomes closely linked with winning and success.

Merchandising in an electrical store

Organising to Achieve Objectives

Public relations

Sponsorship and the promotion of a firm's image and its products are part of its **public relations**. Firms try to make sure that the public see them in a good light. They try to ensure that all publicity about them is good. They want the public to think that they are a reliable company whose products are of good quality and value for money. They probably have a customer relations department to deal with any complaints and to make sure that customers, suppliers and other clients are dealt with politely and promptly.

Activities

1 Spam

To many people, Spam is something they would rather forget. Spam (or spiced ham) was introduced to the British public in 1941. The tinned luncheon meat was very popular during the war years because, for many, it was the only form of meat available. It went on to become a cheap family favourite during the 1950s and 60s, but always suffered by having a downmarket image. This was not helped when in the 1970s the Monty Python television comedy show made fun of Spam in a sketch and a song. Demand for the product fell as people became wealthier and were able to afford better quality food.

In 1998 it was decided to try to recover some of the sales Spam had during the 1960s. The advertising agency asked to relaunch Spam

knew it could not sell the tinned meat as a luxury product. Research found that too many people remembered it from their school dinner days and were put off, even though they could not remember what the meat tasted like.

Instead, the agency stressed the fun image of Spam, its good value and how versatile it was in making spicy Spam burgers and Spam pizza. They used the slogan 'I can't believe I've just eaten Spam'.

Spam now has a cult following, its own fan club (www.spam.com) and its manufacturer, Hormel, has brought out a wider range of products including smoke-flavoured and low-fat Spam.

a Why was it necessary to give Spam a new image in the late 1990s?
b Use the case study to explain these terms:
   - product range;
   - consumer resistance;
   - income elasticity of demand.
c Devise a promotion plan that would increase the number of young people buying Spam.
d **Group activity**
   Produce a short market research questionnaire to determine different age groups' attitudes towards Spam.

ICT Activity

Visit the Spam website and describe how the product is given a fun image (www.spam.com).

Unit 3.5 Protecting the consumer

Arbitration →	using an independent person to settle a dispute. Both sides agree to accept the arbitrator's decision.	**→ Key terms**
Caveat emptor →	'let the buyer beware'. Consumers cannot rely entirely on the law for protection; they still have to be careful and act sensibly.	
Consumer protection →	the laws and organisations set up to protect consumers from unfair practices by traders.	
Inertia selling →	asking people to pay for goods or services that have been sent to them, even though they have not ordered them.	
Regulator →	a person appointed to supervise and control the activities of an industry.	
Self-regulation →	where an industry sets up its own systems to try to control the activities of firms within the industry. Members are expected to follow a code of practice or a code of conduct. The schemes are voluntary.	

It is in the interests of firms to make good quality products and to treat their customers honestly and fairly. Goods should be reliable, safe and meet standards laid down by law. Consumers should also be protected from false or misleading marketing and other information. Most firms try very hard to meet the standards expected of them. However, things do go wrong from time to time.

Firms are well organised and wealthy. They can afford to employ experts and lawyers to protect their interests. Consumers usually have to look after their own interests. They are rarely organised and have little financial support. For these reasons there are a number of laws and organisations that look after the interests of consumers. Consumer protection is provided in a number of ways:

- laws and regulations;
- government agencies;
- local government;
- voluntary and independent organisations.

Caveat emptor

These Latin words mean 'let the buyer beware'. Most of the common ways of cheating consumers have been made illegal. But the consumer still has to be careful. Consumers cannot rely entirely on the law for protec-

tion. The good deal is not always what it seems. The law does not protect the person who buys a new television set for £50 from a total stranger. Consumers are expected to act sensibly. They should read the small print and follow instructions.

Sale of Goods Act

This Act lays down the legal framework covering the buying and selling of goods. The Act only applies to sales by a business to the public. It covers sales in shops and showrooms, and by market stalls, mail order and any kind of direct sales. The Act does not cover private sales. Under the Act:

- Goods must be of 'merchantable quality', which means they should be fit for ordinary use: they must work and be free from faults. The merchantable quality partly depends on the price paid for the goods. More expensive goods are expected to be of a higher quality. There are two exceptions to the rule. Buyers cannot complain that goods are not of merchantable quality if:
  - the seller points out defects when the goods were bought;
  - the buyer has examined the goods before buying them and has been satisfied they were all right.
- Goods are assumed to be 'fit for purpose'. That is, the goods will do what they were bought for,

especially if the buyer has asked the seller for advice before buying the goods.

- Goods must be 'as described'. That is, they must be exactly as they are described in catalogues or other sales material, or by a salesperson. For example, a sweater described as '100% pure wool' must not contain any other fibre.

Sellers cannot take away the rights given to buyers by the Act, for example through guarantees that offer fewer rights or notices such as 'no refunds given here'. The Act applies to goods that have been discounted, or bought in sales or any other kind of special offer.

If there is a problem with goods, the buyer must complain to the shopkeeper, not the manufacturer. This is because the buyer has a contract with the actual seller, not the maker of the goods. It is up to the shopkeeper to reimburse the customer, then get any money back from the manufacturer. The buyer can insist on either having the goods replaced or having a refund. If the goods are faulty the buyer must take them back to the retailer within a reasonable time.

Selling services, for example by hairdressers, garages, dry cleaners, surveyors and auctioneers, is controlled by the Supply of Goods and Services Act, 1982. Services must be delivered:

- with reasonable care and skill;
- within a reasonable time;
- at a reasonable cost.

Other laws that protect consumers

Trade Descriptions Act

This Act makes it an offence for a seller to describe goods and services falsely, in advertisements, notices, sales literature or by a salesperson at the point of sale. False descriptions of all kinds are covered. For example, a photograph that gives a wrong impression, or statements about size, colour, quantity, name of the maker, or purpose of the goods.

Misleading claims about prices are also part of the Act. It is an offence to:

- make a false claim that goods are being sold below the recommended price;
- make a false comparison with a previous price, for example saying that goods have been reduced from

£30 to £20 when they have been sold at £20 for the last three months;

- suggest that the price is lower than it actually is because there are hidden extra costs. For example, the cost of packing and delivery have to be added to arrive at the full price.

Unsolicited Goods and Services Act

This is a law to protect people from **inertia selling**. Someone who receives goods they have not ordered does not have to pay for either the goods or the cost of returning them. If the sender does not collect them within six months the goods can be kept or sold. This is cut down to 30 days if the receiver writes to the sender asking them to collect the goods.

Consumer Credit Act

When goods are bought on credit they cost more than if they were bought for cash. The purpose of this Act is to make sure people know the true cost of credit. Under the Act:

- Consumers must be shown the cash price of the goods. They must be told the APR (annualised percentage rate) for the interest that they are paying. The total cost of the credit must also be given. All advertisements and displays must show the APR when credit is being offered.
- Customers must be given copies of the credit sale agreement. When people sign an agreement at home they have to be given a 'cooling off' period of 15 days. This gives them time to change their minds.
- Only firms licensed by the Office of Fair Trading can offer credit. These include banks, credit card companies and building societies.

Consumer Protection Act

Under this Act the producers, importers and suppliers of goods can be sued if their goods cause injury or damage. Goods have to be as safe as people are entitled to expect them to be. Packaging must warn users of any dangers that might happen through misuse of the goods.

Food and Drugs Acts

All food that is sold has to be 'fit for human consumption'. There are rules about food preparation, labelling and descriptions of food products. For example a pork sausage must not contain less than 30% pork meat.

Weights and Measures Act

The public is entitled to expect that the measuring equipment used by shops and other traders is accurate. The Act allows inspectors to visit traders to test their measuring equipment. Thus weighing scales in shops and pumps at petrol stations are checked regularly. It is an offence to give short weight or short measure. Prepacked goods have to show the weight or other measure on the packaging.

Government agencies

One way of looking after the interests of consumers is to make sure that competition is as fair and open as possible. Monopolies and mergers reduce the amount of competition. Very large firms are powerful and may use their power against the interests of consumers and the public generally. The three organisations listed below work in the interests of the consumer and to try to keep competition as open as possible.

The Office of Fair Trading (OFT)

Set up under the Fair Trading Act in 1973 it is run by the Director General of Fair Trading who is appointed by the government. It has a number of important functions.

- To give general advice to the public about consumer matters. It does not deal with complaints about individual products.
- It looks into complaints from the public about the way that individual traders do business. Firms that fail to behave properly can be made to change the way they do business.
- It advises the Secretary of State for Trade and Industry if a planned merger or takeover should be referred to the Competition Commission.
- It has a duty to stop anti-competitive practices, like price-fixing agreements. It watches out for any practices that work against the interests of consumers. Where it spots such practices firms can be made to stop them.
- Only people licensed by the OFT can give credit.

OFFICE OF FAIR TRADING

The Competition Commission

This used to be known as the Monopolies and Mergers Commission (MMC). Its job is to carry out enquiries into matters referred to it by the Department of Trade and Industry (DTI). It does not decide for itself what to investigate. It may be asked by the DTI whether a proposed merger is in the public interest. It can also be asked by the OFT or DTI to look into any activity that might reduce competition. For example, it has looked into the pricing policies of the car industry. The Commission does not have the power to enforce its decisions. Only the DTI can do that.

Regulators

The industries that were privatised during the 1980s and 1990s used to be state-run monopolies. There were worries that, as private sector companies, they might try to exploit consumers. As a result, a **regulator** was appointed for each privatised industry. The regulators' jobs are to look after the interests of consumers by:

- controlling the prices companies charge;
- bringing more competition into the industries;
- laying down rules about how the companies are to be run.

Thus electricity companies can now sell gas, and gas companies can sell electricity. Any new companies that join the industries also come under the regulator's control. Examples of regulators are OFTEL for the telephone industry, OFWAT for the water industry and OFGEM for the energy (gas and electricity) industry.

There are other industries whose products are hard for consumers to understand. They need a regulator to lay down rules and to make companies tell consumers what they need to know in a way that is easy to understand. An example is the financial services industry where the regulator is the Financial Services Authority.

There are also some voluntary regulators appointed by an industry for self-regulation. For example, the Advertising Standards Authority and the Insurance Ombudsman.

Local Government and consumer protection

Trading standards

Most of the laws to protect consumers are enforced by local councils. They do so through their trading standards or consumer protection departments. The laws give trading standards officers very wide powers to make sure that traders stay within the law.

- They buy sample goods and services, for example to check that a garage has done all the jobs it should when servicing a car.
- They test goods to make sure they are safe. They also test scales and other measuring equipment to make sure they are accurate.
- They can order traders to stop selling goods that are unsafe or not up to standard, for example toys painted with lead paint.
- They can commandeer certain illegal goods, such as fake designer goods or pirate videos.

Traders who break the law can be taken to court, which may result in a heavy fine. Officers try to avoid this by giving traders advice so that they do not break the law.

Environmental health

Local councils also employ environmental health officers. Their job is to make sure that places that handle and prepare food do so safely and have high standards of hygiene. They have the power to close a place that does not come up to standard and prosecute traders that break the law.

Other organisations

British Standards Institution (BSI)

We have seen earlier that the BSI lays down standards to which goods should be produced. Goods made according to these standards are inspected and can be advertised as 'complying to BSI Standard'. After inde-

pendent testing goods can also be awarded the 'kitemark'.

Citizens' Advice Bureau (CAB)

Most towns have a CAB. They are mainly staffed by volunteers with part-time help from professional experts. Their services are free. They advise people on their rights and on the best ways to handle a problem.

Consumers' Association

This is an independent organisation funded entirely by members' subscriptions. It is best known as the publisher of the *Which?* magazines, including specialist editions for gardening and holidays. Acting like an ordinary customer it buys goods and services. It tests and compares various makes of a product and recommends a best buy. The Association also acts as a pressure group to stop unfair business practices that work against the interests of consumers.

Trade associations

Many trade associations have codes of conduct or a code of practice. These rules are used in the self-regulation of the industry. They usually include a complaints procedure that can be used by dissatisfied customers. Examples include:

Which? reports offer advice to consumers on which product to buy

- An ombudsman who weighs up the rights and wrongs in a dispute and gives a ruling. Ombudsmen are usually from the industry and may be seen as not truly independent. Examples include ombudsmen for banking, insurance and estate agents.
- An **arbitration** scheme where the two sides in a dispute ask an independent person to suggest a solution. Both sides usually agree to accept the arbitrator's decision. It is often used in the building industry.
- A committee to handle complaints, such as the Press Complaints Authority, that has an independent chairman.

Activities

1 What is meant by 'merchantable quality'?

2 If a trading standards officer visited the following places, what might they be looking for:
  a a public house (pub);
  b a market stall?

3 Name two organisations somebody could turn to for help on consumer protection matters. Describe the sort of help that could be given by each organisation.

4 You work for a local newspaper as a consumer advisor. Readers write to you when they are unhappy with something they have bought. Some of the letters are to be published in the newspaper followed by a reply from you, pointing out their legal rights and giving them advice.

Five letters have been selected for inclusion in this week's edition of the paper. Produce your reply to each of them.

Dear Sir or Madam

Last week I bought a new electric toaster.

When I got home the toaster was nothing like the photograph on the box. The picture showed an appliance with a frozen bread button and a removable crumb tray.

My toaster has neither of these features. What should I do?

Yours faithfully

Mohammed Saeed

Dear Consumer Advisor

My daughter's wedding is coming up soon and I went out to buy a nice hat for the occasion.

The hat I bought is lovely with a beautiful blue feather that sets it off a treat. But would you believe it? Today I saw an identical hat in another shop for less than half the price I had paid.

I returned the hat to the shop I bought it from, but they said they would neither take the hat back nor give me half of my money back.

Surely that's against the law. Please let me know.

Yours

Heidi Walsh (Mrs)

Dear Consumer Advisor

I gave myself a treat the other day and bought myself some strawberries from a greengrocer. The man told me there were 225 grams of strawberries in each sealed packet. When I got home I weighed them on my kitchen scales and found there were only 175 grams.

Is it my own fault for not asking him to weigh the strawberries when I bought them?

Your faithfully

Ms C Watson

Dear Sir or Madam

As I'm getting on a bit in life, I've decided to get a bit fitter by taking up jogging so I bought a pair of trainers from a sports shop.

On my second time out, I noticed that the stitching was coming away on one shoe.

I took the trainers back, but was told by the assistant that I could not have a refund because I had bought 'pub' trainers and not sports trainers. He said the ones I had bought were not intended for jogging.

Do I have a leg to stand on?

Yours

George Evans

Dear Consumer Advisor

When I was in town a few weeks ago, I answered some questions for a young lady who said she was doing some research for a publisher. She asked for my address in case they needed to contact me about my answers.

Imagine my surprise when yesterday I received 20 volumes of an encyclopaedia. The letter with them said I must return them within 10 days, otherwise pay £250 to buy them.

The post office says it will cost nearly £15 to send them back. I'm just a pensioner and can't afford that sort of money.

Please tell me what I should do.

Yours faithfully

Miss J Perriman

Case Study

5 McDonald's

Firms have an obligation to protect their customers from unnecessary harm, and McDonald's is no exception. In August 2000, 20 customers started legal proceedings against McDonald's for selling hot drinks. The proceedings started in Manchester High Court where it was claimed that McDonald's knowingly served tea and coffee at dangerously high temperatures. It was said that if drinks spilled or were knocked off tables they had the ability to scald or hurt customers or their children.

A solicitor for the former customers said that McDonald's is an organisation that attracts and caters for young children. The firm, therefore, was being negligent by serving hot drinks.

A McDonald's spokesperson said that all hot drinks were served in cups with a fitted lid and were clearly labelled with the words 'caution, hot'.

a In what ways might the following organisations be expected to safeguard their customers?
  - a theme park;
  - a manufacturer of an electric blanket.
b Discuss whether McDonald's had taken reasonable care in the above case study.
c In groups, consider ways in which the need to protect the consumer results in the quality of the service or product being reduced.

ICT Activity

Look at the regulator OFWAT's website (http://roof.ccta.gov.uk/ofwat/protect). Produce a list of ways in which OFWAT can protect water consumers.

Unit 3.6 Capital and sources of funding

Assets →	all the things that can be given a money value which are owned by a business, organisation or person. They are shown in the balance sheet.
Bank loan →	a fixed sum of money borrowed from a bank for a named period at an agreed rate of interest. It is repaid either by instalments or in a lump sum.
Bonds →	promises to repay a loan, usually on a fixed date. They are issued by companies as an alternative to shares or debentures and can be bought and sold on the Stock Exchange.
Capital →	the funds invested in a business to enable it to buy the physical assets it needs and to carry on in business.
Credit →	where goods are not paid for at the time they were bought. The buyer is given an agreed period of time in which to pay for the goods.
Current account →	a type of account offered by banks where the money deposited by customers has to be repaid on demand. Money is usually withdrawn by cheque or debit card.
Debentures →	certificates issued by a company that state the company has a long-term loan from the holder, at a fixed rate of interest.
Equity →	the part of the capital of a company that is held in ordinary shares.
Factoring →	a specialist service that allows firms to get cash in advance of a debt being paid.
Leasing →	renting assets from a company for an agreed time in return for regular payments of rent.
Liabilities →	the debts that are owed by a business. They are shown in the balance sheet.
Loan capital →	not strictly 'capital', the term is used for the long-term loans of a company. It consists of bank loans, debentures and perhaps bonds.
Overdraft →	an agreement with a bank that allows a customer to draw out more money than they have in their current account.
Ordinary shares →	the main type of share issued by a limited company. Each share represents part ownership of the company and gives the holder a vote at the Annual General Meeting.
Preference shares →	a type of share issued by a limited company. The holders are part owners of the company and are entitled to a fixed rate of dividend but no vote in company business.
Retained profit →	the part of a firm's profit that is kept in the business and not distributed to the owners. It is the most common way of financing the growth of a firm.
Start-up capital →	the capital needed to meet the costs of a business before it begins trading.
Trade credit →	credit given by one firm to another firm in the same line of business.
Venture capital →	Capital invested in small firms to help them to start up or to grow.
Working capital →	the funds needed for the day-to-day running of a business.

Capital

Capital is one of the four factors of production. It provides the resources that are needed to start and to carry on in business. **Capital** is not just money.

Suppose a person starts in business using their garage as a workshop, using tools they already have and their skills. The garage, tools and the skills are the resources brought into the business by the owner. They are the **assets** of the business and are equal to the business's capital. In this example, the resources are not in the form of money, although they do have a money value.

Organising to Achieve Objectives

All through its life the business buys raw materials, machinery, equipment and other things needed to run the business. This adds to the assets of the business. As the assets grow, so too does the capital of the business.

Money borrowed or debts owing to other businesses or people are the **liabilities** of a business. When all debts and loans have been settled and repaid, what is left over is the capital of the business. Capital therefore equals the assets minus the liabilities of a business. The capital of a business belongs to the owners.

$$capital = assets - liabilities$$

A new business needs money to pay for premises, equipment, stock and raw materials. There are legal costs and things like stationery and office equipment that must be paid for. It must hire and pay workers and produce or buy goods to sell. These are the start-up costs of the business. Many of them have to be paid for before a firm begins to earn income from the sale of its goods or services. These costs are paid for out of the **start-up capital** of a business.

Once a business is up and running it still needs capital:

- **working capital** to enable it to pay its way from day to day;
- capital to enable it to develop and grow.

The kinds of funds it needs vary between the short term, medium term and long term. It obtains these funds from three main sources:

- its own resources – self-financing;
- borrowing;
- new investment in the firm.

Short-term funds

These are funds for use in the business for up to one year. Short-term funds are used to pay for such items as wages and supplies of raw materials or stocks, and for the running expenses of the business.

Sales revenue

The main source of funds for any business is the money it gets from selling its goods or services. Firms aim to pay for most of their day-to-day running costs out of this sales revenue. However, there are times of the year when a firm is more busy than others. Money does not, therefore, come in regularly throughout the year. For example, firms selling seasonal goods such as Christmas decorations or fireworks. When a firm sells goods and services on credit it cannot always be sure how soon it will be paid. There are times when firms need to be able to call on other funds if they have to.

Trade credit

Firms do not often pay cash for the goods and services they need. They usually have between one and three months credit before they have to pay. When one firm gives credit to another firm it is called **trade credit**. During the period of credit, buyers can use, sell or do what they like with the goods. No interest is paid on the credit. The seller, though, has had to pay the costs of producing the goods. The buyer is, in effect, making use of the seller's capital until the goods are paid for.

Overdraft

Banks offer their customers two kinds of accounts.

1 Accounts that earn interest on money placed in them on deposit. These are called deposit accounts.
2 Banks also provide **current accounts**. Customers can have the money deposited repaid on demand. They can go to the bank and ask for their money over the counter. Usually they withdraw their money by using cheques, debit cards, standing orders or direct debits.

Normally banks do not let customers draw out more money than they have paid in to their current account. However, a firm can come to an agreement with its bank to let it draw cheques for more money than it has paid into its current account. The bank allows it to 'overdraw' on its account, up to an agreed limit. The bank charges interest on the amount by which the account is overdrawn.

- Each time the account is overdrawn the firm is borrowing money from the bank.
- Every time money is paid into the current account the **overdraft** is reduced or it may disappear.
- Every withdrawal over the amount on deposit increases the overdraft.
- The size of the overdraft keeps changing, so interest is charged on the daily balance.
- An overdraft is a kind of safety net. It is only used when absolutely necessary.

A branch of a retail bank

Factoring

All firms have debtors – firms or people that owe them money. Some debts can take a long time to settle. Instead of waiting to be paid, a firm can get its money quickly by **factoring** the debt. The factor is a bank or specialist firm. It agrees to pay a firm 80% of a debt, straightaway. The factor then collects the debt when it is due and pays the remaining 20%, after taking a commission for its work. There are advantages to factoring.

- It may be better for a firm to be certain of 80% straightaway rather than the promise of 100% later.
- The 80% received in cash can be used in the business immediately. The commission paid to the factor may be less than the interest on an overdraft.
- The factor takes the risk of the debtor not paying. Factoring also saves the time and cost of chasing debts.

Medium-term funds

These are funds that may be used for periods of up to five years. The money is used for such things as buying machinery and equipment, research and development and for expansion.

Retained profit

Also called undistributed profit, this is the most usual way for companies to pay for the expansion of their business. **Retained profit** is profit that a business has made which has been reinvested in the business instead of being paid to the owners. It is a cheap way to finance the growth of a business. There are no costs, such as the interest on borrowed money or the very large costs of selling shares.

Trade credit

Firms that sell very large machinery and equipment often offer a credit package as part of the deal. For example, buyers of trains are given credit extending over several years.

Bank loans

Banks offer **bank loans** as well as overdrafts. They lend a fixed sum of money for a fixed time at an agreed rate of interest. For example, a loan of £10,000 for three years at 15% interest. The loan may be repaid in a lump sum or in instalments.

- The bank opens a separate loan account for the firm. This shows how much interest is added and when repayments are made.
- Interest is charged on the full amount for the full period of the loan.

The London Stock Exchange

Hire purchase

Firms may buy machinery and equipment, including vehicles, on hire purchase. Instead of the buyer paying for the goods, the seller is paid by a finance company. By paying the seller, the finance company is, in effect, lending the cost of the goods to the buyer. The buyer is allowed to use the goods while making regular payments to the finance company for a fixed period of time.

- The finance company owns the goods until the last instalment is paid. Technically the buyer is only hiring the goods up to the last payment.
- The payments cover the cost of the goods plus interest on the money used by the finance company to buy the goods.
- Hire purchase tends to be used by smaller firms often for single items of small equipment such as photocopiers or computers.

An advert for a finance company

Leasing

Leasing works in a similar way to hire purchase. Goods are bought from a supplier and paid for by a finance company. The hirer makes regular payments to the finance company to cover the cost of the goods, servicing and interest. However, the hirer never owns the goods. At the end of the lease the goods are returned to the finance company. Leasing is used for large items, for example many airlines lease rather than buy aircraft. It is also used for items that have to be replaced regularly. For example, firms lease rather than buy company cars, photocopiers or computer systems.

Advantages of leasing:

- Firms do not have to lay out large sums on capital spending. The goods are paid for out of revenue (see Unit 3.10a) and are part of the firm's expenses.
- Usually all maintenance costs are included in the lease fees.
- It is easy to change to more up-to-date models.

Disadvantages of leasing:

- Leased goods are never owned. Very large sums of money are paid out with no asset to show for it.
- The total cost of the equipment is greater than paying for it outright. The cost of leasing includes the cost of the goods, plus interest, plus the finance company's costs and profits.

An advert for a leasing company

Government grants

These may be available to buy equipment and to fund growth, especially in certain areas of high unemployment.

Long-term funds

These are funds that are used for periods of longer than five years. They are used to fund long-term projects and the expansion of the business.

Owners' funds – shares

This is the main form of long-term capital in limited companies. Public limited companies may issue **ordinary shares** and **preference shares**. Shareholders are the owners of the business and have a share of the profits. Preference shares get a fixed share of profits. The share of the profits paid to ordinary shareholders varies with the success of the firm. They have a higher risk and have a vote at the firm's AGM. All ordinary shareholders have equal rights and an equal share of the profits, so their holding is often called **equity** capital. When a company wants to expand it may choose to issue more shares.

Bonds

These are called corporate **bonds** to show the difference between them and government bonds. When a firm issues new shares, the profits have to be shared out among a greater number of shares so that each share is worth a smaller amount. To avoid this, a firm can raise long-term capital by selling bonds to the public. Bonds are certificates that say a firm has borrowed a certain sum of money.

- Bond holders are creditors of the company.
- They are paid a fixed rate of interest and are usually issued for a fixed term, often 20 or 25 years.
- The interest is an expense and is paid before a firm's profit is finally calculated.
- If holders of bonds want their money back, they can be sold on the Stock Exchange.

Debentures

These are another way of raising long-term capital by borrowing money instead of issuing shares. Like bonds, they are a form of borrowing for a fixed term at a fixed rate of interest. **Debenture** holders are given security against the company's assets. In some cases they can sell the company's assets if the company fails to pay the interest or repay the loan. Debentures can also be traded on the Stock Exchange.

Venture capital

Small firms and people with a good business idea often find it hard to get the capital they need to start or expand their business. In recent years a new type of financial institution has appeared. These firms specialise in funding new enterprises by providing **venture capital**.

Investing in new or small firms is very risky. Before it invests in a business idea or small firm, a venture capital company will look at it very closely.

- It will give advice, for example on how to write a business plan.
- It will invest in a company, either by providing a long-term loan or by buying shares in it.
- In some cases, it will insist on a seat on the firm's board of directors.
- It always works closely with the company, giving it expert advice and support.
- As the firm grows, it may invest more money to finance further expansion. When a firm is ready it helps it to become a public limited company.
- Venture capital firms also help in management buy-outs, when the managers buy the firm they work for.

Activities

1 A company has the following assets and liabilities:

Value of equipment	£12,000
Money owed to suppliers	£7,000
Bank loan	£20,000
Value of vehicles	£10,000
Current overdraft	£4,000
Value of workshop	£18,000

Split the list into assets and liabilities and calculate the amount of capital in the business.

2 Most companies give their customers between one and three months' trade credit when goods are sold. Explain why a system of trade credit is necessary in business.

3 Many firms have higher sales during certain months of the year. Draw the axes shown below for each type of firm. Sketch a graph to show how sales might change each month for:
   a an ice-cream manufacturer;
   b a car maker.

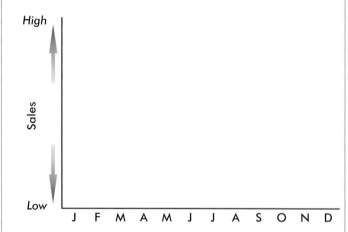

4 Banks want to give firms overdrafts and loans, because firms pay them interest on the money owed. Explain what type of businesses banks may not be keen to lend money to.

5 A factor has been offered two debts from a company. The details are shown in the following table.

	Debt A	Debt B
Amount owed by debtor	£20,000	£30,000
Credit status of debtor	Good	Fair
Time until debt due for payment by debtor	3 months	6 months
Amount paid by factor	95% (£19,000)	?

The factor is prepared to pay £19,000 for Debt A. Consider what you think would be a reasonable price to pay for Debt B. Give clear reasons for the amount you have chosen.

6 A firm has a policy of changing its cars every three years. The firm needs to buy a new car for one of its sales staff. It is not sure whether to lease a car or buy one outright.

The lease would be for three years and the leaser would pay for all maintenance costs.

You have been asked to gather information and decide which would be the better choice: leasing or buying.

	Lease car	Buy car
Cost of buying car	n/a	£18,000
Value after three years	0	£8,000
Leasing costs per year	£6,000	n/a
Maintenance costs each year	0	£1,000
Other costs (e.g. petrol)	£3,000	£4,000

Write a report to the sales manager explaining whether you believe the firm should buy or lease the car. Use the information and anything else you can think of to help you reach a decision.

Case Study

7 BGR Foods plc

Tony Allan runs a successful multi-million pound seafood business, BGR.

Having started his working life as a chef in London, Tony soon discovered that it was very difficult to buy good quality fresh fish. He realised that other restaurants were facing the same problem and recognised that there was a business opportunity supplying fresh fish and other seafood.

As he did not have enough money himself, he managed to borrow £400 from his girlfriend's father to buy a van. Each morning at about 3 o'clock Tony would drive down to the fishing ports of Sussex, returning to London to sell the fish to restaurants.

In the late 1980s he expanded by moving into new areas of business. He formed Cutty Catering, a fish preparation factory, and later bought a salmon smokery and a group of specialist wholesale butchers.

In 1996 Tony realised his dream and opened an expensive restaurant in London called Bank. He funded the £2.8 million costs with a bank loan and cashflow from his other business interests.

Tony had other great ideas for building up his businesses. He wanted to open six more fish restaurants and a food preparation centre in central London. He recognised that raising sufficient finance would be difficult. He eventually decided that he would need to float his company on the Stock Exchange.

a Explain why people starting a business for the first time find it difficult to raise money.

b Tony Allan borrowed £400 from his girlfriend's father to start his business.
   i Comment on why this may not have been a good way to finance his business.
   ii Describe two other suitable ways of raising the money.

c What other start-up costs did Tony probably have besides the cost of the van?

d Many firms are reluctant to turn to the Stock Exchange to obtain money. Explain why they are not keen on this source of finance.

e Tony could have turned to a venture capital company to help him with his expansion plans. Explain how a venture capital company can help firms like BGR.

Unit 3.7 The profit motive and risk taking

Enterprise

Businesses are started because someone spots a business opportunity. A new business opportunity may be:

- a brand new idea that no one has thought of before, for example Trevor Bayliss' wind-up radio;
- a gap in the market that is not being filled, such as the need for a local electrical shop or a new type of vacuum cleaner.

Taking a business idea and carrying it through to the point of starting a business is an act of **enterprise**. Someone who shows enterprise:

- is able to see the possibilities in a business idea;
- knows how and where to get the finance needed to get the business going;
- is able to see the idea through to the point where the business is started;
- can organise and manage the business once it is set up;
- is willing to take the risks of running the business.

There are always risks in running any business. For example, the demand for a product may be less than expected, there may be new competition or the price of materials may suddenly rise. The risks are even greater for a new business that has no reserves to fall back on.

In recent years governments have encouraged enterprise by making it easier to start a new business. Small firms in new industries are seen as being the 'engine for growth' in the UK. They are often run by young, enthusiastic and innovative people. They are seen as the way to keep the country's industry up to date.

The Small Business Service is the Government agency dedicated to helping small firms and representing their interests. Its vision is that by 2005, the UK will be the best place in the world to set up and run a business. Through its Business Link services the SBS provides access to a range of business support and advice. All aspects of running and starting a business are covered, from business planning, exporting, employment issues, information and communication technology and e-commerce. Personal business advisers also help businesses access sources of financial help such as grants, loans, regional funding and venture capital.

Entrepreneur

An **entrepreneur** is someone who:

- spots a business opportunity;
- can organise and manage the resources needed;
- is willing to take the risks of running a business.

Most entrepreneurs start out in business as sole traders. Some grow to become private companies, a few become public limited companies.

Enterprise is one of the factors of production. The other factors of production – land, labour and capital – are of limited value on their own. It is only when they are brought together and organised that they become productive. They have to be combined in the right proportions. Different products need different amounts of each factor. Entrepreneurs have to organise and combine the factors of production in the best way. This involves many risks:

- the combination of factors might be wrong, resulting in high costs, or at least higher costs than those of competitors;
- consumers may not buy the product at the price for which it is being sold.

If entrepreneurs organise the factors in the right way, and produce a product consumers want, they make a **profit**. That profit can be viewed, at least partly, as a reward for taking the risks of business.

Martha Lane Fox and partner

Profit

People only start a business to make a profit. The profit has to be large enough to make it worthwhile taking the risks of running a business. One risk is that it makes no profit, or only a very small one. Business people may be willing to put up with a small profit in the early years of a business. They may also expect to plough back at least some of the profit to help the business to grow. Longer term, those that take the risks of business expect the profit to be more than they could earn by:

- working for someone else;
- investing their money in some other way.

Profit can be seen as the reward for taking business risks. They are the sorts of risks that cannot be insured against. There is an element of chance in all business, for example:

- it is always possible that goods will not sell;
- the product may suddenly become unpopular, for example because of a health scare. Beef farmers were badly hit by 'mad cow disease';
- there could be a sudden change in taste or fashion;
- firms selling summer clothes could have poor sales if the weather is bad.

These are risks that cannot be predicted. Clearly, some businesses are riskier than others. For example, there is more risk in selling a completely new product than a well-established one. Some industries are risky by their nature, for example prospecting for new sources of oil or metals – it is possible to spend millions of pounds and find nothing.

The greater the risk the greater the chance of losing money. In general, the greater the risks in a business the greater the profit the company will expect to make.

Example

A pharmaceutical company may spend millions of pounds on research and development to produce a new drug to cure, for example, asthma. If the drug is found to be unsafe or to cause serious side-effects the money spent on R & D will be lost. There is a high risk. Pharmaceutical companies expect to make high profits on those drugs they eventually bring to the market. The high profits are necessary to pay for the R & D and for the time they have had to wait before being able to start selling the drug.

Types of profit

The term 'profit' is used in two ways:

1 the profit made on a single item when it is sold, that is, the profit per unit;
2 the overall profit made by a firm on the total of its sales.

Profit per unit

The profit on a single item is the difference between the selling price and the cost of buying or making the product. Profit per item sold can be measured in two ways:

1 **As a percentage of the selling price:**
   When profit is measured as a percentage of the selling price of a product, it is called the **margin**.

$$\text{margin} = \frac{\text{profit}}{\text{selling price}} \times 100$$

Example

If an item is sold for £5 and the total cost of making it was £3, then the margin of profit is £2.

$$\text{margin} = \frac{\text{profit}}{\text{selling price}} = \frac{£2}{£5} \times 100 = 40\%$$

The bigger the margin, the more money there is to cover the business expenses. When margins are tight a firm has to control its costs very carefully.

2 **As a percentage of cost price:**

Where profit is a percentage of the cost of making or buying the goods sold. When profit is measured in terms of cost price it is called the mark-up.

$$\text{mark-up} = \frac{\text{profit}}{\text{cost price}} \times 100$$

Example

Using the figures from the example above:

$$\frac{£2}{£3} \times 100 = 66.6\%$$

The mark-up is the standard amount a seller adds to the cost price of an article to arrive at the selling price. A shopkeeper who buys a sweater for £30 may have a mark-up of 66.6%. In that case the sweater will be sold for £50.

Overall profit

The total profit made by a firm is measured by taking away all of the firm's costs from the total value of its sales. The overall profit includes the total value of sales minus the total cost of buying or making the goods sold. It also includes all the other costs of running a firm. These other costs are sometimes called **overheads**. They include things like rent, heating and lighting.

Importance of profit

Profit is often used as a measure of a firm's success. The higher the profit the more successful it is thought to be.

- Firms that have large profits find it easier to expand. They can attract extra resources when they need them. This is especially true of public companies.
- If the profit falls, the price of shares may also fall. The share price is important to a firm because it reflects how people outside the firm view its level of success and future prospects.
- Firms that make a loss will eventually go out of business.

Activities

1 Imagine your school or college is hoping to raise funds by running a summer fair. Identify the risks that will be taken in organising such an event.

2 In what ways could the government help entrepreneurs to start a business?

3 Not all firms set out to make as much profit as possible. Some have other objectives. Explain why, though, it is important that all businesses make a reasonable level of profit.

Case Study

4 Garden Designs

Chris was tired of her job as a technology teacher in a city comprehensive school. She decided that she needed a change of direction in her life. She had always been keen on gardening and felt that she could earn a reasonable living as a landscape gardener. In return for a fee she would design gardens for people, or completely change the design of an existing one.

By leasing a van and hiring any heavy equipment she needed, she hoped to keep her overheads as low as possible. All other tools and supplies she could store in her garage. Her spare bedroom could be converted into an office, where she could produce the plans for her designs.

Chris was lucky. She eventually started her business at a time when television gardening programmes had become very popular. People were keen to improve the look of their gardens. The economy was also booming, with people working long hours. This meant that house owners did not have the time to redesign their own gardens, but they did have the money to pay someone to do it for them. In the back of her mind, Chris knew that she could always return to teaching if things did not work out in business.

Organising to Achieve Objectives

After a year in business, Chris examined her accounts:

Fees received	£40,000
Lease of van	£3,000
Hire equipment	£2,000
Assistant's wages	£7,000
Plants, etc.	£6,000

a Calculate how much profit Chris made in her first year.

b To start her business, Chris gave up her teaching job paying £24,000 a year. Comment on whether it was worthwhile to start the business.

    i What risks did Chris take starting her business?

    ii What did Chris do to keep the risks involved as low as possible?

5 Mathmos lava lamps

Lava lamps were very popular in the 1960s. They are vase-shaped lights that contain coloured oils and water. Heat from the light bulb warms the mixture and creates 1960s-style psychedelic shapes.

Young entrepreneur, Cressida Granger, came across one of these lamps in a Glasgow market. She was fascinated by them so bought some lamps from the manufacturer to sell at her Camden Market stall in London. They sold like hot cakes and Cressida was keen to buy more.

She tracked down the owner of the business and bought the loss-making company from him. She renamed the business Mathmos and set about marketing the lamps to young professionals who were interested in 'retro' fashion. Cressida was successful in selling the lamps and in 1999 Mathmos achieved £18 million in sales.

But it was not all so simple. Cressida's success brought her to the attention of Far East competitors, who realised that there was a new worldwide demand for lava lamps. Within a few months the market was flooded with cheap imitations of the original lamps.

Cressida soon found that she was losing markets to the eastern manufacturers who were selling the lamps at a price that Mathmos found difficult to match. She pointed out to retailers that only Mathmos offered a good quality, safe product with after-sales service. A few accidents with badly made foreign lamps did help Mathmos, but profits failed to reach their 1999 peak.

Mathmos recognised there were four options available to it:

- compete on price with the foreign firms;
- spend more money defending the copyright of lava lamps, so others could not copy them;
- exploit the brand name of Mathmos, the original lava lamp maker;
- start having some of the lamps' components made abroad to lower costs.

Cressida realised that running a business based on just one fashion-sensitive product is very risky.

a Explain why Cressida Granger can be called an entrepreneur.

b Explain the risk Mathmos is taking by concentrating on making just lava lamps.

c Examine each of the four options available to Mathmos, and decide which you would recommend to the business.

Unit 3.8 Budgetary and financial control

3.8a Budgets and their uses

Why keep accounts?

Every firm, large or small, must keep detailed records of money coming into and going out of the business. These records are a firm's **accounts**. The accounts show:

- what the business owns;
- what is owing to the business and by whom;
- what the business owes to others;
- details of the transactions that lead to the business making a profit or a loss;
- what the business owes to the owners.

The accounts are recorded in a ledger. Every transaction always has two effects:

- giving;
- receiving.

When a product is sold for cash, money comes into the business and goods go out. If a firm buys a machine on credit, its stock of machines goes up, but instead of handing over cash there is a promise to pay later. When the debt is paid, money goes out and the debt is cancelled. Recording these two effects in the accounts is called double-entry bookkeeping.

Budgets

Firms that leave things entirely to chance with regard to money are unlikely to be successful. All firms need to plan ahead. At the start of a year they need to have a good idea of what their earnings and costs are going to be. They cannot know what is going to happen. They have to estimate, or forecast, what might happen.

These forecasts are drawn up in a **budget**. A budget is a financial plan. It is one of the main ways of controlling a business's finances. It estimates the money coming into a business and how much is needed to keep the business running. Estimates are based on:

- what happened the year before;
- changes the business knows about, such as changes in tax or the price of raw materials;
- planned changes in a firm's own prices;
- targets set by the firm to increase sales or profits or to cut costs.

Budgets show what resources are needed and how they are to be used over a given time.

- They are usually drawn up for the next year, but may be broken down into shorter periods.
- They can be for short periods such as a month, or for longer periods, perhaps three or five years.
- They are drawn up for a business as a whole, as well as for each department or section.
- They have to be brought up to date regularly to make sure they are as accurate as possible.

Example

If a firm gets a surprise new order, it affects how much it hopes to earn and how much it has to spend on wages and materials. The budget must be brought up to date.

The longer the period covered by a budget the less accurate it will be. This is because it is hard to predict

Organising to Achieve Objectives

what the price of materials and other costs will be in the future.

The word 'budget' is also used when a sum of money is set aside for a particular purpose. If a manager is given a budget of £20,000 to buy a new machine it means that the manager can spend up to £20,000 on that machine. If less than £20,000 is spent the machine has been bought 'within budget'.

Budgetary control

Once a budget has been agreed it provides financial targets for a firm's managers. A department is expected to sell what it said it was going to sell and so earn the income it has budgeted for. It is also expected to spend no more than the amount shown in the budget, for each type of spending.

Checking the income and spending against the budget is called **budgetary control**. Checks are carried out to see that all parts of the business are meeting their targets and not overspending. Managers are not criticised if they earn more than the budget. However, if they spend more than their budget, managers are asked to explain the differences.

Benefits of budgetary control
- Agreed targets are set that everyone knows about. This helps to keep spending under control.
- Problems can be spotted quickly.
- It encourages forecasting and planning and good management of money.

Drawbacks of budgetary control
- Budgets can be rigid and reduce flexibility.
- Departments may be tempted to spend up to their budgets instead of saving money.
- Rising costs are often outside a firm's control, for example the cost of raw materials may rise world-wide.

BUSINESS ASPECTS

There are certain stages in the preparation of budgets which begin with the directors setting certain targets for the firm as a whole.

Target setting: financial plans are agreed by the board of directors or senior managers; targets include items like: cutting costs, increasing sales, a percentage growth rate, increased profits or improved quality.

Information gathering: collecting the facts to see how the targets can be achieved, so that good judgements can be made.

Decision making: agreeing priorities and deciding which of the claims competing for the limited money available to support.

Preparation of budgets: once priorities are agreed budgets can be finalised.

Approval: by the most senior level within the organisation.

Each part of an organisation has its own budget. The manager of each department is asked to draw up estimates for the coming year based on the targets set by the board of directors. Because they know best about their department's needs, budgeting begins with managers drawing up draft budgets for their departments. The departments' draft budgets are agreed with senior managers. Then they are put together to form the firm's budget. Finally this is agreed at the most senior level in the firm.

1 What exactly does 'budgeting' mean?

2 When a business sets its wages budget for the next year, why might it be difficult to calculate just how much it will need to spend on paying its workers' wages?

3 Some people say that budgets stop businesses from being run properly. They say that managers should not have to spend valuable time asking for money and then monitoring carefully how it is spent. The managers would get more done if they were allowed to get on with running the business. Discuss whether you agree with this view.

4 Copy out this paragraph, filling in the missing words from the list.

Budgets

A budget is a financial _____. Each department is given a certain amount of _____. If the department does not spend all of this money, it is said to be _____ budget. The budget encourages managers to be more responsible and not to be _____. It provides _____ on how efficiently the department is being run. Problems can arise if the cost of _____ or labour increases as this is beyond the _____ of the managers.

control   funds   feedback   wasteful   plan
within   materials

5 Group activity

Cookie's Crisps found that sales of its traditional range of crisps and snacks were declining. It was rapidly losing its market to new competitors with exciting snacks that appealed more to children. If something was not done, the company would go out of business.

Working in groups of four, share out the roles of R & D manager, production manager, sales manager and senior manager. Hold a meeting to discuss how the budgets should be allocated. Remember, Cookie's is facing a lot of competition and money is tight.

Memo

To: R&D Department
From: Senior Managers
5 April 2001
Increased budget

Your budget for the next year has been doubled to £400,000. Make sure you come up with a new range of snacks that will give us the lead over our competitors.

Memo

To: Production Department/Sales Dept
From: Senior Managers
5 April 2001
Reduced budget

In order to pay for the extra funds going to R&D we have decided to reduce the Production and Sales budgets by £200,000. Please find ways of economising.

Memo

To: Senior Managers
From: R&D
31 August 2001
New range of snacks

Thanks to the increased budget we have developed a new type of snack called 'Cookie's Crunchies'. Once production starts it should give us a market lead over our competitors in the age 5–12 market segment.

Alternatively:
Write an account on how the problem at Cookie's could have been avoided.

6 Windblown Weathervanes

Windblown is a small business that produces wrought-iron weathervanes and other decorative items. The owner, Bernard Hall, produces three-month budgets for the business, one of which is shown below. The actual figures for January are shown as well as the forecast budgets for all three months.

The firm has a pricing policy of selling its products for twice the amount it costs to buy the materials used to make them.

February

Unfortunately, a welding machine breaks down at the beginning of February and takes two weeks to repair. Workers are laid off, making the wage bill for February only £6,000. The firm is only able to sell goods made that month for £16,000.

March

Production is once again in full swing. The repaired machine works well and produces more goods than normal. The material costs for the month are £18,000 but overtime payments have pushed the wage bill up to £12,000.

a Was the spending on materials in January within or outside the budget?

b Use the information for February and March to complete the table. You may want to put the budget onto a spreadsheet.

c Calculate how the actual profit for all three months differs from that forecast by the firm.

d Explain two possible reasons why the firm budgeted for an increase in sales revenue for March.

e Use the case study to explain how budgets have got the potential to demotivate the workforce.

ICT Activity

Produce a graph to show the difference between the actual and budget gross profits for each of the three months.

All figures are £s	January		February		March	
	Actual	Budget	Actual	Budget	Actual	Budget
Sales revenue	28,000	30,000		30,000		32,000
Costs						
Wages	10,000	10,000		10,000		10,000
Materials	14,000	15,000		15,000		16,000
Overheads	2,000	2,000		2,000		2,000
Gross profit	2,000	3,000		3,000		4,000

Unit 3.8 Budgetary and financial control

3.8b Cash flow forecasting and stock control

Cash →	the notes and coins used to settle debts. Cash also includes cheques, credit cards and debit cards, standing orders and direct debits.
Cash flow →	a specialised kind of budget that shows the cash flowing into and out of a business over a given period.
Stock →	the value of the goods and raw materials held by a firm. Stocks may be of raw materials and components used to produce goods, of work in progress, or of finished goods waiting to be sold.
Stock control →	keeping records to make sure that there are enough stocks to keep production going or to sell to customers. It also tries to ensure stocks are not too large.

→ Key terms

Cash flow

It is rare for money to come into a business in equal amounts throughout the year. In most firms there are months when they earn more cash than in others. **Cash** here means payments by cheque, credit card, debit card, standing order and direct debit, as well as notes and coins.

The way money flows into a business depends to some extent on the kind of business. A retail business has a regular flow of cash. But it may have more coming in at weekends than during the rest of the week. A newsagent collects fairly small amounts of money regularly. A furniture shop collects larger amounts of cash, though less often. A firm making Christmas decorations has a lot of cash coming in from September to the end of January, but during the rest of the year it may receive very little.

Firms may have to wait several weeks or months after they have produced goods before being paid for them. Meanwhile, a firm has regular outgoings that need to be paid for. It has to pay its workers every week or every month. Rent, telephones, electricity, gas and so on have to be paid every month or every quarter, although the bills may vary in size. Other bills, such as for transport or materials, vary according to how busy the firm is.

Forecasting cash flow

Firms can estimate those times of the year when they are going to have a surplus or a shortage of cash. They base their estimates on past experience and on the targets they set themselves. The flow of money into and out of a business is shown in a cash flow forecast.

Example

Phillip Reynolds spent several years training as a tailor. He has saved £10,000 and is going to set up in business making high-quality trousers. His bank has let him have an overdraft up to £1,750.

He plans to sell direct to the public through his own shop and to other shops. He already has a contract to sell 50 pairs a month to each of three shops. One of the shops has promised to increase the order to 75 in April; another shop will buy 25 pairs in May, rising to 50 in June. They will all pay for the goods one month after delivery. Phillip estimates sales in his own shop at 350 pairs in March, 325 in April, 370 in May and 400 in June.

He estimates that he can produce 125 pairs of trousers a week. He plans to sell them at £50 a pair in his own shop and for £30 to other shops.

Phillip has rented a shop, with a large workroom at the back, where he will produce the trousers. The rent for the shop and workshop is £500 a month, paid in advance. He has bought machines and equipment second hand, for £3,000. To get started he has bought £3,000 worth of fabric on one month's credit, and expects to spend a similar amount on materials every month. He employs five people in the workshop and pays them each £150 a week. In March he employs someone to run the shop at a salary of £150 a week. He pays 10% National Insurance on all wages and salaries. To start with, Phillip is taking a salary of £200 a week from the business. This increases to £250 in May.

His other costs include rates at £300 per quarter; electricity is estimated at £200 and telephones at £100 a month. He has made a rough estimate of other costs he might have.

To make sure he has a big enough stock of trousers, the workshop opens on 1 January. The shop opens on 1 March. He makes his first delivery to the three other shops at the end of January.

We can use this information to prepare a cash flow forecast for Phillip's business (see below).

In January, the only money coming into the business is the money Phillip invested in the business, that is, his capital.

In the first month his outgoings are the start-up costs of the business and some production costs. In this month the business is not earning anything. However, production has started and the workers have to be paid. All the costs are met out of capital.

In the second month, the business is still building up its stock, and sales are very small. Most costs are again paid out of capital. In fact the capital is not big enough. The net cash flow – the difference between what is coming into the business and what is going out – is a negative amount. The firm is spending more than it is earning. Even so, it still has to pay its bills and needs to draw on the overdraft from the bank.

When Phillip opens his shop his sales increase and the net cash flow becomes positive. He no longer needs to borrow money from the bank and he can pay all his bills from the money coming into the business.

Value of cash flow forecasts

Cash flow forecasts are a useful planning tool.
- If a firm knows in advance that it is going to be short of cash it can arrange an overdraft with its bank. Banks charge less interest on agreed overdrafts than when a firm simply allows itself to go 'into the red'.

Cash flow forecast for Phillip Reynolds (six months to 30 June)

	January £	February £	March £	April £	May £	June £
Cash in						
Capital	10,000					
Cash sales			17,500	16,250	18,500	20,000
Debtors		4,500	4,500	5,250	5,250	6,000
Total cash receipts	10,000	4,500	22,000	21,500	23,750	26,000
Cash out						
Equipment & maintenance	3,000		500		450	200
Creditors		3,000	3,500	2,750	2,800	3,350
Rent	500	500	500	500	500	500
Rates			300			300
Wages & NI	3,300	3,300	3,960	3,960	3,960	3,960
Own salary	880	880	880	880	1,100	1,100
Electricity & telephone	300	300	300	300	300	300
Other costs		60	200	500	600	800
Total cash payments	7,980	8,040	10,140	8,890	9,710	10,510
Net cash flow	2,020	–3,540	11,860	12,610	14,040	15,490
add opening balance	0	2020	–1,520	10,340	22,950	36,990
cash balance carried forward	2,020	–1,520	10,340	22,950	36,990	52,480

Apart from their regular spending, firms often need to buy small items of equipment and other 'one-offs' out of their earnings. They can use their cash flow forecasts to plan such spending so that it happens at a time when they have the cash available. Firms whose trade is seasonal can plan to be especially careful when cash flow is poor.

Cash flow and profit

Cash flow is not the same as profit. Cash flow shows money coming in and going out of a business. Profit is the difference between the cost of goods and the selling price.

- A firm sells goods at a profit. If it has to wait a long time before being paid for the goods, it may not have the cash to pay its bills. The firm is making a profit but fails because it runs out of cash.
- Many profitable small firms fail when other, often bigger, firms are slow to pay their debts. The small firm may not have enough capital to pay its bills while waiting for its debtors to pay.
- Some payments reduce cash but have no effect on profits, for example capital expenditure or repayment of a loan.
- Depreciation (see Unit 3.11b) reduces profit but has no effect on cash.
- Credit sales and credit purchases affect profit and cash at different times.

Stock

Firms need to hold stocks. Large stocks tie up capital. This is because all goods in stock have to be paid for. A manufacturer holding stocks of finished goods has had to pay wages, the cost of storage and the cost of the materials that went into the goods. Until they are sold, goods in stock are paid for out of capital.

Firms hold stocks for a number of reasons:
- to meet orders from their customers without delay;
- to prevent delays in production by making sure there are enough supplies of materials and parts;
- to spread production evenly throughout the year. When sales are seasonal, stocks are built up over a long time and then released over a short period when demand is high;

- shops must have enough stock, in all sizes, colours and designs, of the goods they sell. People are not willing to wait for goods to be ordered.

Stock control

Holding stock is expensive. Space used to hold stock might be used more profitably for selling or producing goods. Firms must keep enough stock to meet their needs, but not so much that it becomes a big expense. Stock control is the system of records used by a firm to keep track of the amount and movement of stocks. A stock control system should at least provide:
- a record of the date when goods were ordered and received;
- a record of when goods were taken out of stock and used;
- a method of making sure that new stock is ordered in time to ensure that it is delivered before the old stock runs out;
- a method of making sure that stock is used in the right order. Normally, the oldest stock is used first.

Modern stock control systems have to be very sensitive, especially where firms use just-in-time methods.

IKEA sells direct to the public from huge outlets like this one. Computerisation is essential for keeping track of sales and stock (© Inter Ikea systems B.V.2001)

Activities

1 What is meant by the term 'stock'?

2 Explain why firms usually try to keep their stock levels as low as possible.

3 Describe the particular problems the following businesses might have with stock:
   a a bakery;
   b a ladies' clothes shop;
   c a petrol station.

4 During a recession, many firms continue to produce goods despite there being a low demand for them. Explain, with reasons, why firms may choose to stockpile their goods rather than cut back, or even stop producing them.

❑ Case Study

5 **Wedding Belles**

Rebecca Bell is planning to start her own business as a wedding dress maker. She already has four jobs lined up, but she has decided to keep her prices low to attract business until she has made a name for herself. With fittings and alterations, it takes Rebecca an average of two months before she is paid for her work.

She places £3,000 of her own money in her bank account, and plans to draw out £850 each month to pay herself a salary. She has the following expenses that she needs to cover each month.

Rent on shop	£600
Repayments on equipment	£200
Assistant's wages	£500
Electricity etc.	£100
Advertising	£200

❑ Case Study

Each dress will cost her £120 for fabric. After making the dress she will receive an average price of £500 per dress. She will be paid when the dress is finished.

She expects that she will only get orders for four dresses each month for the first two months, but with her advertising this should increase to seven a month after that.

Rebecca realises that she will have a cash flow problem and will need an overdraft from her bank.

a Why is it important that Rebecca plans ahead by producing a cash flow forecast?

b Why is it usual for a business such as Rebecca's to need an overdraft?

c Rebecca's bank has asked her what overdraft level she wants to have. Produce a cash flow statement for the first eight months of the business to see how large her overdraft should be.

ICT Activity
Produce Wedding Belles' cash flow forecast on a spreadsheet. Produce a graph of the business's monthly bank balance.

d Discuss what could happen to the business that would result in Rebecca needing a larger overdraft than she expected.

Unit 3.9 Business plans

Setting up a new business needs very careful thought. There are a lot of questions that need to be answered before starting a business. Mistakes can be avoided by drawing up a **business plan** before starting to trade. The kinds of questions that need answering include:

- The type of business to open and where it should be located.
- What start-up and other costs will there be, and how will they be paid for?
- Will the cash flow be good enough to meet payments? If not, will a bank overdraft be needed? If so, when and for how much?
- Where will supplies be bought? Will they give credit? If so, how much and for how long?
- Will staff have to be employed and how many?
- How much should be taken out of the business to live on?
- How much will the business need to earn to cover all the costs? How much profit can be expected?
- How soon will the business make a profit?
- Is there a market?
- How strong is the competition?

It is not only new businesses that need a business plan. Established businesses also benefit from having one. Every business should have a business plan.

What is a business plan?

A business plan sets out in detail what a business is going to do in a given time. It includes forecasts of

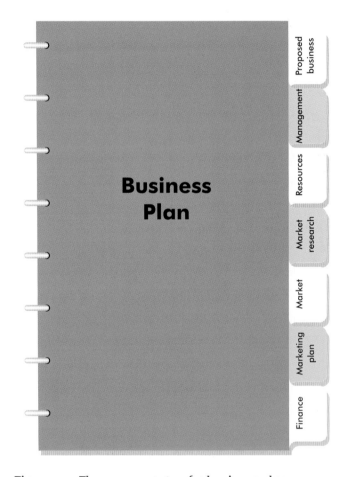

Figure 3.9 The components of a business plan

sales, and budget forecasts for all the main costs. Each part of the plan sets out targets and shows how they are going to be met. Business plans are usually for quite short periods, such as one to three years. It is hard to look further ahead than that with any degree of accuracy.

The main reasons for business plans

- A business plan shows that the business idea is sound. It shows that all aspects of the business have been thought about, and how each aspect can be made to work effectively.
- Banks and other lenders usually insist on a business plan before they lend money to a business.
- People wanting to invest in the business can use the plan to:
  - check that the business is based on sound facts and reasonable expectations;
  - gain some confidence in the management's ability to manage;
  - see that there is a good market for the firm's products;
  - see whether it is worth investing in the firm and get an idea of the return they may earn.
- Plans are also used within the business. Managers can compare what is really happening with the targets in the plan. If the targets are not being met, they may be able to see what is going wrong before it is too late.

What is in a business plan?

In some ways, a business plan is a collection of plans. Not all business plans are the same. What is in a business plan depends on the type of business. It also depends on whether it is a new business or one that has been going for some time. A business plan should contain the following main points.

The business
- name and address of the business;
- for a new business – an explanation of the business idea and why the business is being started;
- for an existing business – a short history of the business and an account of its past performance;
- a statement of the business objectives.

Management
- ownership – whether a sole trader, partnership, public or private limited company;
- main shareholders, and the firm's management structure;

- amount of experience the owners or senior managers have.

The market
- what market research has been done;
- the customers and where they are located – local, national or overseas;
- the competition, if any – how strong it is, where it is located;
- what the product is and how and why it is different from the competition;
- the potential for growth and how it can be achieved.

Marketing plan
- an analysis of the strengths, weaknesses, opportunities and threats (SWOT) of the business;
- how the product is to be sold;
- the marketing mix;
- the cost of each part of the marketing plan.

Resources
- the size and kind of premises needed;
- the number of employees and the kinds of skills that are needed;
- for a manufacturing business, the production methods used;
- an outline of growth plans and estimates of probable future resource needs.

Financial report
- start-up costs (for a new firm) and detailed estimates of running costs;
- main sources of revenue;
- the amount of capital and who owns it;
- details of existing loans and how they are being repaid;
- an estimate of future revenues and costs, also capital needs, including new loans and how they can be repaid;
- a cash flow forecast and the most recent trading, profit and loss account and balance sheet for the firm. A break-even analysis may also be included.

Business prospects
An estimate of the firm's prospects over three to five years. The estimate must be based on facts as evidence that the prospects are realistic.

How business plans are used

- Business plans are useful because they make a business person think through all aspects of the business. A business is more likely to succeed if it has a business plan. It can prevent expensive mistakes from being made. Just writing a business plan may show that a business idea is not likely to be successful.
- They provide a way of measuring a firm's progress. Managers or owners can see whether they have reached the targets they set at various stages in the business plan.
- Banks use them as a basis for deciding whether to lend money to a business.
- Investors use them to help decide whether to invest in a firm and as a way of checking the firm's progress.

Activities

1 What is a business plan?

2 Why is it important that the managers' past experience is included in a business plan?

3 Why would a bank be reluctant to lend money to someone starting a business who had not produced a business plan?

4 Very few businesses expect to make a profit in the first year or longer of trading. Give possible reasons for this.

5 Much research needs to be done before a business plan can be written accurately. Describe three types of research that are needed. In each case say why this research is important.

6 How would these stakeholders benefit from being able to see a firm's business plan:
   a suppliers;
   b investors in the business?

7 **Group activity**
Produce a business plan for an enterprise of your choice. It may be a computer games shop, pop festival, or anything you feel has potential to make money.

The plan should be researched carefully and neatly presented.

Most banks have a small business advisor who may be able to provide you with leaflets or other information to help you get started. You will be able to carry out your research using the Internet or by visiting a bank.

ICT Activity
Research the type of help high street banks can offer people who want to start their own business. An example of a website is www.banking.hsbc.co.uk/smallbusiness.

Case Study

8 Raw Cuts

Steve Hawthorne thought he had it made. He had just received £18,000 from an inheritance and was determined to use this money to start his own business. He had always been a keen collector of music records and CDs, particularly obscure foreign imports, so he thought opening a record shop would be ideal.

The first thing Steve did was to hand in his notice to his employer. This gave him tremendous satisfaction. He then visited his local estate agent and managed to buy a 10-year lease on a shop that was just a short walking distance from his house. The shop was on a quiet road, but it was close enough for Steve to enjoy the benefits of longer lie-ins each morning. Steve paid a lot of money for a sign writer to paint the name of the shop, Raw Cuts, on the front.

Buying stock was more of a problem than Steve expected. He decided to specialise in the music he liked, and importing records from America took longer than he expected. He also discovered that his suppliers were unwilling to give him credit.

A week before he opened he put a notice in the shop window to let passers-by know. On the big day, Steve opened his doors and waited. The only people to visit the shop all day were an old couple who thought the shop was a butcher's. The next day was no better, as was the rest of the week. The few customers who came in did not usually share Steve's musical tastes and were looking for chart music. They also found his prices high and the atmosphere in the shop unfriendly and oppressive.

Six months after opening, Steve had to close down the shop through lack of custom. All his inheritance money had gone and he was forced to try to get his old job back.

a What evidence is there in the case study to suggest that Steve had the wrong attitude to run a successful business?

b Steve did no planning before starting his own business. Describe three mistakes he could have avoided by more careful planning.

c Outline the type of training that would have helped Steve overcome his problems of not having business experience.

d Steve did not need to go to a bank to borrow money. How else could a bank have helped Steve to be successful?

Examination hints

You must read every question carefully. Make sure that you answer the question you have been asked.

Examination hints

- Read what it says on the front of the examination paper carefully.
- Fill in all the information you are asked for on your answer book.
- Always use a blue or black pen in the exam.
- Make sure you know how long the examination will last.

Unit 3.10 Classification of costs

3.10a Types of costs

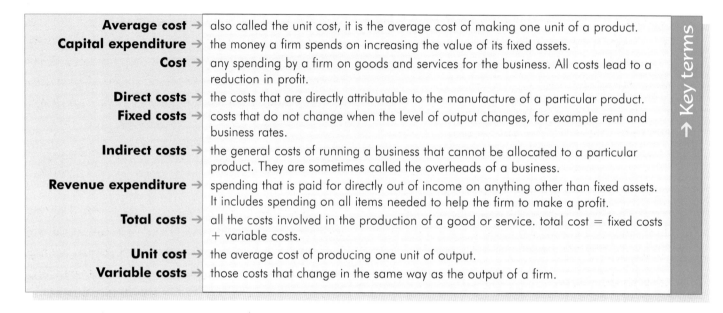

Average cost →	also called the unit cost, it is the average cost of making one unit of a product.
Capital expenditure →	the money a firm spends on increasing the value of its fixed assets.
Cost →	any spending by a firm on goods and services for the business. All costs lead to a reduction in profit.
Direct costs →	the costs that are directly attributable to the manufacture of a particular product.
Fixed costs →	costs that do not change when the level of output changes, for example rent and business rates.
Indirect costs →	the general costs of running a business that cannot be allocated to a particular product. They are sometimes called the overheads of a business.
Revenue expenditure →	spending that is paid for directly out of income on anything other than fixed assets. It includes spending on all items needed to help the firm to make a profit.
Total costs →	all the costs involved in the production of a good or service. total cost = fixed costs + variable costs.
Unit cost →	the average cost of producing one unit of output.
Variable costs →	those costs that change in the same way as the output of a firm.

→ Key terms

Capital and revenue expenditure

Firms have to spend money on a wide range of goods and services, even before they begin trading.

Some of the expenditure is used to buy fixed assets. This is called **capital expenditure**. It is paid for out of capital. The capital comes from the owners (shareholders) or from retained profits. Capital expenditure gives rise to long-term benefits. It is spent on items that last for more than one year. It results in an increase in the value of a firm's fixed assets in its balance sheet. It has no direct effect on a firm's profits. Examples of capital expenditure include:
- the purchase of new or replacement buildings;
- machinery or equipment;
- extending existing premises.

Other expenditure is paid for directly out of income, or revenue. This is called **revenue expenditure** and is used to buy goods and services needed to earn revenue. It consists of money spent on anything other than fixed assets. Revenue expenditure is shown in a firm's trading and profit and loss account. Examples include:

- purchase of raw materials;
- expenses such as wages, telephones, electricity, interest, rent and advertising.

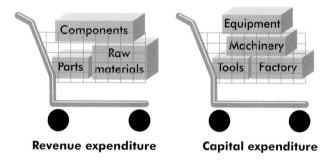

Revenue expenditure   **Capital expenditure**

Figure 3.10 Revenue and capital expenditure

Costs

When a firm uses resources to buy or use goods and services, there is a cost. All firms have costs. Some costs are essential, like spending on raw materials or rent for premises. There is more choice about some other costs. For example, firms do not have to spend on advertising, but it helps the firm to sell its goods and to make a profit. Firms have to incur costs to make a profit. However, costs *reduce* a firm's profit. Lower costs mean higher profits. Costs can be classified in a number of ways.

Fixed and variable costs

Some costs stay the same and do not change with the amount produced. These are **fixed costs**. They include items such as rent and business rates, the interest on long-term loans and the cost of leasing machinery. However, fixed costs do not stay the same forever. There comes a point when a firm cannot produce any more with its existing assets. It may need new machinery or to extend its factory. Fixed costs then rise, but stay fixed over a new range of output.

Other costs change as output changes. If a firm increases its output it has to spend more on raw materials. The cost of running the machines probably changes if output rises or falls. These are examples of **variable costs**. They go up or down in the same way as output. Often they move in the same proportion as output, so that a 20% change in output produces a 20% change in variable costs.

Total and average costs

When variable and fixed costs are added together they are called **total costs**. These costs are shown in detail in a firm's trading and profit and loss account.

One way of finding the cost of one item of output is to calculate its **average cost**, which is also called the **unit cost**:

$$\frac{\text{total cost}}{\text{output}} = \text{average cost}$$

Average cost changes all the time with output. It does so because the fixed costs are spread over a larger or smaller output.

Example

Suppose a firm has fixed costs of £100,000 and variable costs are £2 per item.

Output	Fixed costs	Variable costs	Average costs
100,000	£100,000	£200,000	£3
150,000	£100,000	£300,000	£2

Average costs explains why goods become cheaper when output increases. As output rises, average costs fall and so does the price of the goods in the shops.

Direct and indirect costs

Some of the costs of manufacturing arise directly from the production of a particular product. The **direct cost** can be identified for each item a firm produces. For example, the cost of buying raw materials or components is directly related to the production of a particular product. Similarly, the wages of the workers on the factory floor, and the cost of the electricity used for running the machines, are direct costs. A fall in output results in a fall in direct costs. Fewer raw materials and components are needed, and fewer workers and less electricity are used.

$$\begin{array}{c} \text{direct} \\ \text{costs} \end{array} = \begin{array}{c} \text{cost of raw} \\ \text{materials} \end{array} + \begin{array}{c} \text{direct labour} \\ \text{costs} \end{array} + \begin{array}{c} \text{direct} \\ \text{expenses} \end{array}$$

There are other costs that cannot be identified with a particular product. These are **indirect costs** and are shared across all the activities of a company. They include the costs of telephones, sales and marketing, rent and rates, company vehicles and administration. They are the general costs of running a business and are often referred to as overheads. Firms try to keep indirect costs as low as possible. Higher indirect costs mean lower profits.

BUSINESS ASPECTS

Firms are careful not to include capital expenditure in their revenue expenditure. The effect of doing so is to reduce profit.

It also means that the value of the fixed assets is stated wrongly in the balance sheet. This in turn results in the firm's capital being wrongly stated. This might affect the value of the firm's shares. It might also make it harder to borrow money.

Marginal cost

This is the cost of producing one extra unit of output. It is equal to the increase in total costs resulting from the production of one more unit. In practice, firms rarely produce one extra item, but a given extra volume. Because fixed costs do not change with output, marginal cost is made up of variable costs. Marginal cost is sometimes used by firms when pricing goods, particularly where they charge different prices to different customers.

Example

Suppose a firm sells 1,000 units at £12 each. Its fixed costs are £5,000 and its variable costs are £4 per unit.

	£	£
Sales		12,000
Fixed costs	5,000	
Variable costs, £4 per unit	4,000	9,000
Profit		4,000

The average cost of production is £9 per unit.

If an overseas buyer offered to purchase 1,000 units at a price of £9 a unit, the firm might be tempted to turn down the order. On the face of it there would be no profit in the order at that price. However, it is worth looking at the figures, taking the potential new order into account.

	£	£
Sales (1,000 × £12 + 1,000 × £9)		21,000
Fixed costs	5,000	
Variable costs (2,000 × £4)	8,000	13,000
Profit		8,000

The average cost has fallen to £6.50. The cost of producing the extra 1,000 units is £4,000. The marginal cost of 1,000 units is £4 per unit.

Activities

1 Explain the difference between the terms 'cost' and 'price'.

2 Why are costs such as rent called 'fixed'?

3 Some of the costs facing a fish and chip shop are listed below. Copy the table on the next page and put the costs in the correct columns.
- Potato-peeling machine
- Fish
- Cash till
- Advertising
- Microwave oven
- Plastic carrier bags

Capital expenditure	Revenue expenditure

4 a Explain the difference between a direct and an indirect cost.

  b Give an example of both a direct and an indirect cost that a manufacturer of garden furniture is likely to have.

5 Calculate the values of the missing numbers *a* to *e*.

Output (items)	Fixed costs	Variable costs	Total costs	Average costs
1	£100	£40	£140	£140
2	*a*	£60	*d*	*e*
3	£100	*b*	£180	£60
4	£100	£100	*c*	£50

6 A trader's only fixed costs are his doughnut-making machines that can each produce a maximum of 300 items per hour. Such machines cost £4,000 each. Construct a graph to show the business's fixed costs over the production range 0–1,000 doughnuts per hour.

7 A manufacturer of electric kettles has fixed costs of £10,000 each month and variable costs of £12 for each kettle it produces. The firm sells the kettles to retailers for £20 each.

   a Calculate the firm's profit if it makes and sells 2,000 kettles each month.

   b One month the firm gets an unexpected order for 3,000 kettles, but the purchaser is only prepared to pay £16 per kettle. Show why it would be worth the firm selling these extra kettles at the lower price.

□ Case Study

8 TGB Washers

A dishwasher manufacturer, TGB Washers, needs to replace one of its welding machines when the lease expires. There are two new types available: Samson and Thor. Samson is cheaper to lease at £500 per month but is more expensive to operate, with labour costs of £2 for each dishwasher made. Thor's lease is £800 per month, but labour costs are £1.50 per dishwasher. The normal range of monthly output for the company is between 550 and 800 dishwashers.

□ Case Study

Complete questions a and b below on a spreadsheet.

   a Copy and complete the table below using the information you have been given in the case study.

   b Produce a graph of the average costs against output for both Samson and Thor machines. Your graph should have axes like this:

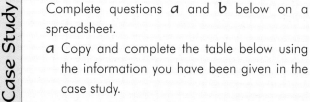

   c Using the information you have been given, and the table and graph you have produced, write a report to the finance manager explaining clearly which of the two machines you would recommend the firm to lease.

Output	Samson				Thor			
	Fixed costs	Variable costs	Total costs	Average costs	Fixed costs	Variable costs	Total costs	Average costs
400								
500								
600								
700								
800								

Unit 3.10 Classification of costs

3.10b Break-even

Break-even →	the output at which a firm's total revenue is equal to its total costs. At this point the firm is not making a profit or a loss. All output below this point is a loss. All output beyond the break-even point is a profit.
Total revenue →	the total amount earned by a firm from its business. Usually total revenue equals total sales.

New firms need to estimate how much they must produce before they make a profit. Existing firms may use **break-even** analysis because they need to know:

- the profit or loss at any level of output or sales;
- the effect on profits of a change in their costs;
- the output needed to achieve a certain level of profit;
- the effect on profit of a change in price.

Break-even is the output at which a firm's total revenue equals its total costs. This output is called the break-even point. At this point the firm is not making either a profit or a loss. Break-even can be worked out either in a table, by graph or by calculation.

Example

Suppose a firm has fixed costs of £20,000 and its variable costs are £5 for each unit produced. It sells its product at £10 per unit. Assume that it sells all its output. What is the break-even point?

The table shows that the break-even point is at an output of 4,000 units. If the firm produces more than 4,000 units it will make a profit; anything less than 4,000 means a loss.

The same information can also be shown as a graph:

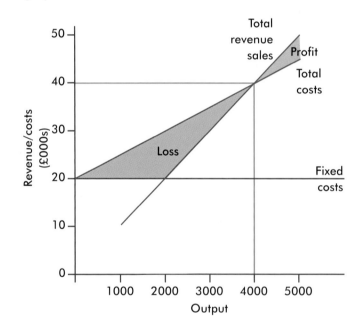

Figure 3.11 Break-even chart

No. of units	Fixed costs (£)	Variable costs (£)	Total costs (£)	Sales (£)	Profit/ loss (£)
0	20,000	0	20,000		(20,000)
1,000	20,000	5,000	25,000	10,000	(15,000)
2,000	20,000	10,000	30,000	20,000	(10,000)
3,000	20,000	15,000	35,000	30,000	(5,000)
4,000	20,000	20,000	40,000	40,000	
5,000	20,000	25,000	45,000	50,000	5,000

- The vertical axis is always revenue/costs and is measured in money terms.
- The horizontal axis is always output/sales measured in units.
- The total costs line always starts on the vertical axis at the fixed costs line. This is because the cost of producing zero units is the fixed costs. There are no variable costs at zero output.
- The firm is making a profit to the right of the break-even point. To the left of the break-even point it is making a loss.
- A graph is easier to use than a table because the cost and revenue lines can be projected forward to show profit at different levels of output.

The formula for calculating break-even point:

$$\frac{\text{fixed costs}}{\text{selling price per unit} - \text{variable costs per unit}}$$

Example

Suppose a firm's fixed costs are £10,000, its variable costs per unit are £5 and its selling price is £7:

$$\text{break-even point} = \frac{£10,000}{(7-5)} = 5,000 \text{ units.}$$

BUSINESS ASPECTS

Contribution analysis

'Contribution' is the amount that is contributed by a sale towards fixed costs and profit. It is calculated by deducting variable costs from selling price.

contribution = selling price – variable costs

For example, if an article is sold for £10 and its variable costs are £6 per unit, the remainder of £4 is a contribution towards fixed costs and the profit for that item.

If the fixed costs are less than £4 per unit, a profit is made. Therefore:

contribution – fixed costs = profit

In this example, profit can be calculated for the firm. Suppose its fixed costs are £600 and it sells 200 units a week:

200 × contribution of £4 = £800
fixed costs = £600
profit = £200

Contribution is a useful tool that can be used to calculate break-even point or to see the effects of changes in sales, fixed costs, variable costs or profit margins.

The formula for calculating break-even point can be restated in terms of contribution:

$$\text{break-even point} = \frac{\text{fixed costs}}{\text{contribution}}$$

Thus a firm with fixed costs of £600 and a contribution of £4 will have a break-even point of £600 ÷ 4 = 150

Contribution is a useful tool to use in 'What if?' situations. It is possible to calculate the answers to questions such as ' What if fixed costs rise by 10%?' or 'What if wages and therefore variable costs increased by 6%?' or 'What if the profit margin was increased from 20% to 25%?'.

Activities

1 Complete the following passage by choosing the missing words from the list below it.

Break-even

A firm needs to know its break-even output, because if it produces any _____ than this it will make a loss. To calculate the break-even point, the business must know both its total costs and its _____. Total costs consist of the firm's _____ costs and its variable costs. Sales (or total _____) is the amount of money the firm gets from selling its products. Fixed costs remain the same regardless of how much is _____, while _____ costs increase as the firm produces more. A firm will make a _____ if it is able to produce more than its break-even output.

revenue	produced	variable	profit	less
	sales	fixed		

2 Using the equation or a graph, calculate the break-even levels of output in the following situations:

a fixed costs: £3,000 per month; variable costs: £15 per item; Price: £25;

b Variable costs: £12 per item;
price per item: £20; fixed costs: £1,000 per week.

3 Breaking Glass

Helen Walsh plans to run a part-time business based on her hobby of engraving glass. She is a good artist and able to produce attractive decorations and inscriptions on wine glasses. In the past she has given these glasses away as presents to friends and family, but she believes that there is a market for selling them.

Taking the advice of a friend, she has done some calculations to see how profitable the business could be. In the past she has bought the glasses individually at £3.50 each, but she has arranged a deal with her supplier for a lower price if she buys more than 20 glasses in a week. She sells the engraved glasses for £8 each to her customers.

Number of glasses purchased each week	Unit price
20 or less	£3.50
21 or more	£2.50

In addition to the cost of buying the glasses, she will need to pay:

- hire of an industrial engraving machine (her old one is not good enough for large volumes) – £40 per week;
- wrapping paper and box – 50p per glass.

a Why is it a good idea for Helen to hire the engraving equipment rather than buying it outright?

b What is Helen's weekly break-even output if she pays £3.50 for the glasses?

ICT Activity

On a spreadsheet show how much it would cost Helen to produce 0, 5, 10, 15 and 20 glasses each week. Add how much revenue she would get from selling the finished products and the profit she would earn. Produce a graph to show Helen's break-even point.

c If Helen discovered she was not selling enough glasses to reach her break-even point, discuss the options that are open to her.

d Why do you think the glass supplier is prepared to reduce the price when a large number of glasses are bought each week?

e Calculate Helen's profit if she sells:
  i 15 glasses each week;
  ii 30 glasses each week.

f If Helen found that she was not making as much profit as she had expected from the venture, why might she still continue with the business?

g Helen feels that she should be earning £12 per hour from the business. If it takes 30 minutes to produce each glass, what price should she charge to achieve this target? State any assumptions you are making when you calculate your answer.

h Helen is not sure what pricing strategy to use. Explain why marginal cost pricing is probably not the best choice for her. Describe another pricing strategy that would be more appropriate.

Unit 3.11 Company final accounts

3.11a The balance sheet

Assets →	everything owned by a business, organisation or person that can be given a money value.
Balance sheet →	a statement of the assets, liabilities and capital of a business, on a certain date.
Capital →	the funds invested in a business that enable it to obtain the resources needed to run the business. Everything used by the owners for the purpose of running a business are part of capital.
Creditors →	other firms or individuals to whom a business owes money. They are shown as a liability in the balance sheet.
Current assets →	assets that change in value each time a transaction is made. They consist of cash (including money in the bank), debtors and stock.
Current liabilities →	the liabilities of a business that must be paid within one year.
Debtors →	those who owe money to a business. They are part of a firm's current assets.
Depreciation →	the amount taken off the value of a fixed asset as a result of wear and tear and the passage of time.
Fixed assets →	the assets of a business that have a long life. They will appear in a firm's balance sheet over more than one year. Examples include premises, machinery, fixtures and fittings and vehicles.
Liabilities →	the money owed by a firm to individuals or other firms.
Liquid assets →	assets that can easily be changed into cash. Cash is the most liquid asset of all, followed by money in the bank, debtors and stock, in that order.
Liquidity →	the ability of a firm to pay its short-term debts as they become due. A firm's liquidity depends on how easily it can turn its current assets into cash.
Net value →	the value of an asset after depreciation has been deducted.
Reserves →	the retained profits in a business that have been built up over a period of time.
Retained profits →	the part of a firm's profit that is kept in the business and not distributed to the owners.
Shareholders' funds →	the part of a firm's funds that is owned by the shareholders. It consists of the share capital plus retained profits held in the reserves.
Working capital →	the funds that are needed for the day-to-day running of a business.

From time to time every business needs to know what it is worth, what it owns and what it owes to others. This information is shown in a **balance sheet**. Every limited company must by law draw up a balance sheet at the end of its financial year and send a copy to the Registrar of Companies.

The balance sheet

The balance sheet shows a firm's:

- assets – what the business owns and the resources used in the business;
- liabilities – what the business owes to other people or firms;
- capital – what the business owes to its owners.

A balance sheet must always balance according to the formula:

$$\text{assets} = \text{liabilities} + \text{capital}$$

The value of each item may change, but the two sides of the formula must always be equal, or 'in balance'. Someone must own the assets of a business.

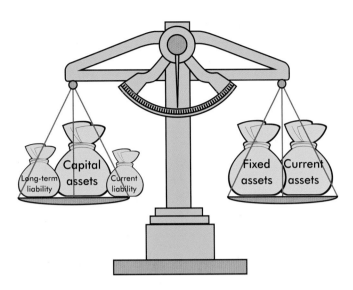

Figure 3.12 Liabilities and assets

Example

If a firm buys an asset for £50,000 and pays a deposit of £25,000 but owes the supplier £25,000, it will have assets of £50,000, liabilities of £25,000 and capital of £25,000. When it pays the rest of the money to the supplier, the firm has assets of £50,000, no liabilities and capital of £50,000.

There are several ways of setting out a balance sheet. A typical example will look like the one opposite.

Strictly speaking, a balance sheet is not an account. It is a summary of the balances in the firm's accounts at a certain date. It is only accurate on that date, so the heading is always 'as at' the date. There are some rules about the way a balance sheet should be set out.

- The **fixed assets** should be shown first, followed by the **current assets**.
- Current assets mainly consist of stock, **debtors**, cash in the bank and cash held in the business, and should be stated in that order.
- It is usual to deduct **current liabilities** from current assets to show **working capital**.
- The net assets employed will be equal to the capital employed in the business.

We will now take a closer look at the main parts of the balance sheet.

Assets

Everything that a business owns, and that has a money value, is part of its assets. A business cannot exist

Haycraft Limited
Balance Sheet as at 31 December 2001

	At cost £000		Net value £000
Fixed assets			
Premises	250		250
Fixtures and fittings	98		80
Machinery	250		190
Vehicles	88		75
	686		595
Current assets			
Stock	84		
Debtors	88		
Bank	77		
Cash	23	272	
Less current liabilities			
Bank overdraft	47		
Dividends proposed	40		
Creditors	75	162	
Working capital			110
			695
Less long-term liabilities			
Bank loan	20		
100 10% Debentures of £1,000	100		120
Net assets employed			£575
Financed by			
Issued capital			
300,000 £1 Ordinary Shares fully paid	300		
200,000 £1 8% Preference Shares fully paid	200	500	
General reserves	63		
Profit & loss account	12	75	
Shareholders' funds			575
Capital employed			£575

unless it has assets. The assets are the resources used in the business. There are two main types of assets:

Fixed assets

Those assets that have a long life. They are likely to appear in the balance sheet over more than one year. Examples include premises, machinery and equipment, vehicles, and office furniture and equipment. Fixed assets are only sold when they come to the end of their useful life. So, for example, a coach company may sell its coaches after seven years. They are at the end of their useful life for that firm, but may be used by the buyer for another 20 years.

Fixed assets can be shown in the balance sheet at two different figures.
- They are shown 'at cost', which is the price at which they were bought.
- They are also shown 'at **net value**', also called the 'book value'. It is the value of assets 'at cost' minus **depreciation**. Fixed assets, other than premises, are worth less as time goes by. This loss in value is called depreciation (see Unit 3.11b). The 'net value' is shown so that the balance sheet gives a true value of the fixed assets.

Current assets

Assets whose value changes all the time. For example, every time goods are sold the stock goes down. Cash sales increase cash, credit sales cause debtors to rise. When a debtor pays a bill the money in the bank or in cash rises. When a firm pays its bills the money in the bank falls.

Current assets are **liquid assets**. They can be turned easily into cash. Cash (which includes money in the bank) is the most liquid asset. It is followed by debtors and stock, in that order. Current assets are always shown in the balance sheet in the reverse order of liquidity. How quickly and easily a firm can change its assets into cash determines its liquidity. An aeroplane manufacturer has

Factory warehouse showing stocks of components

a lower liquidity than a bread manufacturer. Liquidity is important because it affects a firm's cash flow and its ability to pay its short-term debts.

Liabilities

The liabilities are what a firm owes to individuals or other firms. There are two main types of liability:
1 **Current liabilities** are the short-term debts of the firm. These are debts that have to be paid within one year. They are mostly trade **creditors**, that is, other firms the business owes money to. Like current assets the figure changes all the time, as goods are bought on credit and debts are paid. A bank overdraft is also included because it changes as money is put into and taken out of the current account.
2 **Long-term liabilities** are debts that are not paid for more than one year. They are mainly loans such as bank loans, mortgages and debentures. They are sometimes called the loan capital of a business.

Capital

When a business is started money is used to buy or rent premises, stock, tools, equipment and all the other things needed to run the business. These are the assets of the business. They are the resources needed to run that business. The assets all have a value and are equal to the firm's **capital** minus any debts (liabilities).

The capital is equal to what the business owes to its owners. If the business is closed, all the assets are sold. Part of the money is used to pay off the debts of the business. What is left over belongs to the owners and equals the firm's capital.

Working capital

The funds needed to pay for the day-to-day running of a business are called its working capital. The formula for calculating the working capital is:

working capital = current assets – current liabilities

Working capital is important to a business.
- It is used to pay the everyday costs of running the business, such as wages, creditors, expenses such as telephones, heating and lighting, and to buy stocks.
- It is a measure of a firm's liquidity. If working capital is too low a firm will have a cash flow problem.

Working capital must be big enough to ensure these factory workers' wages can be met each week

It cannot pay its bills on time. At worst, if working capital is very low a firm may become insolvent and have to close down.

- Working capital should not be too big. It should be enough to cover all the current liabilities with a little to spare, in case of emergencies. If it is greater than this, resources that could be used for other purposes are being wasted.

Reserves

Profits that are not paid to the shareholders are kept in the business. These **retained profits** are built up in the company's **reserves**, often over several years. Since the reserves are made up of profits that have not been paid to the shareholders, they are shown as part of **shareholders' funds** in the balance sheet. The reserves are not held as cash or in a special bank account. The funds are probably invested. Reserves are an important way of financing a company's expansion.

Making use of the balance sheet

The balance sheet shows the assets of a business and where it gets its funds from. It is useful to three main groups of people.

1 **Managers** – by looking at the balance sheet they can see how well the firm is performing. They can compare one year's balance sheet with those of previous years to see what changes have taken place.

The balance sheet shows:
- the value of the firm's assets, and of its liabilities;
- whether it is using its resources well, for example a firm's stocks may be very high or it may have a great deal of cash that is not being used.

2 **Shareholders** – they use the balance sheet in a similar way to the managers. They also want to see whether it is worth buying more shares or to sell their shares.

3 **Outside parties** – the balance sheet is one of the documents that limited companies have to send to the Registrar of Companies each year. By paying a small fee anyone can look at the accounts at Companies House. Outside parties may be interested for several reasons:
- a person or firm thinking of buying shares wants to be sure that their money is safe and will earn a good rate of return;
- a firm may be thinking of taking over a company. Looking at the balance sheet and the other accounts is a good starting point. They look for assets, like land, that may be undervalued;
- a firm thinking of doing business with a company may look at its balance sheet to see if it is financially sound. For example, it does not want to give credit to a firm that has a low working capital.

Buildings and land – fixed assets

Activities

1 Fill in the missing words to complete each of these statements.

  a The net value of a machine is what it is worth with _____ taken off.

  b Retained profits are the funds left in the business that have not been distributed to the company's _____.

  c If a company is in a position to pay its short-term debts, it is said to be _____.

  d _____ are the people to whom the business is in debt.

  e The difference between a firm's current assets and its current liabilities is its _____ capital.

  f _____ are funds that the company has built up over a period of years.

  g Items the company owns that have a long life are called _____ assets.

  h The total face value of the company's shares is known as its share _____.

2 Rearrange the entries in the table so they go under the correct headings.

Long-term liabilities	Fixed assets
Machinery	Bank loan
Cash	Creditors
Premises	Current bank balance

Current liabilities	Liquid assets
Vehicles	Mortgage
Debtors	Debentures
Fixtures and fittings	Bank overdraft

3 Suggest reasons why a company might choose to invest some of its reserves by buying shares in a competitor's business.

4 It is sometimes said that a balance sheet is out of date as soon as it has been published. Explain why this may be the case.

Case Study

5 National Power plc

The table below shows a summary of National Power's balance sheet for 2000. National Power produces and sells energy both in the UK and abroad. Some of the figures for the 1999 results have been omitted.

Balance sheet of National Power plc as at 31 March 2000

	2000 £m	1999 £m
Fixed assets	4,320	5,027
Current assets		
Stock	57	147
Debtors	647	637
Investments	1,269	824
Cash	855	341
Total current assets	2,828	a
Less Total current liabilities	1,185	d
Working capital	1,643	f
Less Long-term liabilities	3,536	3,023
Total assets Less Current Liabilities	5,963	e
Net assets employed	2,427	c
Capital and reserves		
Share capital	558	620
Reserves	848	783
Profit and loss account	877	1,084
Others	144	142
Capital employed	2,427	b

  a Calculate the values of the missing figures a to f.

  b During the financial year shown in the table, National Power sold off some power stations. Show how the effects of these sales can be seen in the table.

  c Comment on what aspects of the balance sheet look healthy for the company, and which are not so good.

Unit 3.11 Company final accounts

3.11b The trading and profit and loss account

Cost of goods sold →	the cost of making or buying the goods sold by a business.
Depreciation →	the amount taken off the value of a fixed asset as a result of wear and tear and the passage of time.
Gross profit →	the difference between the total income from sales and the cost of the goods sold.
Net profit →	is the gross profit minus all expenses.
Trading account →	one of the final accounts in which the gross profit of a business is calculated.
Opening stock →	the amount of stock held by a business at the start of a new financial year.
Overheads →	the general costs of running a business, including heating and lighting, rent and rates, office expenses and telephones. They are indirect costs that are not directly related to the cost of making or selling a product.
Profit and loss account →	a statement that lists all the running expenses, or revenue expenditure, of a business and in which net profit is calculated.
Purchases →	the buying of all stock needed by a business in order to produce sales.

The main reason for going into business is to make a profit. Thus all businesses need to work out the size of the profit they have made. They usually do so on the same date, at the end of their accounting year. They can therefore compare exactly the same period for one year with another.

Limited companies must, by law, draw up accounts that show their profit during a year. These accounts are sent to the Registrar of Companies and can be looked at by anyone who is interested in the company. Sole traders and partnership need to know whether the business is making a profit, and how much profit it is making.

Measuring profit

There are two kinds or, more accurately, measures of profit.

1 **Gross profit** – the difference between the total money earned from sales and the **cost of the goods sold**. The gross profit is worked out in the **trading account**.

2 **Net profit** – what is left after taking all the expenses of running a business away from the gross profit. The net profit is worked out in the **profit and loss account**.

    net profit = gross profit – running expenses

Trading account

Trading is the buying and selling of goods or services in exchange for money. The trading account shows the profit made by a firm from its trading operations. The main income is from sales. To earn those sales a firm has to spend money on either making goods or services or buying them from other firms to sell.

Business does not stop at the end of one year and start afresh at the beginning of the next. It is a non-stop process. So, apart from new firms, most businesses start their year with stock left over from the year before. These goods are the **opening stock**. During the year the firm buys new supplies. The goods a firm sells during the year consist of the opening stock plus the **purchases**. However, it does not sell all the goods it buys, partly because it needs some stock to sell at the start of its new financial year. The stock left at the end of the year is taken away from the opening stock and purchases. The figure that results is the cost of the goods sold in that year.

The value of the closing stock is found by adding up all the goods left at the end of the year and multiplying them by the price at which they were bought. Adding up the stock is called stocktaking. The closing

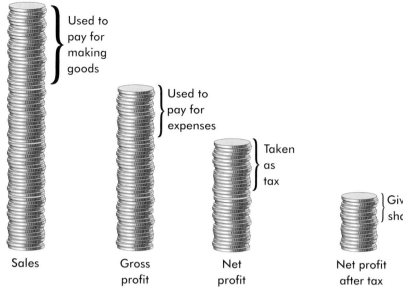

Figure 3.13 Gross and net profit

Sales | Gross profit | Net profit | Net profit after tax | Retained profit

stock from one financial year is the opening stock for the next year.

$$\text{cost of goods sold} = \text{opening stock} + \text{purchases} - \text{closing stock}$$

The gross profit for the year is worked out by taking away the cost of the goods sold from the sales in the trading account.

$$\text{gross profit} = \text{sales} - \text{cost of goods sold}$$

The trading account can be shown as a separate account or, as in the example below, it can be combined with the profit and loss account.

Profit and loss account

The trading account only shows the cost of the goods actually bought and sold by a business to find the gross profit. In order to make that gross profit, a firm has many other costs that have to be met. These are the general expenses of running the business. They include expenses such as rent of premises, rates, telephones, heating and lighting, wages and salaries. The costs of these expenses are listed in the profit and loss account. The total of these costs is taken away from the gross profit to find the **net profit** for the year.

$$\text{net profit} = \text{gross profit} - \text{expenses}$$

The net profit is the true profit for the business. It is the profit made by the business as a whole before taxes have been paid.

The profit and loss account includes only expenses for the year in question. For this reason any expenses paid in advance, such as insurance, have to be taken away. This is shown in the example for Haycraft Limited, given in the table on the next page. In the same way, any money that is owing also has to be added into the account, as in the case of rent.

What happens to net profit?

All firms, including sole traders and partnerships, have to decide how to use their net profit. The way net profit is divided up is shown in an appropriation account at the end of the profit and loss account. Before deciding how to use net profit, limited companies must pay corporation tax. It is taken away from the net profit to show the net profit after tax. Partnerships and sole traders do not pay corporation tax.

Sole traders and partnerships may decide to take all the profit as income from the business. In a partnership it is shared equally or as laid down in the partnership agreement. Limited companies have to decide how much dividend to pay their shareholders. The dividend is 'declared' at so much per share.

Example

In the sample balance sheet on page 184:

- The 200,000 £1, 8% preference shares are paid their dividend first. This is £16,000 and is always the same.
- The 300,000 ordinary shareholders are then paid at a rate of so much per share. If, for example, the

directors decided to pay a dividend of 8p per share they are paid a total of £24,000 (300,000 x £0.08).

- Any profit left over is kept as 'retained profit' and added to the firm's reserves. In the example above, the retained profit is £12,000.

Haycraft Limited
Trading and Profit and Loss Account for the year ended 31 December 2001

	£ 000	£ 000
Sales		758
Less:		
Opening stock on 1 Jan 01	96	
Purchases	385	
	481	
Closing stock on 31 Dec 01	118	
Cost of goods sold		363
Gross profit		395
Wages and salaries	123	
Heating and lighting	34	
Rent	39	
Add Rent due	13	52
Rates		16
Telephones		11
Advertising		18
Insurance	14	
Less paid in advance	2	12
Administration		22
Bad debts		9
Depreciation		
Furniture & fittings at 10%	8	
Machinery at 12%	23	
Vehicles at 20%	15	46	343
Net profit		£52

Depreciation

Suppose a firm buys a new machine for £50,000. After seven years it decides to replace the machine with a new, faster, more efficient machine. The firm sells the old machine for £20,000. The 'loss' of £30,000 is a result of **depreciation**.

Instead of suffering the loss of £30,000 in value all at once, it is better if the cost is spread over several years. Firms do this by making an allowance each year for the fall in the value of their fixed assets. This allowance is called depreciation and is shown in the profit and loss account.

The loss in the machine's value is a cost. It is the cost that the firm has to pay for the use of the machine over the seven-year period it uses it for. Like all other costs, the effect of depreciation is to reduce profit. It is better to reduce profit by a certain amount each year than to do so in one lump sum at the end of the asset's life. In this way, the loss of value is spread over the useful life of the asset. It also gives a more accurate figure for net profit.

Depreciation applies only to fixed assets, other than land. This is because land and premises tend to increase in value. They rarely lose their value. There are three main reasons why fixed assets lose their value:

- the passage of time – a vehicle may work perfectly but it becomes worth less simply because it is older;
- wear and tear;
- obsolescence – equipment of all kinds can become out of date and be replaced by more modern models.

The value of fixed assets is shown in the balance sheet after depreciation has been taken off. This is the 'book value' or 'net value' of the asset. This makes sure that the value of the asset shown in the balance sheet is true and fair.

Calculating depreciation

There are two ways of calculating depreciation:

1 *Straight line method*
Under this method an asset is depreciated by a fixed sum every year during its useful life. The amount that is deducted is found by estimating the value of the asset at the end of its life (the residual value). This residual value is taken away from the cost of buying the asset, and dividing by its expected life.

Formula for depreciation by the straight line method:

$$\frac{\text{original cost of asset} - \text{estimated residual value}}{\text{estimated years of useful life}}$$

Example
A van is bought for £25,000 on 1 January. It is expected to have a value of £5,000 at the end of its useful life of five years.

$$\text{depreciation} = \frac{£25,000 - £5,000}{5 \text{ years}}$$

$$= \frac{£20,000}{5} = £4,000 \text{ a year}$$

The asset is depreciated in the profit and loss account by £4,000 each year. £4,000 is 'written off' its value in the balance sheet each year.

2 Reducing balance method

Under this method a fixed percentage is taken off the net value of the asset as it was shown in the last balance sheet.

Example

A machine is bought for £5,000. It is to be depreciated by 20% a year using the reducing balance method. At the end of three years the value of the machine can be calculated as follows:

	£
Purchase price	50,000
Less	
Year 1: Depreciation – £50,000 × 20%	10,000
Net value end of year 1	40,000
Less	
Year 2: Depreciation – £40,000 × 20%	8,000
Value end of year 2	32,000
Less	
Year 3: Depreciation – £32,000 × 20%	6,400
Value at end of year 3	25,600

Activities

1 Explain the difference between gross and net profit.

2 Not all businesses try to make as high a profit as possible. Outline two other objectives that a business might have.

3 A firm has £6,000 worth of stock at the beginning of the year and £8,000 at the end. The firm spends £30,000 on stock during the course of the year. How much is the firm's cost of goods sold?

4 A business buys a new sanding machine for £12,000. The machine is expected to have a useful life of eight years, after which it would be sold for

£2,000. Using the straight line method, calculate the value of the annual depreciation for the machine.

Case Study

5 Barrow Taxis

Barrow Taxis operates a fleet of 15 cars. The firm has a policy of buying its vehicles new and keeping them for four years. At the beginning of 2001 Barrow Taxis bought four new cars for £60,000.

The firm uses the reducing balance method when calculating the annual depreciation of the vehicle. The firm depreciates the cars at 25% of their net value at the end of the year. The company keeps a record of the amount of depreciation of the four new cars over their life at Barrow Taxis.

Year	Value of car at start of year	Value of car at end of year	Value of depreciation
2001	£60,000	£45,000	
2002			
2003			
2004			

a Why might a car used as a taxi depreciate at a different rate from a car used by a family?

b What is meant by the 'book value' of a company's assets?

c Copy out the table above and complete the missing cells.

d Draw a graph of the amount of depreciation each year.

e Why is it important to Barrow Taxis that their vehicles are depreciated each year?

f Why is the declining balance more suitable than the straight line method when calculating the depreciation of cars?

ICT Activity

Answer questions c and d on a spreadsheet.

Unit 3.11 Company final accounts

3.11c Ratios and the interpretation of accounts

Acid test ratio →	a measure of the money a business has readily available to pay its debts quickly. It is calculated by taking stock away from the total of the current assets and dividing the result by the total value of current liabilities.
Current ratio →	a measure of a firm's ability to pay its debts. It is calculated by dividing current assets by current liabilities. It is also known as the liquidity ratio and the working capital ratio.
Liquidity ratio →	another name for the current or working capital ratio.
Margin →	profit expressed as a percentage of sales.
Rate of turnover →	the number of times average stock is sold (turned over) during a period of time. It measures the speed at which stock is sold.
Return on capital employed (ROCE) →	the profit made by a firm as a percentage of the capital used in the business. It measure how much the owner's capital earned from the business.
Working capital ratio →	another name for the current or liquidity ratio.

Balance sheets and profit and loss accounts on their own do not give a very clear idea of how well a company is doing. The balance sheet, for example, shows the value of the assets and liabilities and whether they have gone up or down. The profit and loss account shows the size of profit a firm has made. But it does not show the profitability of the business.

Most of the stakeholders want to know more than the balance sheet and the profit and loss accounts are able to show. Managers, owners, employees, customers and suppliers want a more detailed idea of how a firm is performing. There are some simple ratios that can be used to interpret the totals that are shown in the accounts. These ratios show the relationships between two or more parts of the accounts. Three important sets of ratios are:

- profitability ratios;
- liquidity ratios;
- business activity.

Profitability ratios

1 Return on capital employed (ROCE)

The amount the owners earn on the capital used in the business is measured by the **return on capital employed** ratio, often simply called ROCE.

$$\text{return on capital employed} = \frac{\text{net profit for the year}}{\text{capital employed}} \times 100$$

The ratio is based on the capital at the start of the year, since that is the capital that was used to produce the profit.

Example

A firm had capital of £600,000 on 1 January and made a profit of £78,000 in the year to 31 December.

$$\text{ROCE} = \frac{\text{net profit}}{\text{capital employed}} \times 100$$

$$= \frac{78,000}{600,000} \times 100 = 13\%$$

ROCE is an important figure because it tells the owners how worthwhile their investment has been. Money invested in a business can always be put to use elsewhere. The owners expect to get a better return than they would from a building society or a bank account. The higher return is their reward for taking the risks of business.

The ROCE in the above example is quite good. The owners would probably compare it with previous years. If it is rising the business is becoming more profitable. On the other hand if it is falling they might expect managers to find ways of improving it.

Someone thinking of buying shares might look at the ROCE of several companies to see where they can get the best return.

2 *Gross profit to sales percentage*

This ratio uses information from the trading account. It shows the gross profit margin, that is, how much gross profit is made on each sale.

$$\text{gross profit to sales percentage} = \frac{\text{gross profit for the year}}{\text{sales revenue for year}} \times 100$$

Example

Using the figure from the trading account on page 190, the gross profit percentage for Haycraft is:

$$\frac{\text{gross profit}}{\text{sales revenue}} \times 100$$

$$= \frac{395{,}000}{758{,}000} \times 100 = 52.1\%$$

The gross profit percentage should not change very much from year to year. It does, however, vary from one trade or industry to another. For example, the gross profit percentage is lower for foodstuffs than for furniture or jewellery.

If the gross profit percentage falls, it may mean that the cost of goods sold has risen while sales have stayed the same. This may be because of an increase in the price of raw materials.

3 *Net profit percentage*

This ratio is based on figures in the profit and loss account. It shows the net profit margin, that is, the amount of net profit made on each sale.

$$\text{net profit to sales percentage} = \frac{\text{net profit for the year}}{\text{sales revenue for year}} \times 100$$

Example

Using the figure from the profit and loss account on page 190, the net profit percentage for Haycraft is:

$$\frac{\text{net profit}}{\text{sales revenue}} \times 100$$

$$= \frac{52{,}000}{758{,}000} \times 100 = 6.86\%$$

The net profit percentage should stay more or less the same from one year to the next. It should also be similar to other firms in the same kind of business. If the gross profit margin stays the same and the net profit percentage falls, it means that the firm's expenses have risen. It may have to take action to stop this trend. However, if a firm's net profit percentage increases it has been able to cut its costs.

Liquidity ratios

Liquidity is the ability of a firm to change its assets into cash. The faster and easier a firm can change its assets into cash the more liquid it is. It is also able to pay its debts more easily.

1 *Working capital ratio*

This is also known as the current ratio. As shown above, working capital equals current assets minus current liabilities. This ratio uses figures from the balance sheet to show the relationship between current assets and current liabilities.

$$\text{working capital ratio} = \frac{\text{current assets}}{\text{current liabilities}}$$

Example

Using the figures in the balance sheet on page 190, the working capital ratio for Haycraft is:

$$\text{working capital ratio} = \frac{\text{current assets}}{\text{current liabilities}}$$

$$= \frac{272}{162} = 1.68$$

- Firms need working capital to pay their everyday running costs. Having enough working capital means they can pay their bills on time.
- There is no ideal working capital ratio. A ratio of about 2:1 is thought to be acceptable. That is, for every £1 a firm owes it has current assets of £2. Anything less than this might mean that a firm is unable to pay all its bills promptly.
- A high working capital may mean that a firm's stocks are too high or it has too many debtors (it is using up capital to give credit), or it may have too much cash in the bank. It may also mean that it has too few creditors. That is, it may not be taking as much credit as it could.

2 Acid test ratio

This is sometimes called the liquid capital ratio. It is similar to the working capital ratio but does not include stocks. Stocks are not included because they are the least liquid of the current assets. It may take time to change stock into cash. Stock may be sold on credit and become part of debtors, and then it may be some time before the debtor pays.

$$\text{acid test ratio} = \frac{\text{current assets} - \text{stock}}{\text{current liabilities}}$$

Example

Using the figure in the balance sheet on page 190, Haycraft's acid test ratio is:

$$\frac{\text{current assets} - \text{stock}}{\text{current liabilities}} = \frac{272 - 84}{162} = \frac{188}{162} = 1.16$$

This ratio shows the balance between liquid assets and the current liabilities. Ideally it is about 1:1, which means that a firm has just enough current assets to meet its current liabilities. Anything less than this would mean that it would struggle to pay its creditors if they pressed for payment.

Business activity ratio

It is expensive to keep goods in stock. A business may have to pay for the goods it holds in stock before it has sold any of them. Even if it has sold some of them, the firm may not have been paid by the time it has to pay its suppliers. A firm needs more capital if it keeps goods in stock for a long time.

The **rate of turnover** measures the number of times a firm turns over (sells) its average stock in a year. It is the speed at which a firm sells its stock. The information needed to work it out is found in the trading account.

$$\text{rate of stock turnover} = \frac{\text{cost of goods sold}}{\text{average stock}}$$

The average stock is found by adding the opening and closing stock together and dividing by two.

Example

If the cost of goods sold is £363, and the opening stock is £96 and closing stock is £118, what is the rate of stock turnover?

$$\frac{\text{cost of goods sold}}{\text{average stock}} = \frac{363}{(96 + 118 \div 2)} = 3.4$$

This figure can be divided into 52 weeks (or 365 days) to find the average time goods are held in stock. In our example this will be 52 weeks ÷ 3.4 which is about 15 weeks and 2 days.

The rate of stock turnover varies from trade to trade. A market trader selling fruit and vegetables may sell all his or her stock each day and will have a high rate of turnover. A furniture shop, on the other hand, has a fairly low rate of turnover.

As with most of the other ratios, firms compare the rate of stock turnover with those of previous years. A firm that increases the rate of stock turnover is improving its efficiency.

Activities

1 Complete these formulae by including the missing terms:

   a $\text{ROCE} = \frac{\text{net profit}}{?} \times 100$

   b $? = \frac{\text{net profit}}{\text{sales revenue}} \times 100$

   c $\text{working capital ratio} = \frac{\text{current assets}}{?} \times 100$

   d $? = \frac{\text{current assets} - \text{stock}}{\text{current liabilities}}$

2 A firm with capital of £300,000 makes a net profit of £20,000. Calculate the ROCE for the business. The interest rate offered by banks and building societies is currently 7.5%. Comment on whether the firm should be content with its ROCE.

3 A firm asks you for advice on its working capital. The business has current assets of £20,000 and current liabilities of £6,000. Calculate the working capital ratio and comment on whether the firm should be happy with its value.

4 Explain the difference between the working capital ratio and the acid test ratio. Why do firms feel that they need to have two different measures of liquidity?

5 Leamington Plastics

The directors of Leamington Plastics were pleased with themselves when the company accounts for 2001 were announced. The board had made a decision in 1999 to borrow money from the bank to buy new machinery for the factory. As the company's accounts had shown increases in revenue and profits over the last three years, it felt that this decision had been a good one.

They were just about to celebrate when the financial director, Celia Hill, interrupted them. She pointed out that Leamington Plastics' financial situation was not as promising as the other directors seemed to think. Ms Hill pointed out that some of the company's account ratios were showing that the business was actually getting into a worse position. Shocked, the directors asked Ms Hill to explain what the problems were.

Summary of Leamington Plastics' Balance Sheets and Profit and Loss Accounts, 1999-2001
All figures are £000

	2001	2000	1999
Fixed assets	4800	4300	3900
Current assets (including stock)	240 (70)	250 (50)	230 (40)
Current liabilities	220	200	180
Long-term liabilities	1500	1200	1250
Capital employed	3320	3150	2700
Sales revenue	6000	5400	5200
Gross profit	1450	1340	1300
Net profit	400	390	380

a Why is a company's gross profit higher than its net profit?

b How is the capital employed calculated?

c Why is stock shown separately as a current asset?

d Calculate the following figures for each of the three years:
- working capital ratio;
- gross profit to sales percentage;
- net profit to sales percentage;
- acid test ratio;
- return on capital employed (ROCE) percentage.

ICT Activity

Copy the table of Leamington Plastics' finances onto a spreadsheet. Use the spreadsheet to help you calculate the figures required for question d. Then produce suitable graphs to show the changes in the ratios over the three years.

e Write a report to Leamington Plastics. In the report:
- Explain why the company is not in a good financial position. Use the ratios you calculated in question d to help you with this.
- Discuss ways in which the company might improve its position.

Unit 3.12 Improving profitability

Firms have to be aware of how well other firms in their business are doing. It is part of being competitive. They must keep up and not get left behind. If they do, the price of their shares may fall and they may become the target of a takeover bid.

For these and other reasons, firms compare their performance with other, similar firms. Other firms, shareholders, banks and fund managers also watch their results. They are compared not only with other firms in this country but also with similar firms from other parts of the world. Because business nowadays operates on a global scale, people can invest in firms from any part of the world. This puts firms under pressure to improve their profits.

Profits depend on two main factors, sales and costs. They affect profit in opposite ways.

Figure 3.14 Effect of sales and costs on profit

There are three main ways that a firm can use to improve its profits:
- by increasing revenue;
- by reducing costs;
- by expanding.

Increasing revenue

A firm can improve its sales revenue, that is, its income from sales, in three ways.

1 Increasing sales volume

This means setting out to sell more. By selling more at the same price, a firm can earn more. There are various marketing methods it can use to increase sales volume.
- By having an advertising campaign.
- Through sales promotions such as competitions, special offers, gift or token schemes. Sometimes firms change the packaging and the image of a product and relaunch it. Whatever plan they follow, the extra revenue must be greater than the cost of the marketing.
- By opening new markets. Many products are known only in a particular area or region. Many firms in the service industries are known in one part of the country only. For example, there are few estate agents that operate nationally. Sales volume is increased if firms extend their markets by trading regionally, nationally or internationally. Firms can increase sales by exporting.
- Improving the rate of stock turnover. If goods are sold faster there is an increase in the total number of sales and of sales income.

Firms can also cut prices to increase sales. Sometimes prices are reduced for only a short time to boost sales. Firms hope that at least some of the new customers they attract will stay with them, even if they increase prices back to what they were.

2 Raising prices

A firm's ability to raise its prices depends on its market and the actions of its competitors. In a competitive market, firms lose sales if they raise prices and other firms do not. In general, a rise in price usually leads to a fall in demand. A rise in price can, in theory, cause sales to fall so far as to lead to a fall in revenue. This does not usually happen, but the rise in revenue from higher prices might be less than was hoped.

3 New products

Bringing out a new product, or updating an existing one, usually increases sales. Firms bring out new versions of their products because they want to be seen to be modern, or at the 'cutting edge'. For the same reason there are always people who want to own the latest version of a product. Some industries regularly introduce new products, for example:

- the fashion industry;
- car makers;
- firms that produce computers and other technology-based products.

In all cases, the main reason for bringing out new products is to increase sales. In some industries, firms that fail to bring out new models can quickly lose sales, for example computer games.

Reducing costs

Profit depends on sales on the one hand and costs on the other. One way of increasing profit is to cut costs.

- There is nearly always some scope for reducing costs. Very efficient firms may find it hard to cut costs without harming the business.
- Not all costs can be cut easily. It may be impossible to cut fixed costs, at least in the short term.
- Some costs are outside the control of a firm, for example the cost of raw materials.
- Wages and salaries are the largest single cost in most companies. Firms often look first to cutting jobs when they need to cut costs. They may do this by:
  - cutting jobs and dividing the work up among the remaining workers who then have to do more work;
  - cutting the number of managers (de-layering);
  - replacing people with machines (automation). Reducing labour can be expensive because of redundancy costs. To keep redundancy costs as low as possible firms may rely on 'natural wastage' to reduce the number of workers. This means firms wait for workers to retire or get other jobs and then not replace them.
- Putting out certain jobs to other firms instead of doing them 'in house'. For example, many firms use computer services companies like Cap Gemini instead of employing their own computing experts.

Expansion

One of the reasons why firms want to grow is to make larger profits. In general, if a firm is bigger it ought to make bigger profits. In Unit 2.4a we noted that firms grow in two main ways:

- internally;
- externally.

Firms grow internally by increasing their production and sales. They may do this by developing new products and new markets.

Firms expand externally by taking over or merging with other firms. It is often easier for a firm to grow in this way rather than internally:

- Growth is very fast – a firm can double in size almost overnight through takeovers, for example Vodaphone.
- Profits grow automatically because the profits of the two firms are added together.
- It can increase those profits even more in due course by cutting costs. Most of this cost cutting comes from getting rid of duplication. For example, it only needs one headquarters staff. Advertising is for one firm, not two. The larger firm may be able to buy its supplies more cheaply because it is buying in larger quantities.

Activities

1 Give two reasons why it is important that a business makes a profit.

2 In one year a business has these costs and revenue:

Costs	Revenue
£40,000	£50,000

   a Calculate the profit the business earns that year.
   b How much profit would the business get if:
      i both costs and revenue went up by 10%;
      ii costs fell by 25% and revenue remained the same;
      iii revenue increased by 20% and costs fell by 10%?

3 A house-building company attempts to increase its profits by using cheaper building materials. Explain why its profits might not necessarily increase as a result of this policy.

4 Going Gnome is a business that makes concrete garden gnomes. It costs £3 to make each gnome in labour and materials, and they are currently sold for £8 each.

The business knows that the number of gnomes it sells each month depends upon the price it charges. This relationship is shown in the table below.

Price of gnomes	Number of gnomes sold each month
£4	3,000
£5	2,400
£6	1,900
£7	1,300
£8	1,000
£9	600
£10	250

a How much monthly profit does the business make at the moment?

b Calculate the price Going Gnome should charge to obtain the highest profit.

5 Sportz Gear is a national retailer of sports clothing and equipment. Its target market is young people in the 14–30 age group. The company is doing well and has plans to expand to increase its profits. The business is considering two options:

- Open more Sportz Gear stores in different parts of the country.
- Move into another area of retailing – golfing products, aimed at the older, more upmarket golfer.

Give two points in favour and two points against each of the two options.

Examination hints

In questions where you are asked to 'Calculate ...', there are stages you should follow in your answer. The examiner can only mark what is on the paper, so show that you understand what you are doing:

- write out the formula;
- substitute the appropriate numbers for the formula;
- show each stage of your calculation in the right order;
- put each stage under the previous one.

If there is more than one mark to the question, show your working, even when you are not specifically asked to do so. Very often there is only one mark for the correct answer, the rest of the marks are for the correct method, or showing the formula or for showing the right stages in the answer.

Unit 4.1 The nature of organisations

4.1a Organisations

→ Key terms

Centralised organisation →	an organisation in which most decisions are taken at head office, who keep strict control over their branches.
Decentralised organisation →	an organisation in which most decisions are passed down to branches or divisions of the organisation, and not taken by the head office.
Delegation →	passing on responsibility and authority to someone at a lower level in an organisation.
Function →	a key task within an organisation, such as marketing, production or finance.
Manager →	a person responsible for the control and supervision of an activity or group of activities.
Organisation →	any body or group that has a common purpose and an identity that is separate from any other body or group.
Organisation chart →	a diagram that shows the internal structure of an organisation.
Profit centre →	a division or department of an organisation that is given the task of operating at a profit. It is given a profit target and the power it needs to reach that target.

What is an organisation?

An **organisation** is any body or group that has a particular purpose or interest, and has its own identity. It decides its own structures and who it wants as members. From a business studies point of view, there are four main types of organisation:

- **Public sector organisations** – these are set up or run by central or local government. They usually provide a service for which there is no direct charge, for example education, roads, street lighting and healthcare.
- **Business organisations** of all kinds and sizes, whose main object is to make a profit.
- **Voluntary organisations** such as charities and clubs. They depend on people working for them on a voluntary (unpaid) basis. They do not aim to make a profit. Any surpluses they make are used to meet their objectives. There are some large voluntary organisations that employ people as well as using voluntary help, for example Oxfam, the Red Cross, Doctor Barnardos and the National Trust.
- **Special interest organisations** such as trade unions, trade associations and pressure groups.

Nearly all organisations have some kind of business aspect to them. For example, they all need to buy goods and services, keep accounts, have bank accounts and have some form of administration.

Some features are common to all organisations:

Objectives
They state what the organisation hopes to achieve, or the overall purpose for which it has been set up. They are the reasons for which an organisation exists.

Culture
This refers to the style of the organisation, its traditions, working practices and ethos.

Resources
Every organisation has some resources. They employ people or use volunteers (human resources). Most use premises, equipment or machinery which they own or rent (physical resources). They collect or earn money

and use it to further their purpose (financial resources).

Organisation

Organisations have a system of working methods and administration used throughout the organisation.

Functions

These are the various roles within an organisation. For example, finance, sales, personnel, production and administration. In small organisations these functions may be carried out by just one or two people doing several jobs. Large organisations have separate departments for each function and employ specialist people.

External environment

All organisations are affected by events that happen outside the organisation, over which they have no control. For example, they are affected by the actions of the government, local councils and competitors. Changes in the law, taxation and the economy also affect them, locally, nationally and internationally.

Internal organisation

Every organisation has some kind of structure. This is different for each organisation. The structure depends on size, and will usually be based on one or more of these four factors:

1 **Objectives** – these affect the way organisations are structured and organised. The structure of a manufacturing firm will stress production. In a service industry firm the emphasis may be on marketing and customer relations. A voluntary organisation may base its structure on fundraising and giving aid.

2 **Functions** – many firms are organised according to key tasks such as personnel, sales and marketing. These key tasks are known as **functions**. Each function is run by a department. The kinds of functions into which a firm is split depends on the objectives.

3 **Product** – some firms produce many different kinds of products. They often group similar products into divisions. This kind of firm's structure is probably based on product rather than on objectives.

4 **Geography** – very large companies with branches all over the world may have divisions based on regions of the world.

Departments

The basic unit of internal organisation is the department. The number of departments that a firm has depends on its size. Each department is usually run by a **manager**. A sole trader is very unlikely to have departments. The owner will be both the manager and probably the main worker. Partnerships can be quite big and have many departments, with a partner in charge of each department. For example, a firm of solicitors might have a department for each branch of the law.

The organisation of a small private limited company is often similar to that of a sole trader. Other limited companies vary greatly in size, and therefore in the way they are organised.

Large companies are divided into many departments. Each department is responsible for a specific task or function for the whole organisation. Many departments are split into sections. Sometimes sections are further broken down into sub-sections. Departments that do similar tasks may be grouped together to form a division.

Organisation charts

The way a company is organised can be shown on an organisation chart. It shows how the organisation is split up into various departments, sections and sub-sections.

An organisation chart gives a kind of snapshot of the whole organisation.

- All departments are shown, including the way each one is broken down into parts. The number of people employed in the various parts may also be shown.
- It shows the levels of responsibility. All the people of roughly the same level of responsibility are shown on the same level in the chart. It shows how departments relate to one another.
- It shows the lines of communication in an organisation. Information is passed down from managers to the next level below. In the same way, it shows how matters are passed upwards from the 'shop floor' to top managers.

No two organisations are the same. In some, all control and responsibility is held by a head office. Others

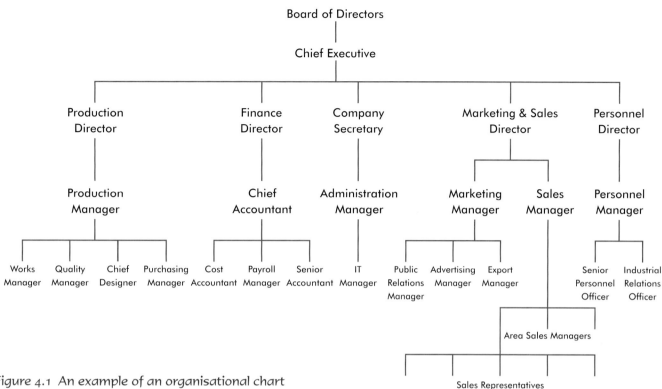

Figure 4.1 *An example of an organisational chart*

have a small head office with little control over strong divisions or subsidiary companies.

Centralised organisations

Some organisations centralise control in a head office where a small group of managers take all the important decisions. Branches and departments have to follow instructions from head office. They have very little power and are kept under strict control. There is very little **delegation**, so decisions can be made quickly. Banks, supermarkets and retail store chains like BHS and Boots tend to be centralised.

- Branch managers are told exactly how to run their branch. They order supplies from head office. They have no control over finance.
- Branch managers' main job is to see that their branch is run along the lines head office lays down. They may be able to hire staff, but only with head office permission.
- Managers send regular reports to head office. They are used to measure the success of a branch. Daily reports may be sent to order fresh supplies.

Benefits of centralisation:

- The small number of head office managers means decisions can be made quickly.
- Everything is done in exactly the same way throughout the firm. Staff can therefore be moved easily and know exactly what to do at any branch.
- There are economies of scale from central buying.

Drawbacks of centralisation:

- The people who make the decisions are not in touch with local conditions.
- Business opportunities may be lost because the people actually doing the job are not allowed to make decisions.
- Branch managers may lose interest in the job because they have little chance to use their initiative.

Decentralised organisations

In these organisations branch managers make most of the important decisions about the running of their branch. Head office makes the policy, gives advice and has overall control. Each branch may be a **profit centre**. The branch managers are allowed to make the decisions needed to reach their profit targets.

Benefits of decentralisation:

- Managers understand local conditions and are better placed to make the right decisions.
- Fewer people have to be asked for an opinion, so decisions can be made quickly.

- Managers are allowed to take initiatives and develop their own ideas. They are less likely to lose interest in the job. If their branch does well they will get credit for it.

Drawbacks of decentralisation:
- The organisation as a whole is hard to control.
- Local decisions may not fit in with company policy. They may not take account of the interests of the firm as a whole.

Activities

1 Which of the four types of organisation is most likely to:

a be run to make a profit;

b provide a service for which it is difficult to charge directly;

c represent the interests of a small group of people;

d rely on unpaid helpers to keep the organisation going?

2 Copy out and complete the table below. Include at least two examples for each of the four types of organisations.

Name of organisation	Type of organisation	Function of organisation
Oxfam	Voluntary	Raises money through its shops to help relieve the effects of poverty in less developed nations
Pilkington plc	Private sector	Provides sheet glass and other glass products worldwide

□ Case Study

3 The Oak Hotel Group

The Oak Group runs a small chain of hotels located in 12 towns around Britain. Stephen and Pauline Peters started the business when they opened their first hotel in Leeds in the 1970s. The business expanded in the 1980s and 1990s, but Mr and Mrs Peters decided to keep tight control of the chain of hotels from their Leeds base.

A manager is responsible for running each of the hotels, but they are all run along the same lines. The company has decided to have the same pricing policy throughout the chain. Stephen Peters even decides the monthly menus available in the hotels' restaurants. The Peters say that guests will receive the same service and facilities whether they are at the Bournemouth or the Manchester Oak Hotel, or indeed any of their other hotels.

Profits have been declining in recent years and some hotel managers have been asking the Peters for permission to be able to alter their prices and offer different events, such as theme weekends. Mr and Mrs Peters have always been reluctant to see any change, believing it is in everyone's interests that all the hotels are the same.

a Use the case study to explain what is meant by centralisation.

b Give two reasons why Mr and Mrs Peters may wish to run all the hotels in the same way.

c What advantages might the Oak Group gain by giving more control to the individual hotel managers?

d Describe why the guests in the Bournemouth Oak Hotel might want different services from those staying in the Manchester Oak Hotel.

4 Waterstone's Booksellers

High street bookseller Waterstone's made a decision some time ago to decentralise control in its branches throughout Britain. Waterstone's believes that each store's ability to say which books will appear on its shelves brings benefits to the company and its customers.

Waterstone's has an 18% market share of the book retail market. There are a huge number of different titles available for Waterstone's to sell in its branches, too many, in fact, for every store to carry each title. Each store has to select between 50,000 and 150,000 different titles. The mix and variety of these books will depend upon the type of people who visit the store. Books by a local author will probably sell well in the author's home town, but be of little interest outside it.

Waterstone's branch managers also have the authority to control their own budgets. This means they can respond more quickly to changing market conditions. For example, they could run promotions and special offers if they found that people were not buying their books. Under a centralised system, they would have to wait for head office to approve this decision, which could take many weeks.

a How do Waterstone's customers benefit from the company decentralising control?

b Why does the nature of bookselling make decentralisation a good idea?

c What problems could decentralisation bring to Waterstone's?

Examination hints

- Make sure you use business studies terms in your answers.
- Your ability to use business studies terms correctly is one of the things that examiners are looking for. It shows how well you understand the subject.

Unit 4.1 The nature of organisations

4.1b Departments

There are certain functions that have to be carried out in every business. The main ones are:

- accounting;
- administration;
- personnel;
- marketing;
- sales;
- purchasing.

There are other functions that vary with the type of business. For example, a manufacturing firm will have a production department, and service industry firms may have a customer relations or customer services department.

In larger firms each function may have its own department. Sometimes functions are combined into one department, for example sales and marketing. Smaller firms can also be split into departments, though there may be only one person working in a department. In a sole trader one person may carry out all the functions.

Accounting and administration

Every business, large or small, must have a detailed record of all the money coming into and going out of the business. Without these records a firm will not know whether it has made a profit or a loss. In a small firm the owner may keep the accounts or use a part-time bookkeeper. A large firm will have a chief accountant to manage the accounts department. Very big firms will have a finance director who will be in charge of every aspect of the firm's finances.

Many large firms have a central administration department. It provides all the clerical and secretarial support. It keeps and controls all the firm's records and general paperwork. Much of the work, such as collecting sales data from branches, is now dealt with using computers online.

Public limited companies have a company secretary who has to make sure that all the firm's legal requirements are met. This means looking after the share register, returns to the Registrar of Companies and all things related to company law.

Personnel

The personnel department deals with the people who work in, or want to work in, a firm. It controls the number of employees in the firm. The quality of workers will largely depend on the way it chooses staff. The department is usually run by a personnel manager. Large companies may also have a personnel director and a number of personnel managers. The department must work closely with all parts of the firm to make sure they have enough staff of the right kind. Its work falls into four main parts:

1 *Employment matters*
- Recruiting, selecting and appointing all new staff.
- Terminating employment through redundancies, retirement or dismissal.
- Negotiating grievance and disciplinary procedures with trade unions and applying them where necessary.
- Organising staff appraisal systems, where they exist.

2 Record keeping

This department keeps records of all the firm's staff, for example application forms, references, details of courses and promotions.

3 Industrial relations

- Negotiating wages, salaries and working conditions with the trade unions.
- Working with the trade unions to try to solve industrial relations problems. They try to avoid the problems from becoming disputes.
- Speaking on behalf of the firm at industrial tribunals.

4 Welfare and training

- Organising welfare facilities for workers. These include things like childcare, medical centres and first-aid rooms, sports and social centres.
- Organising training so that staff are kept up to date and have the skills the firm needs.

A staff appraisal interview between a manager and an employee

Human resources management (HRM)

Many firms have a human resources management department instead of a personnel department. Personnel departments deal with the routine parts of employment such as 'hiring and firing' staff and keeping staff records. The personnel function is only part of human resources management. HRM puts more emphasis on making the best use of people through career planning, staff development and training. It seeks to find ways of motivating people. It tries to provide for all people's needs at work through social and welfare facilities.

Marketing

The marketing department gives the consumer's point of view within a firm. It acts as a bridge between consumers and the production department.

- It sets up market research.
- It works with design and production departments to make sure that the firm's products are of a design, quality and price that consumers want.
- It organises the advertising, promotion and distribution of goods and services.

A marketing presentation

Sales

This is an important department since firms depend on selling their products. It plans, organises and administers sales. There are four main parts to this function:

- Selling the firm's products, usually to other businesses. It does so through sales representatives who not only take orders but also find new customers and keep in touch with existing ones.
- Receiving orders, acknowledging them and passing them on to the production department or the warehouse. It deals with any letters from customers, including complaints.
- Making sure all sales documents, such as delivery notes, invoices and statements, are sent out at the right time. It also receives payments from customers and passes them on to the accounts department.
- Acting on reports from the salesforce. It sorts out complaints and passes on suggestions for new products or changes to existing ones to the production department.

An open-plan office

Production

This is the department that plans, organises and carries out the manufacturing of a firm's products. It must make sure that goods are produced:

- as efficiently and as cheaply as possible, and
- that they are of good quality.

The department works closely with:

- the marketing department in planning and developing new products;
- the purchasing department to make sure that it has enough supplies, in the right amounts, at the right time;
- the sales department to make sure that there are enough goods of every type and style to meet demand.

Purchasing

All firms have to buy in supplies. Large firms use perhaps many hundreds of different components and supplies. To gain the benefits of bulk buying large firms have one purchasing department that buys all the materials, components and other supplies they need.

A sales meeting

Activities

1 Which departments are responsible for these tasks? Redraw the table matching the tasks with the correct departments.

Task	Department responsible
Visiting customers to demonstrate the company's new product range	Marketing
Producing letters and other documents the company requires	Purchasing
Keeping a record of when and how much customers pay the company	Administration
Negotiating with suppliers to get the best deal when buying materials	Human resources
Conducting market research surveys to determine the best price to charge	Accounts
Ensures that employees are fully trained for the jobs they have to do	Sales

Case Study

2 Tenby Timber Products

Tenby Timber Products is a company that designs and constructs wooden buildings, such as garden sheds and garages. The business has grown over the last 10 years and Huw Davies, the main shareholder and managing director, has felt it necessary to change the company's management structure during that time.

The management structure for both 1991 and 2001 can be seen in the diagrams below.

Case Study

a Describe the work performed by:
  i the accounts department;
  ii the transport department.
b What difficulties could Tenby Timber Products have experienced, had it retained the old departmental structure as the company grew?
c Huw Davies is thinking of having a human resources department in the company.
  i What are the responsibilities of a human resources department?
  ii What are the arguments in favour of having a human resources department in a business such as Tenby Timber Products?

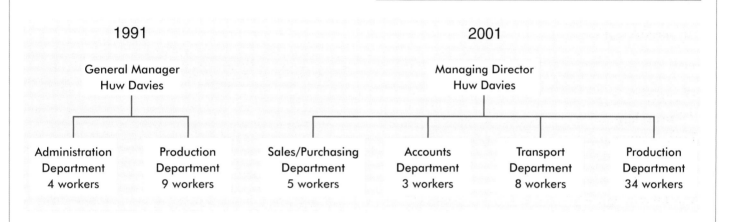

1991

General Manager
Huw Davies

Administration Department 4 workers

Production Department 9 workers

2001

Managing Director
Huw Davies

Sales/Purchasing Department 5 workers

Accounts Department 3 workers

Transport Department 8 workers

Production Department 34 workers

Examination hints

The examination is designed to test you in four skills. Examiners call them:

- Knowledge – what you know and understand.
- Application – whether you can apply or use your knowledge in a business situation.
- Analysis – your ability to break down a business problem or issue into various parts.
- Evaluation – your ability to weigh up the pros and cons of a situation or the two sides of a point. You must then draw a conclusion and support your answer with evidence from the case study.

Questions that carry high marks test all four skills.

Some questions only test one or maybe two of these skills – they will carry fewer marks.

Unit 4.2 Roles in the workplace

4.2a Management

Chain of command →	the route through which managers issue instructions to their staff, and matters are passed upwards from staff to their managers.
De-layering →	cutting down the number of levels of management within an organisation.
Delegation →	passing on responsibility and authority to someone at a lower level in an organisation.
Function →	a key task within an organisation, such as marketing or production.
Hierarchy →	an organisation where responsibility is built up in layers. The upper levels always have more power than the levels below.
Manager →	a person responsible for the control and supervision of an activity or group of activities.
Span of control →	a measure of the number of people over whom a manager has direct control.

→ Key terms

We saw in Unit 2.2 that, in large limited companies, ownership, control and management of a business become separated. Shareholders own the business, they appoint a board of directors to set policy, and to have overall control of managers appointed to run it.

What managers do

Managers are employees of a firm. They run the firm from day to day. The board of directors decides the policies and the objectives of the firm. The managers have to carry out those policies and make sure that the objectives are met. In large companies the most senior managers will also be directors. They provide a link between the board and the managers. Effective managers mean better profits.

Being a manager means trying to keep at least four groups of people happy:

- **board of directors** – expect their policies to be carried out effectively and the objectives they set to be met;
- **shareholders** – expect good profits and the value of their shares to increase;
- **customers** – expect goods or services to be of good quality and good value for money. Customers may be other departments within the organisation;
- **employees** – expect to be treated fairly, have good working conditions and be reasonably paid.

To meet these demands there are certain things that managers do in their jobs:

- **Planning** – this means having to look forward all the time. Planning is on a daily, weekly, monthly and annual basis, sometimes even further ahead.
- **Organising** – making sure that all the things needed to do a job are there at the right time.
- **Directing** – telling people what to do so that they do the job in the way the managers want.
- **Coordinating** – making sure that the various parts of a job fit together so there are no delays or inefficiencies.
- **Reporting** – communicating to senior and other managers and staff. Reports may be in writing or verbal.
- **Budgeting** – a form of planning, to make sure that there are enough resources to do the work.
- **Staffing** – making sure that there are enough people with the right skills to do all the work that is required.

Managers have to carry out a wide range of activities. Their job can be summed up as the control and supervision of an activity or group of activities.

Levels of management

Large companies have many managers. Each department has a manager. The most senior managers may also be executive directors. Some departments may be broken down into sections with each section having a manager. Some sections may be broken down into other sub-sections with each sub-section having a supervisor. Thus there are **layers of management**.

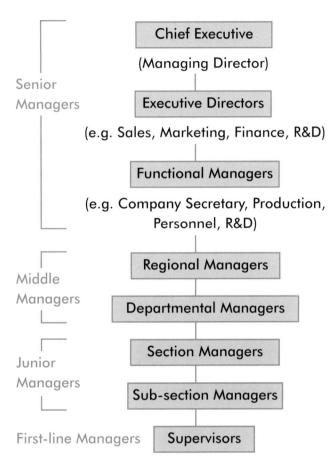

Figure 4.2 Levels of management

Hierarchies

Where power and responsibility is built up in layers in this way, it is called a **hierarchy**. The most powerful manager is at the top of the hierarchy. Those at the bottom have the least authority. A hierarchy can be thought of as a pyramid, with the ordinary workers at the bottom. The pyramid builds up in layers. The bottom layer has most people in it, but they have the least responsibility. As you go up the pyramid, each layer has fewer people with more responsibility than the level below. At the top are the people who make all the big decisions.

The number of layers varies between firms. If there are a lot of levels it is known as a tall hierarchy. If there are only a few levels it is called a flat hierarchy or organisation.

Span of control

The **span of control** is a measure of the number of people over whom a manager has direct control. The chief executive is responsible for all the people working in a

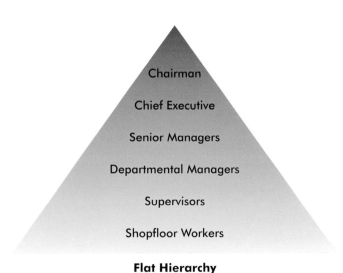

Flat Hierarchy

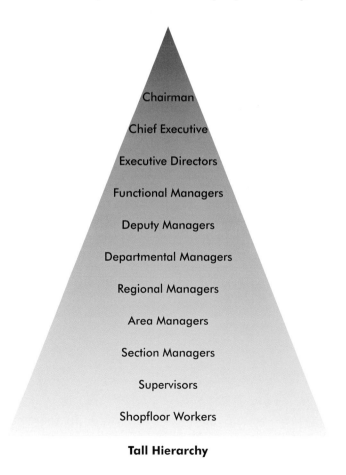

Tall Hierarchy

Figure 4.3 Hierarchies

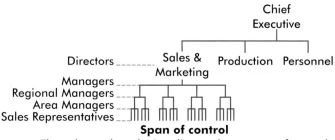

Span of control

The sales and marketing director has a span of control of 4 regional managers, and responsibility for 36 people

Figure 4.4 *Span of control*

company but cannot supervise or control them all. Only a few senior managers come directly under the chief executive's span of control. They receive instructions directly from the chief executive and report to him or her. Other people in the firm come under another manager's span of control. All the people who work in a firm come under someone's span of control. The person to whom an employee reports is known as their line manager. The number of people over whom a manager has control depends on two things:

- The nature of the work. Work that needs very close supervision leads to a narrow span of control. If little supervision is needed it may be wider.
- The structure of the firm. A flat organisation with only a few layers creates a wide span of control. A tall organisation has a narrow span of control with each manager having direct control of only a few people.

Delegation

Delegation simply means 'passing on'. In a small business all decisions can be made by the owner – there is no delegation.

As the business grows the owners cannot do everything themselves. They have to pass on some of their authority to someone lower down the organisation. The board of directors concentrates on policy. All authority and responsibility comes from the board. It passes on the day-to-day running to the executive directors. They, in turn, delegate some of their authority to other managers within their span of control. In this way authority is passed down through the organisation.

The amount of authority that is delegated goes down at each level. Delegation only works if some simple rules are followed:

- those given a job to do must also have the authority to be able to carry out their duties;
- everyone must be clear about what authority and decision-making power has been delegated;
- those given responsibility must have the confidence of their boss. The boss should not interfere once he or she has delegated tasks to someone else.

Chain of command

Managers have to keep in touch with at least two levels within the organisation:

- the people within their span of control, who work for them;
- their immediate boss into whose span of control they fall.

A **chain of command** shows the communication routes in an organisation. It shows how instructions are passed down through the layers of management. It also shows how matters are passed upwards for a decision. Matters have to be passed up the chain when they are outside the responsibility delegated to a particular person.

The length of the chain depends on the number of levels of management. Some departments, for example finance, have a short chain of command. Others, like production, may have several levels of management and a long chain of command.

De-layering

At one time, managers' jobs were thought to be fairly secure. In recent years this has become less true as organisations have tried to be more 'lean'. To be able to compete more effectively firms have to be efficient. One way of increasing efficiency is to speed up the way decisions are made. Decisions can be made faster if there are fewer people involved in making them. By cutting down the number of layers of management, firms can speed up decision making and cut costs. Cutting down on the levels of management is known as **de-layering**. One effect of de-layering is to make a tall organisation into a flat one.

Figure 4.5 Chain of command

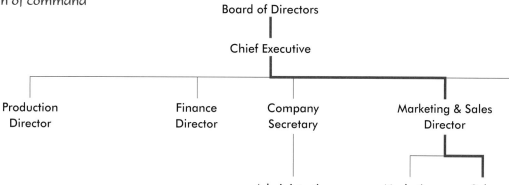

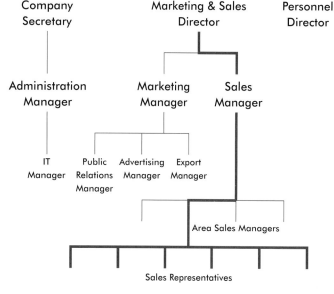

Activities

1 What is meant by a 'management hierarchy'?

2 The production manager at a small brewery has persuaded the board of directors to replace the company's old brewing equipment with a modern stainless steel system. The new equipment is very expensive to buy, but there will be some cost savings as it is semi-automated, so will require less supervision by workers.

Explain how the manager's decision to alter the way the beer is made could affect the company's:

a workers;

b shareholders;

c customers.

3 **Group activity**

Stan and Andrew are two senior managers at Abbey Engineering Company. Stan joined the company as an apprentice 35 years ago when he left school. He made a name for himself as an ambitious man. He very slowly climbed the management hierarchy and was appointed as a senior manager three years ago. Andrew, on the other hand, joined Abbey as a graduate recruit after university when he was 23 years old. He joined as a trainee junior manager but was 'fast tracked' by the company. He studied part-time for an MBA business degree and is now a senior manager at the age of 31.

Stan and Andrew are both on the senior management team. They work together well, but they do have some criticisms of each other.

Consider the different routes Stan and Andrew have taken to become senior managers. Identify the benefits and drawbacks of the two different routes. Which route do you think produces the better type of manager?

4 In-Flight Caterers

Judith Greenlow is the main shareholder and general manager of In-flight Caterers (IFC) Ltd. The business, based near Heathrow, prepares passengers' food for several airline companies. IFC has grown as the demand for air travel has increased. The firm used to employ just five workers, but more than 80 employees are now needed to produce the quantities of food that the airlines need. At first, Judith managed the business on her own, but she now needs a team of managers.

IFC has established a good name in the airline catering business by providing good quality food and delivering it to the airport on time. There are many other firms in the industry, though, and Judith is constantly looking for ways of reducing costs to remain competitive.

The company needs to provide fresh food 24 hours a day, so operates three daily shifts for its workers.

Judith recently paid a management consultant to examine IFC's management systems and to make recommendations on how management in the business could be improved. IFC's current management hierarchy is shown below.

The two main recommendations in the consultant's report were:

- There were too many managers. The company would save money by abolishing the position of assistant manager. The work of these three managers could be shared between the shift managers and supervisors. This would create a flatter management hierarchy.

- Judith did not delegate authority fully. She was still trying to run the business as if it were a small concern. The managers felt that they were being watched all the time and were not trusted to do their jobs properly.

a Use the case study to explain the meaning of:
  i de-layering;
  ii delegation;
  iii span of control.
b What problems could arise in the future if Judith agrees to remove the assistant manager layer of management?
c What are the benefits of having a flattened hierarchy?
d Discuss the reasons why some senior managers find it difficult to delegate responsibility down the hierarchy.

IFL Management Hierarchy

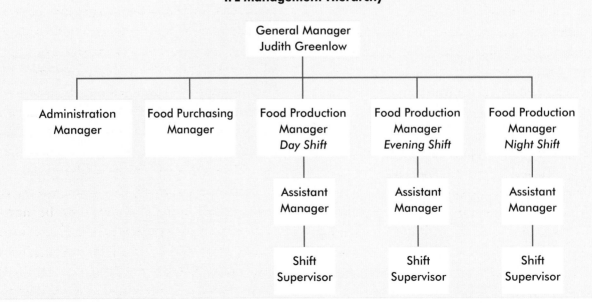

Unit 4.2 Roles in the workplace

4.2b Styles of management

Consultation →	asking people, who may be affected by a decision, for their views.
Leadership →	the ability to take charge of people, so that they perform their tasks to the best of their ability.
Management →	the planning, organisation and control of resources in order to gain a stated objective.

→ Key terms

Leadership

A good leader gains the support, hard work, loyalty and respect (affection, even) of other workers. **Leadership** is the ability to see what needs to be done and to get people to work willingly to get those things done as well as possible.

Being a manager means having to be a leader. Some are better leaders than others. There are some managers that people enjoy working for, and who they trust and are willing to follow. There are others that people find it hard to get on with and are unwilling to follow.

Managers vary a great deal. A manager may be good at planning and organising but not be very good at handling people. Different situations need a different approach. There is no one way that is always right. In some situations people expect to be told what to do. At other times, people like to be asked for their opinion and to have some effect on the final decision. Managers tend to have their own style of leadership.

Leadership styles

The style of leadership depends mainly on the personality of the leader. There are four main styles of leadership that are widely recognised:

1 **Authoritarian** – people are told what to do and how to do it. They are not trusted to do things properly and may not be asked for an opinion. Decisions are not explained. There is no consultation and little delegation.

2 **Democratic** – decisions are based on the views of as many people as possible. Decisions are made only after hearing and taking into account the views of other people who are involved.

3 **Paternalistic** – the leader acts like the head of a family, deciding what is best for the firm and its workers. Unlike the authoritarian leader, this kind of leader listens to others and explains the reasons for his or her decisions.

4 **Laissez-faire** – the leader plays very little part in making decisions. Those who run things day to day take most of the decisions. Such a style seems attractive, but it may mean the firm has no clear direction.

Management styles

Management style may refer to the style of an individual manager, or it may be the style followed by all the managers in a firm. The way managers carry out their jobs is affected by their style of leadership.

1 **Autocratic** – managers tell people what to do and how to do it. Once made, a decision must not be questioned. This style assumes that all decisions should be made at the top. Decisions are made quickly but there is little or no delegation.

Authoritarian managers do not usually consult. Paternalistic managers may also be autocratic. However, they may consult staff and take their views into account when making decisions, and explain their reasons for them. A paternal company often has good social and welfare facilities for their workers, for example Cadbury's and Rowntree's built villages for their workers to live in during the early 1900s.

The main benefit of autocratic management is that people know where they stand and decisions are taken quickly.

2 **Participative** – workers are invited to take part in making decisions. As a first step, workers are kept informed, often through a house magazine or newspaper. They need to know what is going on before they can help to make decisions. In a participative system the workers may make decisions jointly with the managers. Participation may be through:

- works committees made up of management and workers. They discuss matters that are of common interest. These can vary from the menu in the canteen to ways to improve delivery times;
- quality circles, where workers can suggest ways to improve quality;
- cell production, where the workers in the team solve production problems;
- suggestion schemes.

3 **Consultative** – managers ask for the views of other managers and their workers before making a decision. Workers are again kept well informed. They are asked for their opinions through committees, such as works councils. However, they may not be involved in actually making the decision.

Consultative and participative styles of management are very similar. Both are based on a democratic style of leadership. But not all decisions are suited to a democratic approach.

- The firm's objectives and its policy are best decided by the board of directors and senior managers. Workers may, however, have a say in the way the policy is put into effect.
- Workers may not be interested in problems that do not directly affect them.
- Often decisions have to be taken quickly, so there is no time to consult. Urgent and technical decisions are usually made by managers.

Benefits of a participative or consultative style of management:

- People are more willing to accept decisions that they have had a say in.

- The people who actually do a job are often best at deciding how the process should be carried out.
- It draws upon valuable experience and expertise that would otherwise not be given a voice.

The main drawback of participative or consultative styles of management is that decisions may be slowed down.

Activities

1 Identify which of the leadership styles are being used by each of these four managers.

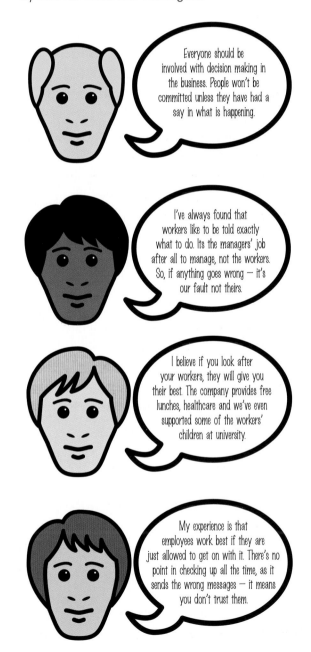

Everyone should be involved with decision making in the business. People won't be committed unless they have had a say in what is happening.

I've always found that workers like to be told exactly what to do. Its the managers' job after all to manage, not the workers. So, if anything goes wrong – it's our fault not theirs.

I believe if you look after your workers, they will give you their best. The company provides free lunches, healthcare and we've even supported some of the workers' children at university.

My experience is that employees work best if they are just allowed to get on with it. There's no point in checking up all the time, as it sends the wrong messages – it means you don't trust them.

People in Organisations

2 Auto Components Ltd

When Brendan Callaghan was appointed as the new chief executive of Auto Components, he called the company's senior and middle managers together. "This company needs some changes," he said. "We can no longer expect our employees to be treated as if they were unimportant. I'm a great believer in a democratic style of management and I want to see these changes straight away." Brendan then listed what he called his five-point plan.

The five-point plan

1 Every manager is to have an open door policy. Workers should no longer need to make an appointment to see their line manager.

2 Workers are to be kept better informed about what is happening in the company.

3 No major decision is to be made without first seeking the workers' views.

4 Quality circles will be introduced into each section so workers can meet in company time and discuss ways the business could be improved.

5 There is to be greater equality. For example, the managers' restaurant will be scrapped and everyone will eat in the same canteen.

As the managers left the meeting it was clear that they were not happy with the plan. One said to another, "He's got no idea what our workers are like. They'll abuse this power and we'll have all sorts of problems with them". The other comments were not quite as polite as that.

a Describe two ways in which the workers could be informed about what is happening in the company.

b Why do some managers prefer not to have an 'open door policy'?

c Explain how quality circles can help a business.

d How could closing the managers' restaurant help motivate workers?

e Explain why the managers were unhappy with the five-point plan.

f Comment on the way Mr Callaghan introduced his plan to the managers.

Examination hints

Every question has a word or group of words that give you a clue about the kind of answer you should write. Examiners call these words 'trigger' or 'command' words. They tell you what to do.

- **Give, Name, List, Define, State, What are, What is meant by** – These are all words used to test what you know.

- **Apply, Calculate, Describe, Examine, Why, Give an example of, From the graph/data..., Outline, Show how** – These are words or phrases used to test your ability to apply your business studies knowledge to a business situation.

- **Advise, Analyse, Compare, Describe, Examine, Show how, Which** – These are some of the words or phrases used in questions where you are being asked to break something down into its parts.

- **Assess, Comment on, Discuss, Do you think, Give reasons why, Do you agree with, In your opinion** – These are some of the words used in questions where you are expected to weigh up the pros and cons of a problem, or situation.

(For a more detailed list of trigger words and what they mean see *GCSE A-Z Business Studies Handbook* by Arthur Jenkins published by Hodder & Stoughton Educational)

Unit 4.3 Why people work

Fringe benefits →	parts of an employee's reward, in addition to their salaries, given in the form of, for example, a company car, life assurance or discounted goods.
Job satisfaction →	the extent to which an employee enjoys and is fulfilled by their job.
Motivation →	the factors that make a person want to do something.
Working conditions →	the physical environment in which a person works.

People work so that they can earn money. They work to live.

However, many people expect more from their job than just money. For example, they want to be happy and valued at work. They may work hard because they want to gain promotion or earn the respect of their bosses or fellow workers. Others work for social reasons, for example they may be bored at home or enjoy being with other people. People do voluntary work because they want to use their skills to help other people.

Motivation

People's reasons, or motives, for doing something are called their **motivation**. To get the best out of their workers firms need to understand why people work and what might make them willing to work harder. Well-motivated workers are more likely to work harder. There are a number of ways firms can motivate their workers:

- good pay, holidays and fringe benefits;
- incentive schemes such as bonuses and performance-related pay;
- good promotion opportunities;
- training schemes to keep workers up to date and to give them the chance to learn the skills needed to gain promotion;
- job security and job satisfaction.

There are a number of theories about what motivates workers. Among the best known are the theories of three American psychologists, Abraham Maslow, Frederick Herzberg and Douglas McGregor.

Maslow

Maslow tried to explain why people need to work. He said that people have five types or sets of needs that they try to satisfy. Once the first set of needs has been satisfied, it no longer works as a motivator. So people move on to the next set of needs. Each new set of needs depends on meeting the previous set. These needs therefore form a 'hierarchy of needs'. The five sets of needs are often shown as a pyramid. (See Figure 4.6.) They are:

1 Basic

Food, clothing and shelter – the basic necessities of life. People must have these things if they and their family are to survive. People either grow or make the basic necessities, or they earn enough money to buy them.

Application:

- Basic wages have to be enough to cover the costs of basic needs. Otherwise, there is no reward for work – they may be better off on benefits.
- Pay is not a big motivator for those who are already well paid.

2 Safety

Once people have satisfied their basic needs they then need to feel safe. They need to be sure that they can continue to survive. This means that they want their jobs to be secure. If their jobs are safe they can carry on providing food, clothing and shelter for themselves and their family. They can plan for the future.

Higher order of needs

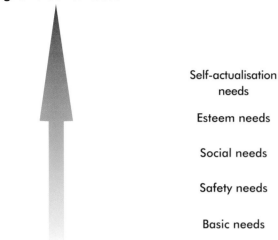

Self-actualisation
needs

Esteem needs

Social needs

Safety needs

Basic needs

Lower order of needs

Figure 4.6 Maslow's hierarchy of needs

Application:

- Good pension schemes offer long-term security for workers; they make the job attractive and motivate workers.
- Many firms offer employees insurance in case of illness, accident or sudden death. It offers them, and their families, continued security.
- Such schemes make employees feel valued. They are in addition to the basic state benefits.
- Threats to security, such as the fear of redundancy, act as demotivators.

3 Social

Once people have met their basic needs and feel sure they can carry on doing so, they develop their social needs. People need to feel they belong. They want to be part of a group and enjoy friendship and companionship. At work they want to feel they are part of a team.

Application:

- Many firms provide subsidised social clubs for their workers and their families. This develops a bond between the firm and its employees.
- Firms may have family outings, Christmas parties and leaving parties for long-term employees to develop the idea of the firm as a family.
- They use team-building exercises through residential and 'outward bound' type activities.

4 Esteem

People need to feel respected by others for their abilities. They need a sense of status, and to feel confident in what they do. They need to feel valued in their community and at work. Most important is to feel the self-respect that comes from being useful and successful.

Application:

- Recognition of an employee's abilities and the possibility of promotion motivates them to work harder.
- Having to wait a long time, or being passed by for promotion, acts as a demotivator.
- Many firms offer training for the next level of job to encourage people to work hard.
- People can gain high esteem in quite low paid jobs, especially where special skills are recognised.

5 Self-actualisation

This is people's highest need, according to Maslow. It is the satisfaction gained from realising personal ambition or personal targets. People need to feel that they have realised their potential. There is satisfaction from doing an important job and taking responsibility.

Application:

- People are motivated to work harder if they feel there is a chance to realise their personal ambitions.
- Ambitions may be outside work as well as at work. For example, to be a local councillor or captain of the local golf club.
- Self-actualisation may come from possessions. For example, it may come from owning a big house, having a second home in France or owning a Ferrari. In this case, the target depends on earning

enough money, not necessarily from being successful at work.

Herzberg

Herzberg developed the idea of **job satisfaction**. This is the pleasure that people get from their work. To gain job satisfaction, Herzberg thought four factors need to be present:

1 **Recognition** – having good or hard work recognised, especially by managers.
2 **Achievement** – the personal feeling gained from knowing that a job has been done well.
3 **Promotion** – this comes from recognition and achievement which then lead to a more senior job.
4 **Responsibility** – this comes from promotion, and increases a person's sense of recognition. It results in a greater sense of achievement.

If people are to enjoy their work and be well motivated, each of these four factors ought be present. Herzberg also noted that there were 'hygiene' factors that are essential for a happy workforce. These include good pay and working conditions, as shown by a clean and safe workplace, the control of noise and fumes and good rest breaks. If these factors are missing, morale and motivation are lower and can lead to unhappy workers and a fall in output. The hygiene factors do not motivate workers but they can demotivate them if they are not present.

McGregor

Workers can be viewed in one of two ways. A firm's policy towards its workers will depend on which of these ways it views its workforce.

One view is that workers cannot be trusted and work only for money. They do not like work and will do as little as possible if they can get away with it. They therefore have to be supervised closely, told what to do and made to work. McGregor called this Theory X.

The other view of workers is through Theory Y. From this point of view workers enjoy their work and work hard for a fair reward. They like to be given responsibility, can be trusted and are reliable.

Firms that believe in Theory X have many rules and regulations. There may be few chances of promotion and workers are not valued.

People's motivation is affected by the way they feel they are treated. If they think they are being treated fairly they are more willing and more likely to enjoy their work. Thus workers are more likely to work hard for Theory Y managers. Firms that believe in Theory Y encourage their workers. They want to see them grow and give them opportunities for further training and experience. They allow them to use their initiative to gain promotion.

Theory X	Theory Y
Workers cannot be trusted	Workers enjoy their work
They work only for the money	They work hard and expect to be reasonably paid
They do as little work as possible	They are honest and trustworthy
They cannot think for themselves	They are able to organise themselves
They cannot be relied upon	They can take initiatives
They have to be told what to do	They enjoy responsibility
They must be supervised closely	They are willing to take decisions
They avoid responsibility	They can work without close supervision
They lack ambition	Money is not their only motivation

Activities

1 Outline what you understand by the term 'motivation'.

2 Explain three ways in which a well-motivated workforce is better for a business than a poorly motivated one.

3 List three things a company could do to improve the hygiene factors faced by workers.

People in Organisations

4 Look back at the leadership style in Unit 4.2b. Which style of leadership is most likely to assume that workers are McGregor's:
  a Theory X type;
  b Theory Y type?

5 Discuss the view that giving bonuses to workers is expensive and reduces the company's profits.

6 Richer Sounds

Companies use a variety of methods to motivate their employees. Some ways are more imaginative than others. Paying good wages is, of course, an important motivator. But there are other things that can be offered to workers to keep them loyal and keen to help the company achieve its objectives.

Julian Richer, the leader of the hi-fi store Richer Sounds, has many ways of getting the best from those who work for his company. He opened his first store when he was 19 and he has always recognised the importance of good staff. His employees have access to the company's nine free holiday homes in the UK and Europe. The three best-performing stores are each lent one of the firm's luxury cars to use as they like for a week. There is a healthcare scheme for employees, as well as a hardship fund available for employees if they run into financial difficulties.

Employees who have been with the company for five years or more are taken out to a restaurant by Julian Richer and go with him on a free two-day activity break each year. Here they do caving, hang gliding or some similar activity. The company also has some unusual ideas. Every month all the employees are sent to the pub with £5 each to 'think up new ideas to improve the business'. Julian Richer promises to personally consider any suggestion to improve the business and gives money to anyone who comes up with an idea that is used.

a One way to measure whether workers are motivated is to examine the level of absenteeism in the company.
  i Explain why the level of absenteeism might be a good measure of motivation.
  ii What other measures might be used to show the level of motivation in a business?
b How might Julian Richer's idea of giving his workers money to sit in a pub help Richer Sounds?
c Describe the type of benefit a company like Richer Sounds might give its workers if it wanted to encourage its workers:
  i to stay with the company for a longer period (remain loyal);
  ii to work harder at their jobs.
d Discuss whether Richer Sounds' employees have the ability to reach all of the levels of Maslow's hierarchy of needs.

Unit 4.4 Recruitment and selection

4.4a The labour market

Labour is one of the factors of production. Labour is the human resources available for use in economic activity. Labour is made up of the people that are available for work as well as those in work. Labour includes mental as well as physical work.

Types of employment

- **Full-time** – a person is employed for the full working week, throughout the year.
- **Part-time** – a person is employed for only part of the usual working day or week. Part-time workers are usually employed for an agreed number of hours each week.
- **Permanent** – a person's employment carries on indefinitely. There is no date fixed for the job to end.
- **Temporary** – a person is employed knowing that it is for an agreed, limited period of time only. Usually there is a fixed date given when the employment will end. Work may be temporary because the work is seasonal, or extra workers are needed to meet an order or to cover for someone who is off work due to, for example, sickness or maternity leave. Both full-time and part-time work may be permanent or temporary.
- **Self-employment** – someone runs and owns their own business. They are their own boss.

Supply of labour

This is the number of people available for work in an area or in the country as a whole. It is the total supply of labour. But an employer needs to know the variety of skills that are available in an area. The supply of labour depends on four things:

1. The size of the population, but the total labour supply is not the same as the total population.
2. The age structure of the population. This determines the part of the population available for work. The number of people over 65 and those in full-time education or training affect the labour supply.
3. The number willing and able to work. There are always some people who are not able to work, perhaps due to ill health. There are also people who do not want to work. This may be temporary, perhaps because they want to stay at home to look after young children or they are ill.
4. The type and quality of skills to be found in an area.

Some parts of the country have a greater supply of available labour than others. For example, areas where old industries, such as mining, shipbuilding and heavy engineering, have closed have high unemployment and a good supply of labour. Other areas, such as south-east England, have low unemployment and a low supply of labour.

Labour market

The number of people able and willing to work is only one aspect of labour. There also has to be someone willing to employ labour.

In reality, there are many labour markets. The market for shop assistants is different from the market for computer programmers. It also varies between different parts of the country.

The state of the labour market can be seen by the number of unemployed. If there are more people than jobs available there is unemployment and the labour market is depressed. If there are more jobs than people to fill them, unemployment is low and the labour market is tight.

Labour mobility

The labour market and the supply of labour are affected by how willing people are to move job or to a new area. Shortages in one part of the market can be made up by recruiting people from another part of the country or from other firms. The extent to which people are either able or willing to move from one place or job to another is the **mobility of labour**. The ease with which people can move jobs or area depends on their skills, qualifications and experience. Those with few qualifications, skills or experience find it hard to move. There are two kinds of labour mobility – occupational and geographical. There are certain factors that make it hard for workers to move.

- Some jobs need special talents or skills and are not open to those who do not have them.

- Some jobs need high qualifications and long training, for example dentists. Training is expensive and income may be lost while in training.
- Moving to a new area can be difficult and costly:
  - housing at the right price may not be available. People may be reluctant to move to an area with high house prices;
  - there are moving costs, such as legal and estate agents' fees and the cost of new carpets and curtains;
  - people are unhappy to leave family and friends and move to a place where they do not know anybody;
  - many parents do not want to disturb their children's education by moving them to a new school.
- Age makes it harder to change jobs or area. It is harder for an older person to change jobs, especially if training is needed.
- People on benefits may be caught in the 'benefit trap' where it may pay them to stay on benefits rather than get a job. The government has tried to reduce the effects of the benefit trap.

Labour turnover

This is the rate at which people enter and leave jobs in an organisation. It is usually measured as a percentage of the number employed.

$$\text{labour turnover} = \frac{\text{number of leavers}}{\text{total employees}} \times 100$$

High labour turnover may be a sign of poor management and poor motivation. It can be expensive due to

the cost of training new staff. It can lead to lower output since new workers need time to learn the job and to be as fast as other workers. There are a number of factors that affect labour turnover:

- rates of pay compared with other firms for similar work in the same area;
- working conditions – whether the job is clean or dirty, hard or easy;
- the number of other job opportunities in the area.

Why labour may be lost

There are a number of reasons why firms may lose labour:

- **Retirement** – people leave work when they have reached a certain age. Traditionally men retire at 65 and women at 60 years of age. These are the ages when they can draw their state retirement pensions. More recently, firms have offered workers special deals to retire early. Older workers are replaced by younger workers with more up-to-date skills who may cost less.
- **Dismissal** – a person might be 'sacked' or 'fired'. Maybe the person cannot do the job. Poor time-keeping, bad behaviour and poor quality work are all reasons for dismissal. Employers must normally give notice of dismissal. If a person is sacked on the spot without notice it is called summary dismissal. Dismissal is not the same as redundancy.
- **Redundancy** – employees might be dismissed because their jobs are no longer needed by their employer. In a redundancy it is the job that comes to an end. It is not redundancy if the worker is replaced by someone else. Redundancies happen because a firm needs fewer workers.

Except for redundancies, loss of labour usually results in a job vacancy.

Activities

1 Labour is one factor of production. What are the other three?

2 Explain why these businesses might prefer to employ temporary workers:
   a a civil engineering company building a new motorway;
   b a hotel at a holiday resort;
   c a new dot.com company.

3 Why do fast-food restaurants, such as Burger King, often prefer to employ part-time workers?

4 An unemployed former miner from the north-east of England sees a job advertised in Kent. Why might it be very difficult for him to move to take the job?

5 It is sometimes said that it is not the person but the job that is made redundant. Explain what this means.

6 The restaurant chain, McDonald's, employs mostly people who are under the age of 25. B&Q, on the other hand, actively seek out workers in their 50s and 60s. Why do you think these companies have such different approaches to the ages of their workers?

7 **Group activity**
The average age in Britain is increasing. In 1998 the average age was calculated to be 38.6 years. This figure is estimated to be 44.0 years in 2040. The increase is the result of fewer children being born and people living longer.

Working as a group, consider ways in which an ageing population affects the labour market. Present your ideas as a report or as a group presentation.

Case Study

8 **Young's Nursing Homes**
Young's Nursing Homes is a thriving business. Run by one of the company's partners, Doreen Young, the firm operates five nursing homes for older people in the north of England. Most of the residents stay there on a long-term basis. Demand for places is high and each home has very few vacancies. But there is a problem. The company finds it difficult to keep its workers. As a result, the firm's labour turnover is very high.

Year	No. of staff employed	No. of staff leaving in year
1999	42	13
2000	46	18
2001	50	23

Mrs Young examined her staffing figures for the last three years. Concerned about the level of staff turnover, she looked at results of the questionnaires that leavers are asked to complete.

Main reasons given by staff for leaving

Main reason for leaving	No. of people
Poor pay	9
Bad management	32
Unpleasant work	8
Too long hours	12
Few opportunities to socialise	21
Poor promotion prospects	18

a What is the most common reason given by workers for leaving Young's Nursing Homes?

b The workers at Young's are only paid the minimum wage, yet money does not seem to be an important reason for leaving. Explain reasons why workers may stay with a company despite being able to get a higher wage elsewhere.

c Calculate the labour turnover for each of the three years.

d Why would a high labour turnover cause problems for Young's?

e Using the evidence given in this case study, explain three ways in which Mrs Young could try to reduce the number of workers leaving.

ICT Activity

Present the labour turnover statistics and reasons for leaving as graphs.

Examination hints

In questions where you are asked to 'explain' you are being asked to do more than define something. A question such as 'Explain what is meant by...' should be answered by starting with a definition and then adding to your answer to show that you understand. It is also a good idea to include an example. If it is in Section B of the examination the example should be taken from the case study.

Unit 4.4 Recruitment and selection

4.4b Recruitment

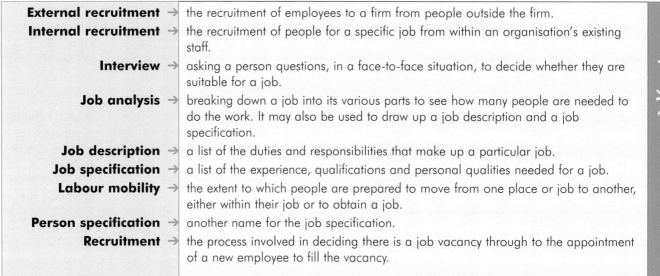

External recruitment →	the recruitment of employees to a firm from people outside the firm.
Internal recruitment →	the recruitment of people for a specific job from within an organisation's existing staff.
Interview →	asking a person questions, in a face-to-face situation, to decide whether they are suitable for a job.
Job analysis →	breaking down a job into its various parts to see how many people are needed to do the work. It may also be used to draw up a job description and a job specification.
Job description →	a list of the duties and responsibilities that make up a particular job.
Job specification →	a list of the experience, qualifications and personal qualities needed for a job.
Labour mobility →	the extent to which people are prepared to move from one place or job to another, either within their job or to obtain a job.
Person specification →	another name for the job specification.
Recruitment →	the process involved in deciding there is a job vacancy through to the appointment of a new employee to fill the vacancy.

→ Key terms

The success of a firm depends to a great extent on the people it employs. Labour is usually the biggest single cost of a firm. Therefore it must take great care when choosing its employees. The process used by firms for taking on new employees is recruitment and selection. It begins at the point where a firm decides it needs to employ a new worker and ends at the point where the person chosen starts work. It means finding and then choosing the best person for the job. The bigger the choice the more likely it is that the right person is found.

How firms recruit

There are a number of methods firms can use to recruit staff:
- use the personnel department, if the firm has one;
- use a recruitment agency;
- use a Job Centre or an employment agency;
- internally from existing workers or externally from outside the firm.

Why firms need to recruit

Vacancies arise and new workers are needed for many reasons:

- **Expansion** – an expanding firm may need extra workers to cope with the extra work, maybe at all levels, from managers to shop-floor workers.
- **Change of product** – a form of expansion where a firm starts a new line or model and needs new workers to deal with the extra work.
- **Replacing workers** lost through retirement, workers moving or being dismissed.

Stages in recruitment

The way firms recruit new workers varies between firms, but there are stages they all follow.

1 Deciding if there is a vacancy

When someone leaves, the job may be filled or the vacancy used for something else. The job may be new, because the firm is expanding or because a job has grown so much that it has to be split. Firms use **job analysis** to decide how many workers of each kind they need. It is also used to work out details of each job. Job analyses are used to prepare a **job description**.

2 Job description

This is a detailed list that describes the duties and responsibilities of a job. It is sent with an application form to each applicant for the job. They can use it to decide whether they want to apply for the job. The job description should include:

- the job title, the job's grade and the person to whom the job holder reports (the line manager);
- the day-to-day tasks that make up the job;
- whether the job holder is responsible for other people, and if so how many and their job titles.

Once the person is appointed, the job description cannot be changed without that person's agreement.

3 *Job specification*

This is a detailed list under two headings, 'essential' and 'desirable', of the qualifications, experience and personal qualities needed for a job. It may include the attitude expected of the employee, for example to equal opportunities. Qualities such as the ability to take initiatives, use judgement or manage people may also be included. It is sent to applicants with the job description and is also known as the **person specification**.

4 *Job advertisement*

This invites people to apply for a job vacancy. Internal vacancies are advertised within the organisation only. Most jobs are advertised externally and are open to anyone, including internal candidates. Advertisements may be placed in several places.

- **Local newspapers** – used for junior, shop-floor, part-time and temporary jobs. They appear in the 'Situations Vacant' part of the local papers, and are for vacancies in the local area. Some management jobs may be advertised in local papers, especially regional papers.
- **National newspapers** – used by organisations that want to recruit from as wide an area as possible. The daily and Sunday 'heavy' papers such as the *Guardian*, *Telegraph* and *Sunday Times* advertise job vacancies in special supplements on certain days. The jobs are for directors, chief executives and senior managers where there are only a limited number of people who have the background needed for such jobs.
- Trade papers are used to recruit specialist staff.
- Job Centres and employment agencies. Firms advertise usually through cards in their offices. The Job Centre or agency may also have someone suitable on their books.

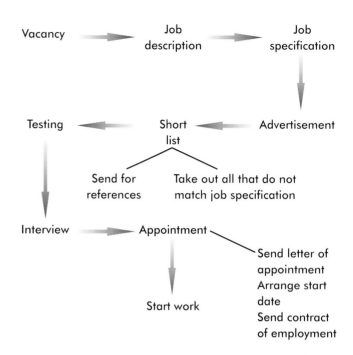

Figure 4.7 Stages in recruitment

Internal recruitment

In most cases firms recruit new employees from outside the firm. However, there are times when it might recruit people from among its existing employees.

There may be a number of reasons why firms decide to recruit internally:

- temporary or part-time staff may be invited to apply for a permanent or full-time job;
- management jobs are often filled by people within the organisation by internal promotion;
- people working in one part or branch of an organisation may be invited to apply for jobs in other parts of that organisation.

Many of the stages are the same as for external recruitment. The jobs are advertised within the organisation on notice boards or in internal newsletters. Some jobs may be advertised internally first, and if no one suitable applies, the job is advertised more widely.

The benefits of internal recruitment:

- The company already knows the applicants. It knows the quality of their work and can judge whether they can fit into the new job. Some companies take on staff on a temporary basis to see how good they are. If they are good, they may be offered a permanent job.

- Internal applicants know where things are and how things are done. Therefore they need less training and get used to the job faster.
- It is a fast and cheap way of recruiting. There is no need for expensive advertising or to pay the costs of bringing people from long distances for interview. There are usually only a few people to consider. The person appointed can start almost straight-away.

The drawbacks of internal recruitment:
- There is less choice if only internal people are considered. This may affect the quality of employees.
- It may slow down change. New ideas from outside are not brought in.
- Other parts of the organisation may suffer if their best people are taken to work elsewhere.

Recruitment agencies

Some employers prefer to use an agency to help them find staff. They usually deal with full-time, senior job vacancies. The employer gives the agency a detailed job and person specification. The agency tries to find people that match up to what the employer wants. They find suitable people through:
- advertising in trade papers and national newspapers;
- headhunting – where the agency approaches individuals employed elsewhere, asking them if they are interested in the job. At this stage they describe the job, but do not give the name of the employer.

The agency carries out the preliminary interviews. It then provides the employer with only one or two people to interview. The final choice is made by the employer, not the agency. The agency is paid a fee for its services.

Job Centres

These are government-run offices found in most towns. They are set up to help the unemployed to find jobs and local firms to fill vacancies. Their services are free. Vacancies are usually for low-level local jobs notified by local employers. They are displayed on cards at the Centre. Someone interested in a job is given a short interview. If they are thought to be suitable they are sent to the employer for a further interview.

People who register as unemployed must report to their local Job Centre. Thus, Job Centres are in touch with a large pool of local people looking for work. They are a cheap way of filling vacancies quickly and can save firms a lot of time and work.

Employment agencies

These are private companies that do a similar job to Job Centres. They try to match people to available jobs notified to them by employers. The agencies hold lists of suitable people for various jobs. Many of them specialise in, for example, clerical or nursing, computing or even teaching staff.

They are widely used to fill part-time, temporary and seasonal jobs. If a regular employee is off work the employer can telephone the agency for a temporary worker. The employer pays the agency a fee that includes payment to the 'temp', who is paid by the agency.

Activities

1 Give two ways in which a job vacancy can arise.

2 A large company needs to appoint the following staff:
- head of a major department (annual salary £60,000);
- graduate trainee manager (annual salary £16,000);
- factory operative (wage £260 per week plus overtime);
- canteen staff (18 hour a week: hourly wage £4.80).

Discuss the most appropriate way to recruit each of the four people needed.

3 Luxury Autos has a franchise to sell Jaguar cars. A vacancy has arisen for a salesperson following the promotion of the previous post holder. The job description for the vacancy is shown below.

Job description

Job:
Junior car showroom salesperson – selling the full range of Jaguar cars.

Pay:
£4,500 plus 1.5% commission on sales.

Reports to:
senior salesperson

Outline of responsibilities:
Demonstrating features on new and second-hand cars to prospective buyers; negotiating value of trade-in cars; arranging finance for purchaser; keeping cars and showroom looking smart.

Hours:
40 hours per week, Wednesday–Sunday

From this information, write a job specification showing the type of person the company wants. You need to remember that Jaguar prides itself on high standards. The cars are expensive and tend to be bought by wealthy people.

ICT Activity

Design an advertisement on the computer to attract applicants for the job described in question 3.

4 McDonald's

McDonald's has to make sure that there are enough workers suitable to staff its restaurants. As each of McDonald's restaurants will be open for possibly 15 hours a day or more, and

for 364 days a year, each restaurant will need to have enough workers to cover many different shifts throughout the week.

There are two types of employees at McDonald's, crewmembers, who prepare the food and ensure the restaurant is kept clean and tidy, and managers, who make sure that the restaurant runs smoothly.

When many crewmembers are needed, such as when a new restaurant opens, McDonald's will probably recruit the workers from the local Job Centre. Recruiting this way saves McDonald's time and money. If only a few crewmembers are needed at any one time, the restaurant may recruit by word of mouth or by placing a notice in the restaurant. Current crewmembers may be encouraged to get their friends to apply. Most of the crewmembers are young and usually work part-time.

Recruiting managers is more difficult as the workers need to be more skilled. When a new restaurant opens managers will usually be brought in from another restaurant to fill the vacancies. If a manager leaves, the restaurant will often try to replace the person by recruiting from experienced and promising crewmembers.

a Why does McDonald's use a different method to recruit a manager from that used to recruit a crewmember?

b Explain how McDonald's can save both time and money by using Job Centres to recruit crewmembers.

c What are the advantages of recruiting crewmembers by word of mouth?

d Discuss whether you feel McDonald's should be advised to recruit older crewmembers.

Unit 4.4 Recruitment and selection

4.4c Selection and appointment

Contract of employment →	a legal document that sets out the rights and duties of both employers and employees with regard to a job.
Curriculum vitae →	often just called a 'CV' it is a summary of an individual's personal details, qualifications and job experience.
Interview →	asking a person questions, in a face-to-face situation, to decide whether they are suitable for a job.
Referee →	a person asked to provide a reference for a job applicant.
References →	written reports given by two or three people who know a job applicant and who can give an opinion about that person's suitability for a job.
Shortlist →	the list of applicants for a job that have been chosen for interview.
Selection →	the last stage in the recruitment of new employees, when the successful candidate is chosen for a job vacancy.

→ **Key terms**

Applying for a job

Most people learn about a job vacancy from an advertisement. The advert usually gives a telephone number and an address from where you can get more details of the job, and a closing date for applications. The details include the job description, job specification and an application form.

The application form asks for personal details, such as name and address; education and qualifications; experience, including previous jobs; and the names of two referees. For some more senior jobs, the applicant is asked to include a letter setting out in more detail why they wish to be considered for the job.

The completed application form is usually the first contact that a possible future employer has with a person. The form should be filled in carefully and neatly, so as to make a good impression.

Curriculum vitae (CV)

Some organisations ask applicants to send them a curriculum vitae instead of, or occasionally as well as, an application form. The CV gives the same details as an application form. The main difference is that it is written by the individual and can be used for any job.

Like an application form, the CV is the first contact a possible employer has with an applicant. It should,

therefore, always be wordprocessed and kept up to date.

A sample application form

SARAH BROWN

Key Skills
- I am a motivated and quick learner
- Good teamwork
- I am charismatic and have a good sense of humour
- I enjoy helping people

Employment History
Temporary work
July 2000 to date

I have been temping with various agencies, in order to gain experience within the office environment, I am currently working for a large insurance company.
Saturday sales assistant
Handling cash, helping people with enquiries, helping with stock control

Hi-Life Clothes Shop
September 1998 – April 2000

Voluntary work

Helping at an old peoples home;general duties included, shopping for the residents, talking to them, helping them with light housework

Babysitting

I regular babysit for two small boys, aged 6 and 7.

Education
Greenfields College   A level Maths   C
Barking Street   A level Business studies   B
Kent   A level English   C

St Marks   8 GCSEs including English and Maths
Trolley Road, Kent

Personal Details
Date of Birth   24/03/82   Address   29 Settlebrooke Lane
                                           Tonbridge
                                           Kent
                               Telephone   01732 867867

Hobbies and Interests
I am currently learning to drive, I still enjoy doing voluntary work two evenings a week, and I am doing an evening class in computers.

A sample CV

Selection

There may be a large number of applications for a job, perhaps a hundred or more. The employer cannot see everyone; it would be too expensive and a waste of time. The employer, therefore, has to choose from the application forms or CVs which applicants to interview. Selection should always be on the basis of the job description and the person specification. There are a number of stages in selection.

1 Shortlisting

The employer or the personnel department (if there is one) goes through all the applications and draws up a list of up to perhaps six candidates to interview.

- Applications are considered in relation to the job description and job specification. Those shortlisted should have the qualifications, experience, attitudes and qualities set out in the job specification as being needed to do the job shown in the job description.
- Those with poorly presented applications and those without the right qualifications and experience are usually eliminated.

2 References

When applying for a job it is normal to be asked for the names and addresses of two or three people to act as **referees**. Referees should never be relatives. They are asked to comment on the applicant and his or her suitability for the job. These comments are known as **references**.

- One referee should be the person's current or last employer.
- Another may be a previous employer, a teacher or some other person who knows the applicant well.

Once a shortlist of candidates has been drawn up, the employer asks for references for each shortlisted applicant.

- The request for a reference may be a form asking specific questions, with perhaps a space for a short general comment, about the applicant.
- Alternatively, the referee may be asked to write general comments about the applicant and to say whether they think the person is suitable for the job. Sometimes referees are asked to comment on things like reliability, honesty, health and absence record.

Some organisations ask for references before finalising the shortlist. Others only use them after the interview, before offering the job, just to check there is nothing they have missed during the interview.

3 Testing

Some firms use aptitude and other tests to weigh up a person's suitability for a job. This is usually done before the interview.

4 Interviews

The purpose of the interview is to choose the most suitable person for the job. The style and length of the interview varies according to the job. If it is a fairly junior post the interview may be carried out with one or two people present. For a more senior job there may be several interviews with different senior managers or groups of people, or a panel of interviewers. The interviewers judge the applicants for the job in a number of ways:

- They judge whether they have the knowledge, skills, experience, attitudes and qualities they are looking for and which are needed to do the job.

- They judge the applicant's physical appearance, the way they dress and present themselves. Firms often expect staff that deal with the public to dress well.
- The interviewers will judge social and communication skills. Is the person polite and able to put their thoughts clearly into words? These skills are more important in some jobs than others.
- They try to decide whether the applicant fits in with the way the firm works and with the people they would be working with.

Interviews are not just a one-way process. The person being interviewed also has to decide whether or not they want to work for the organisation.

5 Appointment

Once all the shortlisted applicants have been seen, the interviewers decide whether to appoint one of them. Once one of them has been chosen the employer has a number of steps to follow.

- The successful person is offered the job. The offer is often made first by telephone or face to face, but it must also be made in writing. This letter of appointment sets out the terms of the job offer. The letter includes salary, holidays and any other benefits. The person appointed must also confirm in writing that they accept the job.
- A starting date has to be arranged. For some jobs, there may have to be a medical.
- A **contract of employment** must be prepared.
- Once the letter of appointment has been received the person appointed has to resign from their present job.

Contract of employment

This is a legal document that sets out the rights and duties of both the employer and the employee with regard to a job.

The employer must give every employee a written statement of the terms and conditions of their employment within 13 weeks of starting a job. Among the things to be included in the contract of employment are:

- the names and addresses of the employer and the employee;
- the job title and a brief statement of the nature of the job;
- the date on which employment begins;
- details of pay and the pay scale that applies, how and when wages or salaries, bonuses and overtime will be paid, details of fringe benefits;
- hours of work, holidays and holiday pay, details of pension schemes and the arrangements for sickness and maternity leave;
- arrangements for ending the contract and the length of notice.

Activities

1 Why do companies make shortlists of people who have applied for a job with them?

2 Why do firms usually want more than one reference for a job applicant?

3 What are likely to be the main sections of information in a CV?

4 Why is it important that a worker has a contract of employment?

5 Name two jobs where staff should be well dressed, and two jobs where this is less important.

6 You see this job advertisement in a local newspaper:

JOB VACANCY

Woman required as Sales Assistant at city centre shop. Must have good qualifications and experience.

Successful applicant will need to work flexible hours.

Send letter of application and CV to:
CLW Ltd, Longfellow Road, Holmefield, IP7 8SD

Give as many reasons as you can why this is not a very good advertisement.

7 A television company has advertised for someone to train as a researcher for its popular chat show. The job involves finding suitable guests and providing the interviewer with a list of questions to ask. The company receives more than 60 applications.

In order to produce a shortlist, it is decided to compare the applications using a checklist. Each person's letter of application and CV are read, and the appropriate boxes ticked on the checklist. Part of this list is reproduced below. Those with the highest scores on the checklist will be shortlisted for an interview.

Copy and complete the checklist with the types of qualities that the company should look for in a researcher.

Applicant's name:	Excellent	Good	Satisfactory	Poor
Application form completed neatly and without mistakes?				
Suitable school/ college qualifications?				

8 Group activity

Testing is often used to find out if someone who has applied for a job is suitable. Within your group, brainstorm ideas for suitable tests for the jobs below. Write up these tests so that someone else would be able to assess the applicants.

a taxi driver

b school receptionist

c sales assistant at a supermarket

□ Case Study

9 BUPA

When the private healthcare company, BUPA, introduced its 24-hour telephone help line, the company thought carefully about what type of people would be suitable to staff the telephones lines. If BUPA members were not feeling well and wanted to discuss their symptoms before seeing a doctor, they could phone the call centre and receive advice on what they should do.

BUPA realised that the person taking the call had to have medical training, so the person needed to be a qualified nurse. Other skills were written into the person specification.

BUPA used a variety of tests to select the most suitable of the applicants. The first stage was to phone each applicant and hold a conversation with him or her. This was used to assess the person's telephone manner. The next stage consisted of an interview when candidates would be tested on their medical knowledge. Then a letter-writing exercise to test the applicant's literacy skills would follow after that. The final stage involved the person visiting a call centre to get an impression of what the working environment was like.

a Why is it important that each person employed at BUPA's call centre has a good telephone manner?

b Besides having medical knowledge, what other skills would appear in the person specification for someone working at the call centre?

c Why do you think letter writing was considered to be a suitable test?

d Write a list of suitable questions that could be asked at the interview.

ICT Activity

Wordprocess a suitable contract of employment for someone about to start a job at a BUPA call centre.

Unit 4.5 Training and re-training

Modern firms have to use new methods if they are to stay competitive. Thus firms need a workforce that can adapt to change quickly and easily. Workers at all levels have to be flexible. This means they have to have good basic skills. They must be willing and able to learn new methods and new skills as the need arises. To be able to respond to change, workers have to be trained more than once during their working lives. Firms that want to stay up-to-date have to invest in training and be willing to bear the costs.

Reasons for training

- To provide workers with the skills they need to be able to do their jobs.
- To keep up with changes in technology. For example, if new software or a new CAD/CAM machine is introduced the operators have to learn new skills.
- To improve the level of workers' knowledge and skills so that they become more effective and efficient. Firms want workers that can do more than one job. They need workers who are flexible and trained in more than one set of skills, that is, to be multi-skilled.
- To provide workers with the qualifications they need for their job.
- Changes in the law mean that workers' knowledge has to be brought up to date. For example, electricians have to show they have done a course in the latest electrical regulations.
- To train workers to cope with new work situations. For example, a worker moved from one job to another, or a different job in the same firm.
- To prepare people for promotion. This may mean having to gain higher qualifications.

Re-training

In recent years many industries have disappeared. As a result many skills used in those industries have also gone. The workers need to be taught new skills, to do different jobs. In these cases the government has provided local training schemes to teach workers new skills. For example, in shipbuilding, coal-mining and steel-making areas.

Re-training older people in the use of new technology

Changes within a firm may mean that some jobs are lost. Rather than make the workers redundant the firm may re-train them to do different jobs, for example:

- There is no longer a use for certain skills, maybe because the job has been automated. For example, welders may be replaced by robots that can do the job faster and more accurately. Rather than make the welders redundant they may be re-trained to do a different job.
- The introduction of new technology may mean a job is done in a different way. For example the introduction of new software means that operators have to be trained to use the new package.
- Some jobs in a firm may be lost because of reorganisation. Instead of making the workers redundant the firm may re-train them to do another job.

Induction training

It takes time for new workers to settle down and feel happy in their jobs. The employer wants them to be working at full speed as soon as possible. New workers are given **induction** training as soon as they join the firm.

- To help new workers 'find their way around', they often start with a tour of the site.
- They are told about the firm, its history, how it is organised and who the main people are. They are also told about the firm's policies, for example on quality and towards customers.
- Their conditions of employment are explained in more detail. They are told the firm's rules, for example about breaks, and what to do if they are sick or late. They are trained in health and safety procedures.
- They are introduced to the people they are going to work with and others they may need to deal with in their job.

Off-the-job training

There are two main methods of training. One of these is off-the-job training. It includes all training carried out away from the workplace. Very often it is a college course paid for by the firm. It may be on one day of the week, on day release, when workers are paid as normal although they are at college. Very often the theory work is done in college while the practical

work is learnt 'on-the-job'. There are also specialist training companies that provide courses, often on a particular topic. Big firms may have their own training centres. They may also have residential centres where they provide longer courses, usually for managers.

Off-the-job training at a local college

On-the-job training

The other method is on-the-job training, where training takes place while doing a job. It may consist of being shown the job step by step by an experienced worker. The trainee practices the job, watched by the experienced worker, until he or she can do it properly.

- On-the-job training is cheaper than off-the-job training and easier to organise. It is the most common way of training.
- Employees are taught to do a job in the way the company wants. It is mainly practical parts of the job that are taught on the job. Any theory that is needed may be taught off the job.
- Not everyone is good at showing other people how to do a job. There is also the danger that existing workers pass on their bad habits to the new workers.

Staff development

This term is sometimes used as another word for training. **Staff development** can mean the personal development of staff. This may be to meet the needs of the firm or of the individual.

Staff that want to get better qualifications are supported by their firms. They may have their course paid for by the firm or be given time to study.

Staff chosen for promotion or a higher grade of job are given a programme to develop the skills they need. For example, many large firms choose staff or recruit people as management trainees. They follow a planned, personal programme that may last a year or more, to prepare them for their next job. The programme may be in three parts:

- working alongside experienced people doing similar jobs;
- being given experience that will help them do the job;
- taking training courses to give them the knowledge they will need to do the job.

Forms of training

Modern apprenticeship

- This is a form of training offered to 16 and 17-year-old school or college leavers. Modern apprentices are usually employed and are paid wages. The employers pay the wages; training is mainly paid for through government grants.
- Apprenticeships provide a chance to gain high-level skills and qualifications to NVQ Level 3 (A level standard). The length of the apprenticeship varies. It mainly depends on how long it takes to reach the NVQ Level 3 qualification.
- They follow a scheme of training agreed for their industry. The schemes are flexible. Minimum standards are laid down for the industry. Actual training schemes can be varied to meet the firm's needs. They can include multi-skill training and a foreign language, for example.
- The skills learnt should mean that trainees can get jobs as technicians in industry and become future managers.

The government and training

From 1 April 2001 all post-16 education and training, up to university level, is being controlled and paid for through the Learning and Skills Council (LSC). As well as the national Learning and Skills Council there are 47 local Learning and Skills Councils in England. A big part of their role is to provide funds to the further education colleges and school sixth forms. They also pay for all the training schemes that were paid for by the Training and Enterprise Councils. They are also responsible for adult and community education and for links between business and education.

The role of the local Learning and Skills Councils is to ensure that the UK has a modern, well-trained workforce. It does this in several ways:

- making sure that there is training available to provide the kinds of skills that local employers need;
- improving people's chances of getting a job (their employability) by providing them with the skills employers want;
- helping employers to improve the skills of their workforce;
- ensuring that all 16- to 19-year-olds are entitled to stay in education and training. The local Learning and Skills Councils must ensure that the kinds of courses they and employers want are available;
- making sure that all the education and training on offer is of a high quality.

Learning+Skills Council

BUSINESS ASPECTS

Training is a large cost for business. When a business pays for someone to be trained it is an investment. It can be a large investment, for example the estimated cost of replacing a bank clerk is £5,000, £10,000 to replace a deputy manager of a supermarket and £50,000 for a tax inspector at the Inland Revenue.

---

1 What is meant by a 'multi-skilled' workforce?

2 Give two reasons why businesses need to keep their workforce well trained.

3 Imagine a new teacher has been recruited to your school or college. Her first day is to be used for induction training. Think about the things that the new teacher would need to know, and the key people she would need to meet. Devise a day's programme of training for the teacher.

4 Autoglass

Autoglass is a company that repairs and replaces damaged vehicles' windscreens and other windows. Like many companies, Autoglass recognises training as being important, not just so that its employees have the skills to do their jobs properly, but also because it is a way of motivating workers.

The windscreen replacement industry is changing all the time. So Autoglass tries to create a culture of constant training within the business. Training is seen as a normal part of the job, rather than something you just do when you first start work.

New recruits joining Autoglass have to follow an induction training programme called 'Startline'. Here the new employees are taught the skills they will need to do their jobs efficiently. They also have to spend some time in each part of the company – at a local branch, the call centre and different departments at the head office – to give them a better idea of how the company works. This helps them to realise how their jobs fit in with others. Somebody who takes customers' telephone calls at the call centre will need, for instance, to be able to answer questions about the different ways of making repairs to small cracks in windscreens.

Much of the training is linked to a recognised national qualification. Fitters are awarded an NVQ when they have successfully completed their training. Senior managers undergo training to improve their management skills. Many senior managers study for a degree at university as a way of improving their management skills.

Since introducing its extensive training programmes, Autoglass has benefitted in other ways as well. Labour turnover has fallen, which means that workers, on average, are remaining with the company for longer. Also Autoglass has found that it can now fill more of its management positions from within the business, as improved training has allowed workers to take on more demanding roles.

a Outline how the skills needed by someone working in the Autoglass call centre would be different from those required by fitters.

b Explain two reasons why training can be more successful when it is linked to a recognised qualification.

c Autoglass believes that providing training is a way of motivating their employees. Explain how training can act as a motivator.

d Explain why it is better for a company if:
   i its labour turnover is low;
   ii it recruits its managers from within the company.

Unit 4.6 Methods of remuneration

Basic pay →	the amount paid to a person for working an agreed minimum period of time. The pay earned for working a basic week, before any overtime or bonuses.
Bonus →	an extra payment on top of the normal rate of pay, usually as a reward for meeting a target.
Commission →	a method of payment usually based on the value of sales achieved. Normally paid as a percentage of sales.
Deductions →	money taken out of a person's gross pay, mainly income tax and National Insurance contributions. The amount left is net pay.
Flat rate →	another name for the basic rate of pay.
Fringe benefits →	benefits given to employees in addition to their wages or salaries, for example a company car, life insurance, and free private health insurance.
Gross pay →	the total pay earned before any deductions have been made.
Income tax →	the tax levied on an individual by the government on all income, above a certain figure. It is based on gross income earned from all sources.
National Insurance contributions →	money deducted from workers' gross pay, used to pay for the system of welfare benefits provided by the government. Part is paid by individuals and part is paid by employers.
Net pay →	the money shown on a person's payslip, stating the amount actually paid after deductions. It is 'take-home pay'.
Overtime →	a payment made for working more hours than the basic working week.
Performance-related pay →	an extra payment made to employees when agreed targets have been met. It is very like a bonus and is usually paid to salary earners.
Piece rate →	an amount paid to workers according to the amount they produce. Workers are usually paid a fixed amount for each item they produce.
Profit-related pay →	a form of bonus which is linked to the size of a firm's profits.
Salary →	a method of paying employees for their work. It is calculated on an annual basis and normally paid monthly.
Time rate →	an amount paid to workers according to the amount of time they work. It may be stated as a rate per hour, day or week.
Wages →	a method of paying employees for their work. They are mainly paid to shop-floor workers on a weekly basis.

For most people one of the most important things about going to work is the amount they are paid. People are not all paid in the same way, even within the same firm. Some are paid every week while others are paid every month. Pay may vary because of the amount of time worked or because a certain target was reached.

There are two main methods of paying people for their work, **wages** and **salaries**.

Wages

Wages are usually paid to shop-floor and manual workers. They are normally paid weekly and very often in cash. Wages are based either on **time rates** or on **piece rates**.

Time rates

Someone paid on time rates is paid according to the time worked. Usually, they are paid so much an hour or so much a week of an agreed length, perhaps 40 hours. The rate they are paid for a week's or an hour's work is their **basic rate** of pay. It is also called their flat rate of pay.

The flat rate does not depend on how much work the worker produces in the time worked. Flat-rate pay is used where it is not possible to measure how much work should be produced in a given time. It is often used to pay skilled workers where it is not possible to measure how long a job will take. The main drawback is that there is no incentive for workers to work harder or faster. Flat rate does not include bonuses or overtime.

Employees paid on time rates may be able to earn more money by working **overtime**. Overtime is paid for working more hours than the basic week. Overtime is usually paid at a different rate from the basic rate of pay. For example, it might be paid at time and a half, while overtime at the weekend might be paid at double time.

Example

Suppose Ian and Jane are paid at an hourly rate of £9.50 an hour for a basic working week of 38 hours. They both work five hours overtime during the week for which the rate is time and a half. They also work four hours on Sunday for which they are paid double time. What would their wages be for that week?

Basic pay	= £9.50 x 38 hours	= £361.00
Overtime,		
weekdays	= £9.50 x 1.5 x 5 hours	= £71.25
Overtime,		
Sunday	= £9.50 x 2 x 4 hours	= £76.00
Total pay for week		£508.25

Piece rates

Piece rates are based on the amount produced or processed by a worker. Workers are paid a fixed sum for every item or piece they produce. A worker who produces 5,000 items a week is paid more than one who produces 3,000 items. Piecework can only be used for jobs where the work of one worker can be counted or measured. It is not suitable for all jobs. For example, most clerical jobs are not suited to piece-work, but production-line jobs are.

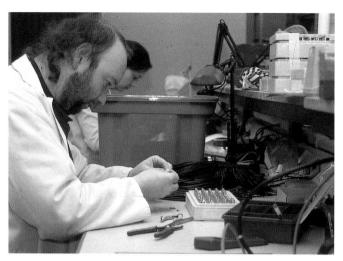
This worker is paid a piece rate, based on the number of components he makes

Benefits of piece rates:

- Workers work harder because the more they produce the more they are paid.
- It is a fairer system than flat- or time-rate pay because the hard working workers are paid more than the lazy ones.
- People can work at their own pace if they want to. Some may prefer to work at a speed that suits them rather than be worn out going for higher wages.

Drawbacks of piece rates:

- So that they can earn high wages, workers produce as many items as they can. This may result in poor quality work. It can mean that much of their work is below standard and has to be rejected. Work may have to be thrown away or time taken to correct it. This is expensive for the firm.
- Workers may also lose money, since they are not paid for work that is rejected or has to be corrected.
- Firms have to spend more money on quality control. Inspectors have to be employed to make sure work is up to standard. Rejecting work reduces workers' pay and can cause disputes.
- The rate for the job has to be agreed with workers, through their trade unions. This can be difficult and may cause disputes. The rate is usually fixed using work study. This means timing the work and fixing a rate based on the time taken to do the job.

Salaries

Salaries are usually paid to managers and office workers. They are usually stated at so much a year, although they are normally paid monthly. Thus, someone earning £21,000 a year will be paid:

$$\frac{£21,000}{12} = £1,750 \text{ a month (before \textbf{deductions}).}$$

Salaries are usually paid straight into employees' bank accounts rather than in cash. Salary earners are not usually paid overtime. They are expected to put in any extra time necessary to do the job.

Payment by results

The more workers on piecework produce, the more they get paid. It is a form of payment by results. There are also other forms of payment by results.

Commission

Many sales staff are paid a commission on their sales. It is calculated as a percentage of the value of sales. Examples of commission payments are:

- Salespeople may be paid a basic salary, plus a commission on any sales above a set target.

Example

A salesperson may be paid £10,000 a year plus commission of 3% on all sales over £5,000 a month. Suppose sales were £8,000 in a month. Pay would be:

salary of $\dfrac{£10,000}{12}$

= £833.33 + commission of (£8,000 – £5,000) x 3%

= £3,000 x 3% = £90

Total pay for the month would be £923.33 (gross).

- Some salespeople work on a commission-only basis. They are likely to be paid a higher rate of commission than in the example above.
- Estate agents and travel agents are paid commission on the value of the houses and holidays they sell.

Bonuses

These are extra payments over and above the basic wage or salary. They are often paid as a reward for reaching a target. The target may be a certain level of production, good timekeeping, low absence rates or even long service. The promise of a **bonus** can act as an incentive to encourage workers to reach a set target.

Performance-related pay

This is a payment for reaching an agreed target. The target may be a personal target agreed with an individual. It can also be a target for the firm as a whole. It can be seen as a kind of bonus. For example, if a firm makes a profit of £5m or more, 5% of the profit may be shared amongst its workers.

For some senior managers, **performance-related pay** is part of their pay 'package'. They are paid a basic salary to which is added a further amount that depends on them personally, or the firm as a whole, reaching agreed targets. In this case it is not a bonus but part of their pay.

Fringe benefits

Often known as 'perks' (short for perquisites) these are benefits, other than money, paid in addition to wages or salaries. They are given as part of a pay package. The best known **fringe benefit** is the company car. Other fringe benefits include health insurance for employees and their families, payments into a pension fund, free life assurance, discounts when buying the firm's goods and cheap loans. Fringe benefits are liable to income tax.

Gross pay

Gross pay is a worker's total pay before any deductions are made. It is always greater than take-home pay. For a person paid an annual salary, paid monthly, it will be:

$$\frac{\text{annual salary}}{12}$$

For a worker paid each week, on time rates, it is:

$$\begin{array}{c}\text{basic weekly}\\\text{hours}\end{array} \times \begin{array}{c}\text{rate per}\\\text{hour}\end{array} + \text{overtime} + \text{bonuses}$$

Deductions

Deductions are taken away from gross pay to arrive at net pay. The two main deductions are income tax and National Insurance. They are statutory (compulsory), and all workers that earn above a certain amount must pay them. The amount paid varies according to a person's gross earnings in a year. Other deductions might include superannuation or payment to some other pension scheme. Some deductions, such as trade union dues or donations to a charity, are voluntary.

Net pay

This is the amount that a person is actually paid. It is their take-home pay, as shown on their payslip.

net pay = gross pay – all deductions

Activities

1 Give an example of a statutory deduction from a person's wages, and a voluntary deduction.

2 A firm pays its hourly paid workers the following rates:

	Rate of pay
Basic rate (up to 40 weekday hours)	£8.00
Weekday hours after 40 hours	Time and a half
Sunday working	Double time

Calculate the gross wage of these three workers:

	Number of hours worked		
	Ahmed	Pauline	David
Monday	8	9	9
Tuesday	8	8	9
Wednesday	8	8	0
Thursday	10	9	9
Friday	8	8	8
Saturday	3	0	4
Sunday	4	4	0

ICT Activity

Set up a spreadsheet to calculate the wages due in the exercise above.

3 Firms do not usually like to pay wages in cash. They prefer to pay by cheque or by crediting the employees' bank accounts. Why do firms not like paying people in cash?

4 A carpet salesman is paid £9,000 each year. He also receives 5% of any sales above £10,000 that he makes each month.

a Calculate how much he would receive each month if he failed to sell enough to be paid commission.

b In January he sold £14,000 worth of carpets and in February he sold £22,000 worth. How much would he be paid for each of these months?

5 A firm agrees a performance-related pay scheme with its employees. If the firm's profits exceed £6.5 million, 2% of the total profit will be shared between the 50 employees.

If the firm made £7 million that year, how much profit-related pay would each employee receive?

Case Study

6 **Amazing Glaze**

Amazing Glaze is a company that makes and fits double-glazing windows. Most of its business comes from the replacement windows market. The industry is very competitive and double-glazing companies always need to keep their costs as low as possible.

Amazing Glaze has decided to try to improve the efficiency of its workforce by introducing a system of piecework pay for its workers. The firm currently employs two types of workers, assemblers, who make the windows, and fitters, who put them into houses. Amazing Glaze believes that both types of workers are not working as hard as they should be.

At the moment the company pays these hourly wages:

Assemblers £6.00 per hour
Fitters £7.50 per hour.

The company conducts a study to time how long it takes its workers to make and fit three sizes of windows. This information is then used to determine the rate per window they will pay. The results are shown in the two tables below.

a Explain what is meant by 'piecework'.
b How could Amazing Glaze save money by introducing piecework rates of pay?

c How might the quality of the product be affected by the introduction of piecework pay?
d Discuss whether the workers would be pleased with the new pay system.

| Size of window | Average time taken by worker | |
	Making window	Fitting window
Large window (more than 1 m²)	90 minutes	60 minutes
Medium window (0.5–1 m²)	60 minutes	45 minutes
Small window (less than 0.5 m²)	45 minutes	30 minutes

| Size of window | Suggested piecework rates per window | |
	Making window	Fitting window
Large window (more than 1 m²)	£8.00	£7.00
Medium window (0.5–1 m²)	£5.50	£5.00
Small window (less than 0.5 m²)	£3.50	£3.00

People in Organisations

Unit 4.7 Employment and the law

The law affects the ways firms recruit and the way they deal with the people who work for them.

Equal opportunities

People have a right to be treated fairly and equally. They should not be ruled out of applying for a job or from doing a job due to their colour, race, gender or because they are disabled. **Equal opportunities** laws are meant to stop **discrimination**. They apply to people looking for work and those already in work, and affect the ways firms recruit. Internally as well as externally advertised jobs should always be given to the best person for the job. There are three main equal opportunities laws:

1 **Sex Discrimination Acts** – these Acts make it unlawful to treat men and women differently.
2 **Race Relations Acts** – these make it unlawful to treat people differently because of their nationality, race, colour or ethnic origin.

These two sets of laws affect employment in a number of ways:

- Jobs should not be advertised in a way that limits who can apply. In general, jobs cannot be advertised as being specifically for a man or for a woman, or for a person from one ethnic group. An advert asking for a 'woman secretary' or 'a person of European origin only' would be breaking the law.
- Men and women employees, of all races, must have the same chance of gaining promotion within a firm. This often means advertising the job internally, so that everyone knows there is a chance for promotion.
- Men and women must be given the same opportunities for training.
- There should not be a difference between the ages or terms on which men and women or any other class of employee retires.
- When there are redundancies, every person should be dealt with in exactly the same way.
- Under the **Equal Pay Act** men and women should be paid equally for doing the same work. They should also have the same overtime rates, bonuses, holidays and conditions of service.

3 **Disability Discrimination Act** – this Act makes it unlawful for employers of 20 or more workers to discriminate against people with disabilities. This applies when they are recruiting new staff, in promotions, training or when dismissing employees.

Getting help

The Equal Opportunities Commission deals with cases under the Sex Discrimination and the Equal Pay Acts. The Commission for Racial Equality was set up under the Race Relations Acts and helps to enforce these Acts. A person who feels they have been discriminated against can go to one of these bodies to get help. They will give advice and support the person against an employer. They will pay to take the case to court or to an **industrial tribunal**.

Employment Protection Acts

These Acts were passed to make workers' jobs safer. There are four ways that the Acts help to increase job security:

1 Employers must give all employees contracts of employment.
2 **Unfair dismissal** – an industrial tribunal decides whether the reason a worker has been dismissed is unfair or not. Every case is different and is decided according to the circumstances of the case. The reason for ending a worker's employment is only unfair if a tribunal says it is. There are some criteria that have to be met before a claim for unfair dismissal can be made:
   - a full-time employee must have worked for the employer for at least two years;
   - a part-time employee must have worked more than eight hours a week for at least five years;
   - some reasons are automatically unfair. For example, dismissal on the grounds of colour, race, gender or for trade union activities.
3 **Constructive dismissal** – if an employer acts in such a way that an employee feels they have to resign, there may be a constructive dismissal. It is grounds for applying to an industrial tribunal. A tribunal will decide according to the facts of the case.

Example

An employer has asked Jane to do a job that up until then had been done by another employee, Ben. Ben has been left with very little to do. The employer has not dismissed him. But, because of the way the employer has acted, Ben feels that he has no choice but to resign.

4 **Industrial tribunals** were also established under these Acts. They are made up of three people. A lawyer always chairs them. They are much less formal than a court. Both sides present their case for the tribunal to rule on. Employees that 'win' their case may:
   - get their old job back (reinstatement), or
   - be offered a new job (re-engagement), or
   - be paid compensation.

Health and Safety at Work Act

This Act covers every kind of place of work. Factories, offices, farms, schools and colleges are all included. It sets out the duties and responsibilities of employers and employees for health and safety at work.

What the lawyers call a 'general duty of care' is placed on everyone in a place of work. This means that everyone in a place of work, including visitors, is responsible for his or her own and other people's health and safety.

Health and safety symbols (reproduced by permission of the Health & Safety Executive)

Employers' duties

- To provide a safe place to work, including safe machinery and safe working methods. For example, making sure there are no trailing wires and that entrances and exits are not obstructed.
- To enforce safety regulations and safety standards. For example, machines must be guarded and workers made to use a machine only when it is guarded.
- To provide safety training and adequate safety supervision. All accidents must be recorded and investigated and the cause put right.

Employees' duties

- To report any defects in machinery or equipment, or in working areas.
- Not to interfere with anything provided for their own safety and that of others. For example, machine guards can slow a worker down. Interfering with a guard is dangerous and may lead to an accident.
- To protect themselves and others in their work area. For example, by wearing safety clothing and not leaving things around that might cause someone to bump into or fall over them.

Activities

1 Explain how the law is being broken in each of these situations:

  a A job is described as unsuitable for a physically disabled person because there is no door ramp for wheelchair access.

  b A woman is asked at a job interview whether she plans to have children in the near future.

  c A woman is made redundant because the man doing the same type of work has a family to support and so needs the job more.

  d A foreman removes fire extinguishers to avoid them getting in the way of forklift trucks.

  e A worker does not wear the safety glasses issued to him because he thinks they make him look silly.

  f A manager makes fun of an employee's work and bullies him into taking a less responsible job in the firm.

Case Study

2 Telford Telesales

Telford Telesales is a company that specialises in selling other companies' products and services over the telephone. Firms that lack the expertise to sell in this way pay Telford Telesales to 'cold call' potential customers to promote anything from time-share holidays to car insurance. The company employs about 200 workers, many of whom work part-time. The training given to employees consists of developing a good telephone manner and learning about the products and services that are sold.

The business has always been worried about the image it has and has taken trouble not to be seen as discriminating in any way. The company recently set itself a series of targets as far as employees are concerned. Telford Telesales stated that within two years, 15% of its workforce should be drawn from ethnic minorities, 20% should consist of over-60s workers and 5% should be registered disabled. This would mean that when someone left the company, preference would be given to someone from one of these groups as a replacement.

These targets received a mixed response from Telford Telesales directors. Some felt that the changes would be good for the company and its reputation, while others were not happy about the plans.

  a Describe what type of worker is likely to be attracted to a job in telesales.

  b Explain how setting employment quotas would help Telford Telesales' reputation.

  c Discuss whether you think companies should set employment quotas.

Unit 4.8 Industrial relations

→ Key terms

Arbitration →	where an independent person is asked to help settle a dispute.
Collective bargaining →	when trade unions negotiate with an employer or group of employers on behalf of their members.
Conciliation →	where the two sides to a dispute try to understand each other's point of view and come to an agreement. Usually both sides get some of what they want.
Industrial action →	when a group of workers decides to take action against their employer as a result of a dispute or a grievance.
Industrial dispute →	when, after negotiations, employers and workers (through their trade unions) cannot find an answer to a problem.
Industrial relations →	the relationship between employers and their employees.
Redundancy →	dismissal of a worker because their job is no longer needed by their employer.
Trade association →	an organisation that draws all its members from one industry or trade. Trade associations share information, act as pressure groups and promote their industry's interests.
Trade union →	an association of workers formed to promote, protect and represent the interests of its members to employers, the government and others.
Trades Union Congress (TUC) →	the central trade union body that promotes the interests of the trade union movement in this country and abroad. Its members are the separate trade unions.
Work to rule →	a form of industrial action where workers follow their employer's rules and regulations to the letter.

Workers want good holidays, pay and working conditions. Employers want a happy workforce. But high pay, long holidays and lots of good facilities for workers cost a firm money. They not only affect costs but also profits and prices. Employers and employees see things in a different way. But they need to get on well together. The way they relate is called **industrial relations**. Workers are usually represented by **trade unions**. They act on behalf of all the workers. Both sides prefer to stay on good terms. They work together to sort out disagreements before they become disputes.

Trade unions

A trade union is an association of workers formed to promote and protect the interests of its members.

Compared to their workers, employers are powerful and have very large resources. In the past, the bad ones treated their workers badly. Conditions and pay were poor. Anyone who 'stepped out of line' risked the sack. Individual workers were too weak to stand up to their employers. But, by joining up with other workers, they could look after their interests better. By acting together they had more power and could take joint action to get a better deal.

Trade union leaders at a TUC conference

Functions of trade unions

- To negotiate with employers on behalf of their members. Through collective bargaining they work to get the best deal for their members.
  - pay and conditions of employment, including working hours, holidays, sick pay, health and safety;
  - working conditions (such as canteens, rest rooms and cleaner work areas);
  - good terms if there are redundancies in a firm.
- To negotiate grievance, dispute and disciplinary procedures with employers. These are meant to make sure things are done fairly and properly if workers feel they have been treated badly or where a firm's rules are broken. Union officers accompany and advise members at hearings under these procedures.
- To give legal advice and protection on matters related to work. They represent members at industrial tribunals and other work-related legal actions, for example a claim for compensation due to an accident at work.
- To provide a range of benefits for members, for example strike pay, injury benefits, retirement homes and convalescent homes.
- To act as a pressure group to put forward their members' views and interests, for example to MPs, the government and the press.

Types of trade unions

1 **Craft unions** were the first kind of union to be formed. All members work in the same craft and have similar skills. At one time these unions controlled membership since only those who had done an apprenticeship could be members. Most craft unions are small, and many have merged to form larger unions.
2 **Industrial unions** represent the workers in one industry, for example USDAW (Union of Shop Distributive and Allied Workers).
3 **General unions** represent workers in any industry. Originally their members were unskilled and semi-skilled workers. Now they are strong in the newer industries and represent workers at all levels. They are very large unions, for example the TGWU (Transport and General Workers Union).

4 **White-collar unions** represent non-manual workers. Examples include the National Union of Teachers, Royal College of Nursing and the Professional Footballers Association.

Pickets

Collective bargaining

When a trade union bargains on behalf of all its members it is acting collectively. Unions may negotiate on rates of pay, holidays, hours of work and other working conditions and methods. Negotiations can be:

- **national** – on behalf of a whole industry or branches of a company, for example nurses or all Ford plants in the UK;
- **local** – at a branch level, often called plant bargaining, for example a Ford plant. Sometimes there may be local agreements in addition to national ones.

Collective bargaining works to the benefit of both employers and employees.

- It would be very difficult for each worker to negotiate with their employer. They would not have the skill or the knowledge to do so. The employer has more resources and is in a stronger position.
- It would take too long and cost too much to negotiate with each worker separately.
- If each employee struck their own deal, it might result in many different rates of pay and working conditions. This would be complicated and costly and might cause disputes.

There are other matters in which trade unions and firms have set up procedures collectively. These are described below.

Discipline

Factories and some offices can be very dangerous places. There have to be rules about the way people behave while at work. Most firms have disciplinary procedures agreed with the unions. They are used when the firm's rules are broken. Serious offences like stealing, fighting or drinking at work may lead to instant dismissal. In other cases there are steps that have to be followed. These go through a series of verbal and written warnings, with dismissal as a last resort.

Grievances

A worker, or group of workers, may feel they have been treated badly or unfairly at work. They may think the firm has acted unreasonably or failed to consult them. For example, they may not have been given a bonus they feel was due to them, or been asked to change jobs. A grievance can give rise to a complaint or even a dispute. Firms and unions agree grievance procedures to deal with such matters.

Dismissals

This is where a worker is 'sacked' by the employer. This may be because of bad behaviour or because they cannot do their job.

Redundancies

There are times when jobs are no longer needed. For example, when a branch is closed, or new technology means fewer people are needed. A skill or type of employee may no longer be needed. Redundancies happen when employees are dismissed because the employer no longer needs their jobs. For a **redundancy** to exist the job must come to an end. If a worker is replaced by someone else doing exactly the same job there is no redundancy.

A redundant person who has worked for more than 16 hours a week for two years at a firm is entitled in law to redundancy pay. The minimum amount depends on the age, number of years at the firm and their basic pay.

When there are redundancies, the recognised trade unions have a right in law to be consulted. They try to find other ways of dealing with the problem. If this fails they try to get the best redundancy pay possible.

Industrial disputes

When **collective bargaining** fails to produce an answer to a problem there is a dispute. Pay is often the main reason for **industrial disputes**. Other reasons include victimisation of a worker, closure of a factory or moving work to another part of a firm. Both sides prefer to sort disputes out quickly and avoid **industrial action**. Disputes and industrial action can be costly for both sides. Firms may lose money through lost production. Workers may lose wages.

Industrial action

When talks have failed to settle a dispute, the unions may take industrial action. It is a way of putting pressure on employers. Before taking action unions must, by law, ballot their members and give notice of their action to employers. There are a number of different forms of industrial action.

- **Action days** – when workers go on strike for a day or two at a time, but on different days each week. This makes it hard for employers to plan ahead. The loss of wages by workers is kept to a minimum.
- **Go-slow** – when workers carry on working but take a long time over their work. They may lose bonuses but still get their basic pay.
- **Overtime ban** – when workers still get their basic pay but refuse to work overtime. Firms often prefer to use overtime instead of taking on new workers when they are especially busy or need to finish an order quickly. An overtime ban may mean loss of production, late orders or cancelled services. The firm and workers lose money.

A group of marchers

- **Strikes** – these happen when workers withdraw their labour. They refuse to work. They may have pickets to try to persuade other workers not to work. Only a limited number of pickets are allowed by law. They also try to stop deliveries and goods leaving the firm. Strikes are a last resort. Workers lose their wages. After a time the union may provide strike pay, but this is probably less than the workers' basic pay.

  Strikes are official when called by the union after a ballot. If a group of workers walk out without the support of the union the strike is unofficial.
- **Withdraw goodwill** – this includes refusing to attend meetings or to do the work of absent staff.
- **Work to rule** – when workers follow the company's rule book exactly. By 'working to the book' they slow work down without loss of wages.

All industrial action means that employers and employees lose money. Any form of industrial action affects production and causes the firm to lose money and have lower profits. A long strike may lose the firm new business. Workers also lose. When they take industrial action their pay is less than usual.

Advisory Conciliation and Arbitration Service (ACAS)

Most disputes are settled through negotiation. There are times when neither side is willing to give way and they need help to end the dispute.

ACAS was set up in 1975 to help to resolve disputes and to promote good industrial relations. Although set up and funded by the government, it is independent. Its services are free and confidential. The services can be used by employers and trade unions. It has three main functions:

1 It gives information and advice about all things to do with employment law and industrial relations.
2 ACAS tries to prevent disputes from developing into major confrontations. The trade unions and the employers can ask for help jointly or separately. ACAS staff help the two sides to work together to solve problems before they get out of hand.
3 It works with both sides to try to settle disputes in two main ways:

- **Conciliation** – an ACAS officer will get the two sides to a dispute to meet. The aim is to get each side to understand and come to terms with the other's point of view. By talking through the problem they hope to find some 'common ground' that can be the basis of a compromise.
- **Arbitration** – if the two sides fail to agree through conciliation, they can ask ACAS to provide arbitration. ACAS will help to find a neutral person, acceptable to both sides, to act as an arbitrator. This person will listen to both sides and suggest an answer to the problem. Both sides will often agree beforehand to accept the answer suggested.

ACAS can only help the parties to a dispute to get over their differences. It cannot impose an answer or even recommend how a dispute is settled.

Trades Union Congress (TUC)

Most trade unions belong to the **Trades Union Congress**. It puts forward the views of the trade union movement as a whole.

- It states the trade union point of view to the government, press and employers. It also acts as a pressure group on behalf of the trade union movement.
- It provides education and training services for union officials and shop stewards.
- It sorts out disputes between trade unions.

Employers' organisations

Employers also find it useful to join together to promote their interests. Some associations put forward the views of business in general, such as the Institute of Directors and the CBI. There are others, known as trade associations, that put forward the views of one industry or trade.

Like trade unions and the TUC, they act as a pressure group to put forward the views of their industry from the employers' point of view.

1 Copy out the paragraph below, filling in the missing words.

Trade Unions

One of the main functions of a union is _____ bargaining. This means the union _____ with employers about wages. Unions can also represent workers who have a _____ . This could be because a worker is being treated badly such as being unfairly _____ . By law, unions must be consulted if a worker is to be made _____ . Trade unions also act as _____ groups, putting forward their members' views to the government. Unions are able to use industrial action, such as _____ , to support their cases.

> redundant   striking   pressure   collective
> negotiates   grievance   dismissed

2 Give an example of a situation when a dismissal would be unfair, and an example of a situation when the dismissal would be fair.

3 What rights does a worker have who is about to be made redundant?

4 What is an industrial tribunal?

ICT Activity

Find out how the TUC is able to support trade unions. The web address is www.tuc.org.uk.

---

5 AEEU/Peugeot

In Summer 2000 many of the workers at Coventry's Peugeot car factory were unhappy. They felt it was unfair that they had to work for 39 hours each week, when employees at the

---

Case Study

company's sister factory in France worked less than 37 hours.

The workers' trade union the AEEU (Amalgamated Electrical and Engineering Union) called for a ballot on taking industrial action. The workers voted in favour of taking action, against the advice of the union leaders. A one-day strike was called. As a result Peugeot lost production of 630 cars worth more than £6 million. The action, however, persuaded Peugeot to reduce the Coventry workers' hours, but with the condition that car workers would need to work Friday evening each week. This condition was felt to be unfair by the employees, so further strike action was planned.

Duncan Simpson, a senior negotiator at AEEU, said that it was important to find a solution quickly as a long strike would damage the industry. This could result in many jobs being lost.

A spokesperson for Peugeot said that the company had factories all around the world and car production could be moved elsewhere if industrial relations at the Coventry plant got worse.

a What was the Peugeot workers' grievance?
b Besides striking, describe other forms of industrial action the workers could have taken.
c Why do you think the AEEU felt it was not a good idea to take industrial action?
d Why did the AEEU hold a ballot before the workers went on strike?
e How could ACAS have helped sort out the dispute between Peugeot and the AEEU?

Unit 4.9 Pressure groups

Pressure group →	an organised group that shares a common interest or point of view, which it promotes by trying to influence others in order to bring about change.

Businesses are under all kinds of pressure most of the time.

- They have to sell their product. The public expects goods to be of good quality for the price. Firms are under pressure to keep their costs down and their prices competitive.
- Firms are always under pressure from their competitors. Their rivals may be bringing out new products, changing designs or selling at a lower price.
- Shareholders want high profits and good dividends. If profits fall, shareholders may sell their shares. If they do, the price of the firm's shares on the stock market may fall.
- Workers expect to be paid well, have good working hours, holidays and employment conditions. Firms that fail to provide them may find themselves short of labour, especially skilled workers. Workers may put firms under pressure to improve pay and conditions, maybe through industrial action.
- Firms are also under pressure from the government, who expects them to meet standards laid down in laws and regulations.

Firms may also be put under pressure by outside groups who, for some reason, may not like what they do. These are often called **pressure groups**.

Pressure groups

A pressure group is an organised group whose members share a common interest, or point of view, which it seeks to promote. Pressure groups try to bring about change by influencing people who make decisions. Pressure groups do not only affect business. They are found where ever public opinion can have an effect on decision making.

Types of pressure groups

There are many different types of pressure groups. Pressure groups can be large or small, local, national or international. They are usually funded by voluntary contributions.

1 **Specific purpose** – these types of pressure group are set up to deal with one issue. They are often local and usually short term. Once the final decisions have been made they disband since they no longer have a purpose. Examples include:
   - residents who set up an action group to oppose the building of a new factory on greenbelt land, the building of a prison close to their homes, or proposals to close a local school;
   - groups that want to gain something, for example a local by-pass, a new pedestrian crossing on a busy road or lower speed limits on the streets of their estate.

2 **Protest** – these can be small local groups dealing with one issue, like those above, or groups that protest on a bigger scale, for example groups opposed to the use of nuclear power. More recently groups have been set up to protest about genetic engineering and the development of genetically modified (GM) crops.

3 **Protection** – there are groups that want to preserve or protect something. Many places have a local Victorian society or a civic society. They want to make sure that local historical buildings and records are not lost. Many pressure groups have a protective element to their work. For example, the National Trust protects parts of the coastline and areas of natural beauty. Trade unions and trade associations protect the interests of their members. Amnesty International protects the interests of political prisoners and human rights.

Supporters of the 'Eat British Beef' campaign in the late 1990s

4 **Promotional** – these include groups such as the CBI, the Institute of Directors and trade associations, which promote the interests of business. Friends of the Earth and Greenpeace promote environmental interests. Trade unions promote the interests of their members. The Consumers' Association promotes the interests of consumers to firms, the government and others.

Most pressure groups fall into more than one of these categories.

Pressure group methods

Pressure groups use peaceful and legal methods to put over their point of view and to try to get change. There are many ways in which they do this:

- **Petition** – a collection of signatures used either to register a protest, or to show support for a cause. The more signatures there are the higher the level of support that is shown.
- **Lobbying** – trying to persuade the people who make the decisions on an issue to take up the pressure group's point of view. This may mean talking directly or writing to those making the decisions.
- **Writing to MPs** – a form of lobbying, where the decisions are being made by parliament or the government.
- **Legal action** – when other methods of protest fail, it may be possible to challenge decisions in the courts. This is very expensive. It can only be used when decisions have been taken that are thought to be against the law or made in a way that broke the law.

- **Advertising** – pressure groups may try to influence the public by putting advertisements in newspapers and magazines. This is an expensive method. They may also try to get articles written which put forward the group's views. They may also use posters and leaflets.
- **Boycotts** – refusing to buy or handle goods or services produced by a certain firm or country, or according to a particular method. For example, when the public objected to GM products, some supermarkets refused to stock them.
- **Demonstrations** – these might be mass demonstrations, rallies, marches or some form of direct action. For example, a sit-in to protest at the closure of a factory.

Amnesty International campaigns for human rights around the world

Activities

1 Describe two ways in which a pressure group opposed to the building of an industrial estate on greenbelt land could get their message across.

2 Fast-food restaurant chains such as McDonald's and Burger King have faced criticism by environmental pressure groups. Outline two aspects of fast-food operations that could be criticised by these groups.

3 Not all the methods that pressure groups use are legal. Some forms of protest are illegal and are often called 'direct action'. For instance, if a pressure group destroys a field growing GM crops this would be breaking the law. Discuss whether you think pressure groups help their cause by taking direct action.

4 The AA

The Automobile Association (AA) is an example of a special-interest group. Many people just think it provides a vehicle breakdown service for its members. However, the organisation has branched into other areas. You can buy your car insurance from the AA as well as using it to book hotels. Increasingly the AA acts as a pressure group, representing the interests of motorists. The AA, for instance, tries to get the government to reduce the tax on petrol and to extend its road building programme.

In 2000 the AA ran a campaign to stop the government increasing the tax on petrol by more than the rate of inflation. The organisa-

tion has also researched the need for a 10-year plan to improve the road network in Britain. The AA recognises the environmental problems caused by car use, but believes that encouraging car makers to develop more environmentally friendly vehicles is better than punishing motorists with high taxes.

a Suggest two possible objectives that the AA might have.
b Describe the way that the AA might get across its members' views to the government.
c Why might the government feel it was right to tax car users so heavily?
d Discuss methods by which the AA might encourage car makers to develop more environmentally friendly vehicles.

ICT Activity

Look at the AA website (www.theaa.co.uk) and describe a campaign being run by the organisation.

Unit 4.10 Communications

4.10a Methods of communication

Communication is the passing of information between people or organisations. Information includes numbers as well as words. All communications have two sides. There is always a sender and a receiver. In some cases there may be a number of senders and receivers.

Internal and external communications

Internal communications take place within the same organisation. For example, between different branches of a firm, or between head office and the branches. They are mostly between those who work together; they may take the form of instructions from a boss, or a meeting.

External communications are with people or organisations outside a business, for example suppliers, customers, trade unions and local and central government departments.

Channels of communication

Information within a firm moves along two channels of communication:

- **Vertical** – information moves up and down through the chain of command. Matters that need to be handled by a more senior person are passed upwards. At the same time, there is communication down from the top when instructions need to be given or work delegated.
- **Horizontal** – information is exchanged between workers at the same level in the firm's hierarchy.

Formal and informal communications

Formal communication means sending or giving information via official channels. There are two kinds of formal communications:

- Those that use the official lines of communication within a firm. That is, through the chain of command. They can be in writing, but if a boss tells someone what to do it is still a formal instruction.
- Official communications, in the name of the firm, with people outside the organisation. They are usually in writing, but can also be telephone calls, faxes or e-mails.

Informal communication is all communication that is not formal. It can be both within a firm and with outsiders. Within a firm, for example, it would include two people talking about work on the telephone, or when they meet in a corridor. Informal communications within a firm can be in writing, for example a memo. Informal communication with outsiders is usually not in writing.

Methods of communication

There are four main methods or types of communication:

- written;
- face to face;
- visual;
- electronic.

- Communications
  - Written
    - Letter
    - Memorandum
    - Report
    - Business form
    - Notice
    - News letter
    - Circular
  - Face to face
    - Meeting
    - Conference
    - Interview
    - Video conference
  - Electronic
    - Telephone – landline / mobile
    - Pagers
    - Fax (facsimile)
    - E-mail
    - Internet

Figure 4.8 Forms of communication

Written communications

The main advantage of written communication is that copies can be kept. There is a record, and therefore proof, of what has been stated. There is also a record of when it was sent and who wrote it.

Letters

These are mainly used in formal, external communications. However, there are some situations when a letter should be used for internal communication, for example:

- to confirm an employee's promotion to a new post, or give notice of a change in salary or conditions;
- a written warning or dismissal.

Business letters are usually laid out according to some general rules.

ASP Pharmaceuticals
River Walk
Alebury
AL4 34P
Tel: 01732 8997766
Fax: 01732 8997788
Email: mail@asp.com

Svanhildur Haraldsdottir
Flat 7, Rowan House
Alebury
AL4 36N

Dear Ms Haraldsdottir

I have pleasure in confirming your promotion to Senior Sales Executive and concomitant increase in salary to £21,600. This is to take effect from 30th August 2001. As Senior Sales Executive, you are entitled to a company car. Please contact Jane Harris on ext 456 for details.

I would like to take this opportunity to commend you for your outstanding work this year, making our decision at interview so much easier, despite the general high standard of applicants.

We look forward to seeing you in your new role.

Yours sincerely

Gita Edwards

Gita Edwards
HR Manager

A business letter

Memorandum

A 'memo' is used for internal communication. It is shorter and less formal than a letter. Memos can be used when departments need to write to one another or to give instructions. They are dated but not signed, although the sender may initial them. Like letters, a copy is usually kept, in case a record is needed.

DDAL Communications

MEMO

DATE: 15.05.01
TO: R&D
FROM: Chris Summers
SUBJECT: Can all staff in R&D please remember that they are required to attend the meeting in room 8 at 9.30 tomorrow morning. It is vitally important that everyone is there, because as you know there is going to be some major restructuring.

A memo

Reports

These are usually about a specific subject. They can be internal or external. Internal reports are prepared within a firm. External reports are provided by outsiders such as consultants or auditors. Most reports are in writing but can be verbal. Reports can be presented in many different ways, depending on the 'house style' of the firm. There are some features they should all include:

- **title** – this should be as brief as possible and show the subject clearly;
- **introduction** – this sets out the terms of reference and background to the report;
- **sub-sections and sub-headings** – the report should be broken down into parts. Each part should deal with different aspects of the subject of the report;
- **conclusion/ recommendations** – these are based on what is said in the report;
- **originator's name** – the name of the writer of the report. This can be at the end or shown on a title page at the beginning. A report should *never* be signed;
- **who the report is prepared for** – this should be shown at the beginning. It can be part of a title page. It might be shown as 'A report prepared for the Managing Director of ABC Co Ltd. Prepared by XYZ Consultants';
- **date** – this is often shown at the end or immediately after the above sentence.

Reports can cover a wide range of topics and have several purposes:

- to give information, for example the **minutes** of a meeting, monthly sales figures or the Annual Report and Accounts;
- to help directors and managers to make decisions. A report may set out the pros and cons of several options. For example, when buying new equipment, the costs and benefits of each option would be explained;
- to comment on or to suggest a course of action. A manager may put forward ideas on how to expand a department or to reorganise it.

Some reports are required by law, for example the Annual Report and Accounts given to shareholders in limited companies.

Business forms

These are used as a way of keeping records, and where information needs to be recorded in a standard form. For example, forms for getting goods out of stock and for job applications. They are also used for external communications like ordering goods from a supplier or sending an invoice to a customer.

Notices

These are a good way of passing information to a lot of people quickly and cheaply. Some notices have to be displayed by law, for example health and safety regulations. They are also used to give notice of possible dangers. Notices may also be external, for example local councils have to put up notices about planning applications.

Newsletters

These are often used by large organisations to inform their employees about events that affect their firm.

Face-to-face communications

When people meet and talk directly to one another, it is called face-to-face communication. It is used to give messages, instructions and to discuss problems. Important decisions can be made during face-to-face discussions. They give both parties instant feedback. By watching a person's face and their body language, it is possible to see how they react. The main drawback to such meetings is that there is no official record of what is said or agreed. Each person present may remember different things in different ways.

Meetings can also be formal. The business of a meeting can be set out in an **agenda**. Decisions, and often the main points in the discussion, are recorded in the **minutes**. There is a chance, at the next meeting, to correct any errors.

Interviews are also a form of face-to-face communication.

Visual communications

Some things are often easier to understand when they can be explained visually rather than verbally, especially things in number form, like statistics. They are much clearer if they are shown as diagrams, graphs, charts or tables. Being shown a demonstration of a product is better than reading about it. It is not always possible to set up demonstrations, so many firms use videos, films and slides to sell their products. Videos can be professionally produced and may be more effective than a salesperson. Overhead projectors are often used at meetings and presentations.

Audio-visual methods are very useful and widely used in training. Although it can be difficult and expensive to make a training video, it is cheap and easy to then set up and use.

Electronic communications

Electronic methods are becoming more important for both internal and external communications.

Telephone

This is often the first point of contact with a firm. People judge a firm by the way they are dealt with on the telephone. It is a quick and cheap way of speaking to a specific person. Telephones are used for internal and external communications, and can be used to speak with someone in any part of the world. Mobile telephones mean that people can be contacted at any time and wherever they are.

The main drawback of telephone communication is that there is no record of the conversation. The two parties may not agree on what was said. For this reason some firms record certain conversations. For example, insurance companies record answers to questions on which a telephone quotation is based.

Pagers

These are used by people who travel or move around large sites. Although still widely used, they have been largely replaced by mobile phones.

Video conferencing

This is the use of telephone links to set up a video network. It allows staff at places far apart to see and speak with one another. The benefits are:

- it is cheap and easy to set up, even between countries;
- it saves time because people do not have to travel to meetings. They can get back to work as soon as the meeting is finished;
- there are no costs of travel, or of hiring rooms or hotels for meetings.

Facsimile (fax)

This is a method of sending and receiving written material rapidly using the telephone system. The fax (or telephone) number of the machine to be contacted is keyed-in and the document fed into the sending fax machine. It is then printed out by the receiving machine within seconds. The advantages of fax are:

- machines do not have to be attended and can be left on so that messages can be received at any time of day or night;
- international companies can ignore the time differences between countries.

The use of fax machines is being reduced by the growth of e-mail.

E-mail

Short for 'electronic mail', e-mail is a way of communicating between computers using the world wide web. Every user has a unique address and mailbox that can be protected with a password. Messages are sent to a mailbox using the telephone system via a modem. Messages are stored in the mailbox until it is opened. Messages can be printed, filed or deleted. Large documents can be sent either as messages or as attachments to messages. There are a number of benefits of e-mail:

- it provides more or less instant communication, and can be used to send files and pictures easily;
- it is secure – many firms have their own national or international networks; messages can be encrypted and password protected;
- it allows 24-hour communication anywhere in the world, as long as the machines are switched on;
- a hard copy can be kept by both the sender and the receiver of messages.

Modern mobile phones are able to send and receive e-mails, thus making the system very flexible. People no longer have to go back to their offices and computers in order to collect or send e-mails.

Internet

This is a worldwide network of databases that can be accessed by computers. Access is through the telephone system via a modem to a service provider. Large firms can become their own service providers. Anyone registered with a service provider can have their own web page. Firms can use it as a method of providing information about the firm and its products. Firms can also use it to sell goods and services through **e-commerce**.

Activities

1 Copy and complete the table below. State which method of communication would be most appropriate in each case, together with a reason for your choice.

Message	Method of communication	Reason for method of communication
Telling a worker he is about to be made redundant		
Reminding workers about where fire extinguishers are located		
Informing the board of directors about a study into buying new machinery		
Getting workers' personal details for company records		
Checking with a customer if a delivery has been made		

2 Explain the difference between formal and informal communications.

3 What is a channel of communication?

4 Write a letter to a job applicant informing her that she has been successful.

5 Why do many companies produce their own company newsletters or magazines?

ICT Activity

Using a presentation software package (such as PowerPoint), produce a series of at least six slides on the main types of communication and when they should be used. Set the slides to run as a continuous presentation.

Examination hints

If you are asked to prepare a report in a question:

● Follow the report format shown in this unit. You do not have to include every point, since it may not be necessary for your answer to that question. At the least, you should:
  1 have an introduction;
  2 break your report into two or three sections;
  3 include your name (but not signed) and the date and who the report is addressed to.

● There are also things you should avoid: make sure it does not look like a letter or a memo.

People in Organisations

Unit 4.10 Communications

4.10b Importance of effective communications

Purpose of communications

Communications are used for a number of different purposes.

- **To provide and collect information** – people who have to make decisions need as much information as possible. The information must be full and up to date. Other people collect the information for them. Firms also provide information to their customers, consumers, shareholders, workers, the government and many others.
- **Public relations** – making sure the firm has a good image. This may mean spending a good deal of money on providing customer service, such as customer newsletters. Advertising is a form of communication.
- **To answer questions** – questions may come from any of the stakeholders in a firm. For example, a supplier may want more details about a specification. Queries should be answered quickly, fully and accurately.
- **To give instructions** – all decisions give rise to some kind of action that has to be communicated. It may mean telling someone what to do, or placing an order for supplies, or issuing redundancy notices.
- **To influence others** – firms may try to influence government through their trade associations, the press and MPs. Pressure groups try to influence decisions. Workers may threaten to strike to stop a firm closing a factory.

To fulfil these purposes effectively, communications should be:

- clear and simple – they must be easily understood, and there should be no doubt about what is meant;
- accurate – mistakes can create problems and cost time and money to correct;
- complete – each point should be fully dealt with at each stage;
- appropriate – different situations need different methods of communication.

Most firms think communications are important. They have to work hard to make sure they are as effective as possible. The larger the organisation the harder it is to have good communications. It is also harder if there are many levels in an organisation.

Why communications may fail

- **Poor skills** – poor language skills mean that a person may not make their point clearly. A strong accent may mean that people who are not used to it find them hard to understand. Using a regional dialect may mean that there are some words people do not understand. Language problems make international communication difficult.
- **Jargon** – technical language and using too many abbreviations may mean a person is not always understood. The person using the 'jargon' should be able to explain it to other people, who are not experts.
- **Distortion** – messages can often get confused, especially when they are passed on by word of mouth. This is made worse if the person who is passing on the message does not understand it. They may miss out something because they do not realise its importance.
- **Delays** – often messages are not picked up, or someone forgets to pass them on. If a firm does not reply to letters or other communications quickly, it is thought to be inefficient and people may be less inclined to deal with it.
- **Faulty equipment** – a faulty fax machine may mean an important document is not sent or is delayed. Similarly, if a computer system crashes important information may be lost.
- **Channels of communication not clear** – in large organisations, it may not always be clear who is the right person to contact for information or decisions. If the wrong person is contacted, or a person is given the wrong information, time is wasted and opportunities could be lost.

Results of poor communication

- **Misunderstanding** – being given wrong or confused information, or being spoken to impolitely, may cause misunderstanding. A firm's relationships with those it does business with can be harmed. Within a firm, working relationships may be damaged.
- **Wasted time** – failing to make contact with the right person straightaway can lead to time and money being wasted. Having to say the same things to several different people is a waste of time. An outsider may give up and the firm may lose business. Having to correct mistakes also wastes time and duplicates effort.
- **Loss of customers** – people often judge a firm by the way it handles its communications. Poor communications or rudeness may lead to customers going elsewhere.
- **Increased costs** – if, for example, a firm sends out invoices that are wrong, time is wasted putting them right. Both parties' costs are increased.
- **Loss of profits** – if customers are lost, a firm's sales income falls. If this is linked to higher costs because of poor communications, profits also fall.
- **Disputes** – poor communications between a firm and its workers can cause misunderstanding. In the worst cases this may lead to disputes and loss of confidence in the firm's management.

Activities

Case Study

1 Fulton Fabrics

Fulton Fabrics was displaying all the signs of poor worker motivation. The rate of labour turnover was high and punctuality and absenteeism were both getting worse. The factory workers showed very little interest in what they were doing, which caused a fall in the quality of the products.

A culture of mistrust had grown between workers and managers. The managers thought that the workers were lazy and needed constant supervision, while the workers thought the managers were incompetent.

Things came to a head when a group of visitors were being shown around the factory and a rumour started on the shop floor that the company was about to be sold. The trade union leader went to see Mr Thomas, the general manager, to find out what was happening. Mr Thomas told him in no uncertain terms that it was none of his business and to get back to work. After a meeting with the union members it was decided to call in a trade union official for advice.

a What evidence is there to suggest that there were poor communications at Fultons?

b Describe the management style of Mr Thomas.

c What action could the union take to support the workers?

d Describe ways in which communications could be improved at Fultons.

People in Organisations

Unit 4.11 Impact of technology

Database →	a collection of data that is set out and collected in a systematic way that suits the needs of the user.
Information and communications technology (ICT) →	the collecting, recording, storing, retrieval and distribution of information using computers and telecommunications.
Spreadsheet →	a computer program designed to record numerical information and to make calculations according to formulae entered by the user.
Teleworker →	someone who works from home using computer links to keep in touch with their base office.

→ **Key terms**

When people speak of 'new technology' they are usually thinking about developments based on the computer. Some of the more recent changes are the result of developments in telecommunications and the way they link computers. Although there are other new technologies, this unit will look at some of the ways computers affect business.

Working methods

Computers have had a big effect on the way people work. Many jobs that were repetitive and boring have been taken over by computers. Many jobs have disappeared altogether. For example, accounts are no longer written by hand and there are very few shorthand typists now working in offices.

On the other hand, computers have resulted in many new jobs. Programmers, systems analysts and jobs in call centres are three examples. New industries have grown based on the new technologies. There are firms that manufacture computers, computer components and mobile phones. Others sell and distribute them. Two examples of where computers have had a big impact are the office and manufacturing.

1 The office

Information and communications technology (ICT) is used in offices for a number of purposes:

- Preparing documents – in most offices, documents of all kinds are written using wordprocessors. The work can be altered easily, corrected, added to or shortened. In the past the work would have been retyped each time there was a change or an error. More complicated documents like reports, newsletters and leaflets can be prepared using desktop publishing software.

- Information can be collected in a **database**. Firms keep records of their customers and other firms they do business with. It is up to the user to decide what and how much information to keep. They keep records of, at least, names and addresses and telephone numbers. Databases of different classes of client can also be bought.

- Financial, sales and other records are collected on a **spreadsheet**. Information is entered in rows and columns. The computer adds, subtracts, multiplies or divides the data according to a formula entered by the user. Quite complicated calculations can be done easily and quickly. The information can also be shown in charts or graphs.

- Computers can store very large amounts of information in a small space. This reduces the need for large areas of office space to store large numbers of paper records. This may reduce a firm's costs.

- Computers can be linked together in networks through servers. Networks may be local, where all the computers in a branch or building are linked. They can also be wide area networks, where all the branches throughout the country are linked through the telephone system to head office. Big firms have international networks.

Through these links, information can be fed back to head office. For example, the tills in supermarkets are computer terminals. Every item rung up on the till feeds back to head office. Head office is able to use the information to keep track of stock in the branch, and re-order new stock as it is needed. They can also keep a close track of sales figures for each store.

The factory

- Computer-aided design (CAD) can be used to design products and components much more quickly than by hand. Designs can be viewed from any angle. They can be fitted to other components on the screen.

- Once the design is finalised it can be transferred directly to computer-aided manufacturing machines. This saves time setting up machines. The machines are able to make the item more accurately than machines operated by people.

- Robots are widely used for some operations. For example, to weld metal joints or to spray car bodies. They are more accurate and produce less waste than human-operated systems.

- One person can often operate a number of machines at the same time. Machines can also operate 24 hours a day. This reduces the number of jobs and cuts costs. Increased use of robots and automation makes firms more competitive by cutting costs.

- Machines often replace skilled craftsmen, resulting in de-skilling of the workforce.

New technology plays a major part in the car manufacturing industry

Home working

Working practices

The use of computers and improved telephone-based communications have brought about changes in the way people work.

- Employees that work away from their office can remain in contact via their mobile telephones. As long as their mobiles are switched on, they can be contacted and given information. They, in turn, can give instructions, ask for urgent information, or report to their boss. They can also receive and send text messages. Newer mobiles can send and receive short e-mails. New generation mobiles can be linked to laptop computers to get the full range of Internet and e-mail services.

- One result of being able to keep in touch in this way is that people do not have to work normal office hours. They can work from home, travel widely and still stay in touch with their base.

- There are some people who do most of their work from home. **Teleworkers** are linked to their offices through computer links. Their working hours can be fixed to suit themselves. They work from home or anywhere they choose. Their computers are linked to a base so that they can give and be given work, and receive instructions and whatever information they need. They can be contacted wherever they are via the telephone.

Many experts expect teleworking to grow. There will be less need for huge, expensive offices. Head offices will need fewer staff. People will work for themselves and be hired by firms to carry out particular jobs. Working from home saves travelling time and costs, and fewer cars on the roads makes it more environmentally friendly.

Globalisation

In recent years there has been a trend for firms that operate in many world markets to merge. By merging they are able to operate in most countries in the world. By being very large they can make huge profits. They are less likely to be takeover targets. This globalisation has been made possible by better communications through:

- the Internet;
- better and faster telecommunications using satellite links.

These make it possible for firms to set up international networks to keep in touch with their operations anywhere in the world at any time.

- Data can be fed back to head and regional offices at any time of the day or night. Branches in different time zones can provide feedback information during their normal working hours.
- Firms can use the Internet to promote their activities anywhere in the world in more or less any language.
- They can be informed instantly about any kind of change that may affect them.

A wap phone

E-commerce

Many people now own computers and access to the Internet is cheaper. At the same time, firms have recognised the potential of the Internet for selling goods and services. The buying and selling of goods and services on the Internet is known as **e-commerce**. There are three main types of firms selling in this way.

- Traditional firms that have developed an Internet trading arm. Firms like Tesco, Sainsburys, high street banks and building societies are offering the same goods and services on the Internet as they do in their shops and offices.

Tesco's Internet shopping delivery service

- Other companies that have diversified by opening a different service. For example, Egg, an Internet bank, was set up by the Prudential insurance company.
- The new dot.com companies. They have been set up just to sell goods and services on the Internet. Examples include Amazon and lastminute.com.

So far, very few of these newer companies have made a profit. Many are expected to fail. However, some experts think that in time many people will prefer to do their shopping from home on the Internet. Some think that this will mean the end of shopping as we know it. The benefits of e-commerce include:

- because they do not have to rent shops in expensive shopping centres, Internet firms can sell goods more cheaply;
- shopping is easier and hassle free – people can shop when they like, and avoid crowded shopping centres and the cost of travelling and parking;

the same choice of goods and services is available to everyone. It is therefore ideal for those unable to get to shops, for example, the elderly and disabled and those living in rural areas.

Activities

1 Describe some ways in which modern technology has changed the way that your school or college is run.

2 What is meant by 'globalisation'? Give an example.

3 Explain three ways in which e-commerce can save money for a business.

4 Organisations such as EasyJet do not operate a paper-based system when customers book tickets for its flights. What are the advantages to the company of using an electronic system?

ICT Activity
The Data Protection Act limits what a company can do with the personal details it holds on people. Find out what the law says about holding personal details. A useful website is:
www.dataprotection.gov.uk.
Write a short account of your findings.

5 **Group activity**
Investigate the reasons why some people are unhappy about buying products using e-commerce. Work together to produce a questionnaire on people's attitudes towards e-commerce.

Case Study

6 **Teleworking**
Advances in ICT have changed the way that many people work. Simon is one such person.

Simon works as a manager for an insurance company. Until recently the company was based in the centre of London. Traditionally, insurance companies have located in central London so that they can be close to other firms in the industry. When computers were introduced into Simon's office in the early 1980s, it was thought that they would just make it easier to produce and store documents. However, the introduction of electronic communication completely changed the nature of Simon's job.

Simon found that he could supervise his team of insurance salespeople by communicating with them using e-mail. Documents could be sent electronically and he could easily keep in touch with what was happening in the insurance world through the Internet. So it was not long before Simon's company decided to sell its London offices and have its managers working from home as teleworkers.

Teleworking was welcomed by Simon. He took the opportunity to move from where he lived in the south-east of England to Yorkshire where he had been brought up. He found he no longer had to spend two hours each day commuting to and from work and he thought that the quality of his life was much better in Yorkshire than it had been in London.

Simon still sees his sales team fortnightly when they meet at a hotel in Manchester, but he suspects that it will not be long before these meetings will be held using video conferencing.

a Give three ways in which Simon's company saved money by introducing teleworking for its managers.

b Teleworking would not be possible for all jobs. Describe some types of employment that would be unsuitable for teleworking.

c Besides the points mentioned in the case study, why might Simon prefer teleworking?

d Explain two problems that Simon could experience as a teleworker.

ICT Activity
Research teleworking and list the types of equipment somebody such as Simon would need to telework from home. Websites include:
www.wfh.co.uk/workingfromhome and
www.tca.org.uk.

What is a case study?

A case study is a story. It may be one based on actual facts or it may one that has been made up. It is a story about some aspect of a business. Case studies may cover many issues or points or they may just look at something specific. They aim to get you thinking about business problems and situations.

The main purpose of a case study is to illustrate some general principles or ideas that you have covered, such as raising finance, marketing a product or motivating workers. For example, there are many possible ways of marketing a new product that you could suggest, but a case study provides a context which limits the number of ideas that will actually work. Marketing a new software product designed for use in a small business is very different from a new game for the Sony Playstation.

Case studies that you cover in your course will also provide you with examples that you can use in your examinations. Most examining groups set questions in which you are asked to define or explain something **with the aid of examples**.

In Business Studies you will find you use case studies all the time. They can be found in every unit of this book. Your teacher/tutor will probably show you video clips on businesses from programmes such as the *GCSE Bitesize Revision on Business Studies*. You might be asked to access the Internet to find examples to include in your coursework, classwork or homework. Examining groups also use case studies to test you. They may, for example, want you to:

- define some term or concept;
- explain why a situation has arisen;
- discuss your suggested solutions to a particular problem.

Examinations and case studies

The examining group AQA uses a case study of a real business as the basis for its examination paper. In recent years it has used Chesterfield Transport, Tesco and McDonald's, and the 1999 case study on The Broadford Manor Hotel was based on a real business in the west of England. These case studies cover a lot of aspects of the business. For example, the 2000 case study of Tesco covered:

- business objectives;
- the development of Tesco from a market stall in London's East End to the multinational business it is today;
- opening a new Tesco store and the various types of store;
- ICT in Tesco including stock control and the Tesco Clubcard;
- working for Tesco;
- marketing the business;
- customer services;
- financial information;
- the environment and the community.

Other examining groups use shorter case studies in the examination paper to test different areas of the syllabus.

Using the AQA case study to improve your examination result

The AQA case study should arrive at your school sometime during the March before you sit your examination. This should give you plenty of time for preparation and revision. What follows are some suggestions for activities you might like to carry out after you have been given your copy of the case study by your teacher/tutor. Some of these activities might be done as part of your general revision programme in class in the weeks leading up to the examination. However, some you might like to do on your own or with a few of your fellow Business Studies students. You must always remember to keep your own set of notes as an aid to your revision.

- You will need your own copy of the case study that you can write on and annotate.
- Start by reading the case study through. Don't mark it at this stage. It is simply to help you identify any major themes and issues such as how the company began and has grown, what is its market, how the business was financed, etc.
- If it is a real business, then there may be an Internet website you can visit. This could contain up-to-date information on the firm. Remember, your case study would have been written at least one year before you received it and that circumstances might have changed since then. However, you might find there is too much material available at the website. (If you use the search engine Yahoo! (UK sites only) and typed in 'Tesco', the 2000 case study, you would get over 150 possible sites to look up!) Also, remember the AQA stresses that **you must not contact the company directly to get more information, and that all the information about the firm that you need to answer any questions set can be found in the case study.**
- Newspapers are also a potentially useful source of information if the case study is of a well-known company. Again, the Internet might prove useful because you can access the archives of all the well-known daily papers.
- Now read the case study again very carefully. With a highlighter pen, pick out the key terms (it is useful to do this in a group because you might miss some points).

  When you have picked out the key terms and phrases and made your own list, then using your textbook or a business dictionary write out a **clear** and **precise** definition in a notebook or on cards. These will prove excellent for revision nearer the examination. There are certain to be some questions in which you are asked to explain a term or phrase. **However, remember that section A of the AQA examination paper tests all areas of the syllabus, not just the terms found in the case study.**

  It is vitally important that your definitions or explanations are accurate, so use a handbook, such as the *GCSE A–Z Business Studies Handbook* by Arthur Jenkins, to help you.

You will have quite a long time before the examination to work on the case study. It is a good idea to break the case study down into manageable chunks to help you plan your revision. As mentioned earlier, each AQA case study is broken down into sections. These will vary depending on the nature of the business, but the main ones are likely to be:

1 history;
2 organisation;
3 sales and marketing;
4 human resources;
5 finance and financial performance;
6 external environment;
7 future plans.

A useful exercise that you could carry out on your own or with a group of fellow students is to study each of these areas carefully and make a list of the key points or issues raised. You could do this by using, for example, a spider diagram or a mind map. These also should be fairly brief and can be used for quick revision and self-testing nearer to the examination. You can use your own class notes and the textbook to help you revise these areas.

Revising, though, is not just about learning information such as definitions. To pass your examination you will also need to be able to demonstrate skills. Examinations are about showing the person marking your Business Studies paper what you know, understand and can do. The four main skills written down in the GCSE Busines Studies syllabus are:

1 your knowledge and understanding of Business Studies, for example what does the term 'marketing mix' mean?
2 your ability to apply this knowledge to specific situations, for example if Walkers launched a new range of snacks what marketing mix might it use?
3 your ability to explain and analyse problems, events and situations, for example if sales of Golden Wonder crisps had fallen in recent years, how might the company change its marketing mix to improve this situation?
4 your ability to offer your own judgements, solutions and comments on an issue backed up by clear and sensible explanations. Examiners call this

'evaluation'. For example, Golden Wonder decides to cut the price of all its crisps by 20% to improve sales. Discuss the possible benefits and drawbacks of this decision. Do you think this is a good idea?

In the AQA GCSE Business Studies examination you will be asked to demonstrate these skills through your use of the materials and information in the case study.

An example of a short case study

The case study given below comes from information found in a newspaper article and on the Internet. The website for the company can be found by typing E. Botham and Sons into a search engine such as Google or Yahoo. It is much shorter than a typical AQA case study, but you can look at it and study it in the same way that you might analyse your actual examination case study.

□ Case Study

Elizabeth Botham and Sons Ltd

Elizabeth Botham and Sons Ltd is a family-run bakery founded in 1865. It is based in Whitby in North Yorkshire. It produces a wide variety of bread, cakes, biscuits and chutney. It is a traditional craft bakery where many of the products are hand made. It has its own shop, café and a restaurant, building on the successful brand image of the company.

What is unusual about Bothams is that it was one of the first businesses to trade on-line through the Internet. Now about half the sales of its cakes, chutney, biscuits and hampers are sold worldwide. It has customers as far away as Australia, Japan, the USA and Indonesia, as well as in France and Spain. Recently, when a group of Japanese students visiting the UK

□ Case Study

called at the restaurant, they were offered free tea and cakes in exchange for helping to write a Japanese web page for the company.

Bothams went on-line in 1994. It is now sharing its skills and knowledge with other smaller companies through a scheme called 'Compris'. This is a project funded by the government and the EU (European Union). The aim of this scheme is to have 20,000 businesses in the Yorkshire and Humberside area on-line by 2003.

The benefit of the Internet is that it expands the market for a company's products. However, there are problems. It can be expensive to produce a website and a small business might need to find the finance for such a project. Marketing is not just about advertising. Firms must also provide an efficient service because customers want their orders to be delivered quickly.

The exchange rate can also have an important influence. Recently the value of the pound has fallen against the dollar and so sales in the USA have increased. This is not the case with the Euro where the pound has been very strong, making it much harder to sell products in the EU.

Bothams has also linked up with other businesses selling goods on the Internet through the Yorkshire Pantry Group. By doing this the firms involved can gain economies of scale. It also helps to market the region's products. Sometimes supermarket chains do 'regional promotions'. Recently, 24 producers who are members of the Yorkshire Pantry Group got together to make a presentation to the directors of the supermarket chain Somerfields who were interested in selling their products.

Read the case study through carefully then have a go at the following exercises.

First of all, you need to identify the business terms and concepts.

1 The business is a **limited company**. Look this term up. What does it mean? Who owns the business? Are shares generally available?

2 Bothams is a *craft* bakery. What method of production do you think it might use? Would this method be suitable for all the products it makes?

   Working on your own or with a small group of other students, you could list the products that the firm makes. Then think about what would be the most suitable method of production for each of these products and why.

3 Why do businesses like a bakery also own shops, cafés and a restaurant?

4 The company sells its products in many other countries. Working by yourself you could list the general benefits and problems of doing this and then think about how these might apply to Bothams. You could carry out this exercise by drawing two spider diagrams, one for benefits the other for problems. See if you can come up with at least five points for each diagram.

5 The company was one of the first of its kind to go on-line. One of the problems mentioned in the case study is that setting up a website is expensive. What sources of finance might be available to businesses to pay these costs?

   Working in a group, you could see how many sources of finance you can list in one minute then compare them with each other. Put together a master list and discuss which would be appropriate in each situation. Put the top three in order. (**Hint** – you need to think about the amount of money, the fact that these companies are small, whether these

costs are fixed overhead costs, direct/variable costs or both, and the information given in the third paragraph).

6 The 'exchange rate' is also mentioned in paragraph five. What does this term mean? How does it affect businesses trading abroad? You could use mind maps to create a revision aid for this topic.

Second, what business issues does the case study raise? These aspects of the case study are for **discussion**. You are likely to learn most from an exercise like this by working as a group, and remember that the points raised could apply to other businesses.

There are a number of issues raised in this case study, but two of the key ones are:

1 Why do businesses, even those which might be in competition with each other, link together to sell their goods? What evidence is there of this happening in the case study? (**Hint** – there is the 'Compris' scheme and the Yorkshire Pantry Group.) What is the point of doing this? The case study mentions economies of scale. What are they? How might they affect the businesses involved, and in particular Bothams? (See page 265.)

2 Why does the government and EU give funds to help small businesses such as those taking part in the scheme mentioned in paragraph three of the case study? You need to think about the benefits, e.g. in terms of jobs, that might arise and also the location of these businesses. Would the government have given such help if businesses like Bothams had been located in, say, London?

When you work as a group you should always make notes on the key points that you have discussed. These should help to clarify the points in your mind and when it comes to your actual GCSE case study you can use them for revision purposes or even to practice writing a timed answer to a 'typical' question.

Coursework is an important part of the assessment, counting for 25% of the final mark at GCSE. Most candidates taking a two-year course complete coursework in the second year, although it can be done at any time. It gives you the chance to look at something in more depth than you might have done in the rest of the course. You will not be able to do a good piece of coursework without looking at/contacting real businesses.

You can tackle coursework in two ways:
1 You can produce a single item of work. For example, you might wish to run a mini-enterprise or complete a study on retail changes in your area.
2 You can produce a number of items covering different business problems or issues.

An assignment might meet the requirements of more than one option. For example, if you wrote about a mini-enterprise you were involved in you might use ICT to, say, wordprocess a marketing report, or to produce a balance sheet or a break-even chart using a spreadsheet. You could, therefore, submit your work as an Enterprise option or an ICT option.

Assignments should, however, be based on **one** option from the list below. The guidelines and suggestions included under the options are not meant to cover every possibility. They are there to give you a few tips as to what would make a good piece of coursework, and to stress the main pitfalls so that hopefully you'll avoid them.

Business and Change option

It is important that you choose a topic that gives you the chance to explain the reasons for a change and the effects of the change on people, the business itself, other businesses and the community. For example, you might want to study the effects of an out-of-town shopping centre on local businesses. A bad way to tackle such an assignment would be for you to simply give a potted history of the shopping centre. A good way would be for you to look at what local people think of the centre; how the centre has changed the way people shop; how local businesses have been affected during the building of the centre, and after it has been built; etc.

You might, on the other hand, want to study how a local business has changed its use of technology. A bad way to tackle such an assignment would be for you to simply write about the technology used by the business. A good way would be to look at how the technology has changed the way the business works, for example the effects on the number of staff; the need for training; the introduction of just-in-time production; etc.

Business Support Services option

You might want to look at the banking and financial services used by a business. A bad way to tackle this would be to collect leaflets from banks and then simply write about the services provided in purely general terms. This is what is meant by a 'descriptive' answer. It does not get you many marks. A better approach would be to study the service needs of actual businesses, for example the need for a loan or an overdraft, and explain how banks meet or don't meet these particular needs.

Enterprise option

A popular way to tackle this option is to prepare and/or run a mini-enterprise or a Young Enterprise Company. Such a project can be both interesting and a good way of completing coursework. However, there are pitfalls. You must not simply produce a diary approach to your business. Details of what you or your friends did or did not do will not gain you many marks. You need to look at questions and issues that are involved in setting up and running a business, for example:
- What should the business do? You can carry out market research to answer this.

- Where should the business be set up? Simply saying 'we would use room X in school' misses out the problems that a real business would face.
- Should the business be a sole trader, a partnership or a limited company? You can then write about the pros and cons of the different kinds of business ownership from your business's point of view. Don't just copy out the advantages and disadvantages from a textbook.
- Where can the money to set up the business be found?
- How can the business be marketed? You can write about issues such as ways of fixing the price of the product or service your business produces, and how your business can be promoted.
- What is the cash flow forecast and actual cash flow for the business? You must remember to write about where the figures you use have come from – what have you assumed?

Human Resources option

You might like to study how a business chooses its workers, how it trains them, and how it encourages them to work harder/more efficiently and stay with the business.

Once again, the main mistake you might make here is to simply describe what the business you are studying does. You must give **reasons** for what the business does. You could look at how technology has changed what businesses do generally, and the numbers and kinds of staff they need. You need to write about what you think about the way workers are recruited and trained etc. You could carry out a survey with workers from a variety of jobs to compare how different businesses treat their workers. You could come up with some ideas of your own about recruiting workers and how to encourage them to work more efficiently.

Information and Communication Technology option

There are two ways of tackling this option:

1 You could study the ICT particular businesses use today. Be careful not to simply describe the ICT they use. You need to look at issues such as:
   - How is the ICT they use chosen?

- What effects does ICT have on the people who work for the business, for example the numbers and kinds of workers they need? What training is needed?
- What effects does ICT have on the way the business works, for example the way it deals with its customers and other businesses? What is the effect on costs of using ICT?
- What do you think about the way ICT has affected business? What about the future?

2 You could use ICT to produce your coursework. For example:
   - You could use the Internet to find out about a business or business issues.
   - You could use a spreadsheet to produce a balance sheet, or graphs of your survey/questionnaire results. You should then explain the balance sheet or graphs.
   - You could use a database to record your survey/questionnaire results. You should then write about what you have found out and why it is important.

Whichever way you tackle the ICT option, you must not simply show that you know how to wordprocess, or how to set up and search a database, or how to set up and use a spreadsheet, etc. These skills are not what your teacher and the moderator are looking for, so if you merely produce examples of database searches or spreadsheet printouts of accounting ratios etc. you will get few marks. What you must do is use ICT as a way of answering a business problem/issue. ICT can be used to help you collect information, and then to present it.

Production option

This option gives you the chance to study issues such as the ways or possible ways businesses can increase how much they produce, and how businesses aim to produce what consumers want.

You must be careful not to simply describe terms such as specialisation or economies of scale, or to simply write about what specific businesses do. You need to find out about particular businesses and explain issues such as what is involved in increasing production or developing a new product.

You could give your views on these issues, and the various ways businesses try to deal with them.

How your coursework will be marked

When you are deciding on the assignment(s) you're going to do as your coursework it is essential that you choose carefully. You must give yourself a number of opportunities to provide the type and quality of evidence your teacher/tutor and moderator are looking for when they mark your work.

Your teacher/tutor and the moderator will be looking for evidence of your understanding of the world of business. You must remember that the various pieces of evidence should not be looked at separately. They do overlap and are linked.

However, coursework does not need to be of great length. Quality is more important than quantity. Coursework is marked out of 63, initially by your teacher/tutor. A moderator working for the examining group may also mark your coursework.

Coursework evidence you need to provide

1 Knowledge and understanding of business terms/ideas/problems/issues (maximum 8 marks)

- You need to collect information and research from a number of different places:
  - textbooks;
  - surveys/questionnaires;
  - company reports;
  - accounts;
  - observation etc.;
  - visits.
- You need to show that you have used primary and secondary research. Both types are equally important. This means that you must collect enough information on the topic you are studying.
  - Primary research covers information you have collected by asking people using questionnaires, in-depth interviews with people or observing the business world.
  - Secondary research covers information that somebody else has collected or written about such as company reports or textbooks.

- To make sure that you collect enough information you might have your own checklist to record what primary and secondary research you have done.
- It is important that this research is carried out to help you deal with a business problem or issue you're studying. You must then use the information to answer the problem. You will not get many marks for simply copying large sections from books or reports, or putting lots of leaflets etc. in your file.
- Research must be for a reason. You might, therefore, find it helpful to phrase your coursework assignment(s) in the form of questions. For example, if you chose to do the Business and Change option about the change in ownership of Asda, you might ask questions like: Why did WalMart take over Asda? How will this affect other large retailers like Tesco and Sainsburys? How will shoppers be affected?
- You need to think carefully about how you will present your information/research etc. The use of reports, graphs, photographs, etc. is a good idea.

Checklist
1 Will I collect information from:

• textbooks	yes/no
• interviews/surveys/questionnaires	yes/no
• reports, e.g. government reports, company reports, newspaper reports	yes/no
• accounts, e.g. balance sheets, profit and loss accounts	yes/no
• other sources, e.g. the Internet	yes/no

2 Will I present my work in a number of ways?   yes/no

3 Will I make good use of the information/ research I've done to answer a problem/ issue/question?   yes/no

To get a high mark for knowledge and understanding, you should be able to answer 'yes' to all the above questions.

2 Application of business terms and ideas (maximum 14 marks)

You need to use business terms and ideas in your answer, linking them to the business problem or issue you're studying. Your teacher/tutor will be looking for evidence that you can use the correct business words clearly and precisely. Show that you understand why these terms and ideas are important to your study. It is also crucial that you select the terms that are relevant to your assignments.

For example, you might be looking at possible locations for a business and how a location is chosen as part of the Business and Change option. You will not get many marks if you copy sections about location from a book. You need to say how things like market pull, government influence, etc. would affect your business. Factors such as industrial inertia may not be relevant in your case.

Alternatively, you might have chosen the Enterprise option and are looking at the most suitable type of business ownership for a possible enterprise. It is not a good idea to write down from a book general points about the advantages and disadvantages of sole traders, partnerships, limited companies, etc. You need to link the general points to the specific enterprise you are hoping to set up. A specific comment, in which you apply the appropriate business terms correctly, such as 'if I set up as a sole trader then I could lose all my personal possessions like my house to pay off my business's debts' is much better than a general one such as 'a sole trader could lose all their possessions'.

The most common mistake candidates make is to produce work that is very descriptive. For example, writing about what you did on work experience; writing a diary of events about your mini-enterprise; writing about the history of a business or shopping area. If you approach coursework in this way you will not gain many marks.

Checklist

1 Will I use the relevant business terms and ideas to answer a problem/issue/question? yes/no
2 Will I link these terms and ideas to the problem/issue/question? yes/no
3 Will I choose carefully the terms I need to use? yes/no
4 Will I give reasons for the terms and ideas I use? yes/no

To get a high mark for application, you should be able to answer 'yes' to all the questions above.

3 Selection/organisation/interpretation of information you've collected (maximum 22 marks)

You have to decide what information/research you need to do, and explain how it is linked to, and why it is important to, the problem/issue/question you are tackling. You must always try to give reasons for what you are saying.

When you have collected information and research you need to analyse and interpret it. For example, if you've conducted a survey you need to write about what you've found out and how the information answers the problem you've been set.

Checklist

1 Will I choose carefully the information/ research I will collect? yes/no
2 Will my work be clearly organised, for example divided into different sections? yes/no
3 Will I explain the information/research I collect? yes/no
4 Will I examine the relevant factors to a problem/issue/question? yes/no
5 Will I give reasons for comments I make? yes/no

To get a high mark for selection/organisation/interpretation, you should be able to answer 'yes' to all the questions above.

4 Evaluation/judgement (maximum 16 marks)

It is important to provide evidence that you have made decisions or reached judgements/conclusions following your research. You need to weigh up and explain the things that have influenced your decision. For example, deciding on the location of a business, choosing whether to set up as a sole trader or a partner, etc.

Conclusions and judgements can occur at any place in your coursework – not simply at the end. There is not always one answer to a business problem. Marks are gained by explaining why you have chosen a particular answer or solution to a problem. For example, if you choose a particular location for a business as part of the Enterprise option, you should give reasons for your decision. This might include why you didn't choose other possible locations or sites for the business.

Checklist

1 Will I have to make business decisions?   yes/no
2 Will I have to give reasons for my decisions?   yes/no
3 Will I have to reach conclusions/provide opinions/make recommendations?   yes/no
4 Will I have to give reasons for my conclusions/opinions/recommendations?   yes/no

To get a high mark for evaluation/judgement you should be able to answer 'yes' to all the questions above.

5 Spelling, punctuation and grammar (SPAG) (maximum 3 marks)

You can gain extra marks for using a wide range of business terms correctly and precisely. Good spelling and correct punctuation are also rewarded.

And finally …

Please remember that your teacher/tutor is there to help and advise you. Always check that the evidence you are providing answers the questions or problems you are looking at. However, your coursework must be your own work. If you work as a group, say in running a mini-enterprise, you must produce work on your own. For example, you could individually examine issues such as business ownership, how to finance the business, marketing strategies, etc.

Good luck!

Option 1 Business and Change

Pressures to change

Businesses are subjected to many different pressures. If an organisation is to prosper, or just simply survive, it must respond to these pressures by changing how it operates. Sometimes the changes can be quite small, such as altering the way in which advertising is carried out. Occasionally a substantial change needs to be made, for instance a company may find it needs to uproot and move to another country where costs are cheaper.

Some businesses seem better than others at adapting in response to these pressures. Adaptable companies tend to be the ones that thrive in the long run. Those businesses that try to ignore pressures for necessary change until the last moment will probably find themselves spending an increasing amount of time managing one crisis after another. Companies that resist change at any cost will probably fail.

Internal and external pressures

Sometimes it is the business itself that causes the change. For instance, a firm may find it would be more profitable to switch from producing one good to another. Or the need for change could be because something outside the firm's control has happened. For example, when the government's minimum wage came into effect this meant that some firms with low-paid workers had to increase their employees' wages. They had no option but to change, as it was the law of the land.

> Internal pressures for change are those that a firm creates for itself and over which it has some control.
>
> External pressures for change are factors that a firm has no influence over.

Proactive and reactive businesses

A business needs to be prepared to make changes when they are necessary. A good business will also carefully monitor the changing business environment, so the need for change does not take it by surprise. If, for example, a business suspects that the demand for one of its products is falling, it will monitor its sales figures regularly, looking for a downward trend. If the firm believes that consumers are no longer finding its product attractive, something can be done before the situation becomes critical. Planning ahead in this way allows changes to be made in a calm and calculated manner, rather than responding urgently when a crisis arises. Firms that behave in this way are described as proactive.

Reactive organisations behave quite differently. A reactive business will wait for the pressure to build up before it feels the need to change. It may not even notice the pressure for change until the last moment. For instance, a business may still be using manual production methods when its competitors moved several years ago to automated machinery. Costs of production will be higher for this firm so its profit margins will be cut. Each year will find it less competitive until the business is no longer able to recover. As an unprofitable business, it finds it difficult to raise funds to invest in new machinery. It could probably have survived had it monitored the situation and planned more carefully.

> A proactive business will monitor the business world carefully and will be aware of any need for change before the pressures for change become overpowering.
>
> A reactive firm will respond to the pressure for change only when the effects are already being felt and it has no choice but to change.

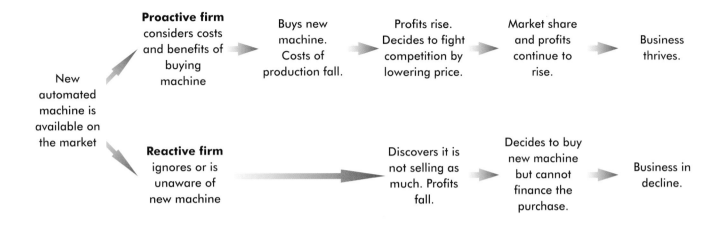

The effects of change on the company's stakeholders

When a company changes, it will probably affect its stakeholders in different ways. This can be explained by using an example.

Imagine the government passes a law banning the use of a certain type of fertiliser on farms. This may be because the chemical used in it has a bad effect on the environment. Any farm that uses the fertiliser needs to look at alternatives. The reason the original fertiliser was used was probably because it was cheaper than others, so the farm will now have to spend more growing its crops. The farm may try to get some of the extra costs back by charging higher prices for its crops, but this will depend upon the prices charged by its competitors.

Alternatively, the farm may take this opportunity to become organic, where only natural fertilisers are used. This will mean that the total amount produced will not be as high as with artificial fertilisers, but many consumers are prepared to pay extra for organic produce.

How will this pressure for change affect the farm's stakeholders? Unfortunately the effects on stakeholders may not be very clear. The change may simply have a good or a bad effect, but it is not always as clear-cut as this. The overall effects are not always easy to predict.

Shareholders: the owners of the farm may find that their dividends are lower because the profits the farm makes have been reduced. However, there is a possibility that if the farm moves to organic production, this may improve the farm's long-term prospects.

Employees: there is a possibility of being made redundant if the farm declines because its costs have risen. Lower profits would also make it more difficult to demand high wages. However, workers may gain increased job satisfaction from working on an organic farm.

Customers: prices could increase, which consumers will not like. But as an organic producer there will be more organic food being supplied which could help bring prices of this type of food down.

Competitors: of course, other farms will be stopped from using the banned fertiliser, which will also increase their costs. However, some competitors may be located abroad where the ban is not in operation, so this will give them a cost advantage. If the farm does become organic, there will be one less competitor in the mainstream business, so competitors' market share would increase.

Managing change

Very few people like changing the way things are done. Most of us are creatures of habit and do not look forward to altering the routines with which we are familiar. So when a business decides that change is needed, it will have to manage the situation very carefully.

A reactive firm will probably find it easier to manage change than a proactive one. The pressures for change will be so obvious, the workers will realise that without change the firm will fail and they will lose their jobs. A proactive firm may find change harder to bring about because workers may not be able to see the reason for change. Some may view the situation as managers being incompetent and changing things without good reason.

Some managers believe that the best way to introduce change is gradually, making slight changes every so often so nobody really notices. This way, there is no major upset when a completely different system is started all at once. For instance, if a firm wanted to change its workers' pay from piece rate to hourly rate of pay, it may start with a few willing volunteers. As other workers get used to the idea more and more can be changed over time.

Other managers believe that it is far better to make the change in one jump, getting it over and done with in a shorter period of time. This is sometimes called the 'big bang' method. This way, the benefits of the change can be gained at once, rather than spread over a longer period.

Change and management style

How a manager presents the change will often depend upon his or her management style. An autocratic leader will simply tell the workers that it is happening, probably without even offering an explanation. This is the 'like it or lump it' approach. This method may work if the rewards (usually wages) the employee receives are high enough to compensate them for the change.

A democratic or consultative manager, on the other hand, would recognise that change would be easier if workers were made aware of the need for the change. In this case the workers would be told about the change well before it happened. The reasons for the change would be explained and the workers' opinions would be sought. This type of manager believes that unless those who will be affected by the change have the chance to express their opinions, they will not work towards making the change successful.

Option 2 Business Support Services

Businesses depend upon each other in many ways. They need to buy their supplies from other companies, and quite often it is other businesses that will buy their goods, rather than individual consumers. Businesses also need the financial services that are provided by banks; they may need overdraft facilities and mortgages as well as a convenient way of paying their creditors. By law a business requires a certain amount of insurance to protect it and its employees. So a firm also needs the services of an insurance company.

At one time, most businesses would have provided any other commercial service they required themselves. It

would have been unusual, for instance, for a company, other than the largest ones, to use an advertising agency. Advertising campaigns would have been devised within the organisation, probably the sales department. When goods needed to be transported, the firm's van would have been used for the purpose. If new employees were needed, the business would have recruited and selected suitable people itself.

Increasingly, businesses are taking specialisation one stage further and drawing on the expertise that business support services can offer. Many companies realise that it is more economical and less stressful to contract specialist work out to another business rather than undertake the work themselves. For instance, a software design business that employs mostly university graduates may find that it is better to contract out its cleaning to a specialist office cleaning company than employ its own cleaners. Similarly, a food wholesaler may choose to use a specialist computer company to maintain its ICT equipment rather than employ its own technicians.

The main forms of business support services are:

Financial

Banking is an important service. Banks provide a convenient way of raising money both to solve cash flow problems and for funding the purchase of equipment and premises. In addition, other specialist financial organisations have developed to meet the needs of businesses. Venture capital companies concentrate on lending money to high-risk businesses, such as those with a new idea that has not yet been tested. There are businesses that provide specialist debt-collecting services, and others that buy a company's debts then collect the money on its behalf (known as factoring). Each business needs to produce annual accounts for shareholders and for tax purposes. These must be audited and certified by a professional firm of accountants.

Insurance

Besides the basic levels of insurance required by law to protect the public and the employees against anything the company might do, many businesses will extend their insurance to cover other things.

All insurance is based on the idea of pooling risks; the many helping the few who suffer a loss. Those who suffer a loss should not make a profit from their misfortune – insurance is intended to put them back financially to the position they were in before the loss. This is known as indemnity. The relationship between insurance companies and the people they insure depnds on mutual trust (utmost good faith). Anyone who takes out an insurance policy pays a fee, known as a premium, to the insurance company. Only people with an 'insurable interest in an event' can take out insurance.

Most things that involve a risk can be insured against. An ice-cream manufacturer might want to insure against the effect on sales of a cold summer. A business might want to have insurance in case it loses all its data in the event of a computer failure. However, it is not possible to insure against the normal risks of business, such as failing to make a profit. Otherwise, firms might be tempted to make less effort to sell their products, or to try out ideas that have very little chance of succeeding.

Specialist insurance companies will also underwrite share issues. This means the insurance company agrees to make up any shortfall of money if a firm does not sell all the shares that were available for sale.

Technical

These services have become increasingly important as technology has developed and become more complex. Many firms now sell their products through the Internet. Rather than set up and maintain their own website, many choose to pay a specialist company to do this for them. Keeping a company's computer system functioning is an important job. Many businesses do not feel they have the necessary skills within their company to do this job, so they contract the work out to a specialist company. Advances in technology mean that a firm's equipment soon becomes obsolete. Businesses do not want to keep buying expensive machines that may be out of date within a short time. So instead they may choose to lease the equipment from one of the leasing companies that have grown up to provide this service.

Advisory

There are many organisations that are prepared to offer advice to businesses. Some are voluntary, such as

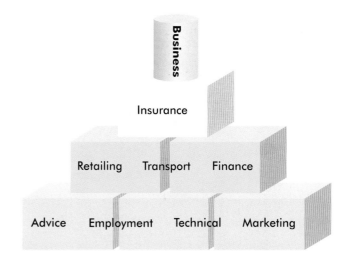

Live Wire and the Prince's Trust, which offer help to young people starting up in business. Others are organisations that provide the service purely to make a profit. Many accountants offer advice to businesses for a fee. Sometimes the advice can be free, but the organisation giving the advice may be trying to sell other services as well. All the main banks, for instance, are prepared to give advice to new businesses as long as their owners have accounts with them.

Retailing

Very few businesses rely on selling their products from the place at which they were made. Most need at least one organisation between them and the eventual consumers of their goods. Wholesalers make the chain of distribution easier by buying in bulk from manufacturers and selling in smaller quantities to retailers. Other specialist companies provide services, such as freight carriers and personal selling services. Telesales, where an agency telephones potential customers to tout for business, is a recent business support service. Some entrepreneurs prefer to use the services offered by a franchisor rather than start from scratch. Franchising can offer support and remove much of the risk associated with starting a business.

Marketing

Agencies are also available that can take on aspects of marketing. These organisations are able to undertake market research for their clients or provide them with databases of potential customers. Other agencies will undertake promotional campaigns for businesses, giving a more professional feel to how the product or service is presented to its target market.

Employment

It can be very expensive if a company makes a mistake when recruiting a senior person in the organisation. It is often difficult to remove an unsuitable manager and damage can be done to the firm's profits and reputation. To avoid this, businesses will sometimes use headhunters to find a person who matches what the company is looking for. Once found the employee will be encouraged by the headhunters to leave his or her current job. This recruitment process is known as poaching. Businesses also use employment agencies for other levels of employment. There are agencies that are able to provide temporary workers ('temps') to cover short-term illnesses and holiday periods. Job Centres are frequently used to recruit staff.

Transport

Good transport is vital to all firms. It ensures that they get their supplies on time. It also gets the goods to the customers. There are two main types of transport used within a country – road and rail. Water and air transport are also used, though mainly for international trade. The kind of transport used by a firm will depend on the type of goods it produces. It also depends on where the firm is located. In recent years, specialist tranport firms such as parcel and courier services have emerged.

Benefits to a business of using business support services

- **Economies of scale** – because the company specialises, average costs are reduced. For example, a recruitment agency would get better rates when placing job advertisements than an individual company.
- **Increased expertise** – specialists find it easier to keep up to date with developments in their fields. They are able to have the most modern equipment and know about new techniques. As a result, jobs can be done more quickly and efficiently. This allows firms to concentrate on their core business and not have to worry about things they are less confident about.

Using a business support service is worthwhile if the benefits outweigh the costs. These costs and benefits may be financial, but there are non-financial considerations as well, such as peace of mind and knowing that a good job has been done.

Option 3 Enterprise

Enterprise is that magical ingredient that allows factors of production to be assembled into an organisation in order to produce a good or service. Without the vision, drive, skills and hard work of the people we call entrepreneurs, businesses would not be created. Nobody can really be sure if a business idea will be successful. There will always be an element of risk involved – far more businesses fail than become long-term successes. However, it may be the excitement of the risk involved, the sense of doing something worthwhile or satisfying, the prospect of making money or a combination of these things that attracts entrepreneurs.

It is not clear if entrepreneurs are born with the necessary characteristics to make them risk takers and organisers, or if the skills needed can be taught and developed through training courses. There are, nevertheless, certain practical things that can be done in order to make sure that a business idea stands a good chance of success.

Identify a business opportunity
There must be a good idea for a business. The good or service must be in demand otherwise it will not be bought. The presence of other firms producing the same product will indicate that there is a demand, but competitors will make it difficult to become established. This may not be so great a problem if the new business has a distinctive or unique selling point.

Often the business opportunity comes about by observation. An entrepreneur may notice that certain shops or services appear to be more busy than usual, or he or she may personally want to buy something that it is difficult to find. If the product is new, the entrepreneur may have a hunch that demand will be created once the product is on the market.

Market research is essential to find out the likely success of the idea. It will also give feedback on the best way to market the product. If it is done properly the research will inform the business on:
- the possible demand for the product;
- what potential customers see as an acceptable price;
- the best way to promote the product;
- any changes that are needed to make the product more attractive.

Produce a business plan
The business plan gives the entrepreneur the chance to try out his or her idea on paper. Many assumptions have to be made such as how much the business's costs and revenue will be. The temptation is to exaggerate these figures to the advantage of the business. So people say that more will be sold than is likely, and costs will be lower than will actually be the case. It is safer to reduce the likely revenue and increase the costs.

The business plan should evaluate the idea and determine whether it is worth taking it further. It should not be seen just as a means of raising money from banks and other sources. It is more of a checklist to make sure that all the factors needed to increase the chance of success of the business are in place.

Have a marketing strategy
The four Ps of the marketing mix need to be planned carefully. Price, product, promotion and place need to be considered in the light of the market research. This should include both a short-term plan for when the product is introduced and a longer-term plan.

Obtain sufficient finance
Without enough money to see the business through the initial stages when its costs will be high and revenue low, there will be little chance of success. The business plan and cash flow statement will inform just how much money is needed and for how long.

Know when to stop
Not all businesses will be successful. In Britain, when a business closes it is often seen as a failure. This may not be the case; the closure may be the result of a change in demand. Other countries are less critical when businesses fail. Sometimes, businesses in the UK continue long after the warning signals have been flashing, because people do not wish to be seen as failing. They continue with a lost cause, hoping that something will turn up.

Option 4 Human Resources

Labour is one of the factors of production. Labour, or human resources, is quite different from the other factors of production, land and capital. The quality of labour will depend upon the abilities, experience, training and the degree of motivation of each worker. Companies are able to develop labour, which many say is their most important resource. As human resources are central to the success of a business, most firms recognise that they need to ensure that they get the best out of their workers. Businesses use many different strategies to achieve this.

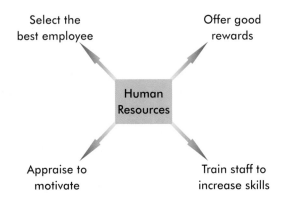

Selection

Businesses must select the best people from those available to work for them. The quality of labour varies tremendously in terms of abilities and potential. It is therefore important that great care is taken in the selection procedure. Companies are relying less on a single interview to determine the most suitable workers. They are increasingly likely to use various tests, observations and references to help them decide. Often a worker is employed for a probationary period of say three months to check his or her performance during that time. If potential is shown, the worker will be kept on permanently.

Rewards

At its most basic, this means the wages the workers receive. These should be at least enough to attract them to the business in the first place. However, wages need to be sufficiently high to encourage workers to remain with the company and to motivate them. Rewards do not just include wages, there are other benefits that a worker might receive. Profit sharing is one such example, as are perks such as company cars and private health insurance. Workers do not work just for financial benefits. There are many other benefits than can be gained from work. If people are able to socialise in their work, gain satisfaction from what they do and achieve a sense of purpose to their lives, they are more likely to work well.

Appraisal

In many companies workers have an annual appraisal interview. At this meeting a more senior employee will discuss with the worker how well he or she has performed since the last appraisal. The meeting is an opportunity to find out if the worker has any training needs and to assess his or her potential for promotion. If conducted wisely these regular meetings can both motivate the worker and provide valuable feedback to the company on workers' concerns.

Training

If workers are to become more efficient and safe when doing their jobs they need to be fully trained. Training also allows workers to adapt to changing working practices, which allows them to undertake different jobs, and can act as a motivator. Training, however, is expensive for several reasons. First, while someone is training, the person is not doing his or her proper job, so output is lost. This is more severe if another employee is away from work training the person. Second, courses and training materials have to be paid for, and third, the trained worker will become more valuable to the company, so his or her wages may need to be increased. The company may need to pay higher wages to stop the worker being poached by another firm.

Option 5 Information and Communication Technology

Advances in information and communication technology over the last 15 years or so have revolutionised the world of business. Computers can undertake many business practices that were once performed by skilled workers. So great are the changes, that it is often said that business has undergone a 'technological revolution'.

Information technology

Businesses have to deal with a great deal of information. Customer details have to be stored, accounts kept for each customer and supplier, details of stock held kept up to date, employees' wages calculated – the list is almost endless. Before computers were cheap enough for firms to afford, businesses used paper-based systems. All details would be stored on cards or ledgers and updated by hand. Whilst this system worked well for hundreds of years, it did have problems.

Specialist workers, such as clerks and bookkeepers, were needed for keeping accurate records. It was not always easy to understand the figures, so access to them was a problem other than for the specialists. It took time to collect the information, which meant it was usually out of date. It was also difficult to cross-reference the information. For instance, when a customer ordered some goods, many departments would be affected and they would each need to keep separate records. Notes would go to transport to deliver the goods, the sales department would have to inform accounts to invoice the customer, the production department would need to record that the stock level had fallen, and so on. A computer-based system allows each of these separate records to be linked together.

A computerised system can also be used to look at the consequences of a proposed change in the business. For instance, if a firm is considering increasing the production of one or more of its products it will have an impact on many departments. More supplies will be needed, as well as more labour, machine time and transport. The change can be explored or 'modelled' on the computer to test its effect. By doing this, a firm can avoid making costly mistakes.

Information technology makes it far easier for complicated data to be presented in tables, graphs and other ways. This allowed non-specialists to spot trends, recognise unusual figures and get an overview of different aspects of a business. The presentation of data is particularly useful for interpreting and explaining market research results and for setting targets within the company.

Communication technology

Businesses discovered the potential of computers for communication after they had used them for IT. A firm's computers can be linked, or networked, to each other to create an intranet. This makes it as easy for employees in different branches of the company to communicate as it is for those in the same building. Messages can be sent from person to person almost instantaneously but, unlike fax, the receiver can edit the document that is received. Workers can also have access to central records and documents. For instance, if a customer telephones an insurance company, anyone who takes the call can access the customer's file, even if it were kept many kilometres away at head office.

Intranets also allowed businesses to monitor the performance of different branches of the company. Vital information can be sent frequently from each part of the company to its headquarters by a system know as EDI (electronic data interchange). If, for example, the Newcastle branch of a chain store were selling less of a particular product, the head office would pick this up very quickly. This means that the company can identify problems a lot more quickly than under the old system.

Many firms have discovered the potential of the Internet. Having a website is a cheap way of advertising the company and its products. This greatly expands the business's customer catchment area. Providing the product can be transported, the market for the product can become national, if not international. Similarly, firms can check they are getting the best deal by going to the websites of different suppliers and comparing prices.

Option 6 Production

There has been a large fall in the number of people who work in secondary industries. These are industries that produce goods, such as household items, and equipment needed by other businesses. This does not mean, though, that the amount of goods produced has declined over the years. Many industries are now making more with far fewer workers than they were 25 years ago. This has been achieved by increases in productivity.

$$\text{Labour productivity} = \frac{\text{number of items produced}}{\text{number of workers employed}}$$

Productivity is a measure of how much output can be produced from a certain amount of resources. The more that can be made with the available resources, the higher the level of productivity. For example, if a car manufacturer can make 10,000 cars a year with a workforce of 2,000 workers, each person on average makes five cars a year. If the same number of cars can be produced with just 1,250 workers, this average rises to 8 cars per worker.

The advantage of increasing productivity is that it becomes cheaper to make the goods, as less has to be spent on the resources needed to produce them. This means that a firm's profits will increase. As a result, firms have devoted much time and energy to finding ways of increasing productivity.

The reasons for the increase in productivity can be put into three categories. These are improvements caused by:
- advances in technology;
- better production methods;
- better motivation of workers.

Technology advances

These have revolutionised the way goods are produced. Businesses are now able to use computers to operate machines that once needed to be controlled by skilled workers. Once a computer has been programmed to run a machine it is able to continue to produce goods without a break. Labour costs are reduced as one technician can oversee many machines at once. Computer advances have also allowed specialist software to be produced that has taken much of the hard work out of the design and development of products.

Production methods

Many changes have occurred in the way goods are made in an attempt to increase productivity. Flow production, for example, allows large numbers of a product to be made with a high productivity. This process ensures that the full advantages of division of labour can be obtained, as well as other benefits such as kaizen and just-in-time stock control. Companies have often experimented with methods of production to test ways of keeping costs low. Cell production is an attempt to retain the advantages of large-scale production while avoiding the workers having to do dull, repetitive work.

Workers' motivation

The quality and quantity of employees' work depend to a large extent on how motivated they are. Poorly motivated workers need more supervision, and quality control to check their work. Well-motivated workers, on the other hand, take pride in their work and produce high quality goods. Such workers are also less likely to be absent from work and more likely to work productively when they are there.

Much has been written on how workers' motivation can be improved through changing working conditions and practices. These can be found in Section 4 of this book.